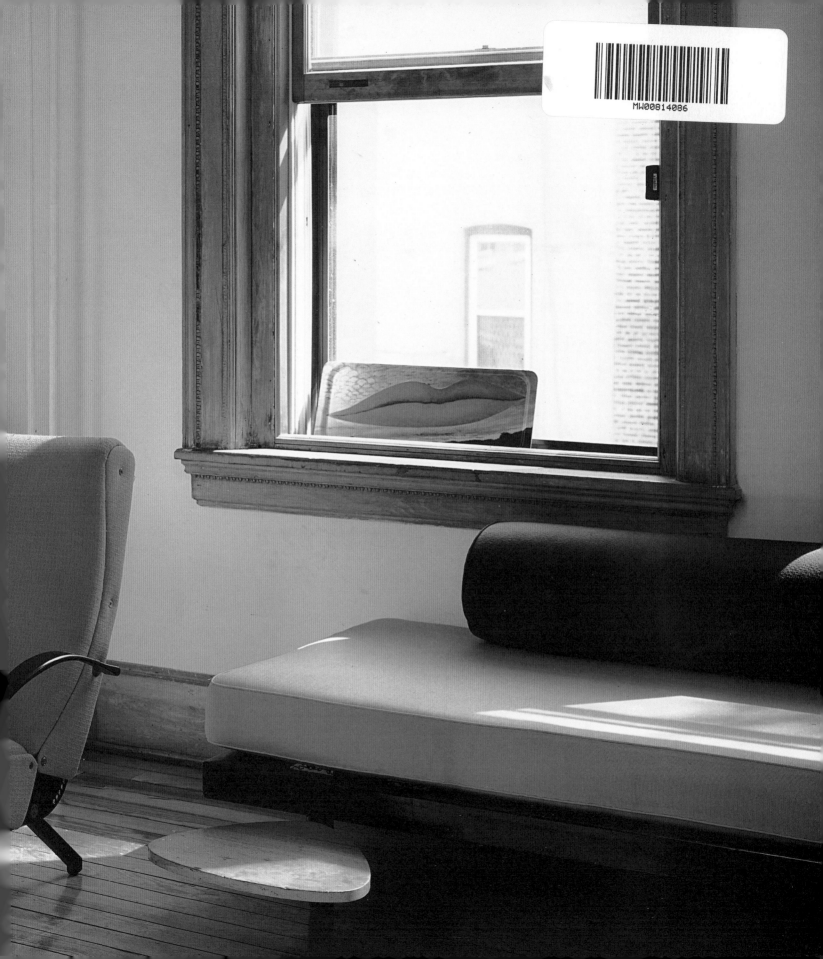

IN YOUR

SPACE

PERSONALIZING
YOUR HOME AND OFFICE

For my mother and father
from deep in my heart

Front Cover: Jenette Kahn's media room in her Harlem house
defined by color, sports themes, and contemporary art.

Back Cover: In her Harlem house, the author reclines
on her favorite piece of furniture beneath a tree of grinning
vinyl beasties.

Editor: Susan Costello

Art Director and Designer: Julietta Cheung

Production Editor: Marian Appellof

Copyeditor: Miranda Ottewell

Production Manager: Louise Kurtz

First edition

2   4   6   8   10   9   7   5   3   1

Library of Congress Control Number: 2002100197

ISBN 0-7892-0757-5

Printed in Hong Kong

IN YOUR
SPACE

PERSONALIZING
YOUR HOME AND OFFICE

JENETTE KAHN

PRINCIPAL PHOTOGRAPHY BY
JASON SCHMIDT

ABBEVILLE PRESS PUBLISHERS
NEW YORK LONDON

Contents

1.

Introduction:

The Dawn of the Century— My First Real Apartment

The twin towers of the Century rising majestically over Central Park.

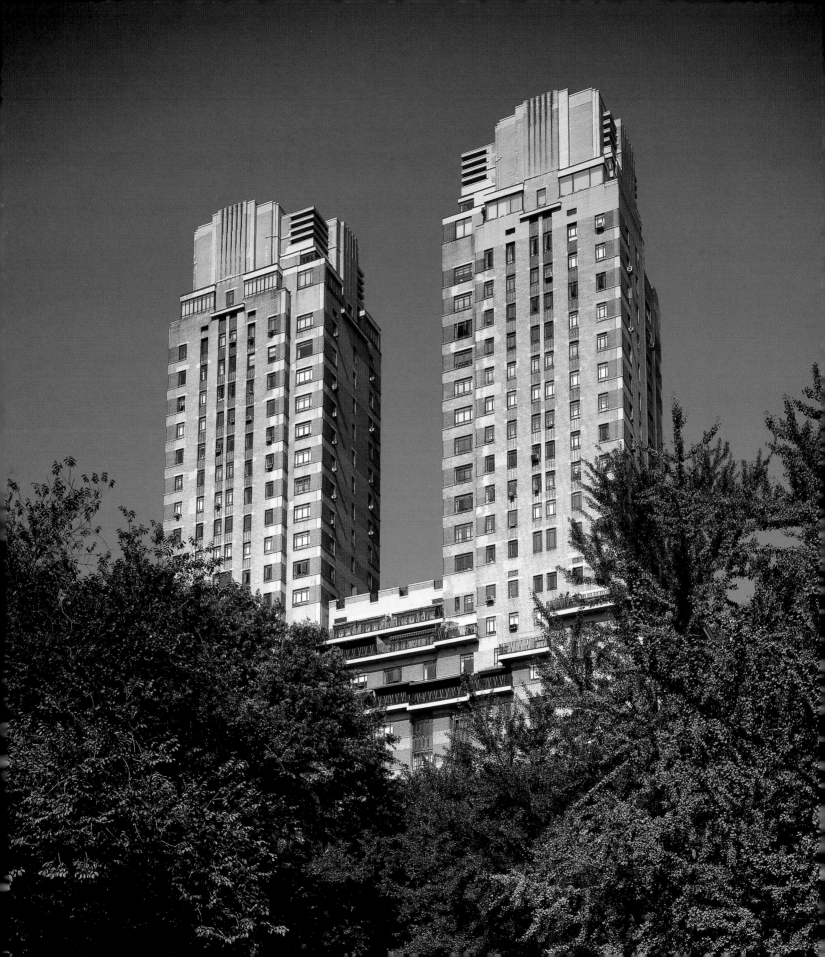

I have a passion for design, for all the innumerable components that separate a single object from a cast of thousands, whether it's a can opener or a glittering chandelier. Line, color, materials, and form are the visual and tactile ingredients. But for me, the elements that raise a design beyond the generic, beyond the well made and the functional, even beyond the aesthetically pleasing, are the intangibles—concept, invention, risk, surprise, wit, and wonder. When an object combines these components, the best results are thrilling. Great design, like great art, fills your heart and mind.

But long before I consciously began to appreciate design, before I knew about artists, icons, or movements, I had another passion. I wanted to personalize my own space, to surround myself with items I loved, with colors and objects that gave me joy. This desire was rooted in an instinctive knowledge that no place could make me happier than a room of my own, a room that expressed my feelings and impulses, a room filled only with things I cared about and that gave me deep, abiding pleasure.

Humble Beginnings

I say a room, because that is how I started. As a child I had my own bedroom, and I was lucky in that it was unusually large. But my mother, as mothers do, picked everything in it—the blue walls, the plain white furniture, the white chenille spread on my bed, and the curtains, for which I harbored a silent but enormous dislike. These were printed with rows of paper dolls rendered so schematically that today, forty-five years later, they could be read as universal signage symbols. My mother deserved credit for their graphic sophistication, but I hated

the colors—turquoise, fuchsia, chartreuse, and black. Even when I was five, I knew which colors made me uneasy and which made me feel good— clear, vivid primaries, oranges, yellows, reds, true blues, bright greens. I loved my mother, but I thought my room was boring and tame. And had it not been for one single piece of art on the walls, I could have felt as transient as a boarder. But this one picture made all the difference in the world. And my mother chose it, too.

My father cut a mat for the picture and hung it on the wall over my desk. It was a poster by Matisse extolling the sun-drenched pleasures of Nice. A combination still life, interior, and landscape, it shows a large window suffused with the bright green fronds of a tree. It's flanked by an orange shutter, a strip of pink triangles, and a wall so black that it pops every other hue. A portrait of a woman in a circular frame highlights the upper right, while a warm sienna table gives life to the bottom. On it is a sky blue plate scattered with fruit in apricots and yellows, and a single open fruit whose red flesh is speckled with black. Behind the table is a decorative pattern, gay and colorful and loose.

I loved this poster with all my heart. Morning and night, I would lie in bed and stare at it, never tiring of it, never absorbing enough. And although my mother may have chosen it, it was the one thing in the room I felt was truly mine. I couldn't explain how or why, but this picture gave voice to my deepest, most joyful feelings. Looking at it validated all of the instincts and emotions for which I had no words.

It wasn't until my first year at Harvard that I finally had a room I could decorate on my own. My budget was no larger than any other student's, but I was still able to create a space that gave me the same sense of unadulterated pleasure I'd found in my childhood Matisse. Like every freshman, I ransacked the inexpensive stores in Harvard Square where the only affordable bedspreads came in corduroy colors so bland, you wondered why anyone had ever bothered to manufacture them. One of the shades, however, was brown, a deep, dark brown at that. Ordinarily I would have dismissed it as just another institutional color, but I had learned something from the sienna table in my Matisse. Brown on its own may not be particularly interesting. But brown with other colors can look unexpectedly rich. I bought the bedspread and transformed it with cushions in different shapes and bright colors.

From a remnant store, I bought a piece of golden yellow carpeting that became my area rug. At a junk store, I found a homemade cribbage bench in plain, unfinished wood, which I painted black and set on the yellow rug in front of the bed, with its brown bedspread and multicolored pillows. In addition to these, I purchased another staple of college living, a butterfly chair with its black, wrought-iron frame. But the canvas cover I picked for it was a pure, emphatic red, as red as the opened fruit in the Matisse.

When I could, I added vibrant accessories, like a cobalt blue teapot I would fill each week with flowers from the florist nearby. I wanted to move color all around the room, using brown and black as anchors to ground the lighter, brighter hues.

My next question was what to do for art. If students bothered at all, they bought posters from the Harvard Coop, which they tacked or pasted to the walls. No one could afford frames, so although the posters were copies of famous paintings, they looked makeshift, and even cheaper than they were. In addition, most of them were just a fraction of the size of the originals. I wanted pictures on the walls that I loved, but I also wanted them to have presence and scale. And insofar as one can achieve this in a dormitory room, I wanted them to look purposeful.

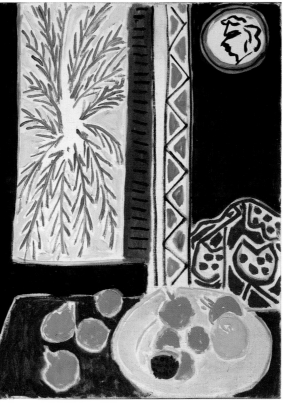

My first and lasting inspiration—a Matisse poster advertising Nice that hung in my childhood bedroom.

But how would this be possible? Once again, I was indebted to Matisse. As a child, I had very few opportunities to see his art in person, but on our occasional family trips to New York we always visited the Museum of Modern Art, which owns some of his finest work. I loved Matisse's seminal **Dancers**, an early picture of a circle of naked women dancing on green grass against a bright blue sky. And I was enthralled by the extraordinary cutouts he made late in life out of prepainted paper. In these cutouts, or **coupées**, Matisse reinvented not only himself but painting itself. In 1947 he published **Jazz**, a limited-edition book based on some of the best of this work. Years later the Modern reissued a small volume of **Jazz**, which I bought and always kept close to me.

Matisse's cutouts became my inspiration. If he could create paintings out of paper, why couldn't I do the same? At least I could re-create pictures out of paper. I thought of two of my favorite paintings that were geometric enough to be reproduced with scissors and colored paper, both Picassos—**Three Musicians** and **Girl before a Mirror**. Although I have very little skill in drawing, it was amazing how much easier it was to cut paper into these well-defined shapes, most of them straight-edged, and piece them together like a puzzle with glue on posterboard. I reproduced both paintings in this fashion, making them as large as would fit in my room. **Three Musicians**, which I placed over my bed, was approximately three feet high by four feet wide. **Girl before a Mirror**, which went over my desk in a small alcove you came upon almost by surprise, was close to three feet wide and four feet high. I edged both of them with black electrical tape. The tape worked as a strong framing device that not only helped define the borders of the images but even made them look somewhat permanent. I also re-created Matisse's **Dancers**, although more clumsily, because those figures could not be reduced to geometric forms. Instead of gluing them onto posterboard, I tacked them with pushpins to a bulletin board. The wooden edge of the board, like the tape, served as a frame, giving the picture substance.

At college I loved the fervor of my classes, the low-key hubbub of Harvard Yard, and the whispered intrigues one could always pick up while studying in Widener Library. But the place that felt like home, that I was always happy to wake up to in the morning and return to with pleasure at night, was my room. I had decorated it solely for myself, with no thought to how others might react, yet it became a nocturnal center as classmates meandering through the halls dropped by and stayed for hours.

Why did my room become the hangout of choice, even though I'd banned smoking there at a time when cigarettes were badges of our budding sophis-

tication? Because, I believe, it was more than a way station, a place to sleep and study. There was an energy to the decor, a liveliness that came from creativity, a welcoming spirit. Although my peers, had they thought of going to similar lengths to decorate their rooms, would have made very different choices, they still respected the genuineness and originality of mine. Even if they wouldn't choose to live in my room, it was still a great place to visit. This, I think, was the most unexpected lesson I learned from that time. If you create your own space, if you invest it with your dreams, then other people will come, finding in it some of the same pleasure it gives you.

This book is very much a personal journey. It is about many things—my growing awareness and appreciation of design, my countless gropings, my innumerable visions and revisions and mistakes. It is about honing my taste, developing passions, finding collaborators and artists, discovering sources, and opening up new arenas of collecting. And it is about learning to trust my instincts and finding the creativity inside myself.

But this book is not just about me. It is for everyone who wants to individualize his or her own space. The things I learned can be shared, whether you prefer neutrals or colors, traditional furniture or contemporary design, simplicity or complexity. Although the photographs in the book show my office, and my houses in the city and the country, this is not a manual on how to replicate my style. Rather, it is a book about the creative process, and how you can use it to personalize your own interiors. You'll find that expressing your interests and personality can give you more pleasure than you ever dreamed.

It's okay to be a beginner. I started out knowing next to nothing, and although the first results were flawed, nonetheless, I learned a tremendous amount.

Far from being discouraged, I looked forward to every opportunity to try again. I never stopped making mistakes, but each wrong turn only helped me to find the way the next time. With every new step, I discovered more about the world and more about myself. The journey turned out to be as rewarding as the finished rooms. It is amazing how much a quest to personalize your space can enrich your life. And whether you adorn your walls with Daumier cartoons or inexpensive, colorful maps, whether you line your shelves with rare art glass or cheap flea market bottles, if they're what you love, then you will also love the various places where you live and work.

The Century: The Early Years

The first real apartment I got the chance to decorate was in one of New York's premier buildings, the Century on Central Park West. At the age of twenty-five, I became immersed in a romance so heady that we decided to live together. My other half in this adventure was considerably older than I and separating from his wife. For him, among many things, this meant moving out of the substantial Park Avenue apartment of his marriage. I, on the other hand, was giving up very little by way of a home. The first magazine I'd created had faltered financially, and I could no longer pay the rent on my brownstone floor-through. Luckily, I had friends in abundance, all of whom generously offered to take me in. I became an urban nomad, leaving a trail of possessions behind me as I lightened the load with each move.

Because both of us were in transition and our own relationship was so new, we opted for a solution that seemed as temporary as our circumstances. We decided to sublet a furnished apartment.

The apartment we chose was only a one-bedroom,

although it had nearly a thousand square feet of living space. It was on the second floor and faced a courtyard instead of the park. But the apartment still had wonderful features, even for two people who viewed it simply as a place to land en route to something much larger and more permanent. For one thing, despite its relatively small size, it had a capacious circular layout that made it possible to orbit the apartment without catching sight of each other. I often mused that it was the ideal backdrop for a French romantic farce. It had a large living room, high ceilings, a good-size foyer, and a small, separate dining room, all amenities quite rare in a one-bedroom apartment. And it had five closets, a fact that certainly was not lost on me.

The Century was one of New York's great apartment houses. Built by Irwin Chanin in 1931, the twin-towered Art Deco edifice massed its different height components with such subtlety and grace that the look was imposing but never overpowering. I always thought that Chanin had named it the Century because he believed his building, fusing as it did new engineering techniques with farsighted architectural forms, would hold its own for the next one hundred years. If so, he was right; the Century was awarded landmark status and remains one of the most coveted places to live in New York even now, as the twenty-first century replaces the one in which the apartment house was built. In truth, as I learned only much later, the Century actually took its name from the Century Theater, which had once occupied the site.

We had wonderful times in the apartment, even with someone else's furniture. But a year later, when we broke up only to become lifelong friends, each of us volunteered to move. Was it by the flip of a coin? I can't remember, but I was the one who stayed. Even so, because the apartment was a sublet, my occupancy was tenuous. Ever mindful of the scouting motto,

I revved myself into a state of perpetual preparedness, ready to pack for that inevitable moment when my landlord wanted her apartment back.

Luck, however, was on my side. After a year during which I languished in residential limbo, she miraculously decided to give the apartment up. Now my task was to convince the Century that I was a worthy tenant, a harder feat than one might imagine, since I'd been living all along with my cats and the lease prohibited any pets. Despite this glaring contradiction, precedent prevailed. The Century abounded with quadrupeds, and my felines were just three small furry creatures in what could pass as a sizable petting zoo. Suddenly, the apartment was in my name, and the furniture was gone.

Learning about Design: The Saga of a Total Novice

And so I began to decorate, recycling whatever furniture I had, since my budget was practically nonexistent. Without realizing it, I had already bought my first designer piece, a sinuously curved chaise and ottoman covered in deep orange velour. I purchased it because I loved both the color and the lines and only incidentally because it happened to be quite comfortable. It was years later that I learned that the chaise was by Jan Eskëlius, and a classic of early 1970s design.

Looking back on this time, I realize that I was totally unschooled in furniture design. Oh, I had definite responses to what I liked and what I didn't, but I was unaware that there were artists behind these household basics: tables, chairs, and lights. There was one exception. In Cambridge, Massachusetts, where I was an undergraduate at Harvard, there was a wonderful store called Design Research. It was a light-filled and inviting space, full of fresh tulips and bright Marimekko fabrics, dishes and flatware, rugs and furniture, all in a modernist vein.

I had a boyfriend who loved the store for one particular reason. In the window was a chair and ottoman of bent plywood and black leather that was the perfect synthesis of masculine grace and comfort. It was priced beyond the imagination of any college student except those with independent incomes. But Design Research had a laissez-faire attitude, and my boyfriend would blithely walk in every day, settle himself in the chair, and read the **New York Times**, believing, for at least thirty minutes, that the chair was his.

He mentioned his morning jaunts to me and referred to his daily perch as "the Eames chair." Had he used the names Pesce or Deskey, Loewy or Prouvé, I would have been in the dark. But I knew the name Eames and had since childhood, because my parents had given my brother an Eames construction kit. It had large geometric shapes in bright primary colors, supported by dowel sticks. A paradigm of invention, it leapfrogged over all other building sets to bring a child of the 1950s astonishingly close to erecting his very own geodesic dome.

So the Eames name was familiar to me, and now I was able to match it to the luxurious bent-plywood chair in the window of Design Research. Yet this was an isolated instance. Looking back, it amazes me that I knew about painters, sculptors, and architects but was ignorant of the people behind furniture and lighting design, many of whom were architects themselves.

My exposure to design happened during my first semester of college, when I spent two weeks in the Harvard Health Center, recovering from double pneumonia. The Health Center was an anomaly, as it faced the redbrick Georgian buildings that dominated Harvard Yard. It was designed by José Luis Sert, the Spanish architect who was close friends with the painter Joan Miró and who, in fact, also designed the Miró Foundation in Barcelona.

Two weeks in the Health Center were more than enough time to take in my surroundings. The furnishings were as modern as the building, but I remember the couches most vividly. Both the back and the seat of each couch were composed of independent padded circles that looked like giant cushy Lifesavers minus the holes. I loved the form of the sofa—it felt so new, even though I was later to learn it had been designed in the 1950s. What I didn't really like was the mix of orange, fuchsia, and violet cushions, which, like the dolls' colors in my childhood curtains, seemed dissonant to me.

Years later I discovered the couch was conceived by the American designer George Nelson, and was known as the Marshmallow sofa. It came in many color combinations, or could be ordered in a single color, like orange or white.

Although I have no place to put a Marshmallow sofa, every time one comes up for sale, I start to scheme about how I might buy it. It must be my design gene raging out of control.

Two Lessons, Maybe More

Lesson One

First, important and innovative design transcends ignorance. The Jan Eskëlius chaise and the George Nelson sofa grabbed my attention despite my woeful lack of consciousness and education. They were simply that good. Knowledge is a powerful and invaluable tool, but art in its highest form shines a light even on the most benighted.

Lesson Two

Design has tended to be shunted aside by other arts like an unwanted stepchild. Except in specialized schools, such as New York's Parsons School of Design, the Pratt Institute of Technology, and the newer Bard Graduate Center for Studies in the Decorative Arts, Design, and Culture, it is not often included in the teaching of art history. Luckily, today one can teach oneself. Any bookstore worth its salt has a department devoted to illustrated books on contemporary design as well as the design of earlier eras. Although they can be relatively expensive, these are books to be revisited over and over again. Somehow, the pictures never get boring.

All of the major auction houses devote sales to different periods of design, and you can buy old catalogues from them for a potpourri of reference about styles and prices. You can also purchase catalogues of upcoming sales if you want to tempt yourself to buy. Numerous decorating magazines devote at least a few pages to new developments in lighting, furniture, and accessory design. There are important annual design shows, like the Winter Antiques Show or Modernism at the Park Avenue Armory in New York, and the design, or shelter, magazines will often alert you to a countrywide calendar of similar events.

At these shows individual dealers are usually glad to explain the history of a piece to you, although you should be aware that some of them are closer to used car salesmen than experts. Try to talk to other people who have dealt with dealers before taking them at their word. And always ask to see documentation of the piece, like a photo reference from a book or magazine. If you buy it, ask for copies of the documentation. It will get you the best price if you ever decide to sell.

It's important to trust your instincts and purchase only objects that elicit in you a strong emotional response. If you do, you may also unknowingly discover some designer pieces. This happened for me even as I decorated my apartment on a shoestring.

In an Art Deco store behind the American Museum of Natural History, I found two spun-aluminum torchères on long, tapered wooden stems that the owners said had been designed by Russel Wright, and this proved to be true. I also bought a round table for my dining room that stirred my interest because it had a solid piece of wood connecting the top and the base on one side, and several chrome pipes doing the same on the other.

When the table was lacquered black, it had a spirited Art Deco resonance. This wasn't the most efficient dining table—any unfortunate guest seated near the vertical slat either had to straddle it or list to one side—but it looked terrific, and was the perfect size for my nine-by-nine-foot dining room. Some years later, when I had married and the table was being ousted from the new decor, a noted Art Deco dealer identified the designer as James Mont, and speculated that it had most likely been built in the 1930s or '40s for a window display of one of the great New York department stores. With the provenance established, I was able to sell it for five times what I'd paid.

Of course I've been wrong, too, and at least twice have spent far too much money for items that were either fakes or so altered by the dealer that they lost all their residual value. Spotting substitutions requires not only a good eye but tremendous familiarity with each object. It's rare that we ordinary mortals have both. Try to befriend reputable dealers and ask them to check out the piece both for authenticity and fair market price.

Starting to Collect: Another Beginner's Journal

Only a few years before I began my awkward gropings in furniture and lighting design, I had embarked on my very first collection. In this I was somewhat

of an anomaly. Most collectors started when they were children, whether they amassed stamps or coins, comic books or baseball cards, dolls or stickers. But I came to collecting relatively late, at the age of twenty-one, when I had a summer fellowship at the Museum of Modern Art.

My assignment was to lay the foundation for an interdepartmental exhibit tentatively titled 1908–1918. The museum's director, Bates Lowry, believed those were watershed years in all the arts that the Modern represented: painting, sculpture, photography, and film. I had studied the painting and sculpture of that period, but Harvard's art history program didn't include classes on photography. I was eager to learn about this area, so shortly after I arrived at MoMA, I introduced myself to John Szarkowski, its legendary director of photography. In a season of immense generosity, he took me under his wing and shared his passion for this relatively new art form. When artists brought in their photographs, John allowed me to sit with him while he viewed their work. When he was mounting a show, he'd take me into the exhibition rooms, where the photos would be spread on the floor, and he'd ask me how I'd hang them. He listened intently as I replied, then hung the show his way without explanation. I was left to draw my own conclusions.

It was during that summer that the Modern acquired Eugène Atget's extraordinary turn-of-the-century images of Paris. The American photographer Berenice Abbott had sought out Atget before his death, and it was she who had rescued his work. Every few years she offered to sell her Atget collection to the museum, and every few years the Modern would turn her down on the grounds that it was too expensive. As time went by, the price of the collection continued to rise. Finally, when it reached $85,000, an incredibly low sum by today's standards for such historic photographs, John Szarkowski realized that the museum would always find the Atget collection unaffordable. He took an "acquire or perish" attitude, and the photos at last found a permanent home in the Museum of Modern Art.

It wasn't just the content of Atget's pictures that made them so compelling and often so poetically surreal. It was also the tones of the prints themselves, soft, burnished sepias that gave the images a dreamlike intimacy. The quality of these tones owed as much to the chemicals and paper available when Atget was alive as it did to Atget himself. Any later attempts to strike prints from the original plates—with one very limited experiment staged by the Museum of Modern Art—resulted in harsh black-and-white images that seemed as many miles away from Atget's own work as present-day Paris seems from the Paris Atget documented so lovingly. Atget's prints were coveted not just because he made them, but also because there was such an aesthetic difference between them and later prints.

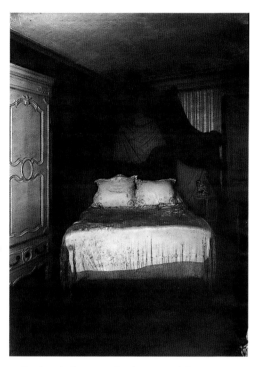

An Atget photograph of a turn-of-the-century French bedroom, its sepia tones as sensual as the satin coverlet.

The Modern was still reeling from paying $85,000 for the collection when a wondrous thought occurred. In cataloging Atget's photographs, the curators noticed there were a number of duplicate prints struck by Atget himself. Did the museum need two or sometimes three of the same image? No, of course not. The duplicates would go to a gallery to sell and the proceeds would help defray the cost of the acquisition.

And so it was that a large number of Atget prints went on sale at the Robert Schoelkopf Gallery.

Soon my feet were headed up Madison Avenue to check them out. Did I really plan to buy one? That idea was still an embryo whose existence I was trying to deny. But there is no such thing as being just a little bit pregnant.

The most famous Atget prints had already been sold. Those that remained—less celebrated, certainly, but still beautiful—ranged from $250 to $300. That was a fortune to me then, but I was spellbound by the images. I wanted to own an Atget, and I believed that somehow I'd figure out a way to pay for it. I visited the gallery every week, trying to decide which picture would give me the most lasting pleasure. In the end I chose a photo of an interior marble stair, gleaming and cold even through the sepia. The only concession to "prettiness" was the somewhat ornate metal banister that flowed beside it. I bought the picture and cherished it, and found I was on the path of true collectors. I couldn't help myself. There would be many more photos to follow. And more of everything else. The damage was done.

Work with Dealers Who Will Work with You

As I was struggling to make my decision, the Schoelkopf staff only grudgingly brought out the Atgets for me to see. Their attitude guaranteed that I would not return unless, as with the Atgets, they were the exclusive representative of something I dearly wanted. A good dealer will try to cultivate a customer, spending time with her or him, and share his own knowledge and enthusiasm. When I began to collect in earnest, I never returned to the Schoelkopf Gallery. If there is more than one place to find what you are looking for, it is best to seek out dealers who welcome you no matter how inexperienced you are. They can be among your best teachers even long after you've become familiar with an area. And good dealers will always try to work with you. A 10 percent discount is not unusual. But many dealers will also let you pay for a piece in installments, making it possible to afford something over time that you could never buy if pressed to pay at once.

The Atget triggered my interest in collecting, and it was not long before I was buying more photographs. About a year later, I was back in Boston, making a weak-kneed stab at graduate school. I didn't really want to be there, but it was a place to pass the time while I figured out what I really wanted to do. Nonetheless, I wasn't totally idle. My experience at the Museum of Modern Art had been seminal, and I now had an abiding love for photography. Although the range of my taste was to widen as I grew older, the first photographs that interested me were in a realistic tradition that showed actual people, places, and things, transformed only by the photographer's eye and the sleight-of-hand of the camera.

At that time, contemporary photography in Boston was dominated by abstract expressionism. The photographs captured real things, like tree trunks and roots, but they were shot so closely that one was aware only of crystalline swirls, not of the objects themselves. I had an inflated, youthful sense of mission, a desire to bring the kinds of photos I'd come to love to a city that seemed unimpressed by them.

Motivated by this ideal, I got reinforcements from a fellow graduate student, Francine Trachtenberg, and together we applied for a Kress Foundation grant to mount a show of these naturalistic pictures. And while we weren't as surprised as we should have been — one of the many flaws of being only twenty-two — we actually received it. Soon after depositing the check, I was on a plane to New York to meet with as many photographers as I could. First on my list was the groundbreaking and lyrical Hungarian artist André Kertesz, who at that time was already in his seventies. Kertesz was somewhat frail, but as charming and gracious as his wife was warm and gregarious. As we talked in their apartment high above Washington Square Park, I explained to them the exhibition's concept. And Kertesz, with his customary generosity, agreed to participate, despite the fact that I was an untried curator and far too young to inspire any confidence.

Knowing that Kertesz was on board, I went to see photographers who had become friends during my summer at the Modern: Garry Winogrand, Joel Meyerowitz, and Tod Papageorge. They too became participants, allowing me, as Kertesz had, to select particular photographs, at times with some urging, often with none. At the top of my list, in that same rarefied pantheon occupied by André Kertesz, were Henri Cartier-Bresson, Walker Evans, and Robert Frank. In retrospect, I don't know how it happened, but — full of excitement and anxiety — I actually met with Evans and Frank and secured their participation, too. Cartier-Bresson was in Paris, but I worked with his gallery, which agreed to lend me pictures for the show.

Back in Boston, Francine had found exhibition space at Boston University and arranged for security for the photographs. We sent out the photographs to be matted and framed and then set about painting panels in two different shades of gray on which to mount the pictures. I loaned one photograph to the show, which sat by itself under the caption, "The

Descriptive Tradition." It was my Atget, of course. If a picture is truly worth a thousand words or, in the best case, fewer, more incisive ones, then the Atget was installed instead of a wall label to illuminate the fundaments of the exhibition.

The exhibit was up for a month, and every day I went to it to take in the photographs. In part I was propelled by a sense of personal achievement, but primarily it was the pictures themselves. I couldn't see them often enough. The photos were all for sale, but I was nothing more than a window shopper. And then, depending on your point of view, a miracle happened. Or a disaster.

My grandfather decided to give each of his grandchildren $2,000. I'm sure we were meant to invest it, probably in Israeli bonds, but it arrived without any explicit instructions. Suddenly I was a woman of means. Now I looked at the photos in a new light. Which ones would I like to live with? Which ones would I like to own?

As I had agonized over the Atget, so too did I agonize over each and every one of the pictures in the exhibition. I wanted to have at least one from every photographer, but which? It's hard to know why one makes certain choices and not others. I finally arrived at some sixteen photographs I loved. But even today, so many years later, other images from the show drift through my mind and provoke an inexpressible yearning that makes me question my earlier decisions. I try to get over it. Deep in my heart, I know that had I chosen sixteen other photographs, I'd still be suffused with a longing for those I didn't pick.

Material Girl: The Beautiful Fabrics of Quilts

The photographs, of course, became part of my decor at the Century. And so did quilts, the area of collecting I next embraced. My fascination with quilts began by accident. I was walking on a street in Manhattan's East Seventies when I saw a tiny subterranean shop. Its window was colorful and engaging, and in no time I was headed down the stairs to explore the world of America Hurrah.

America Hurrah was owned by Kate and Joel Kopp. They were passionate about folk art, and their narrow store was lined with piles of folded quilts. I knew nothing about them, but I was attracted by the charm in some, the bold graphics in others, and the color, always the color.

Although I was a novice, Kate unfolded quilt after quilt for me, giving a brief introductory course as she did so. She shared both the history and diversity of this extraordinary medium, in which nearly all of the practitioners have been women working in anonymity. On the most superficial level, the quilts seemed governed by issues of practicality. Fashioned from recycled fabrics, scraps of clothing that had long ago served their primary usefulness, they were made for warmth, padded comforters to shut out the winter cold, especially in an era where heat was a precious commodity.

Yet there was so much more to the quilts. Kate pointed out the complex stitching, which not only held the padding in place but was in itself a beautiful element of design. Even if these women did not call themselves artists, it was clear that many were. And some of them, rightfully proud of their work, defied convention and did sign their quilts, even shunning traditional designs to create their own with a breathtaking level of invention.

Recent decades have seen a surge of interest in quilts, in no small part because there are parallels in modern painting. The color field and minimalist painters of the 1950s and '60s—Mark Rothko, Kenneth Noland, Frank Stella, Morris Louis, Jules Olitski—caused art lovers to look at quilts, nonfigurative Amish ones especially, in a whole new light.

More recently African-American quilts, disdained because of a different underlying aesthetic, have begun to be given their due. It's now clear that some men made quilts as well. And today, many contemporary quilt makers are continuing to expand the possibilities of the medium.

I felt welcome at America Hurrah and came back again and again to look and to learn. I bought books on quilts and quilt calendars and studied the images, trying to refine my taste. Finally, I bought my first quilt from Kate and Joel. It was still a safe quilt, not strong enough to be mounted on a stretcher and hung as art. But it was made of beautiful nineteenth-century fabrics with a subtle play of pattern and color. It was perfect for my bed, the centerpiece of my bedroom, and I began to decorate around it. I was now in love with quilts, and as is the case with everything I become passionate about, this one was only the first.

The next quilts I bought from Kate and Joel were a major step up. They were both Amish, one from Ohio, one from Indiana, and I had stretchers made for them, attaching the quilts with Velcro, so they could be displayed on the wall. The Ohio quilt followed the traditional cactus-basket pattern, but the blues, blacks, and occasional lavender in the fabrics gave it a transcendent richness.

I was amazed that a quilt that was so seemingly dark on the surface could be so vibrant. There was a sheen, like polished cotton, in the black, and the other colors pulsed against it. This was a quilt made within the constraints and devotion of the Amish way of life, and in its visual depth one could find spiritual depth as well. The quilt was large, perhaps six by eight feet, and it took up most of the far wall of my dining room. When you turned from the living room, it was the first thing you saw.

Drama in a Tiny Dining Room

My furnishings and the objects I loved were beginning to come together. The James Mont Art Deco table that I'd lacquered black gleamed against the quilt, as did the 1930s clear plastic and chrome hat stands I placed on it as a centerpiece. Right after college, I had bought dishes that I'd longed for in a pattern called Anemone. They were made by Arabia, a Scandinavian manufacturer, and they had a dove gray center circled by two bands of cobalt blue. Something about the color combination moved me; I found it rich and provocative, just as I had the colors of the cactus-basket quilt. Although purchased five years apart, the quilt and the plates complemented one another perfectly. Accidental associations can sometimes yield even greater rewards than those that are planned.

The final additions to the dining room were two tall lamps that began on bamboo poles and spread out into giant fans. I had seen them and a number of variations first in a lighting fixtures store called George Kovacs, and then in Bloomingdale's. When lit from behind, they were simultaneously sensuous and grand. There was no designer attribution, and in those early years I wouldn't have known to inquire who made them. But in assessing the caliber of a work, the most important factor is not the identity of the designer, although this has a value of its own. Too often people judge a piece of art by the creator's name. But even a great designer can make an unsuccessful work. First and foremost, you have to trust your eye.

These lamps were extraordinary; of that there was no doubt. I bought a pair, one for each corner of the dining room. When dimly lit, they were radiant, with an elegant presence, giving the room an exotic and otherworldly feel. It was only many, many years later, when I became friends with Ingo Maurer, the poet of light, that I learned that he, although choosing to remain anonymous, was responsible for the lamps. But by then, it didn't matter.

Suddenly the dining room had drama, based on just five elements. The quilt contributed the greatest impact. Rather than overwhelm the space, its large size gave the small room an unexpected sense of scale, and emphasized one of the apartment's pluses, the height of the ceilings. For me, it was also the emotional center. I loved the tension in the quilt— on the one hand, it was enormously sophisticated, on the other, clearly homemade. Against it, the lacquered table with its unusual structure and chrome pipes added a slicker, more urban sense of style. The coloration of the plates tied the two together, and the lamps brought an ethnic glamour to the space. Finally, there were the Lucite hat stands, capped with chrome, that I used as a centerpiece. I had purchased them because they were sculptural, abstract, and spare. It was nearly impossible to imagine their true function, and they therefore added mystery, lifting the room beyond the literal.

Looking back on my first decorating attempts as a quasi-adult, I think the dining room really worked. But the rest of the apartment was less successful and underscored how inexperienced I was. I was grappling with many things that later, with practice, became easier for me—color, invention, and spatial relationships. There was one, however, that I never quite seemed to master—my budget, or more accurately, my questionable ability to stick to one. Untried, without so much as a correspondence course to coddle me with decorating tips, I experimented as I went, and in doing so, I made my share of mistakes. In hindsight, I realize that this was simply part of the process. Even my errors showed someone striving to break out of the box.

The Error of Her Ways

I began the dining room from scratch, and perhaps for that reason it reflected a surer hand than the living room and bedroom, where finances dictated that I recycle whatever furniture I had. Even so, I inadvertently created my own impediments, and the resulting effects were flawed. I had a handful of furnishings that I couldn't afford not to use. There was a butcher-block sofa with clean, simple lines, and sailcloth cushions in a strong bright blue. I had gotten it at Design Research, the home of the Eames chair and Marimekko fabrics. The second was a black-and-white checkerboard-patterned straw rug, which I'd bought for a floor-through rental that I'd started to decorate and then been forced to move out of before I'd gotten very far. With a stretch, it could be called my first custom rug. When I was in college, it was common for students to have some version of this floor covering, largely because it was the cheapest rug around. It was made of woven, straw-like squares that were sewn together, and one more or less ordered them by the piece: eight squares by ten squares, six squares by nine. Not only did the material look like straw, so did the color.

When I was buying items for my floor-through, Bloomingdale's was having a rug sale in its New York store, and I decided to check it out. But even with prices slashed, the quality rugs I could afford were the size of bath mats, and I needed to cover a large area. Although the prices were prohibitive, I nonetheless ambled over to the panels where good-size rugs were mounted for easy viewing. There amid the florals, geometrics, and ethnic rugs of many lands, I saw the straw squares of my college days. Only this time they came in a variety of colors: the obligatory wheat, a deeper brown, bleached white, dark green, burgundy, and black.

As in college, these rugs were sold by the

square. I gazed from the black to the white and back again. An upscale vision flashed through my mind of checkerboard marble floors, a staple in stately homes of the rich. For me, the attraction was not their gleaming message of money but their graphic strength. Within seconds I'd found a salesman. I had an idea.

"So," I broached the subject, "these rugs are available by the square?"

"Of course," the salesman replied, sounding piqued that I'd dragged him over to ask such an obvious question. But I was just warming up.

"If, then, I wanted to order the rug in alternating squares of black and white, would that be possible?"

He looked weary and skeptical. "I really can't answer that. I mean, no one ever has. I'll have to ask the manager." He disappeared to a desk somewhere between the kilims and the dhurries. At a distance I could see he was talking on the phone. I couldn't tell if he was rolling his eyeballs, but I felt sure he was.

Finally the salesman returned. He looked as if he'd been hit by a truck, but he made a supreme effort to get the words out. "Well, it looks like it's possible. It will take longer to get, and there will be a slight extra charge, but if you want it, I can go ahead and order it."

I did want it. And a couple of months later the rug arrived, brightening the large and harmonious proportions of my front room and giving it something more: drama and energy. But when I brought the rug to the Century, its dimensions were wrong—too square for the long, narrow living room. Luckily, this was a rug made of squares loosely sewn together, so I cut a number of them off on one side and made it fit as best I could. The butcher-block sofa happily looked good, and once I'd changed the rug's proportions, it lifted my new living room as much as it had the old. The orange Jan Eskëlius worked, too.

But now I began to make mistakes. I saw a couch with a light and graceful open back that looked as though it were constructed by lashing sticks of bamboo to one another. Its cushions were covered in a clear and sunny yellow cotton. The sofa had quickened my pulse, and it was clear I needed more seating. So I bought it. But in making this purchase, I had forgotten a critical detail. My apartment had only one bedroom. If I wanted to have guests spend the night, I needed a convertible sofa. Now there is nothing wrong with two couches in a living room, but only a demented person would have three. I had doomed myself to having multiple sofas in a twelve-by-twenty-four-foot living room.

Gloomily accepting my fate, I scoured the convertible sofa shops until I found the least offensive representative—no small task, since this species of furniture clearly has mating rituals based on escalating scales of ugliness. To the salesman's horror, I covered it in pink cotton. The pink somewhat softened my mistake. It didn't shout: I'm a sofa! Look at me! the way the bright blue and cheery yellow did. But, even so, three sofas in my living room gave it the distinct atmosphere of a budding furniture warehouse.

Art on the Walls to Art in the Stalls

Despite the calamity of the couches, there were other bright spots as I began to acquire the tools to personalize my space. Two of them I owe to a close friend of that time, Rachelle Epstein. Shelley had studied art at Tyler and Yale. Later she would become a jewelry designer at Tiffany's before gaining her own boutique at Bergdorf Goodman, but at that time she worked in a gallery while pursuing painting when she could. Shelley called one day to tell me that there was a show at the gallery that she thought I'd like. It was an exhibit of the work of young emerging artists, many of whom Shelley knew personally.

I had always felt that a singular piece of art was beyond my reach. I counted myself lucky to have discovered photographs for many reasons, but one of them was their low prices. Because it was possible to strike unlimited prints from a single negative, the market value of photos tended to be depressed. Not so with paintings. So when Shelley added that I might even want to buy something from the show, I was quick to exclaim, "Oh, I couldn't possibly afford anything."

"You never know, Jenette. Some of the pieces are really reasonable."

My interest roused, I showed up for the opening at the Willard Gallery. Shelley was right; there was some wonderful work on display, and at least several of the artists represented in that exhibit went on to have important careers. I was struck in particular by the art of a woman in her twenties who had the unlikely but prophetic name of Lois Lane. Among the paintings and sculptures in the show Lois had several works on paper, which combined pencil and paint with images cut from magazines. They had a clean freshness, and joined whimsy and mystery in a way that felt appealing and new. Each, of course, was one-of-a-kind. But because the art was on paper instead of canvas, they were priced as drawings, not paintings.

Yes, despite all my protestations, Shelley was right. I could afford them, and I bought two on the day of the opening. Thanks to Shelley's urging, I had broken through to acquiring a broader base of art. Despite my limited income, I found that by buying sparingly (and usually paying for my purchases over time) I could afford:

designer furniture and lighting
photographs
quilts
works on paper (posters, drawings, silkscreens)
crafts
and, ultimately, even paintings and sculptures.

I collected all of the above, and other things as well. Every area had a separate learning curve, and I made more than my share of mistakes. But there was always keen pleasure in the pursuit, and in most cases, even greater pleasure in living with what I bought. Although we all have to find our own way, I'm happy to share my helpful hints. But that's for another part of the book.

It was Shelley again who opened up another field to me. Or perhaps I should say fields; she introduced me to outdoor flea markets, which, rain or shine, would take place on several acres of grassy land on a Sunday, a weekend, or as in the case of the legendary flea market in Brimfield, Massachusetts, for a week at a time. But Shelley was suggesting something a little less daunting and closer to home, a flea market in Stormville, New York.

Although hard-core buyers arrive at shows like Stormville long before sunup, moving from table to table with flashlights to get the jump on everyone else, Shelley and I drove up at a somewhat saner hour, but early enough that not all the best things were sold. As we clambered to the top of the knoll, where the market was in full swing, I was startled to see row after row of jury-rigged stalls piled high with what anybody at first blush would have to call junk. And to be fair, a lot of it was junk. But, depending on your taste, there amid the clutter were wondrous things to discover: old advertising signs, humorous salt and pepper shakers, World's Fair souvenirs, ancient Steiff stuffed animals, luminous Bakelite jewelry, tinkling tin toys, and gewgaws, gimcracks, and bibelots of every sort and quality. I felt an enormous rush of excitement and, like everyone else at the market, hurried from table to table, raking each surface with my eyes to get an overview, then combing through objects more slowly, picking them up, holding them, turning them over, trying them on. And always calling out: "Shelley! Look at this! What do you think?"

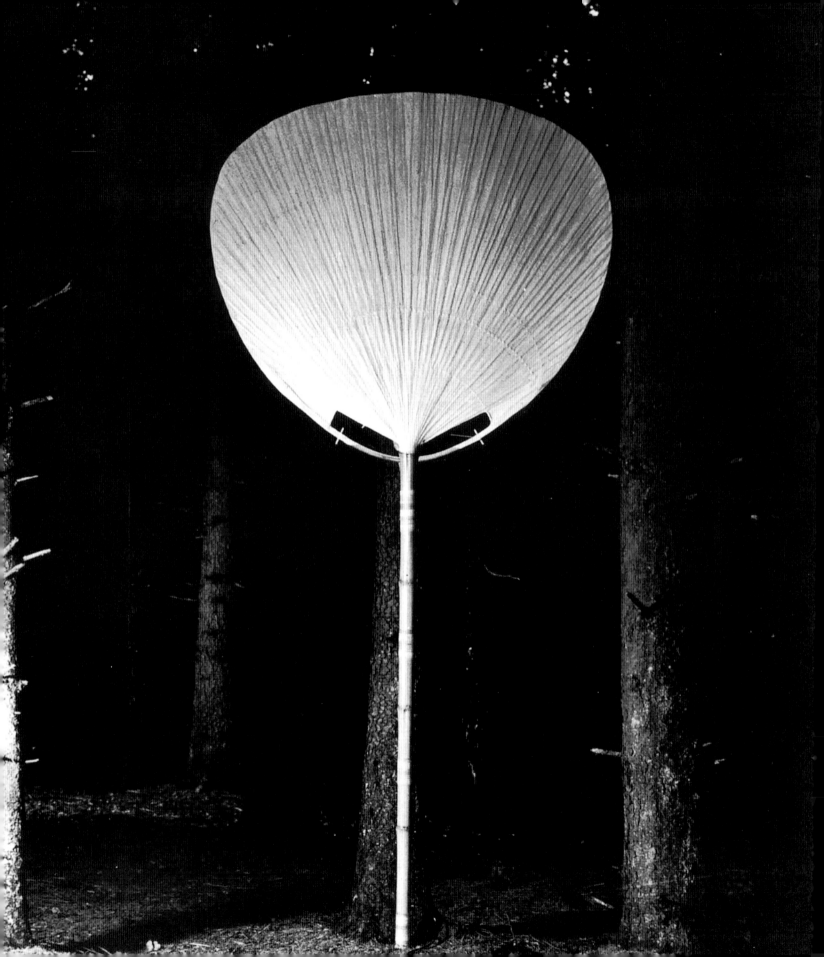

What did I buy that day? Two Art Deco clocks, one with a coin that commemorated Guglielmo Marconi's first wireless transmission inset between the rim and the center, the other with the 1939 World's Fair Trylon and Perisphere painted on a circular blue field. An electrified Lucky Strike counter display predating World War II, when the package was still green. A pair of signs fashioned from rectangular boxes faced with glass, one for a ladies' room, one for a men's. These I had wired, as they originally were, so that the images on them lit up. I placed one above my bathroom door on the left, one on the right. The signs had Art Deco type and graphics that echoed the bathroom's still-intact 1930s tile. I began to see how a little money and a little wit could transform an otherwise predictable space. Flea markets, I quickly learned, are a vast resource for implementing this equation.

So looking back, what did I learn in these early years? More than I would have ever imagined.

Lessons Learned Along the Way

1. I discovered that conviction is one thing, impulsiveness quite another. It's a lesson that's taken me years to learn, and to be honest, I'm always falling off the wagon. The important thing to keep in mind is that you can walk away from most things, and they'll still be there when you return. Needless to say, the stakes are higher when the piece is rare or one-of-a-kind. You can always try putting a hold on it for a specified period of time, and if the dealer refuses, you can weigh the odds of reflection versus the chance that you might lose it.

But clearly, when something is contemporary and readily available, you don't have to jump at it. Anybody who does that will inevitably end up with three sofas in her living room.

2. Significant art can be affordable, even on a very limited budget. You have to have passion, the desire to learn, and a belief in your own taste. But the art is out there, and so are the dealers and artists who are willing to work with you.

3. Fight for your vision. Some things on the surface may seem carved in stone, but a little push can reveal the San Andreas Fault just inches below. What otherwise was an ordinary inexpensive straw floor covering became both an interesting checkerboard rug and a strong design statement. But it would never have occurred if I hadn't questioned whether it was possible to depart from the usual way the carpeting was sold. When you ask someone to make an exception, the answer often is no. But you never want to miss the times when the answer is yes.

4. Tag sales and flea markets can yield personal and original objects without overtaxing your budget.

5. Mistakes are part of the creative process. You always hope they're not crushingly expensive, but errors simply come with the territory. Although there's always a cost involved, each mistake is also educational and helps you move to the next level.

6. Everything is source material. It's critically important to see and read and experience as much as possible. This is the best way to hone your taste. The larger your intellectual and emotional databases, the more possible connections you are able to make when trying to find a creative solution. As with the other five points, this is a truism you'll see borne out in your own design adventures.

Ingo Mauer's proud and poetic fan lamp inspired me to use two to create drama in my tiny dining room

2.

Mid-Century Modern

The Eames Eiffel Tower chairs, whose
metal construction brings to mind the soaring
Paris landmark.

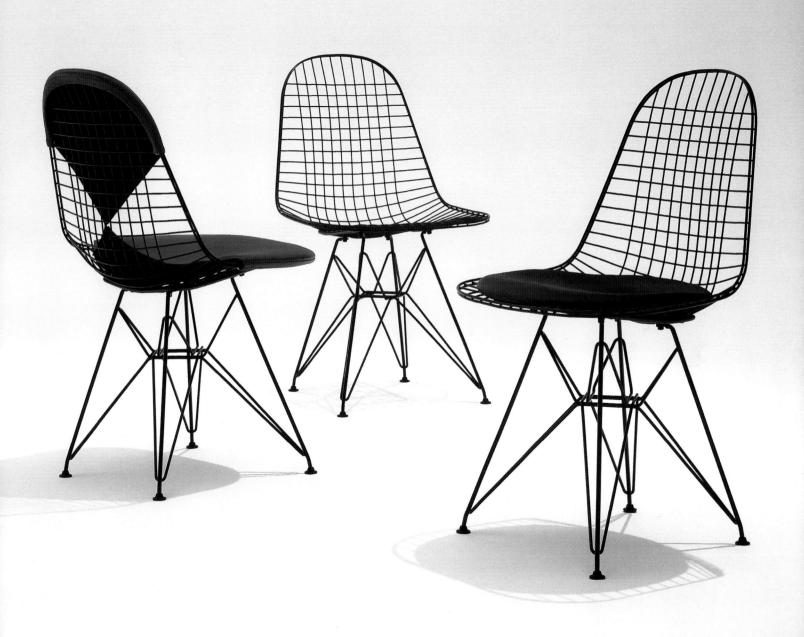

Somewhere between my first incarnation at the Century and my last, I got married. In addition to imposing a more adult decor, this also meant having to compromise so that two people with very different tastes could be comfortable in the same space, or at least a little less miserable. My husband was so convinced that I couldn't decorate, he insisted on a professional designer. And although I felt he was wrong in this assessment, I really couldn't blame him. After all, when we met, I had three couches in the living room. On the other hand, I had seen his decorator-designed house, which I thought was about as imaginative as an Ethan Allen model room. Temporarily, at least, we were at an impasse.

Skipping a Period: Jumping from 1930s to 1950s Design

Meanwhile, my collecting urges were forcing me into the streets. Eager to find new sources, I combed the yellow pages under Galleries and Antiques. Anything that seemed potentially interesting I put on my list. This was nearly twenty years ago, and my focus at that time was on Art Deco and Art Moderne. The places and people I chose to visit all specialized in those areas of design. One of them was Alan Moss, a private dealer who then was working out of his loft on Sixteenth Street. I made a date and, at the appointed time, arrived at his door. Although Alan lived there, it was hard to imagine where; the space was crammed with coffee tables, dining tables, chairs, sideboards, couches, daybeds, table lamps, ceiling lamps, bookcases, bureaus, and decorative objects too numerous to count. But somehow, with Alan navigating, I began tentatively to negotiate the territory, scanning the Art Deco pieces I'd hurried

down to see. So much was extraordinary—Alan has remarkable taste—but nothing caused me to vocalize that ill-advised collector's cry when passion overtakes judgment: "Oh, my God, it's fabulous! How much is it?" Instead I moved through Alan's storehouse as rapidly as I could, knowing that every other foot was mined.

Suddenly I halted, struck dumb by a tiny oasis of what seemed to me incomprehensible beauty. In front was a round plywood coffee table stained red. Near it was a fabric-covered chair that momentarily made you think of airline seats but was ever more graceful and clearly had been designed by someone whose gift was form as much as function. Not far away were five aluminum standing lights of different heights whose bases interlocked. They made me think of musical notes. All were wonderful. And none of them was Art Deco.

"Alan, tell me about these."

"Well, the coffee table, it's often called the Flying Saucer table, is by Charles Eames. It's from the fifties, made of bent plywood, and also came in natural and black."

"And the lights?"

"Italian. From the fifties, too. Osvaldo Borsani designed them."

"And the chair?

"It's also by Borsani. The back has numerous settings. So does the footrest. Or you can tuck it right under the seat. It's called the Tecno chair, and ads for it in the fifties show how it reclines so far back that you can practically sleep in it. Oh, and look at the arms. They're made of a hard rubber, but they're also flexible."

And so saying, Alan pushed down on one of them so that it seemed to collapse. Rather than a raised support for the sitter, it now was a black concave line following the curve of the chair.

Why did these pieces look so startling, so

amazingly new and so contemporary? Next to them, my passion for Art Deco objects began to ebb. In a flash, they seemed to me like anachronisms, rich and elegant ornaments of a bygone age. It is hard to explain these sea changes, when your taste shifts in a moment of epiphany from one era to another. It is like meeting a potential new lover and deciding in seconds that he has all the sparkle and verve, all the edge, that you now are sure has been missing for years with the old love, blunted by time and familiarity. I merely know that in that downtown loft jammed with a thousand Deco suitors, I gave my heart to another and never looked back.

Needless to say, I bought the Eames table, the Tecno chair, the Borsani lamps. It was the beginning of a personal revolution, and my next experience only took me further down the road.

Mort, my husband-to-be, was in L.A. on a business trip that encompassed a weekend when one of the grand, three-pier antiques shows was being held in New York. I arrived on my own, late, far too late for any self-respecting collector, on Sunday afternoon when the piers were closing at six. Nonetheless, there was a

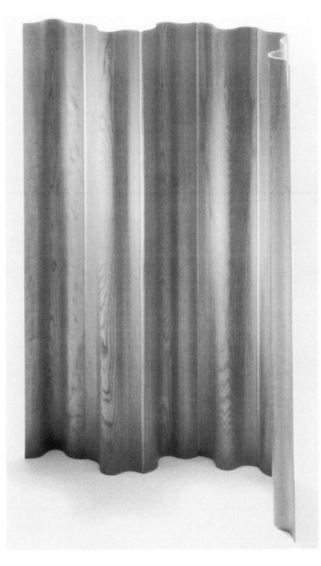

Another Charles and Ray Eames icon, a luminous bent-plywood screen hinged by vertical canvas strips.

tremendous amount to see, and I hurriedly whizzed up and down the aisles.

Despite the abundance and variety of objects, nothing altered my pace until I was struck by a spare and elegant column of bent plywood that looked more like a minimalist sculpture in the Museum of Modern Art than a piece of furniture. Eager to know more, I vied for the dealer's attention, managing at least to catch his girlfriend's eye.

"Excuse me, but what is that—I don't know what to call it—that tall curved piece of wood?"

"Larry," she signaled to her companion, "this woman would like to see the Eames screen."

At that, he turned around, lifted the wooden column off the pedestal on which it stood, and carried it into the vast middle aisle, empty now except for the occasional last-minute shopper. And then, with the suspense of a stage magician, he unfolded the column into two, then three, four, and finally five sections, forming a simple but magnificent curvilinear wall of wood. Each panel had the same gently rounded form, and each was connected to the next not by hinges but by a strip of linen-colored canvas.

The canvas, it seemed to me as I tried to take it all in, was a stroke of genius, combining pragmatism with aesthetics to such an intense degree that it was hard to know where one left off and the other began. The strips broke the wood into component parts, emphasizing the lean but sensuous shape of each panel. They had a rhythm of their own, too—straight, clean, vertical lines that played against the plywood's curves. The naturalness of the canvas, so raw as to seem almost primitive, made the wood gleam all the more.

Larry must have heard my sharp intake of breath. "It's beautiful," I finally managed. Followed by the fatal question: "How much is it?"

"Well, it's $3,600, but the show's about to end, and I wouldn't mind not having to ship it back to California. So if you pay for it now and take it now, I'll give it to you for three."

Eames. Charles Eames. There was that name again. The chair in the window of Design Research, my brother's construction kit, the Flying Saucer table. This was the first I'd seen or heard of an Eames screen. I had no idea what it was worth. But $3,000 suddenly seemed like a bargain—except for one problem. I had no money.

"Let me see what I can do. Do you know where the pay phones are?"

Miraculously, Mort was in his hotel room on a Sunday afternoon. "The show's about to close. It's incredibly beautiful. We can get it for three thousand instead of thirty-six hundred. What do you think?"

To his credit, without having a clue what I was talking about, he trusted me and okayed the purchase. Five minutes later we were the owners of an Eames screen. The course was set. We would collect 1950s furniture and redo my apartment with it.

When Mort returned from L.A., we started seeing dealers together. We trekked down east and south of the Lower East Side in search of another Tecno chair. From Tony Delorenzo, who specialized in exquisite, often one-of-a-kind Art Deco pieces, we bought a Tecno sofa. Tony, too, had suddenly been bitten by the 1950s bug, and he was bringing in beautiful designer furniture from Europe. From him we also bought an elegant desk by Jean Royère, and two grand palette chairs by Royère as well. From Bill Webber, a dealer who unfortunately died many years ago of AIDS, we got a refined cabinet by Maurice Pré with alternating sliding bands of clear and dark glass. In Paris we bought a Serge Mouille totem pole lamp. Somewhere in New York we picked up a Noguchi dining room table and six Eames wire Eiffel Tower chairs to go around it. For a one-bedroom apartment, we had almost all the furniture we needed.

Still Flirting with the Thirties

Simultaneous with our 1950s fascination I stumbled on two other areas of collecting. Interestingly, although I had turned my back on Art Deco in favor of the more forward-looking designs of a later decade, both of these pursuits were planted firmly in the 1930s, the era when Art Deco flourished.

The first occurred in, of all places, a department store—Barney's, when Barney's was located on Seventh Avenue and Seventeenth Street, before there was also a Barney's on Madison Avenue. It had been founded as a discount store for men's clothing by the family patriarch, Barney Pressman, but by that time, control had passed to his son, Fred, whose vision for Barney's was more comprehensive. Fred had made Barney's a family affair, and everyone—from his wife, Phyllis, to each of their children—became a decision maker, expanding its inventory and raising the bar on style for all other department stores.

While most people traveled to Barney's for the cutting-edge designer clothes that Gene, one of Fred's sons, was importing from Europe, I was mesmerized by Phyllis's concentration on antique jewelry, silver, and British china. As you entered the store from Seventh Avenue, all these things were immediately on view to your left. Phyllis's taste was superlative, and I would quickly scurry toward the displays to see what new treasures she'd unearthed.

One day I spied a round ceramic pot about ten inches high and twelve inches in diameter, resting on several half-moon feet. In shape alone it had simplicity, scale, and presence, all of which greatly appealed to me. But what seized my attention was the way it was painted. The background was cream, and on it were several childlike green trees with black trunks, and a little house, with a black door and chimney and an orange roof, that sat on a gen-

tle knoll of grass. The clouds that floated near the top looked as though they had been taken from the pages of a comic book, each one a simple notation made from curved black lines. Everything, in fact, was outlined in black: the grass, the house, the green, ballooning puffs that were shorthand for the bushes and trees. Even the one-inch band of orange that circled the edge of the pot had a thin rule of black running next to it.

Looking at these black lines filled in with vibrant but limited paints, it was easy to think of a children's coloring book. But there was nothing crude about the decoration. It was instead enormously sophisticated. The naïveté was indisputably purposeful, the design bold and modern. The cachepot, I discovered, was by Clarice Cliff, a British artist who, at thirteen, had apprenticed at one of the potbanks near her impoverished village of

Five small examples of Clarice Cliff's Inspiration pattern, with its iridescent blues and greens.

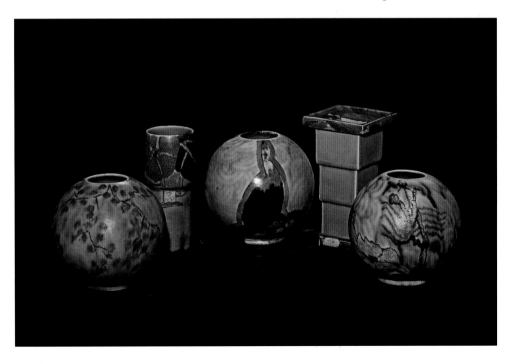

Tunstall. It was there that she learned the craft of hand-painting ceramics.

Women in the potbanks earned far less than men and were not permitted to design patterns or model shapes. But from the beginning, Cliff had been determined to break through the ceramic ceiling. And by the mid-1920s, when she was no more than twenty-six herself, she had not only developed a uniquely personal style but was modeling, designing, and painting, and earning more than any other woman in the factory. Far more importantly, she was impacting British pottery with her bold, highly charged colors, her vivid, modern patterns, and the exciting new shapes that reflected her one trip abroad, to Paris, and the Art Deco exposition in 1925.

Although the cachepot had force and beauty in its own right, its effect on me was heightened by my sense of discovery. It is nearly impossible to describe the thrill of experiencing something for the very first time.

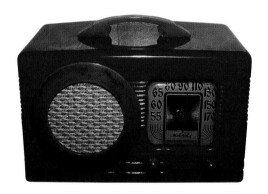

A Bakelite radio, glowing with saturated color.

Whether it's the first ice cream cone, one's first kiss, or the first day at school, these watershed events are etched indelibly in one's mind. The world has expanded: it is not simply about the experience, it is also about a growing sense of mastery.

I conveyed my excitement to Mort, who was infected by my sense of adventure. Not surprisingly, we decided to buy the cachepot. A few days later, hoping to learn more, I returned to Barney's to see other Clarice Cliffs. Although the store's selection represented only a fragment of her extraordinary

output, I was still struck by the diversity of shapes and ornamentation and the freshness of her work. The patterns might be geometric or floral—or even representational, if one could call the abstracted landscape on the cachepot that—but the colors always seemed newly minted, and almost every one had a feeling of experimentation.

I picked up a small spherical vase of pungent greens and purples. It depicted a house with a short black tree, almost a bush, but the image seemed immaterial in this field of saturated color. When I turned it over to examine it, I found not only Clarice Cliff's name on the bottom but also the name of her line of pottery, Bizarre. You had to love this woman.

"This specific design is called Inspiration," said the knowledgeable woman helping me. "It's prized among collectors."

And I could see why. There was an exotic iridescence to the color, as though a rare tropical fish had flashed its deep-sea plumage before disappearing into the depths. It made me think of my mother's oil paints, and the one tube called Thalo green I seized upon as a child. Like the colors on the vase it, too, had a shimmery, emotional quality.

"Mummy, use Thalo green, use Thalo green."

And my mother would patiently explain that Thalo green was a difficult color to employ. It was demanding, it upset the balance, it could be used only very, very sparingly, if at all. Yet here was this vase, seemingly drenched in Thalo green.

The saleswoman interrupted my thoughts. "This piece is particularly rare. If you'll look closely, you'll see that the name Clarice Cliff is not stamped but actually written by hand. That means that Clarice Cliff herself painted this, not one of the girls she taught to execute her designs."

I held the vase gingerly and turned it slowly around so that I could see it from every point of view. It was beautiful—equal parts modern art, ancient artifact, and Scheherezade. And it was unique. I thought it would make a wonderful gift for Mort, and that's what it became. The Inspiration vase could not have been better named; together with the cachepot, it was just that, the impetus to start collecting Clarice Cliff. England, Clarice Cliff's home, was the mother lode. Our wedding and honeymoon were just around the corner, and so was our first stop, London.

Radiohead

Meanwhile, another collection began to form. I had been interested in Bakelite jewelry for quite some time, and dealers, like old-fashioned peddlers, would periodically stop by my office and spread out their wares. Bakelite was a plastic invented as an insulation material in the 1920s by a Dr. Baekeland. A mottled greenish brown, it was easily molded, and everything from flashlights to radios to the handles of irons began to be fashioned from it. Only a few years later, it was discovered that if formaldehyde was added to the formula, this new material could be transformed from humdrum hues into the most brilliant colors. Red, yellow, green, blue—even black—had never glistened with such intensity. A whole new world opened up. Bakelite was no longer utilitarian. It was decorative.

Bakelite objects of every sort sprang up, from sophisticated salt and pepper shakers to magnificent

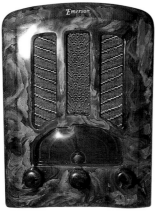

Another Bakelite radio, one of the few vertically shaped examples of the era.

chess sets. But probably nothing was produced in such incredible abundance and diversity as costume jewelry. Pins, necklaces, bracelets, earrings—every ornament possible drew on Bakelite's stunning colors and virtuosity. Suddenly there was Bakelite jewelry in the shape of hearts, hats, Scottish terriers (this was the same period in which the presidential dog, FDR's Scottie Fala, had become the national pet), clusters of cherries, bunches of bananas, scarecrows, pianos, and musical notes. Other pieces were elegant, geometric, and beautifully structured, particularly bracelets and a coveted number of necklaces. It was easy to be hooked, and I was.

Understandably, Mort had no interest in Bakelite jewelry. For him, it was a girl thing. Nor did he like my quilts, although he had generously bought me one when I became president of DC Comics. I disclose his antipathies only because they set the background for what became our next collection.

One day a dealer named John Sideli visited my office with his latest in Bakelite jewelry. I was scanning his new offerings when John interrupted me.

"Do you want to see something really beautiful?" Naturally, of course, immediately. Only ascetics and masochists would decline.

John whisked out a large color transparency, and there in the photograph were some nine to twelve radios, their colors so luminous that they seemed to float off the shelves. I was dumbstruck by how beautiful they were.

My mind racing ahead, I asked John if I could borrow the transparency.

"Sure," he replied. He knew I had taken the bait.

Later that evening at dinner with Mort, I repeated John's question like a Stepford wife. "Do you want to see something beautiful?"

"All right. What is it?"

I flashed the transparency and saw Mort's face light up. These weren't just decorative objects. They were radios. I could feel his Y chromosome kick in.

"They're for sale. We can go see them. It's about a two-hour drive."

And sometime not long after, we were headed north toward a tiny town in the middle of nowhere to a place where plastic was worth its weight in gold. When we arrived at John's house, there were the radios, shiny as jewels, eclipsing all else. John actually had more than thirty and permitted us to make changes in the mix. Mort selected one I secretly thought was duller than dull, but I willed myself to say nothing, understanding that the rules of partnership sometimes require that you just shut up. No money exchanged hands, but it seemed to all we had made a deal.

However, only a few days after Mort was exulting in our purchase of the radios, he took a different stance. "We can't afford them," he said. "The radios are too big an investment."

"But I thought we told John we were buying them."

"I don't care what we said. They're too expensive."

I was shocked, both because of this sudden about-face and because I believed we'd made a promise to John. Nonetheless, it was Mort who had money in the bank, not I. "I'll tell you what," I rejoined after fast-forwarding a number of mental scenarios. "I really believe in the radios. You do, too. On the other hand, you don't like my quilts. I'll sell my quilt collection to finance the radios."

And that's what happened. It was one of those things you do in a relationship you believe is going to last. You give up some things that are strictly personal, especially if they make one partner uncomfortable. For instance, if I were ever to get engaged again and, in a truly deranged moment, actually selected someone who had a trophy collection of animal heads, the wedding would be off unless he agreed to leave them behind. And so it was that I sold my quilts, and the radios were ours.

Decorator Days

Meanwhile, we also compromised on a designer, although at the time neither of us had any idea what an extraordinary compromise it would prove to be. If I wasn't going to be the decorator—and it was clear that the job description excluded family members—then I at least wanted someone with an artistic sensibility. Both Mort and I had worked with Milton Glaser, who, although not an interior designer per se, is unquestionably one of the great design innovators of the last fifty years. Holding him in the highest esteem, we went to Milton for a recommendation. Milton suggested a former student who had embarked on a career of interior design. I can remember only his first name, Phil. It's unclear when I doomed his last name to oblivion, but it was bound to happen, considering the disastrous events that followed.

Mort and I moved out of the apartment so that the floors could be sanded and painted black according to Phil's design. We moved back in while the rest of the work was being done under Phil's auspices and those of a contractor he'd hired. Part of the plan was to modernize the bathroom while keeping the original Art Deco tile in place. This meant building mirrored cabinets the length of the wall and a counter and drawers below them. In the kitchen, new cabinets were also planned. And the bedroom too needed closet and storage space. For all this work, someone, Phil or the contractor, engaged a carpenter. His name, like the contractor's, is also lost to me, another casualty of the renovation wars.

Although Mort and I were gone during the day, signs of unrest began to show. Whichever person was in the apartment when we returned would grouse about the others. The salvos increased in frequency, and in this triumvirate of people working on our apartment, no one was immune. But these were only skirmishes. Full-scale war was declared on the morning that the contractor fired the carpenter and took away his keys. I was in my office some hours later when I got a call from the Century.

"Jenette, you know the man who's been working in your apartment building cabinets or something? Well, he came by this afternoon and said he'd forgotten his keys and could we let him in."

"You didn't, did you?" Although somehow I knew the answer.

"Well, we knew he was working for you, so it seemed okay to help him out. But then someone saw he had a ladder outside your window and he was bringing things out of your apartment. He ran away when we yelled at him, but he may have taken some stuff."

I flew home, filled with dread. What had he taken in his wrath at being fired? Were my clothes still there, the stereo, our TV? Had he hidden one of my cats in the folds of his shirt like the ancient Spartan boy and the fox? But the closets were still full, and all cats were accounted for. What was gone were the cabinets, as much of his handiwork as he could remove before someone in the building caught him in the act.

The blame game was now at its peak. Phil accused the contractor of causing this fiasco; the contractor, in turn, accused Phil. As if to exonerate himself, Phil fired the contractor and promised to get everything back on track. But one week later Phil left a message that he was having a nervous breakdown and leaving New York forever.

If we hadn't been the ones caught in the cross fire, if we hadn't been the ones signing the checks, and if it hadn't been our apartment that now required a Marshall Plan to help us rebuild, the insane swirl of events actually would have been funny. Even at the time I knew this was a quintessential New York story, but it always hurt when I laughed. Today, with years gone by to deaden the blow, I can embrace the events in all their glorious lunacy. But this is now, and that was then.

When the dust cleared, we were able to take toll of the carnage. On the plus side, we had new black floors, some cabinetry, and a state-of-the-art electrical system. (It eventually proved to be something quite else, but that tale belongs to another chapter.) On the downside, we had no designer, no contractor, no carpenter, and no plans. Somewhere, life was going on around us, while we were trapped in a Buster Keaton short without nearly his spunk or resourcefulness.

The weeks dragged into months, and word of our misfortunes spread from friends to acquaintances. One day Alan Moss, the dealer from whom I'd bought my first pieces of fifties furniture, called to commiserate.

"You know, there's a new designer in town. He's young, he's Italian, he's worked for some great people in Europe, and he loves modern design. I think he might have the right sensibility for you and Mort."

Any port in a storm. "What's his name?"

"Claudio. Claudio Motta."

Soon we were meeting with Claudio, and not long after, we engaged his services. The truth is, we liked him. He was warm and enthusiastic and full of ideas and energy. For better or worse, and it was certainly both, we put ourselves in his hands. Despite his infectious bravado, Claudio willed us his own legacy of mistakes. But overall he made a massive contribution, and one that required good nature, fortitude, and a great deal of ingenuity.

He was, after all, left to complete or correct Phil's half-finished, half-aborted efforts. His new clients not only had already selected their own furniture but had a vast number of radios and over a hundred pieces of pottery. And he was dealing with a small space that could barely house all the collections.

But Claudio was unflappable, and his ideas were graceful. First, he wanted to create a unified environment that would visually link all the rooms, create a sense of expansiveness despite the apartment's size, and provide a warm but muted backdrop so that each art form—the furniture, the radios, and the Clarice Cliff—could have clarity and presence. And so he decreed that the black floors would have to go. They were too dark, too heavy, and contradicted his idea of a light and airy space. Claudio made it clear that pale floors were critical to his vision, and although it was a major expense, this was his first request of us. We believed he deserved our confidence, particularly at this early stage. Once again we moved out, and once again the floors were sanded and refinished, this time in cream.

Cream, in various shades of warmth and in various textures and surfaces, became the leitmotiv for the apartment. It was the light motif as well, creating a shell that was weightless but not sterile. One of the large Royère chairs was covered in cream leather and placed in the bedroom. Claudio deemed, rightly, that there was no space for the second one, and it was exiled to storage. Other than the many books on our shelves, there was no color in the bedroom other than cream. The ropelike rug was cream, as were the walls, in a slightly deeper hue, and the fitted spread that Claudio had fashioned out of different pieces of leather, so that the connections formed a subtle tracery. In making these choices, Claudio felt he had created a serene retreat. But I never saw anything wrong with a lively bedroom.

In the living and dining rooms, Claudio chose some color, but not much. He covered the Tecno sofa and the two Tecno chairs in turquoise leather. The Eames Eiffel Tower dining room chairs had what were called "bikini pads," and these Claudio covered in leather, too, but in a warm yellow. One final note of color appeared in the Roman shades, which were made from sailcloth in a bold yellow-and-white horizontal stripe.

The real reservoirs of color and pattern rested in the radios and the Clarice Cliff. To accommodate these, Claudio carved out enormous wall-to-wall niches, two along the right side of the living room, one on the back end of the dining room where once the cactus-basket quilt had filled the space and now there were three-foot–high cabinets built by our wayward carpenter. Claudio ordered unusually thick glass, as thick as the bottoms of Coca–Cola bottles, and turned it into shelves to support the radios and pottery. The living room shelves extended from floor to ceiling and blazed with Clarice Cliff. The shelves in the dining room glowed with the radios.

When it was finished, we had a simple but elegant space that achieved its character through the unique forms of the furniture and the strength and variety of our collections. Not everything was perfect, of course. We had cats, and cats, we were to learn, have a particular affinity for leather. The chairs were easy targets, and soon the custom leather spread on which our felines slept and stretched, stretched and slept, was covered with a fine pattern of scratches infinitely more complex than the one Claudio had originally intended.

The bed, which Claudio designed and had seemed so inspired, came with its problems, too. Claudio had constructed a low platform for the mattress, to make the room look larger and to continue his almost Asian concept of refuge and peace. Hidden below the platform ledge and following its circumference was a thread of tiny lights that, when lit, gave off a subdued radiance so that the bed seemed momentarily suspended in space. It was a novel idea, and the optical illusion was stirring, almost poetic. But Claudio had placed the transformer in the hollow of the three-dimensional headboard, and brown stains soon began to appear on its surface. Before long the lights began to flicker, and not much later, they were as dark as a Broadway theater where the show has closed.

Unable to find Claudio, who had disappeared from our lives as suddenly as he had entered them, we called the Century electrician. The problem was the transformer. Housed in a nearly airless space, it had begun to overheat. The deep stains on top of the headboard were actually scorch marks. Just short of an electrical fire that could have consumed the apartment, the transformer had self-destructed in a miraculous meltdown. The floating bed, like floating weeds, was ephemeral, carried away on a stream of heat.

Like the bed, the apartment, too, glowed for a brief moment and then was gone. Two years later I was getting divorced, and everything under the New York laws of marital property was in dispute. I didn't want to live with objects that I could no longer feel sure were mine. The uncertainty robbed me of my sense of home and place as though I were living in a dreamscape where nightmare troubled the surface. There was only one thing to do: empty the apartment and start all over again.

And so it was that the furniture went to Tony Delorenzo, to be sold and the money put in escrow. The radios and Clarice Cliff were wrapped and put in storage. All I had left were glass shelves and cream-colored walls. And soon these, too, were gone.

Lessons Learned Along the Way

1. No matter how much you love a certain period, your décor will be livelier if you mix it with pieces from other eras. The surprise touches, the unexpected painting or chair or lamp, will energize your favorite style and make it not only more interesting but infinitely more personal.

2. Suppose you'd like to start collecting, but you don't know enough to decide where your passions lie. How do you begin? Well, you can thumb through decorating magazines and illustrated books to find the periods and items that interest you. But nothing compares to seeing objects in person. Just go to your yellow pages, look under various headings like galleries, antiques, and collectibles, and start making the rounds. After several months of looking, you'll have a clear sense of your preferences.

3. One object by itself can be beautiful. But there are times when that same object, seen again and again, even with only the slightest variations, has a power far beyond the individual parts. This is as true for banal, everyday items as it is for rarefied, refined ones. If you install a collection of objects with clarity and deliberation, it will become an important focal point, arresting your attention while providing a source of constant fascination.

3.

A Century of Progress:

Design
of the Times

Naugas cavort on the dining room shelves above
Lloyd Schwan's circular table and Verner Panton's
luminous chairs.

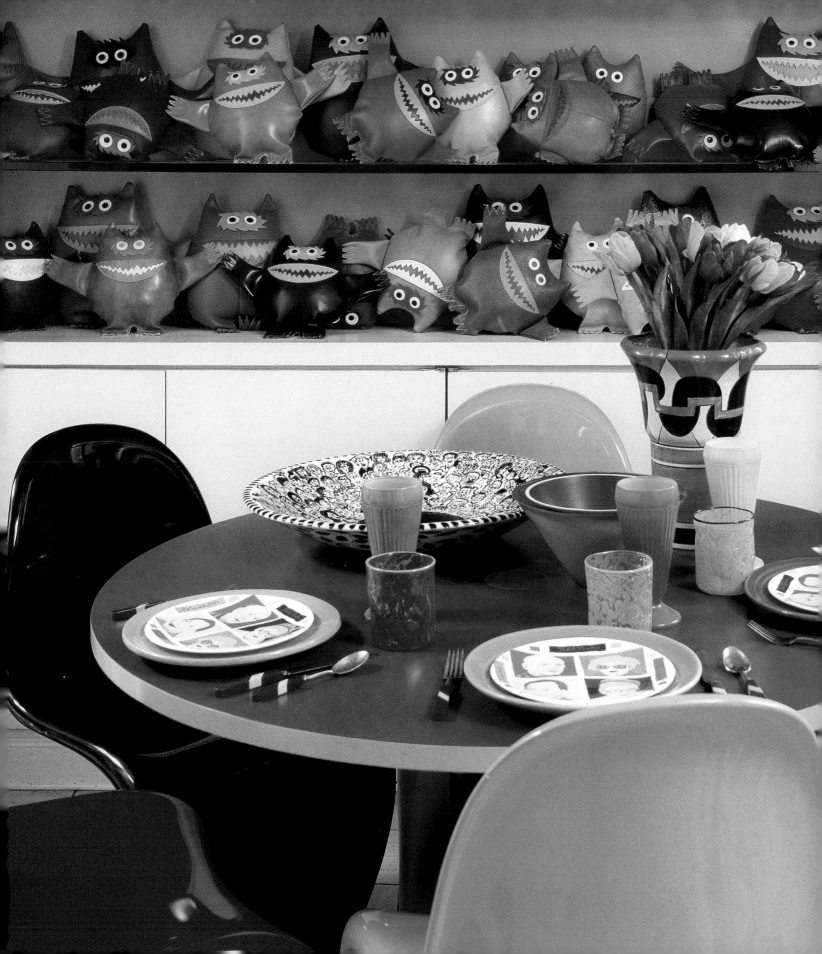

Single again! Single again! Oh, lucky me, I was single again. Where to start now that I was on my own? I bought season tickets once more to the Knicks, visited my favorite galleries, talked up a storm on the phone, sought out art and artists, hung out with old friends and continuously brought new ones into the fold, laughed a lot, opened my apartment to people who needed a place to crash, cruised flea markets and antiques shows, traveled to places I'd never been before, bought a house in the country, and began to decorate not one home but two.

I had emptied my apartment in the Century of all the things my husband and I had bought together. Now it was time to fill it up again and to make it indisputably my own. I respected Claudio's notion of a soft and weightless shell, but cream was never my color. Give me white, bright glistening white, which in its brilliant clarity is no mere backdrop but a presence to be reckoned with. And so the walls did indeed become white, while I splashed color on the ceilings. There was sky blue in the foyer and yellow everywhere else except the kitchen and halls, which served as rest stops until color exploded again in the bedroom.

It would be unfair to say I'd outgrown the 1950s furniture we'd collected when I was married. Even today there are a few select pieces that I own and others that I'd like to have. But I wanted to make an unequivocal break with my marriage and all its representations. I couldn't imagine going backward into 1930s or '40s design. The only course was to go boldly where I hadn't gone before, headlong into the 1960s and hurtling forward to the present day. This was still uncharted territory. It was nearly impossible in the 1980s to find a book in English on 1960s design, let alone on anything later. Where would

someone start? But, as happens so often in life, I found my first pieces by accident—in the small, dark basement of a chic Manhattan shop.

New Adventures in Collecting

On Madison Avenue between Sixty-seventh and Sixty-eighth Streets is a wonderful store called Primavera. It is a tiny jewel box of a shop, and jewelry is what it sells: choice, exquisite vintage pieces that reflect the high taste and selectivity of its owners, Audrey Friedman and Haim Manishevitz. My engagement ring had come from Primavera, and while serious jewelry is happily one of the few vices I don't have, I couldn't help dropping by when I was in the neighborhood. There was always so much to see and marvel at, and I enjoyed exchanging pleasantries with Haim and Audrey.

Primavera also sells lighting, furniture, and glass, most of it stellar Art Deco that is elegant, precious, and refined. But given the store's spatial limitations, one can see very little at any given time. To compensate, Audrey and Haim kept binders of photographs to show customers the many items not on display that nonetheless were still for sale.

One day Haim and I were hanging out in the store when he brought out the binders, so that we could have the fun of leafing through them. Most of the photos showed what one would expect— beautiful pieces by famed Art Deco designers. But there were also photographs of work that had nothing to do with these fabulous Deco objects. These pieces were witty and inventive, sly but good-natured, and always unconventional. And they were, for the most part, plastic. Haim and I were poring over the pictures when I couldn't contain myself: "What are these? They don't seem like you and Audrey. They're so different from everything else you have."

Haim responded with gusto. He rarely got to share his passion for this work, because it wasn't on display. And for me, it was a chance to learn about an entirely new area. Of course, Haim had more than one reason for warming to his subject. As a dealer, he had to know that my interest meant I might also be a buyer.

"We have most of these things in the basement," Haim advised, as the salesman in him quickly replaced the enthusiast. "Do you want to take a look?"

"I didn't know there was a basement here. But sure, let's look!"

In a moment we were clambering down a set of wooden stairs, leaving behind the elegance of the upper floor. When Haim turned on the lights, the room at first glance looked like a basement, anybody's basement. But as I focused more closely, I saw that this cellar was crowded with wonderful things, and soon I was spotting the ones I loved. There were two white molded fiberglass chairs and a love seat by the designer Wendell Castle. They looked like giant teeth and, not surprisingly, were called the Molar chairs. Although Wendell Castle is renowned for his precious one-of-a-kind handmade furniture, no work of his seems more modern than the Molar chairs, commissioned by design impresario George Beylerian in 1968. The large curvilinear shapes unblemished by a seam, the sheen of the fiberglass, and the subliminal dental references— dental references? in furniture?—combined to put the Molar chairs on the cusp, or bicuspid, of things to come. Today, no permanent design collection worth its salt is without them.

I had never seen the Molar chairs. They appeared as fabulous to me as they looked uncomfortable. It didn't seem possible that you could sink into the hard plastic, and of course you couldn't. But they were better than I had imagined. The back of the chair was actually at a good angle for support,

and you could prop your elbows on its rounded arms.

I wanted the love seat and chairs and paid a fortune for them. Audrey and Haim have never been known for modest pricing, and unlike most other dealers, they leave little room for negotiation. A babe in the woods of 1960s design, I committed the same cardinal sin I did when I bought my first Nauga (see page 47), thinking I'd never see one again. I accepted Haim's price and assumed it reflected the market—if in fact there was one. It is hard to be more naïve. Even with values rising in the last ten years, my Molar chairs are still the most costly ones in captivity. I will write on the blackboard one hundred times: Never buy something without doing research first…

In addition to the Molar chairs, I purchased a wonderful 1950s French rug woven out of sisal. Its background was black, and the field was articulated by an interplay of variegated geometric shapes in varying shades of primary colors. Powerful and light at the same time, I saved it for the house I had bought in the country. I also purchased a 1970 French Plexiglas lamp whose three-dimensional geometry seemed to expand when it was lit. The designer, as with that of the rug, was unknown, but it was beautiful. Years later my friend and design guru, Jim Walrod, discovered that it was by Architecture Luminaire. The firm's name could not have been more apt; the light, which I treasure, has a constructivist form that one associates with the logic—and magic—of illuminated buildings at their best.

Ferreting Out New Sources

I had now exhausted my one small source of 1960s design. Yet clearly, if Primavera had a stash in its basement, then there must be other repositories secreted throughout the city. I thought of Tony Delorenzo, who, although he specialized in European pieces from the 1930s through the 1950s, was always plugged in. Tony had also been unflaggingly honest and kind in his dealings with me. Perhaps he knew of someone who was handling more contemporary work. I gave him a call and struck gold. Tony suggested a shop called Modern Things run, he said, by two kids (kids meant people in their twenties and thirties) who had just started to deal 1960s design out of a storefront on Lafayette Street. "As far as I know they're good guys," said Tony. "And they've got good stuff."

I phoned, got the address, and was soon downtown at Modern Things. Jim Walrod, a lanky young man with blue eyes and strawberry blond hair, was manning the shop and introduced himself. Jim was hip and fun, with a love of pop culture and a passion for design. And Tony was right. He and his partner, Christopher Chestnutt, had good stuff. Almost all of it was European, some of which I was familiar with from an unexplained past life, most of which I wasn't. But right away, I knew I was in my element. The colors, of course, were key—bright oranges, Mercurochrome pink, neon green, sunshine yellow, Norell red, turquoise straight out of Howard Johnson's. But just as important were the materials—Plexiglas and fiberglass cut and molded to create unprecedented forms—and the art, the wonderful, exuberant, irrepressible art.

Although it was small, Modern Things was light and airy and jammed with furniture. What wasn't on display could be seen in photographs. I selected a Gae Aulenti lamp, the magisterial King Sun table light with a heavy domed orange base studded with tall half-moon pieces of clear plastic. A cylindrical bulb of the sort one finds in fish tanks ran up the center. When lit, it sent light around the edges of the Plexiglas and shot onto the ceiling a radiating pattern that looked liked the rays of the sun. There was a molded orange fiberglass table by the Danish designer Nana Dietzel, and the Gherpe ("shrimp")

lamp, with hot pink Plexiglas pieces that crawled on top of each other, like something scuttling on the bottom of the sea. I bought them both, and then turned to the photos Jim kept of things he might, just might, be able to get his hands on. Time stood still while I was lost in Pee-wee's Playhouse.

If American pop art flourished in painting and sculpture in the 1960s and early '70s, it seems to have burgeoned simultaneously in Europe in lighting and furniture design. There were lamps in the shape of giant pills, foam chairs fashioned to look like the capitals of fallen Greek columns, sofas in the shape of succulent lips. I wanted the pill lamps, the foam capitals, and something else the same company, Gufram, made, the Pratone or Big Meadow, a human-size pincushion of giant foam blades of grass. Jim pledged a search-and-destroy mission, and eventually came up with them all.

I Can Get It for You Wholesale

I saw Jim often. We talked about everything, but design always wove in and out of our conversation, and I continued to buy from him. Our relationship was founded on a commonality of interests but also on a base of loyalty. Early on, when I was buying furniture and lighting from Jim's store, Tony Delorenzo—who had directed me there in the first place—gave me a call.

"Jenette, I realize you're buying sixties from the kids on Lafayette, but I wanted to tell you that I know their source. I'll give you the number of the dealer where they're getting the stuff, and you can buy it direct for less."

I knew Tony only had my interests at heart, but I declined. "Tony, I really appreciate it. But the guys have been great to me, and they're just starting out. If you hadn't called me, I'd never know their supplier, and I don't want to undercut them."

To some people this might sound foolish. Why pay retail when you can get something for less? But I've always felt that many things are far more important than money, and being honorable is one of them. Tony respected my decision, and when Jim heard about it, it meant the world to him. Even if my relationship with Jim had gone no further, I would have been glad that I took this path. But my goodwill toward Jim was always answered by his equal goodwill to me.

Nicola: Pop till You Drop

When there was something Jim didn't have that he knew I wanted, he'd make introductions or give me leads, and it is to his generosity that I owe other wonderful pieces. Jim was aware that I loved the work of an exceptional French artist who goes only by her first name, Nicola. Nicola now lives in New York, and her creativity ranges from painting to performance to film. But she also makes furniture, and in Paris in the 1960s, Nicola was renowned for a number of seminal pieces. One of these was a pole lamp in the shape of an eye. The eyelid, made of plastic, opened and closed so that one could adjust the amount of light emanating from this dis-embodied orb. It was ingenious, surreal, and a little spookier than I wanted to live with. But it was memorable.

And although I didn't want to go about my appointed rounds under the glare of an all-seeing eye, I did want to live with Nicola's lip lamp, a sen-suous, ripe red mouth that, when lighted, must have inspired someone to say "eye candy" for the very first time. I also wanted one of Nicola's monumental sofas made out of body parts that one could assemble in any way one wished. There were male versions and female versions, some with faux hair in very pointed areas, others more chastely nude. I had my

preferences, but all of them were great.

Jim never forgot that I wanted Nicola's giant body sofa. So when he heard of one in major disrepair in the warehouse of another dealer, I was the first person he called. We were able to liberate the sofa for a reasonable sum, and Nicola was ecstatic. The sofa needed to be reupholstered, and Nicola lobbied to cover it in pink. But I went with my instincts and chose a bright, sunny yellow vinyl. Unlike the many things I purchased that were designated for the country house, the sofa from the start was meant for the Century. I couldn't wait for it to arrive. It already had a lot of company fast in place.

Going with the Flow

When you write about decorating, the process tends to sound linear. Yet it is anything but that, especially if you're doing it on your own and you're willing to ignore the constraints you might impose on someone else, like a time frame, or the ones someone else might impose on you, like a house style. If you're able to let the experience unfold organi-cally, then things occur as they occur, sometimes simultaneously, sometimes in tiny, consecutive baby steps, sometimes in isolated giant ones. All paths and combinations are possible if you allow them to happen. So while it might have seemed that I was on a single-minded quest for 1960s and '70s furni-ture, I was at the same time casting a very wide net of interest and curiosity, and into that swam the most remarkable things.

I Am Curious Yellow: Recent Color Photography

At twenty-one I had bought my first photograph, and within a few years I had a small but provocative collection. The photos that I'd purchased were black and white, and their scale was intimate. These were pictures that one stood close to see, just as one might hold a book at half an arm's length. Although I'd long since stopped buying photographs, the ones I continued to look at, the ones I cared about, always had something in common with the ones I already owned.

It wasn't until some seventeen years later that I experienced the shock of the new, although when I did experience it, the new was not nearly so new as it seemed to me. I had gone with a boyfriend to a benefit preview and auction at Sotheby's on behalf of AIDS-related charities. The items being auctioned were photographs, and I felt immediately at home, strolling the aisles, familiar with most of what I saw. Occasionally, small ripples of surprise brushed up against me, piquing my interest in a way that was both pleasurable and safe. So comfortable was I with this terrain that I was unprepared for two pictures that were as alien to me as the spaceship that lands in Washington in the sci-fi classic **The Day the Earth Stood Still**. Like the movie's inhabitants, who, lacking all reference points, gawked at the craft in awe, I stood before these photos, transfixed.

What made these pictures so thrillingly radical that everything else on the walls suddenly looked tame? One thing was size. They were infinitely larger than the other photos, approximately twenty-five inches high by thirty-two inches long. They were in color, and extraordinary color at that—intense, vibrant, saturated to the point of unreality. And then there was the content, as artificial as the color; every detail, every prop, was unashamedly, seamlessly arranged to create both a portrait of an interior and an interior portrait of contemporary anxiety.

One photo, not surprisingly called **Hangers**, showed walls, a floor, and a door, all covered with blue hangers that create a geometric pattern from top to bottom and from edge to edge. At first the surface whimsy makes the picture seem inviting.

But the candy colors and playfulness are also a lure into a darker, unsettling world.

In the second photograph, a vivid palette once again snaps you to attention. The entire interior is a slightly acid green—not just the floor and walls, but the canister light hanging from the ceiling, the 1960s swivel chair, the rickety table on which the TV sits, the standing lamp with a bowl of green fruit balanced on a circular shelf a foot and a half below the shade. You are immediately aware of only one other color, the chalky lavender leaves of a plant at the bottom of the picture. But there are two other colors in the photograph—the flesh tones of a woman in the chair watching TV and, all over every surface except the woman and the floor, tiny, crumpled pink blobs. What are they? The title is the clue: **Germs Are Everywhere**.

Like the first picture, this photograph is simultaneously inventive, funny, and disturbing. We never see the woman's face. She sits in a housecoat and slippers with her hair in curlers, a drink in one hand, fixated on an imageless green television screen. There are twenty picture frames on the walls—round ones and square ones, ovoid and diamond—but where the pictures should be there is nothing but flat, unyielding green. An overwhelming sense of vapidness hangs heavily over the scene, and, even in this most mundane of situations, germs eat away at the environment.

The pictures were by a photographer called Sandy Skoglund. The name was as unfamiliar to me as were the images. Was the artist a woman or a man? I hurriedly checked the estimates. Even if they sold at the low end, these pictures cost more than I'd ever paid for a photograph. In one of those rare moments of restraint—or maybe of uncertainty, not about the photos but about their value, who'd made them, their place in the history of art—I decided not to bid. But I left Sotheby's that night haunted by the memory of one room where countless colored hangers trisected the space, and another where an immovable woman in rollers seemed to meet the solid green screen of the television set with equally vacant eyes.

The next morning I was on the phone. Who was Sandy Skoglund? A woman, I was told. And where could I find her work? At Leo Castelli downtown, someone said. I called Castelli and was transferred to the gallery's print department.

"Oh, yes," said the enthusiastic voice on the other end. "Sandy Skoglund. She's terrific, isn't she? We used to handle her work. We don't anymore. But I think her dealer now is Janet Borden. You might try there." And wishing me good luck, she signed off.

The Janet Borden Gallery is located on Broadway between Prince and Spring Streets, above one of New York's finest gourmet stores, Dean and Deluca. Janet did indeed represent Sandy, and she had the two photos I'd seen: **Hangers** and **Germs Are Everywhere**. At the first available moment, I made a pilgrimage to SoHo. It was the beginning of a whole new era of collecting.

First, about Janet. I always call Janet the Bette Midler of the gallery set. She is more or less the same size as the Divine Miss M., and there is some similarity in their features, too. But nowhere are they more alike than in their bold, bald, and bawdy speech. With no compunctions at all, Janet cheerfully announces what the rest of us would love to say but only dare to think, and for that vicarious guilty pleasure we are forever in her debt.

Needless to say, I liked Janet immediately. And I loved the work she showed. Janet's gallery was dedicated almost exclusively to recent color photography, most of it large-scale and always with a singular point of view. I've long since forgotten what exhibit was up on that day of my first visit, but I do know that we not only looked at Sandy Skoglund's work but hung out in the gallery's back room and talked while Janet pulled out one picture after another. It was in that room that I was first exposed to a different kind of photography. Like Rip Van Winkle, I had been asleep for far too long, and the world to which I'd awakened was infinitely changed and infinitely wonderful.

In the Helpful Hints Department of Life

All galleries have back rooms, sometimes more than one. There is the show that is up, and then there is everything else: additional works by that artist, works by other artists the gallery represents, art on consignment, prints, drawings, artists' books. The back rooms are off-limits, but exceptions are always made. The key to admission is what you bring. Curiosity, interest, and enthusiasm go a long way. And seriousness does, too. A dealer might truly enjoy your company, but she or he is in the business of selling art, and chatting just for the fun of it is a luxury.

If a dealer is going to leave the main gallery or her desk to show you pieces not on display, she has to believe you're a customer. This doesn't mean you have to buy anything at the time. You don't have to spend a lot of money. In fact, you never have to make a purchase from the gallery. But you must be sincere that if some time you saw something you really liked, at a price you could afford, and on terms that you could manage, you would step up to the plate. If you are genuine, a good dealer will spend time with you and, in fact, be one of your greatest sources of knowledge.

At Janet Borden's, I did become a customer. My first two purchases were Sandy Skoglund's **Hangers** and **Germs Are Everywhere**. But the more I saw of Sandy's art, the more I loved it, and I began to compile a wish list. **Radioactive Cats**, which many consider her watershed photograph, was sold out, but there was always the chance of purchasing it on the secondary market. In the meanwhile, I bought a fragment of the picture—a neon green, three-dimensional papier-mâché cat that Sandy had sculpted for the piece. In a radical departure from traditional picture taking, Sandy built her own installations, which she then photographed to make her final works. Although this was a green and frankly fake feline, it nonetheless had a specific and particularly lifelike gesture. It also looked great on my orange Nana Dietzel table.

I bought another denizen of Sandy's skewed zoo, a violet-blue cast dog who lay, lovable and sleepy-eyed, on his stomach, his ears drooping toward the ground. Again, he seemed as real as he was artificial, his doggy characteristics captured to a tee, his body insistently purple from snout to tail. The dog was a rescue from a huge and brilliant photograph of Sandy's, **The Green House**. This photograph went to my office, but the dog came home with me to take his place under a piece of furniture, his heavy lids barely masking his steadfast gaze at the green cat on the orange table across the room.

I continued to buy from Janet, and not just Sandy's work, but that of other vanguard photographers. But in this first flourish of excitement, where nearly everything I saw thrilled me and made me eager to see and know more, I did add another picture of Sandy's to my collection, **The Revenge of the Goldfish**.

The Revenge of the Goldfish depicts an interior with two young boys, one asleep in bed, one sitting on its edge, awakened trancelike from his slumber. The entire room is a throbbing, mottled blue, and other than the flesh and hair of the boys, there is no additional color except the vibrant orange of the goldfish, who are everywhere: in the bed, in the bureau drawers, flopping on the floor, and floating overhead. It is a surreal but poetic nightmare,

calling up all those goldfish we overfed when we were young and found the next morning at the fishbowl's surface, the goldfish we flushed down the toilet into oblivion. They are back to haunt us, and not just in our sleep, but at that boundary where dream ends and reality tears at its edges.

And, Finally, into the Living Room

I hung **The Revenge of the Goldfish** above **Germs Are Everywhere**, high over the orange table where the neon green cat stood and raised his head. Just in front of the photo, I suspended a sculpted goldfish from the picture. It looked as though it was trying to join the myriad other fish who were swimming from one side of the frame to the other. The cat looked lasciviously up at the fish, while across the room the purple dog stared balefully at the cat. Using the tools she had given me, I created my own Sandy Skoglund installation. It commented on the process by which Sandy achieved her work, the tension between two dimensions and three that exists in flat art, and on the dog-eats-cat-eats-fish world in which we live. I loved my mini-installation, with its layers of meaning and wit, and to my delight, Sandy loved it too; nothing could have made me happier.

I was now in serious collecting mode, and it was open season on everything. While I continued to collect photographs, prints, and paintings, I was also collecting furniture, lighting, rugs, glass, and plastic pocketbooks. But where would I hang the art, considering that heavy glass shelves lined my living room and dining room walls? There was only one answer. The shelves would have to go. To display objects, I left just two low wooden shelves above the baseboard, on either side of a protruding pier. Above them, in one niche, I hung Sandy's photographs. Andy Warhol's spacemen—one silkscreened in yellow, the other in fuchsia—went on top of the other

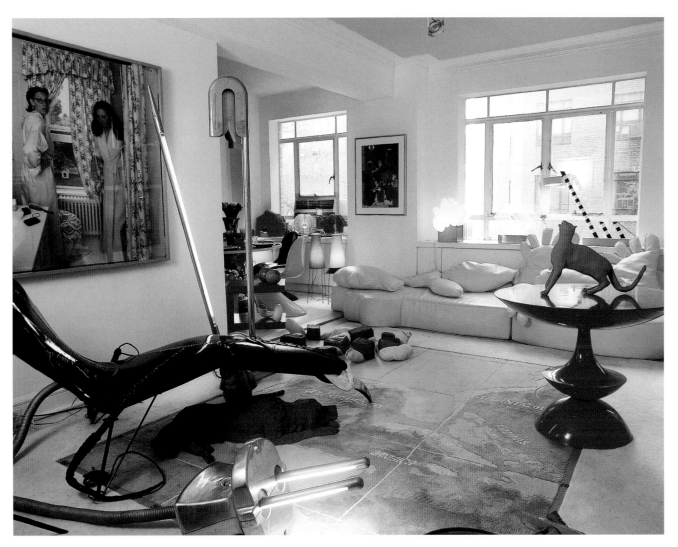

In the living room, color, modern design, and contemporary art define the space.

in the opposite niche. And on the center pier I placed a subtly beautiful Ida Applebroog, a respite from the electric color on either side. When I was buying Jody Harrow's dance-step carpet for my office, I had no space for her smart and elegant map rug (see page 68). But now I couldn't get it out of my mind. I realized it was the obvious rug for the living room, even though Jody's sample was too small for my needs, and I had reservations about the muted colors

she had used and the relationship of the border to the central image. But Jody is a gem. Together we changed the dimensions and proportions. We added new colors and pumped up the volume on those that remained, so the land masses were a yellow as bright as Nicola's sofa and the blues of the water made you feel you were in the Caribbean.

In the living room I now had Nicola's sofa, Jody's map rug, the Nana Dietzel table, and a number of pieces of art. To this I added Alex Locadia's extraordinary Catwoman chaise. Fashioned out of black patent leather (with a smaller piece of matte leather to indicate the boots), corseted in the back, and detailed with whips on either side, it looked like something one could order today from dominatrix.com. But it is also a great piece of furniture, as sculptural as it is wickedly suggestive. Based loosely on Michelle Pfeiffer's costume in the second Batman movie, it had special meaning for someone like myself, whose day job is limned with cowls, capes, and secret identities. Ordinarily, when I see work I like, I try to seek out the artists, many of whom have become my closest friends. But long before there was a Catwoman chaise, the artist had already found me.

Art and the Artist

I met Alex at a very small luncheon for artists and selected guests at the American Craft Museum, across from the Museum of Modern Art in New York. My memory serves up only two details. Wendell Castle, of the Molar chairs and hand-constructed furniture, was at one end of the table. His wife, a ceramist, was there as well. I was at the opposite end, not far from a tall young African-American man who, I imagined correctly, was one of the artists. As the luncheon was coming to a close, he came over to speak with me.

"I hear you're with DC Comics," he said, half a statement, half a query. "I'm Alex Locadia. I did the room with the black leather chaises and the speakers."

"Really? It's great. I especially love the speakers. They look like African totems from some far-flung future."

Alex smiled. He'd passed the first hurdle. "I wanted to talk with you. I'd like to do a line of Batman furniture, but I know I need permission. How would I go about getting it?"

At DC Comics we seldom work with small, individual licensees. But in the case of singular artists, we try to make exceptions. Andy Warhol made several iconic pictures of Superman under license from us, and Mel Ramos created one edition of prints based on Batman and another on a more obscure character of ours, Phantom Lady. Alex wasn't as well known as Warhol or Ramos, but he was immensely talented. Maybe there was something we could do.

"Let me think about it. Do you have a studio in New York?"

"On Canal Street. Why don't you come visit?"

And so we made a date, and I returned to my office, excited and wondering how Alex would transform Batman into furniture and lights.

This was a time between Tim Burton's powerfully atmospheric first Batman film and his second, **Batman Returns**. Warner Bros., the studio that produced it and our parent company, had started to open retail stores, which featured merchandise based on the Looney Tunes and DC Comics characters and, of course, its movies. Batman fit two of these three categories and, with the wild success of the first movie, the Warner Bros. stores were stocking their shelves with Batman products unavailable anywhere else. In addition to embroidered shirts and sweatshirts, snow domes and sculptures, key rings and mugs, the stores were also commissioning artists to fill the more exclusive gallery areas. Robert Lee Morris, four-time winner of the prestigious CFDA fashion award, created a stunning line of silver jewelry and accessories. Jeanette Kastenberg, a hot young designer, produced a small number of showstopping clothes. Brenda White, with her partner, Jesse Rhodes, made enormous ceramic chargers with bold black lines and bright colors. All of these artists were friends of mine. Perhaps the stores would respond if I told them about Alex's ideas for Batman furniture.

And they did. Alex, employing the materials he loved, leather and metal (he had begun his career customizing the interiors of cars), designed not only lights but ingenious chairs based on the musculature of Batman's body armor and, of course, the infamous Catwoman chaise. Of the chaise, Alex made less than ten. But I was lucky enough to purchase one of them, and it ended up in my living room, on the diagonal to break the monotony of all things parallel and perpendicular. Interestingly, the only piece of furniture for which my cats showed a particular affinity was the Catwoman chaise. I would often find one curled up beneath it next to Sandy Skoglund's sleepy purple dog, or lying on it filled with feline insouciance, or cheerfully sharpening its claws on the matte black leather. Was it the material? I always thought so, as my cats had previously left their mark on Claudio Motta's leather spread. But when several years later Alex gave me one of his leather Batman chairs, it remained immune to attack. Had my cats secretly seen **Batman Returns**, and did they sense the feral implications of the chaise? I am dubious, but also at a loss for another explanation.

With the addition of the Catwoman chaise, the living room was almost complete. I hung a wonderful photograph of Tina Barney's opposite the Warhols, and over the closet a proud and provocative photographic triptych by Carrie Mae Weems. On one of the wooden shelves just above the baseboard I installed a colorful collection of plastic pocketbooks by Harriet Bauknight, and on the other, a sparkling assemblage of Memphis glass. And with that, the living room was done.

A Pride of Naugas

It would be misleading to imply that I worked only on the living room, leaving the remainder of the apartment empty until I could formulate each space according to some systematic plan. The living room was the first to be complete, but everything was going on simultaneously and seemingly chaotically, although there was a method to the cheery madness. I had been busy collecting Naugas, and they had grown to vast numbers. Some were in my office, others in the country, but a menagerie of over eighty grinning beasties was waiting to be ensconced in the Century. Like the living room, my small dining room had heavy glass shelves on which not long before had rested row upon row of luminous Bakelite radios. There was something irresistible about putting my Naugas there, a playful, mischievous counterpoint to the more serious art across the way.

Naugas? You are right to ask. Naugas are not found in any dictionary I know of, and although they are animals of a sort, they are conspicuously absent under "N" in any standard bestiary. Perhaps this is because the first-known Naugas were sighted only forty years ago, when their huge smiles, open arms, and pointy little teeth started to appear in the pages of major magazines.

In the 1960s, when Naugas first came to the fore of public consciousness, there was a sudden spate of synthetic alternatives to leather. One of them was produced by Uniroyal, and it was called Naugahyde. George Lois, the brash and inventive advertising legend, was awarded the Naugahyde account. He surveyed the terrain and wondered how he could differentiate Naugahyde from its host of competitors.

And although only a gleam in his eye, it was then, as George pondered, that the Nauga was conceived. As the species' chief spokesman, George let the world know that Naugas were warmhearted creatures who willingly shed their skins for the sake of mankind. Washable, durable, in colors ranging from black and olive to turquoise and pink, their hides could be used on furniture, car seats, and walls. No more dead cows. Naugahyde would replace leather.

I had not seen Naugas when I was growing up, but George was a terrific friend and someone whose work I revered. Naturally, I owned his books, and it was in **The Art of Advertising** that I encountered one of his greatest creations, the Nauga. The book reproduced some of the original pages in which the Nauga was introduced. There he was on the left-hand side of an advertising spread, grinning in all his vinyl glory. On the right side of the spread was a modern office chair covered in Naugahyde.

"The Nauga Is Ugly," intoned the type above the Nauga. "But," it continued over the chair, "His Vinyl Hide Is Very Beautiful."

Forget the hide. I thought the Nauga was beautiful. But, as far as I could tell, Naugas no longer roamed the earth. Like the Brontosaurus and Tyrannosaurus rex before him, the Nauga had become extinct. It wasn't until one day in 1990 that, on the prowl at a giant collectibles show in New York, I encountered what I thought was the last of his race, a red-and-chartreuse Nauga.

"How much?" I asked the dealer, trying to contain my excitement. Every cunning collector knows that the slightest expression of interest is sure to accelerate the price. It is an axiom I cannot repeat often enough.

"How much?" I asked again.

The dealer sized me up. "One hundred and twenty-five dollars."

"Can you do any better?"

"Impossible," he replied. "This Nauga is very rare."

I was certain I'd never see a Nauga again. "I'll take him."

As soon as the Nauga was in my hands, I found myself surrounded by dealers I knew. The babble was eager and supportive. "Jenette, you got the best Nauga." "Yes, red and chartreuse. What a combina-

tion!" "If you knew how much I wanted him myself."

"Wait a second, wait a second." For a moment I silenced the din. "If you thought this Nauga was so special, why didn't any of you buy him?"

"Jenette," they proclaimed in unison. "Only you would pay one-twenty-five for a Nauga."

It turned out there was a Nauga market where one paid $50 tops for a small one, $75 for a large one. I had just paid $50 above the going market rate.

We pause for an educational moment. If you're about to collect something, it's always good to do some research first. Many areas of collecting—radios, dolls, lunch boxes, teddy bears, even salt and pepper shakers—have published price guides. You can find them at collectibles shows and in some bookstores. Other collectibles, like Naugas, have not yet been codified, but you can always poll a cross-section of dealers for their thoughts.

Was it a disaster to pay $125 for a Nauga? No, the $50 overage wasn't going to thrust me into debtor's prison. But in another instance, this could have been a costly mistake. There's a New York clothing store that declares, "An educated consumer is our best customer." I should have followed that advice.

By now I had developed a better sense of Nauga realities. I had also developed a severe Nauga addiction. My Nauga, prized as he was, was not alone. He had vinyl relatives in shelters and foster homes all over the country, if only I could locate them. With missionary zeal, I embarked on my quest, finding a Nauga here, a Nauga there, sometimes even a major cache.

And as I discovered more and more Naugas and reunited them, I observed several very interesting things. The first was that the color combinations rarely repeated themselves. It was astonishing how many variations of Nauga there were. Second, it was apparent that, following Mendel's law, brown was dominant. Out of the nearly one hundred Naugas I'd gathered, only one color combination had blue eyes. Third, I was single-handedly driving up the price of Naugas. But they made me happy. Bright-eyed and grinning, as ready to bite as to embrace, there was nothing quite like them.

The Naugas came in so many colors and so many color combinations, it was difficult to think of what to paint the dining room wall behind them. But because that wall was a focal point, the first thing you saw from the living room, I felt it needed color, both to give it density and to strengthen the dining room. After hours of searching my Pantone book, that wonderful volume of all the hues one can achieve from the four standard printing inks, I finally came up with an orange that worked well with the yellow ceiling, nodded to Sandy Skoglund's more vibrant goldfish on the opposite wall, and seemed to pop more of the Naugas than any other color I could think of. I allowed the Naugas to be as animated as their toothy smiles and outstretched arms implied they would be, if given half a chance. They danced on each other's stomachs, radiated in cartwheels, and overhung the shelves facedown so that they could peer at the goings-on below. Was it art? Well, that would be stretching it. But was it fun? Oh, yes, absolutely, definitely yes.

Dining in the Round

I needed a round dining table, one that would continue the color and esprit of the art and furniture in the living room. It did not seem likely that I would find one ready-made—the jubilant surroundings and small dimensions of the room created criteria that were far too specific. So rather than plow through magazines or haunt my favorite stores, I called Lloyd Schwan, a former neighbor, lifelong friend, and inspired designer. Soon after, Lloyd was at my house with a number of sketches.

Because I had strong ideas of my own, it was hard to embrace Lloyd's first drawings. Instead we seesawed back and forth, until we finally found common ground. In the end, we agreed on a round table whose base was composed of rings of different sizes and colors stacked on top of one another like a child's toy. (When the piece was going to a gallery show, Lloyd said he didn't know what to call it, and asked me to name it in his stead. I dubbed it the Playskool table because it looked like a gargantuan version of the classic Hasbro building set.)

When Lloyd and I first discussed the table, I wanted a light pink surface for the top, and Lloyd acceded—with minimal argument. Maybe he knew something I didn't, because a canvass of suppliers failed to turn up anything in a pink laminate. I was forced to abandon my first choice and with reluctance picked a dark blue as my second.

Without anything on the table, I think the pink would have been softer and more playful, with a welcome sense of airiness. But I laid the table with heavy Bauer ceramic dishes from the 1930s in strong shades of yellow, orange, turquoise, and green. I put smaller, contemporary plates on top of them that featured four artists—Andy Warhol, Picasso, David Hockney, and Salvador Dalí, their visages streaked with vibrant color. Near them I placed bright vintage soda glasses and red-and-yellow silverware.

When the table was set, the blue I'd disdained became a more dramatic background than the pink. Colors swirled on the tabletop, and only the weight of the blue kept them from flying off into space. They had an exuberant energy, and I decided to reinforce it by placing plastic Verner Panton chairs around the table in different colors, too. I chose two in red and two in yellow to add to the carousel-like whirl, and two in black to anchor it. Overhead I hung a multicolored ceiling fixture by Ettore

Sottsass that had one hidden halogen light and a second visible red one, as bright and round as the nose on a clown. Suddenly the dining room, like the living room, was done.

The Joys of a Small Apartment: Only One More Room to Go

There was no theme to either the living room or dining room. Each was simply an aggregation of objects and art that I loved—modern, colorful, witty, and energetic. At least that's what they were at first glance. Hopefully, if one looked closer, there was both order and substance in the arrangement and selection of the work. But neither room was based on any particular motif.

Thus far, only one part of the apartment had a unifying concept. That was the entry foyer. Immediately to the left of the door as you entered were two animation cels. One featured all the characters in Bill Cosby's groundbreaking show **Fat Albert**. The other showed row upon row of futuristic bubble cars—the employee parking lot from **The Jetsons**. Above them was a poster of the American flag that Jasper Johns had created to protest the war in Vietnam. Instead of the familiar patriotic red, white, and blue, its colors were a disturbing orange, green, and black. There was a bullet hole in the center. At the bottom was the word "moratorium."

Against the wall on the right was a curvilinear orange and green cabinet by Lyn Godley and Lloyd Schwan. Over it I hung a set of psychedelic Beatles posters that Richard Avedon had produced around the time that the Fab Four had gone to India. Perpendicular to them, at the entrance to the living room, I placed another cel from **The Jetsons**, this one depicting the exterior of Spacely Sprockets. On the other side of the foyer were two additional images. One was Robert Indiana's classic **Love**

poster, the other a poster by Fillmore West artist Rick Griffin announcing a group exhibition. It showed a pack of marijuana with one cigarette protruding and the label "Joint Show."

What did all of these pictures have in common? Each was an icon from the 1960s and early '70s. Together they summarized the attitudes and issues of the day. **The Jetsons** imagined an idealized and optimistic future at a time when the space race was in its heyday. After years of denigration, when African-Americans were stereotyped or excluded from mainstream media, the civil rights movement had begun to force major social and political shifts. **Fat Albert** was the first animated television show to feature an all-black cast, and it was a success. Now how optimistic was that? The Jasper Johns poster with the flag blemished by a bullet through its heart was a call to end the fighting in Vietnam. The **Love** poster, the Joint Show, the Beatles? Sex, drugs, and rock and roll. The foyer let you know that you were entering the modern world.

But, as I said, that was the exception. Until you got to the bedroom. Like the foyer, the bedroom had a theme, but it was one that evolved only as I worked on the room.

Music, Pattern, and Rhythm

Memphis was a movement initiated by Italian design legend Ettore Sottsass in the early 1980s. Sottsass and his colleagues conceived of Memphis as an international force, and there was representation from different countries, including the United States. The designers were interested in color, pattern, new and often faux materials—usually in combination—and unconventional shapes for conventional objects.

As they sat around discussing their principles and goals, the question arose: what to call their group? The name was avidly debated while records spun in the background. A pause, and the would-be revolutionaries were suddenly aware of Bob Dylan's "Memphis Blues" resonating through the room. "Memphis Blues." Memphis. A movement was born.

I loved Memphis. It was such a breath of fresh air. And although I had not yet seen a piece in person, design magazines continued to document the movement, keeping us on the other side of the Atlantic as up-to-date as possible. Among the people drawn to this new furniture was fashion celebrity Karl Lagerfeld. He hired the designer Andrée Putman to decorate an apartment for him exclusively in Memphis. It looked like a laboratory for the movement and was photographed many times.

And then, in the Department of Unexplained Wonders of the Western World, Karl Lagerfeld decided to put the contents of his apartment up for sale through Sotheby's in Monaco. The auction included a number of prototypes, and I could feel my heart pound as I pored through the catalogue. But I didn't think about flying to Europe to be at the sale in person. Even for me, the notion seemed far too extravagant. Happily, auction houses permit you to bid on the phone, and the phone has always been my weapon of choice. I called Sotheby's, made the arrangement, and waited anxiously for the sale day to arrive. As it happened, when the day did come, I was in Los Angeles on business. The time difference between California and Monaco is nine hours, so, long before it was light, I was up, dialing 011 for an international call.

Bidding can be an incredibly heady experience, so much so that losing your head is an occupational hazard. There is tremendous pressure at auctions because you are constantly forced to make split-second decisions. There are almost always other bidders. How high will they go? How high will you go? And with no time to ponder these questions, the sale continues apace.

Now, rational buyers decide in advance how much they'll pay for a piece, and if the price exceeds that limit, they responsibly drop out. But there is something addictive about the experience. Passion has a way of trumping intellect, and you have to exercise enormous self-control not to get carried away. If you can manage it, restraint is certainly the better part of wisdom, because the price when the hammer goes down is only the beginning. You still have to pay a buyer's commission to the auction house and, on top of that, shipping and insurance. If you're purchasing items from overseas, you have to pay duty, too.

Despite these caveats, nothing could deter me from the Memphis auction in Monaco. Did I get every piece I wanted? Actually, most of them, a certain sign that I'd thrown all caution to the winds. A mature bidder would have won some and lost some, conceding several desired objects to someone with either more money or even less sense. But at the moment, I was giddy with my purchases, which included two Sottsass prototype King lamps, his Atlantique bureau, and a Michele de Lucchi prototype bed. It was only when I got the bill for shipping, especially for the bed, that I took stock of what I'd done. But the damage was irreversible, and had been from the moment the auctioneer said "sold."

On the other hand, when the furniture arrived, I was ecstatic. The King lamps, seven feet high, were both modern and majestic. The Atlantique bureau had black-and-white sawtooth patterns on the frontal façade, translucent gridded glass on the drawers, and curved yellow handles that looked like segments of the Loch Ness monster rising out of the depths. And then there was the bed—the bed of both my waking wishes and my dreams. A black platform floated on a lacquered cylindrical base supported by three gray triangles. The headboard was of a light but warm wood veneer. It rested on top of angular piers covered in a black crisscross laminate that was shaded—almost indistinguishably—in gray.

These objects became the most important pieces

in my bedroom, determining everything else. As I mentioned, Memphis was about pattern, rhythm, and music, principles that guided my remaining choices. I decided to paint the ceiling yellow, as I had in the living room. But for the cove molding surrounding it, I chose a black-and-white design different from both the one on the bed and the one on the bureau. Looser and more painterly, it still had that Memphis vibe. For the bed I found a cotton spread with a black-and-white geometric pattern. To soften it, I stacked pillows up against the headboard: black, black and white like the bedcover, solid yellow, yellow-and-white vertical stripes, yellow-and-white horizontal ones. For some color and humor, I added several Naugas.

Memphis: Mixing It Up

Although many Memphis objects made prodigious use of color, I nonetheless felt that the Memphis interiors I'd seen tended to look sterile. The pieces in Karl Lagerfeld's apartment were thrilling, but I found the environment cold, and certainly not one I wanted to emulate. I tried to add warmth through the art, objects, and materials I chose. Over the bureau I hung a framed 1960s black-and-yellow paper dress, its energetic pattern collaged from phone numbers and ads in the yellow pages. To the left of it I hung Andy Warhol's red Elizabeth Taylor, a poster announcing one of his shows. Over it was Roy Lichtenstein's brushstroke in yellow and black with blue benday dots. It had been folded to send through the mail, an invitation to an early exhibition at Leo Castelli's gallery.

Next to the bed I placed a red and brown 1920s bar that celebrated the Jazz Age, with musicians and dancers in black silhouette. An airborne top hat and cane and the word "Whoopee!" on the front captured the abandon of the era. Above the bar

I hung a Lichtenstein poster from 1967. It was yellow, black, white, and red, and on the top was written "Aspen Winter Jazz." Against the left wall as you entered the room was a low bookcase. On top of that, leaning against the wall, I placed two pictures. One was a French poster from the 1940s of a conductor in tails with his symphony. The other was by Paul Colin, from his book of prints **Le Tumulte Noir**. It, too, showed an orchestra, but this one was composed entirely of black musicians against a lively cubist Paris, the ultimate visual expression of "Le Jazz Hot". At an antiques show I had bought several brass cornets that had been made by hand at the end of the nineteenth century. They seemed like a perfect addition to a room where music was key. I hung them above the pictures with the bell ends up, as though they were tooting at the ceiling in joyous sound.

One of my favorite acquisitions continued this musical theme, a seven-foot-high poster for the 1947 movie **Hi-De-Ho**, starring Cab Calloway. The majority of film posters tend to be representational, and for that reason I am less interested in them. But this poster, solely in red, black, and white, was stunningly graphic. It showed a beautiful woman with ribbons on her ankles and wrists and a polka-dot bow in her hair. Her hands are raised, her head's thrown back, and her teeth flash in a smile that spreads across her face. Her legs are wide apart, and between them is a musical note with a photograph of Cab Calloway's smiling face inside it on an angle, his eyes to one side. At first glance he's charming. At the second, he's looking up her skirt. It is a poster full of sly sexuality and total joie de vivre.

I first saw it, or I should say, a photograph of it, when I was sitting next to some friends at a Christie's auction of animation cels. Next to me was a young man I didn't know, but who knew my friends. He introduced himself to me, Bruce Hershenson.

"Would you like to look at some pictures?" he asked, after we'd chatted a while.

"Sure. Of course."

Bruce brought out a binder filled with photos of movie posters that he was putting up for sale at a later auction at Christie's. Many of them were classic images for classic films. I was appreciative but somewhat detached. Although I am a movie buff, most of the pictures left me unmoved—until I saw the one for **Hi-De-Ho**.

"Oh, my God. This is so incredibly fabulous!"

"Yes," Bruce agreed. "It's the only one I've ever seen."

Bruce was a dealer. So I asked the inevitable question. "Is it possible to buy it?"

"Jenette, I'm sorry, I really am. But I've already committed all the posters you see here to Christie's. If I hadn't, I would have been happy to sell it to you."

"If you ever come across another, will you let me know?"

Of course, I could have bid on the **Hi-De-Ho** poster at auction. But by the time it came around, I was purchasing other things and didn't think I could buy the poster too. This was an adult decision, but nonetheless I continued to feel regret, imagining the poster in my mind and wishing it were mine.

A year and a half went by, and still I thought of the poster, which I was sure had gone into some private collection, never to see the light of day — or an auction room — again. And then one afternoon, Bruce called.

"Jenette, I never, ever thought this would happen. But I've found a second poster for **Hi-De-Ho**. It's in even better condition than the one that went at Christie's, and I'll sell it to you for less."

From the Section of Helpful Hints

It seemed like a miracle. The poster proved as rare as Bruce said. My friend James Wheeler, who has been collecting all his life and has one of the largest treasure troves of black film memorabilia, had never seen it. To what do I attribute my good fortune? Clearly, about 98 percent of it was owing to pure, unadulterated luck. But 2 percent of it came from outreach. I had let Bruce know that I seriously wanted the poster. And no matter how sure he was that he wouldn't find another, my passion had registered with him. When the impossible happened, when Bruce did uncover a second print of **Hi-De-Ho**, I was the first person that he called.

So what is the lesson? Don't be shy. Get the word out there. The more people who know what you're looking for, the better your chances are that someone will turn it up. Doggedness can be man's best friend. If you call from time to time to follow up, your quest might still be on the back burner, but you're keeping the fire going.

And, Last of All, the Bedroom Screens

Although some pieces I own are by artists I've never met, I am nonetheless surrounded by furniture, photographs, sculpture, and lighting by people who already were friends or became friends after their work inspired me to search them out. What could be more rewarding than to live with art you love by people you love? I say this as preface to a long creative process that finally led me to one of the most valued instances of art and artist coming together.

Some years earlier, I had built closets on either side of a window in my bedroom to minimize the amount of furniture and to add storage space that was hidden behind two sets of bifold doors. Bifold doors, of course, are on a track and hinged down the center line so that the halves can either be folded into an angle or pushed back absolutely flat.

By now most of my bedroom was completed, and the bifold doors, like the walls of the room, were

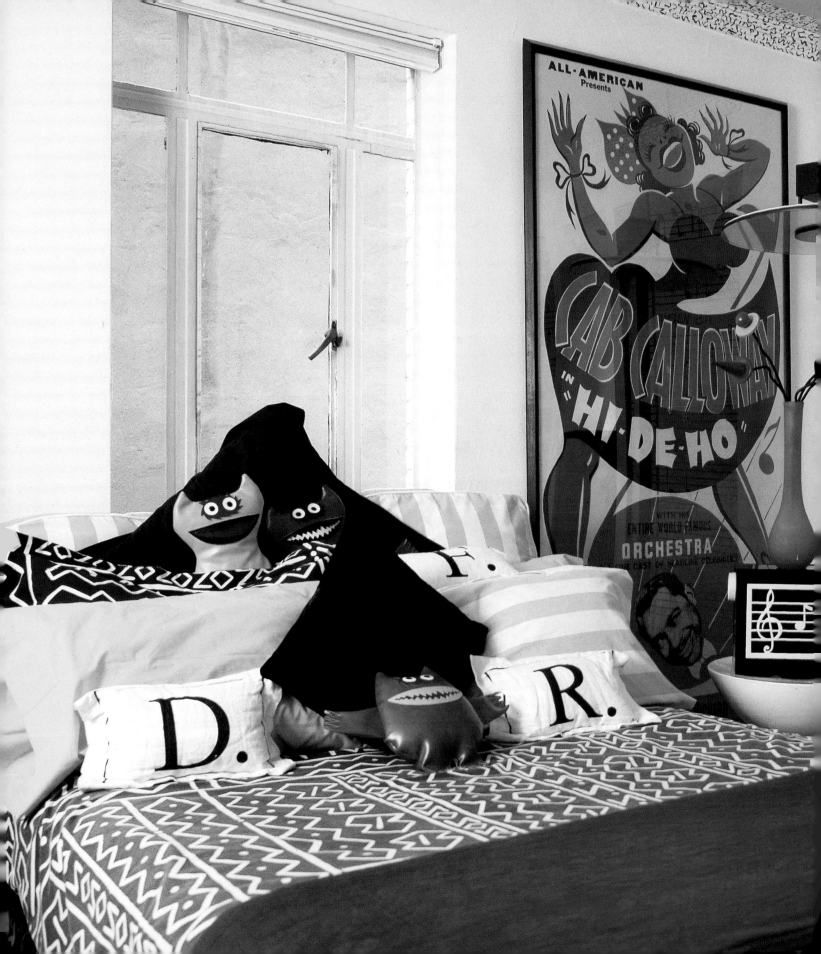

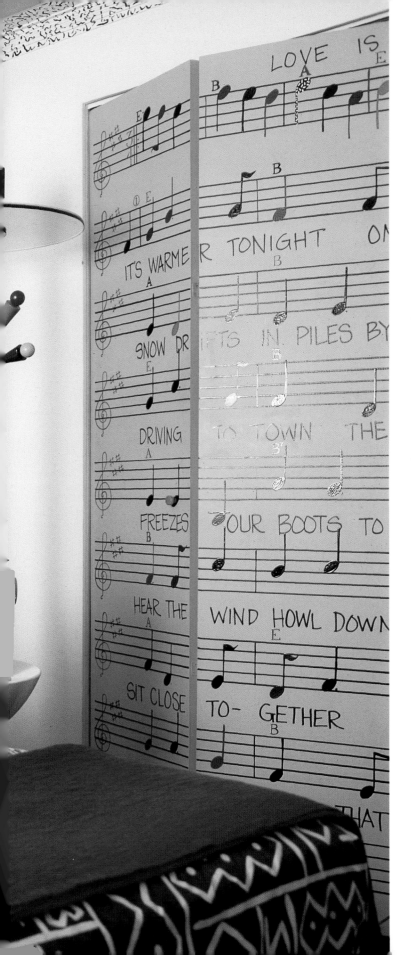

white. However, unlike all the other surfaces, they were unadorned. With the two closets and a window in the center, one entire wall of my bedroom was blank. There was no way, with the bifold doors folding in on themselves, that I could even hang pictures on them.

Relevant Digression Number One: The bed is my favorite piece of furniture. It has never occurred to me that beds were made just for sleeping. I believe they are made for reading, watching movies and basketball, talking on the phone for both business and pleasure, and eating as many meals as possible. With the exception of sprints to the bathroom and raids on the kitchen, I spent most of my hours at the Century either in or on the bed.

Propped up on top of the covers, I found my eyes regularly drawn to the bifold doors, bare and boring, I felt, in a room full of pattern, rhythm, color, and references to music. I wanted them to be part of the whole, but they steadfastly were not.

And then one day, when the doors were not closed flat but angled on their hinges, I was struck by an idea. The bifold doors were like four parts of a folding decorative screen, except that they were sep-arated by the niche, that held the window. I could turn the parts into one large screen with a single image that would jump the niche to be continued on the other side. This revelation kept me up into the early morning hours, searching through various design books to see how artists from Dunand to Fornasetti had graphically played with the form.

I began to fashion ideas, and key among them was that the image would start on the left doors and continue on the right doors despite the inter-ruption of the window. Next, I phoned my friend

My bedroom at the Century, where music and pattern rule even on the bifold closet doors.

A Century of Progress: Design of the Times

Steve Kursh, an excellent artist as well the person I call "The Man Who Can Make Anything." Steve loved the concept of turning the closet doors into a screen, and we both agreed that he would be the designated painter.

However, life as always intervenes. Steve had his projects and I had mine. But I had also developed a serious Zen attitude about things getting done in their own time. Numerous experiences have taught me that as days and weeks and months go by, even one's best-loved ideas can change, and almost always for the better. I forgot about making the bifold doors into a screen, and it paid off.

Relevant Digression Number Two: Most days when I get ready for work, I listen to music. One morning, I put on a CD by my brother and only sibling, Si Kahn. In addition to having spent his entire adult life as a grassroots organizer, Si is also a singer-songwriter who has written well over a thousand songs. As I was drying my hair and listening to Si singing, the thought occurred to me how wonderful an artist Si is. And then I thought about the word artist. I hadn't really considered him this way before because, as a musician, his work doesn't take the form of an object and therefore seems more elusive. But if the joy in my surroundings is most especially the artwork of cherished friends, then somehow I had to include Si's music in my life. How could I do it? When you're working on a solution, even passively, as I now was with the bifold doors, connections are often made swiftly and unexpectedly. I decided to take the score from one of Si's songs and have Steve paint the doors with multicolored notes against a yellow field. As before, I wanted the imagery to start on the left, jump the window, and continue onto the right-hand doors as though they were truly a four-part decorative screen. I listened to all of Si's tunes, looking

for one whose words expressed the warmth and joy of the bedroom. And then I found it, a song where the last lines read, "Love is the quilt that we draw up at night to shelter us safe from the storm."

The Screening Process

It was important that the doors continue the lively Sottsass aesthetic, so I decided to combine traditional black notes with colorful ones painted with Memphis patterns. Steve Kursh and I discussed the concept, but again many months went by between our meeting of the minds and Steve's removal of the bifold doors to bring them to his studio. I gave him a handwritten sheet of music I'd secured from my brother, so that the notes on the doors could actually be sung by anybody who had the dual powers of reading music and perfect pitch. Thus far, very few people with these talents have materialized in my life, let alone in my bedroom. But if any did, I was ready.

A few weeks later, Steve called me to come down to see the screen. Going to see a commissioned work for the first time is difficult. There will always be a discrepancy between the original concept and what the artist has done. Sometimes your idea is transformed in ways so wonderful it far exceeds what you could have imagined. Sometimes, you are disappointed.

For this reason, I headed down to Steve's with both eagerness and anxiety. On the phone, Steve was excited, and I took heart from that. He had already created some magical pieces for me, and I looked forward to yet another tour de force in an ongoing series. But this was not one of those times. When I looked at the doors, there were so few black notes to ground the yellow surface that the colored ones seemed weightless, floating off the screen into some indeterminate space. In addition, Memphis patterns—while highly graphic—have an industrialized geometry about them. The notes Steve had drawn betrayed his personal hand, like painted Easter eggs.

I had to communicate these problems while emphasizing the many things Steve had done so well. Luckily, Steve was open to dialogue without taking offense. Although it's important to be sensitive to an artist's efforts even when you have serious reservations about the outcome of a commissioned work, you are still the client, the one who has to live with the end result. It isn't easy, but you have to convey appreciation without downplaying the changes you feel are necessary to satisfy your vision.

It took another meeting and two more sets of revisions before the screens evolved into what I had hoped for. In the end, they were joyful, graphic, strong, and so very personal. I loved to lie in bed and look at them, ferreting out one detail, then another. Every moment yielded deep pleasure. But none compared with the day my brother came to visit. I led him into the bedroom, and he stopped, in pure amazement and delight. The doors had become more than art. They symbolized the profound love between us. Overcome by emotion, we both, for once, were speechless.

Lessons Learned Along the Way

1. Ceilings are part of the total decorating environment. When you splash color on them, or paint a pattern in a cove molding, you are moving the spirit of your décor around the entire room. Many times a white or neutral ceiling is the best option. But always consider other solutions before making that decision.

2. When you discover an area in which you want to collect, check out market prices before spending any real money. In this age, where collectibles are a billion-dollar industry, almost everything already has an audience, and there is usually a consensus of going rates. Look for price guides, log on to eBay, and talk to different dealers. With a little research, you'll begin to sense whether something's fairly priced or not.

3. For selecting colors, my favorite tool is the Pantone book. A binder with more than 150 pages, it is filled with tiny die-cut stamps that show 1,012 shades you can achieve by combining the four major printing inks: cyan, magenta, yellow, and black. Of course, there are other colors in the world, but this is a pretty good start. To inquire about ordering a book, call Pantone at 201-935-5500, or fax them at 201-896-0242.

4. Auction houses are a great place to buy everything from furniture and lighting to ceramics, art glass, paintings, photographs, and posters. And luckily, you don't have to live in the city where the auction is taking place. Almost every house allows you to bid on the phone. But be prepared: there are pitfalls. A catalog photograph puts the best face on an item. If you can't inspect it yourself, make sure you speak to an expert for a full condition report. In addition, it's important to realize that the price when the gavel goes down is only the beginning. Expect to pay taxes, a 15 percent buyer's commission, shipping, and insurance. If the auction is held outside the country, be prepared to pay duty, too.

5. A successful room should feel unified. Happily, there are many ways to accomplish this, any number of which work well in combination. You can use complementary colors or materials or patterns. Or you can explore a conceptual theme with its countless variations. If you know in advance the emotional tenor you want your interiors to sound, the choices in getting there will come more easily.

4.

Caution: Woman at Work—

Design in the Office

Opposite: The seventh-floor lobby of DC Comics, with Superman flying out of the phone booth to save the day.

Pages 60–61: At home in my office, with its sunny yellow rug and Andy Warhol's **Superman** painting setting the theme.

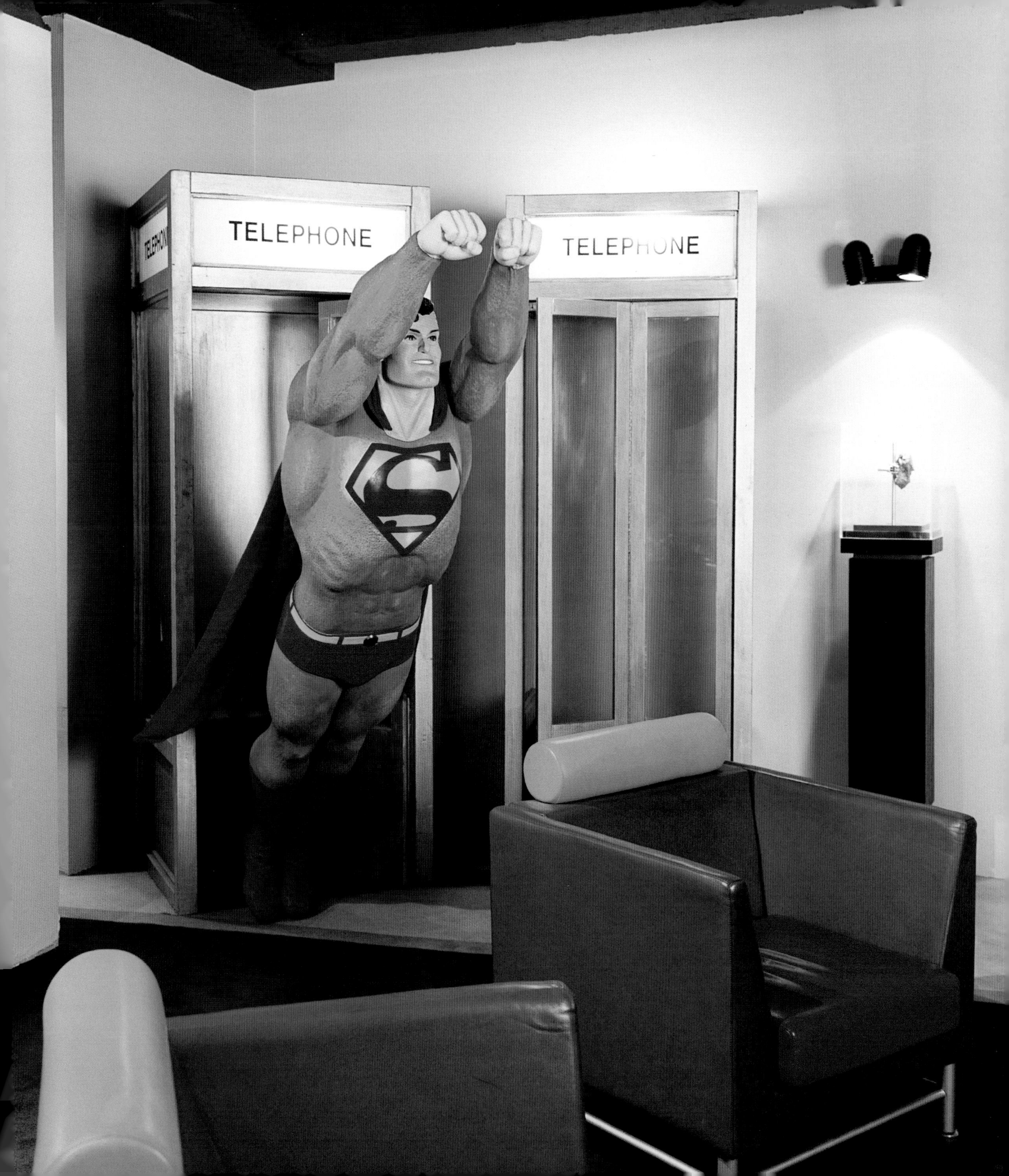
TELEPHONE
TELEPHONE
TELEPHONE

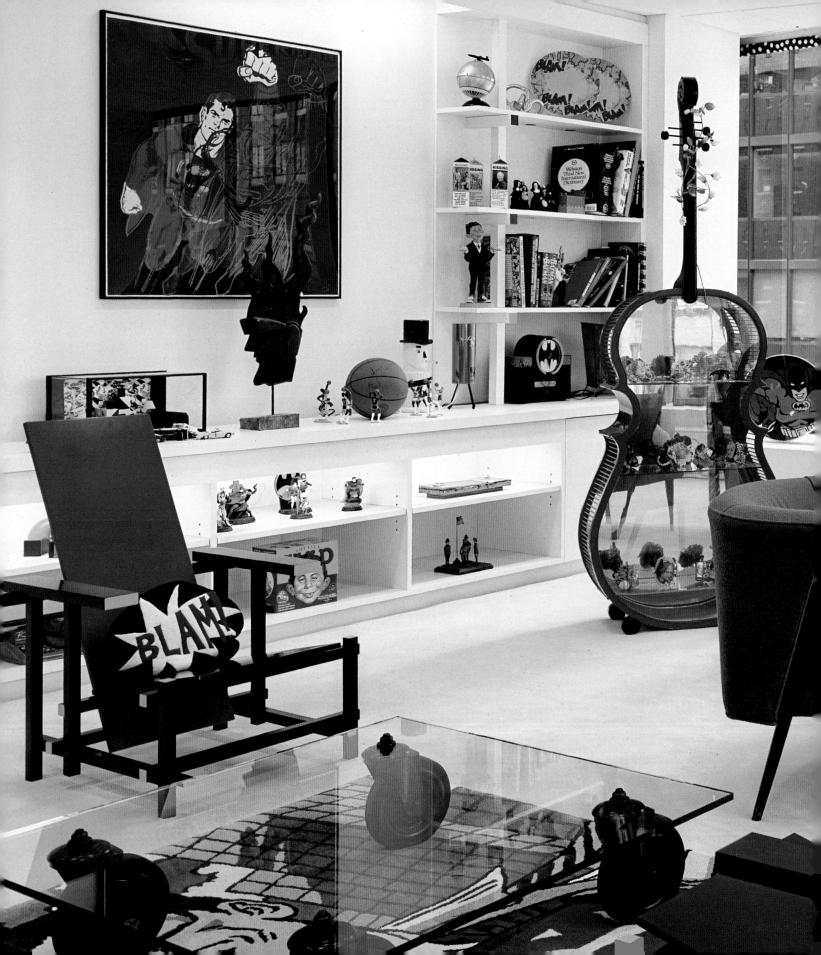

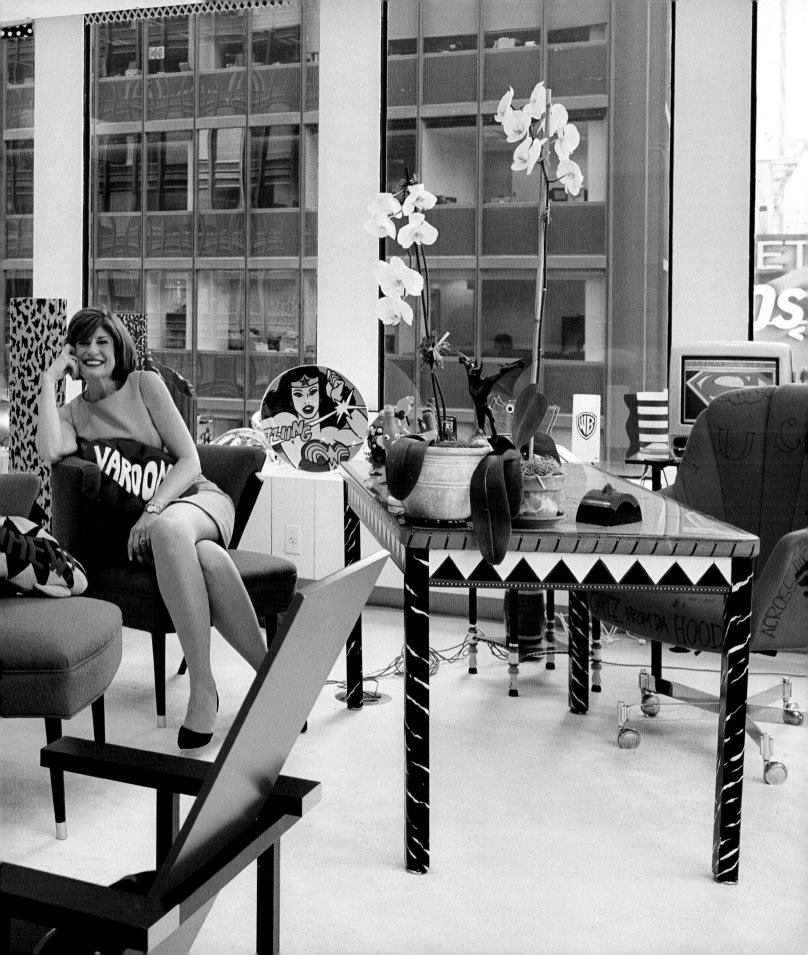

When it came time to decorate my office at DC Comics, I had only one idea in mind. But it became the conceptual center of the space, and most of my other ideas flowed from it.

In 1918 Gerrit Rietveld, a Dutch architect who, like Piet Mondrian, was part of the De Stijl art movement in Europe, created a beautiful wood chair fashioned from two larges planes and flanked by rectangular supports. Sometime between 1923 and 1924, at the suggestion of a fellow artist, he made the chair in color: red, yellow, blue, and black. The Rietveld chair, as it is known, is a classic of modern design; it holds up against any contemporary piece, even eighty years after it was conceived.

I had always loved the chair, which in many ways is a three-dimensional expression of Mondrian's most famous canvases. The bold red and blue planes of the seat and back are enlivened by a small yellow rectangle at the end of each arm, and by yellow squares at the ends of the supporting frame. The frame and arms are black, popping the yellow but anchoring it too.

Yet for all its art historical references and its timeless design, the Rietveld chair had a unique resonance for me. The colors and their relationship to one another echoed those of our flagship character, Superman. In the world of my office, the Rietveld chairs were not just an aesthetic choice but an abstract homage to the superhero whose red cape, blue costume, and yellow-and-red "S" shield limned in black symbolize the field in which I work.

After the Rietveld chairs, everything else seemed to follow without effort. My previous office, although brightened by art, had been more hushed, with gray walls and soft furniture rounded in Art Deco curves. A 1940s table of white-lacquered linen and chrome became my desk. An elegantly witty Eileen Gray rug—black, parsed by white lines of metric measurement—sat on the wall-to-wall gray carpeting.

Primary Colors

But now we were moving, and I could think only in color. I knew immediately that I wanted the walls to be a dazzling, bright white and the carpet a vibrant, sunny yellow without either a hint of green at one end of the spectrum or gold at the other. So while others tended to logistics, I dedicated the intervening months to the process of hunting and gathering. With the Rietveld chairs and yellow carpeting lodged firmly in my mind, everything I saw or heard or did was source material. I frequented galleries and antiques shows, lingered over design magazines, and checked out every feature in the Home section of the **New York Times**.

I don't think I can recapture the order in which I assembled different pieces, and ultimately it didn't matter. Each one was impelled by the bright vision of Rietveld chairs on a yellow carpet. In one way or another, everything was related.

Covering the Basics
1. The Desk

My quest started by accident, when I was in Santa Fe for a weekend, my first trip there. I was with my boyfriend of the time, and we were making the rounds of galleries. Because we both lived in New York, where contemporary art is only a footstep away, we immersed ourselves instead in the rich tradition of Native American art showcased throughout the town. It was a wonderful day. We were still going up and down the streets of Santa Fe when a colorful window stopped me in my tracks.

"Look at that piece of furniture!" I exclaimed, and headed through the door. We were out of the realm of Native American work and into that ambiguous category of handmade objects sometimes known as craft and sometimes as art.

The furniture maker, we found out, was an artist named Tom Miller, who lived in Baltimore.

My boyfriend recalled having seen his work before. Although the gallery had only one of Tom's pieces left, we pored over photographs of old tables, chairs, benches, and screens that he had transformed with wit and boldly colored paints, decorative patterns, and African-American motifs. Although I doubted there was just one Tom Miller in Baltimore, I was

My desk, neater than usual, but not without its obligatory collection of vintage Mr. Potato Heads.

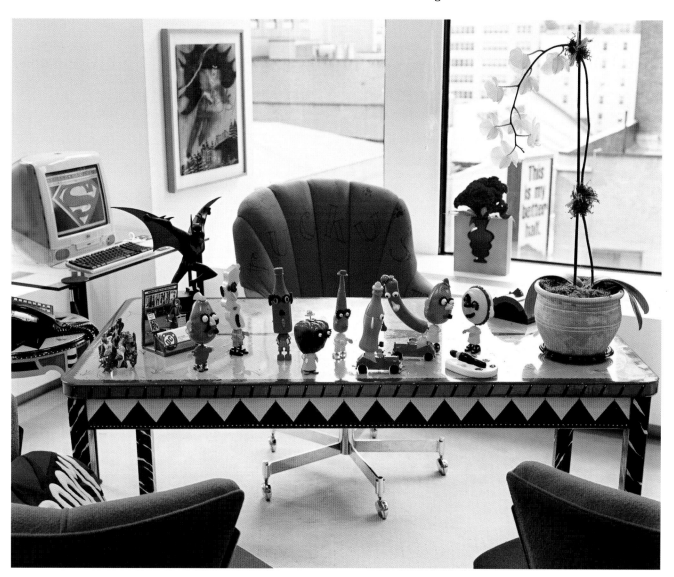

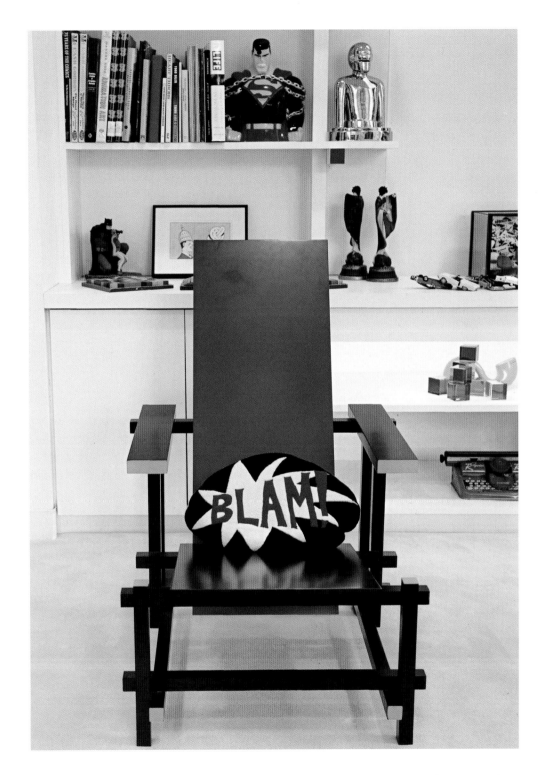

The classic Rietveld chair, in Superman colors:
blue, red, yellow, and black.

In Your Space: **Personalizing Your Home and Office**

still determined to find him. I wanted a special desk, and Tom was just the person to make it.

Luckily, I knew an artist in Baltimore, Joyce Scott, from whom I'd once bought an extraordinary hand-beaded necklace with the provocative title "What You Mean, Jungle Music?" Joyce, like Tom, was African-American. I hoped that Baltimore, like most other cities, had a community of African-American artists who knew one another.

Fortune was on my side. Joyce gave me Tom's number, and I arranged for my boyfriend and me to meet him. The trip from New York to Baltimore is an easy one by train, and soon we were at Tom's home. Although suffering from HIV, Tom was turning out a beautiful body of art, working on city commissions, and organizing a traveling show. It was an inspiring visit.

I explained to Tom what I wanted, and we surveyed his collection of used furniture waiting to be transfigured. I opted for an old schoolteacher's desk that resembled a table, but with a drawer in the center. So that Tom would know exactly what colors I envisioned, I sent him chips from my trusty Pantone book. He responded with a number of Magic Marker sketches, and I chose a design from among them. Whatever comments I had were minimal.

When the desk arrived, it exceeded my expectations. The colors were vivid: red, yellow, blue, black, and white, with a few grass green tendrils that emanated from the abstract crocodile on the tabletop. The surface of the desk was luminous, covered with so many coats of lacquer that it shone with the crystalline clarity of polished glass. When I pulled open the desk drawer, I saw that its base and sides had been meticulously painted red and black in the composition-book pattern made famous by the Memphis movement. Compared to the vibrant surface of the desk, the drawer's interior was even richer and more intense, as though jewels had

been hidden in a beautifully decorated chest. This surprise detail, so complete in its thought and execution, raised Tom's piece to another level of artistry.

2. Rare Chairs

My desk had taken me from New York to Santa Fe to Baltimore. But some discoveries occur much closer to home. I was cruising the Modernism show, an annual New York City event that brings together dealers specializing in high-end twentieth-century design. As always, I came expecting to see furniture, objects, and lighting by artists like Charles and Ray Eames, Le Corbusier, Charlotte Perriand, Serge Mouille, George Nelson, Verner Panton, and Jean Royère. But I also encountered surprises: rare, exquisite pieces by Jacques-Émile Ruhlmann, fifty different Kodak cameras by Walter Dorwin Teague, and great objects by virtual unknowns.

At the booth of Lost City Arts, a New York City store specializing in pop culture collectibles, I spotted two chairs from the 1950s. No one could identify the designer, but they had strong, curved lines, and just happened to be upholstered in Superman blue. What's more, they were genuinely comfortable, a feature for which I am not particularly well known. I bought them, and they became the seating in front of my desk.

The chair behind my desk was another matter. Ward Bennett had designed my previous desk chair, and it was softly curved and unusually plump for its species. It had given me both comfort and support, and I was enormously fond of it.

"Don't switch it," cautioned the decorating team working on the larger DC project. "A good desk chair is hard to find."

That seemed like sound advice. But my chair was covered in gray suede and wouldn't be able to hold its own in the riot of splendid colors that was fast becoming my office. My friend the designer Lloyd Schwan had once instructed me that you can always repaint. I felt sure this maxim extended to reupholstering as well.

How did the idea come to me? I really don't know. Sometimes inspiration simply burbles up unbidden from the hidden places in one's mind. But I envisioned—with unassailable certainty—a chair finished in bright red with black graffiti scrawled all over it. There was just one small obstacle. A good desk chair may be hard to find. A bright red chair covered with graffiti is impossible.

As in so many instances, this meant a call to the endlessly resourceful Steve Kursh. The decorating firm had already struck out in finding the fabric. No problem. Steve bought some material and dyed it. The chair was then sent out to be covered. It came back in all its primary glory, a handsome older woman resplendent in her stylish new clothes.

You might think I would have stopped there. But no, I was dedicated to my original idea, and not even my favorite desk chair in the perfect shade of red could halt me in my path. I came up with the graffiti I wanted: Deco, Ruckus, and Fusion—my cats' names—Chill Hill Annex, Suspects Central. Everything had personal meaning. Steve took my

words and his brush, and soon the chair was covered with painterly black scrawls. I had liked the chair before. I loved it now.

3. And a Sofa, Too

Had it been up to me, I wouldn't have chosen to work on my office with a decorator. But designing all the DC lobbies, all the floors, and all the offices was a humongous task. There is so much legwork and managerial detail involved in moving 250 people into pleasing but functional quarters that an architectural or decorating firm is essential. We hired interior designers, and their efforts included helping me. Occasionally they were a hindrance. But more often than not they made a contribution, and they almost always made my job easier.

One such instance involved my office sofa. The American husband-and-wife design team of Charles and Ray Eames had created a modern sofa that had simple, clean, and unassuming lines. I had seen it both in books on their work and in design anthologies. Now, at the same Modernism show where I had spied my blue desk chairs, I saw the Eames sofa in person.

The Modernism show was running for several days, and the decorators obligingly said they would stop

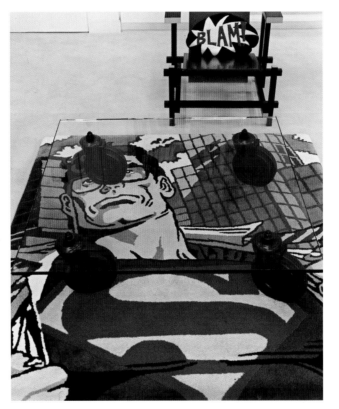

Gae Aulenti's rolling coffee table atop Jody Harrow's heroic Superman rug.

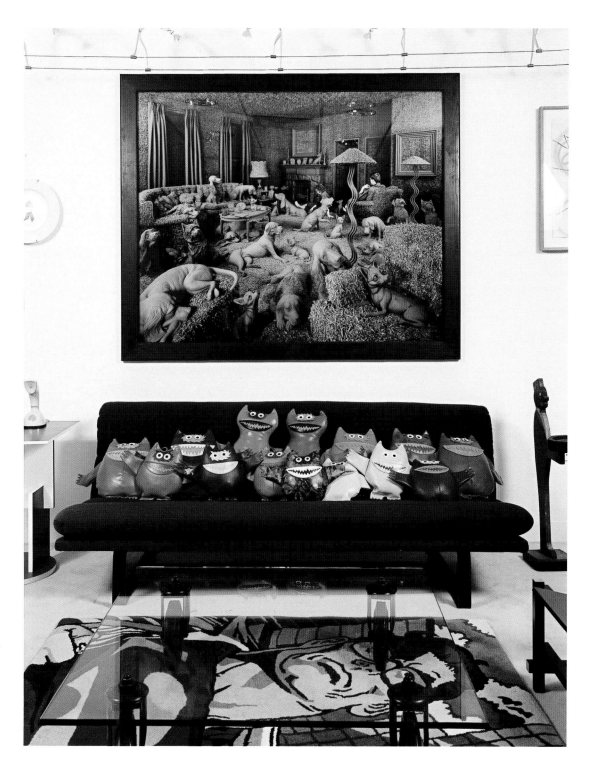

Naugas, posing on the couch for a family portrait, beneath
Sandy Skoglund's provocative photograph **The Green House**.

Caution: Woman at Work — Design in the Office

by to see the couch I'd described. They reported in the next day. Bad news. The sofa was too small to seat enough guests for a meeting—and worse, it was uncomfortable.

Uncomfortable. Oops. My nemesis again. Form over function, form over comfort, form over everything. I digested what the decorators said. Small. Uncomfortable. But then again, I didn't have to sit on the couch. Just my guests. For one brief moment I considered being a truly rotten person. Then it passed.

"Okay," I said. "We have to find another sofa."

Now on a mission, the decorators shone. They had seen what I liked and listened closely when I explained what aspects of the Eames sofa were appealing, even if size and comfort were not highlights on the list. Thus armed, they went looking for a larger couch, a softer couch, but nonetheless a comparable couch. And, in the Will Wonders Never Cease Department of Life, they found something. It was considerably longer than the Eames sofa, it certainly had more springs, but it was still in the family. While its base was clunky, and adjectives like "fresh" and "inventive" didn't exactly leap to mind, it managed to bring together enough of the Eames attributes that I liked.

While unoriginal, the sofa still appeared simple and relatively handsome, which for office furniture is no mean feat. I congratulated the decorators and chose a black fabric to cover the couch. Still, the lengthy expanse of sofa seemed plain, very plain. It needed some color, some animation, and I found both in my still-growing collection of Naugas.

I began to bring them into the office. Soon, they had taken over the couch. There are now something like fourteen Naugas on the sofa (see page 47). Big ones, small ones, even two mutant Naugas I'd found who had necks, bore the name "Waldo," and, quite contrary to Sex and Expression in Nauga Society, wore suspenders and pants. Sometimes, when

I'm not looking, I think they multiply. Whatever the case, there is very little room for humans on my couch.

People come into my office and head for the chairs. The overflow somewhat sheepishly eyes the couch and wonders exactly what it's supposed to do. "Oh, just move the Naugas," I say. "Put them on the floor, they won't mind."

But most guests hesitate, as though they were displacing your beloved pet from his favorite piece of upholstery. They tend to say, "Uh, that's okay," and prop themselves up against this sea of animated vinyl, pretending to look comfortable. Some part of me thinks I should move the Naugas and allow the couch to be functional. It is, however, a very small part. The rest of me says, "I love sitting at my desk looking out at my beaming, toothy brood. Naugas. What would I do without them?"

Cutting a Rug: A Dance-Step Carpet in the Office

When it came to the sofa, the decorating team was terrific. But as I moved on to other things, I discovered in them a latent obstinacy, cunningly disguised as polite efficiency.

One Thursday morning like so many others, I eagerly turned to my favorite part of the **New York Times**, the Home section. For me, it was a banner day. There, on the front page, was a picture of a rug that thrilled me. It had a classic configuration: six black squares divided by thin white lines and framed by a generous white border. But this time-honored format was contravened by a pattern of footprints that started outside the right-hand corner of the grid and ended at the opposite end in the center.

Graphically bold, as witty as a Cole Porter song, the rug was a guide for would-be Fred Astaires. What dance was it describing? The foxtrot? The tango? Only a giant or a contortionist could follow the rug's diagram with ease. The schematic, I was sure, was really a blueprint for Adult Twister. Whatever its hidden meanings, I loved the rug with its classical foundation and contemporary skew. The next day, I showed the photo to the decorating team.

"I'd like to have this rug in front of my sofa. The **Times** says it's by someone named Jody Harrow. It shouldn't be hard to track her down."

Sometime later they returned with two postcard versions of the rug. Jody had done one set of dance steps for men, a second set for women. I thought the one for men was better and was eager to see it in person. But I also wanted to meet Jody and view any other rugs she had made.

"Let's go to her studio," I urged.

"Oh, that's not necessary. We can have the rug brought here." The decorators were determined to be the interface between artist and client, and they made every effort to ensure we didn't meet.

When the decorators arrived at my office the next day, they had postcard versions of Jody's other designs, and a transparency of the dance-step rug. From the soft blacks in the **New York Times** to the rich ones on the postcard to the vivid ones on film, the rug was looking better and better. As much as I'd wanted to meet Jody, there was no disputing that the dance-step rug was great. "Let's get it," I said.

I made only one alteration. Jody's sample rugs used a warm ecru instead of white, a logical defense against dirt. I ignored conventional wisdom and asked for white wherever there was beige. While my colors are not as saturated as those in Pedro Almodóvar's visually electric films, there is no room for beige in my life. At least not yet.

I kept the postcards as shorthand reminders of Jody's work. But there was one I paid particular attention to, a map of North America and the Caribbean.

I took special pains not to lose it. Something told me a time would come when I would want to revisit it. In the meantime, weeks passed, and the dance-step rug finally arrived, looking crisper and more vivid than any photograph could capture.

No matter who visited my office, there was always at least one uninhibited soul among them who could not resist trying to follow the diagram. Inevitably, she or he wound up looking remarkably foolish, since Jody had exaggerated the distance between footprints. All the time the rug was in my office, only one person was able to dispatch the steps with something approaching grace. But then again, she was a dancer.

The Pleasures of Meeting Artists

A year had passed since the rug was in place, stirring ongoing bouts of bumbling athletics. Spring came, and with it, the furniture show at the Javits Center. Only two months earlier, I had made a pilgrimage downtown to meet Lyn Godley, of the furniture and lighting design team Godley-Schwan. My good friend George Beylerian had just returned from the Milan furniture fair, where Lyn and her husband Lloyd had premiered their work. He brought back slides of it for me, sure I would love it. And he was right.

When I called Lyn to ask if I could visit their studio, her resistance was palpable. "There's nothing here," said Lyn. "All the furniture you saw in the slides is still in crates from Milan en route to the Javits show."

Famous Flaws Department of Life: I can be an enormous pain.

"Don't you have any of your work at home?"

"Well, there's a chair and an ottoman," Lyn reluctantly allowed. "But they're totally different from what you saw. Just natural wood. No color."

"I'd love to see them if I could."

Lyn relented. It was less stressful than trying to persuade a Roto-Rooter from its course.

So I made my way down to a loft on Hudson Street where Lyn and Lloyd lived and worked. Lloyd wasn't home, but I met Lyn, Wolfgang, her first baby (two more were to come), and the family cat. Somehow we made conversation, polite and strained at first, warmer and looser toward the end. I left, promising to come to the Javits Center when their work was on display.

Several weeks later I arrived at the furniture show and, with the precise instincts of a homing pigeon, cruised through the hundreds of installations directly to their booth. Lyn was there, and Lloyd, and a phalanx of furniture more buoyant, inventive, and remarkable than the Javits had seen in years. Although Lloyd, who was staunchly cynical, would have been sure to disagree, I believe we all felt a little giddy. It was the furniture. The work was so amazingly good, I felt we were on the brink of a new movement in design. Nothing else in the vast convention center looked like Godley-Schwan.

"By the way," said Lyn. "There's someone here we thought you'd like to meet."

She extended her hand to a very pregnant young

A red bass display case, glittering with Wendy Gell's "wristies."

Julie Harris lookalike, Jody Harrow.

It was a full year since I'd bought Jody's dance-step rug, and now, at last, I was being introduced to her. I had given up pressing the decorators to include me on their visits to her showroom, but I still had the postcards of her other work, and I had begun to fantasize about the map. As I imagined the map rug, it became part of my life. I would talk about it, and one of the people I mentioned it to was Lyn. Lyn and Lloyd knew Jody—design circles are small— and they introduced her to me, as much for Jody's sake as for mine. Maybe I would make another purchase.

Lyn, Lloyd, Jody—they all became my friends. Yes, I did buy furniture and rugs from them. And even now, more than ten years later, we brainstorm and collaborate, and their work has become part of the house I bought on Strivers Row in Harlem. But long before that I purchased a country house on a lake and Lyn and Lloyd decided to rent the house next to mine. There our weekends recaptured the unbounded freedom I had experienced years ago growing up in a small town. We left our doors unlocked and were in and out of each other's homes. Lloyd and I would do the communal shopping, Lyn would cook, or Lloyd would barbecue. I was on cleanup detail. We all pitched in.

When I made my second trip to Senegal, Jody joined me for the first week. I wanted to visit as many artists as I could, while Jody, who had spent several years in Japan studying textile design, devoted herself to finding the weavers of Senegal's beautifully intricate fabrics.

Back in New York, Jody and I now make a tradition of visiting the Javits Center for the annual furniture fair, the spot of our first meeting. We wander the aisles, stern critics of most of what we see, goofy teenagers when we find something we like. And while our ostensible focus is design, we cover the waterfront as we walk and talk. Friends and boyfriends, husbands and children, work, dreams, Africa, art— the themes weave in and out of our conversation as though we were jazz musicians jamming on a late night for the sheer pleasure of it all.

Recently Jody reminded me of something I'd forgotten as the years folded into one another. In buying her dance-step rug, I had unknowingly become Jody's very first customer. Who can explain the mystery and magic of intersecting lives? Lyn, Lloyd, Jody: their art fills my house, but their friendship fills my life.

Against the Wall

While it's true that the Rietveld chairs set the tone for my office, I would be remiss if I didn't mention its other polestar, a silkscreen of Superman by Andy Warhol.

In the early 1980s I received a call from Ron Feldman, a dealer with a well-deserved reputation for intelligence, vision, and integrity. Ron is also warm, unaffected, humane, and very funny. He had phoned because he was working with Andy Warhol on a silkscreened portfolio of ten classic American icons. Their list included Uncle Sam, Mammy, Frankenstein, Mickey Mouse, and of course Superman. Ron was inquiring about the rights.

Andy Warhol doing Superman? It was a perfect marriage of pop culture and pop artist. The chairman of Warner Publishing — to whom DC Comics reported at that time — gave Ron and Andy permission. In exchange, he received a limited number of HC prints ("hors commerce" — not for sale), which he distributed as gifts. I was one of the lucky recipients.

I first saw Andy's work when I was a young teenager in Washington, D.C. I had gone with my parents to a gallery on or near Connecticut Avenue. I don't remember its name, and my dim recollection of the space is that it was a walkup on the second floor. But I do have a strong memory of sunlight pouring through the windows and of one painting in particular, a large, unstained canvas with row after row of Coke bottles, each with a different amount of cola in it.

For me, it was love at first sight. And a defining moment: my parents hated the painting. They dismissed it and everything else in the show with the angry contempt of art lovers who feel their values have been assaulted. My mother had a passion for modern art, and her taste was liberal. She revered Rothko and Franz Kline almost as much as she worshiped Cézanne. Mummy's responses were emotional and visceral. She was moved by the arc of a brushstroke, the sensuality of color, the tactile quality of paint. And she eschewed analysis of any work she loved, believing that deconstructing a painting or a poem would destroy its beauty and power. If my mother had to explain why she liked a picture, she would offer some vague generalization, that the work was, well, painterly.

Andy's art, with its banal popular imagery and machine-like execution, was an affront to everything my mother held dear. My father, although taking it less personally, was of similar mind. "This isn't art," they declared. "This is a sham, a con game, a disgrace. All hype and no substance. A scheme to bilk the public of its money."

My parents weren't aesthetic boors, far from it. They were educated, thoughtful, and cultured, enthusiastic in their enjoyment, fair-minded and benign in their criticism. Yet Andy's work had provoked anger and outrage. Their reaction, which I only came to understand years later, mystified me. It's not that we hadn't disagreed before. But this time my parents and I stood on opposite sides of a chasm, without any bridge between us.

As I grew up, I never lost my love for Andy's work. I met Andy in my late twenties, and we were friends until he died. Over time, my father met him too, lunched with Andy and visited him at the Factory, the enormous loft space that was the hub of Andy's creativity. (My mother was long since deceased.) Andy was immensely fond of my dad, and even thought they looked alike, a notion that left Papa a little nonplussed. "I'm not so sure that's a compliment," he observed. But despite the good times we had together, Papa's estimation of Andy's work remained the same. It wasn't art.

The first Warhols I owned were all gifts, either from Andy himself or, in the case of his **Superman**, from the head of Warner Publishing. The ones from Andy I framed for home. But the **Superman** was different. How could I hang it anywhere but in my office?

As he did with almost all his work, Andy experimented with the Superman image before arriving at the final version for the portfolio. He made two spectacular paintings, five feet square, one on a blue background, another on a green. He silkscreened the image against different colors, too. In the end he opted for black, a choice that grounds Superman's primary colors in an atmosphere of sober mystery. One can feel the Man of Steel piercing the shroud of airless, darkened space.

The figure of Superman was based on a drawing by the late comic-book artist Curt Swan, who penciled the Man of Steel for so long that countless generations of adults, including Jerry Seinfeld, still value his rendition above all others. Many artists have followed Curt with their own compelling versions of Superman. But for those who grew up on Curt, there are no rivals.

Curt's drawing showed Superman in flight, his body listing to one side to give the sense that he is cutting through the sky, his left arm raised and ending in a disproportionately large fist. It is a distortion that conveys power, just as the oversize hand of Michelangelo's **David** has stood as a metaphor for the untried youth who felled a giant with his slingshot.

Equally effective is a second ghost image, which Andy added by silkscreening the same Superman contours in pastel shades of diamond dust.

The ghost image is somewhat lower than the original, and partially overlaps it, so that Superman's head and body seem embedded in the outstretched arm of the original rendering. The foreshortened arm, the overlarge fist, were indices of strength in the Curt Swan drawing that Andy appropriated for this work. But now the arm seems to signify more. It feels imbued with the essence of Superman, with something metaphysical: his heart, his energy, his spirit.

Andy's **Superman** is more than a picture—it is a symbol. On the surface, it feels like a magisterial interpretation of a classic Superman pose. But the Warhol version pumps up the volume, adding what Dostoyevsky, in describing the power of the church, called Magic, Mystery, and Authority.

In my earlier Art Deco office, I had hung the **Superman** to the left of my desk in the middle of the wall. On either side, I placed long, brushed-aluminum sconces that had supposedly come from the Woolworth Building, a New York City landmark built between 1910 and 1913. There was no ignoring Andy's Man of Steel. I took to calling it the Altar.

When we moved offices, I needed, as I had in the

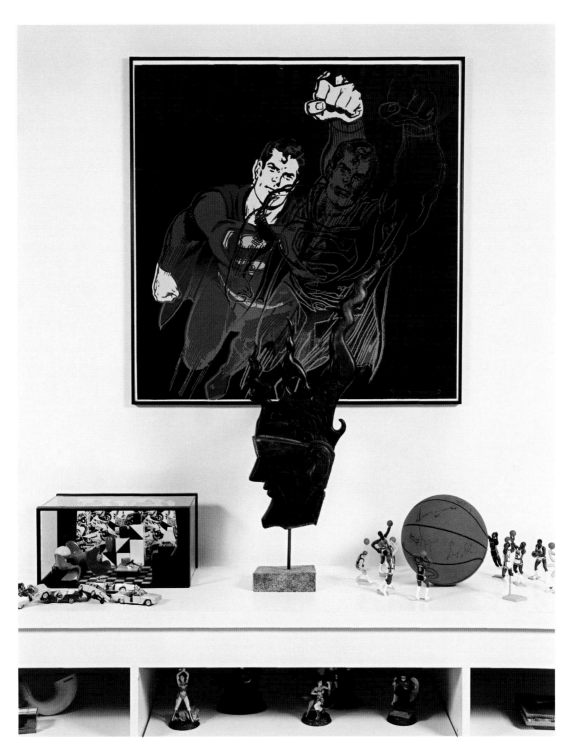

Superman presiding over several skewed tableaux: a classic car pileup, a model 1960s room, the Olympic Dream Team around a giant basketball, and, center, Pucci de Rossi's self-portrait radio.

73

Caution: Woman at Work— Design in the Office

past, a combination of built-in bookshelves and cabinets. The design firm took on the task, looking for its inspiration to the Rietveld chair. The cabinetry it designed was white instead of black, but at certain intersecting points, flat, outward-facing squares echoed not only the chair's construction but its colors: yellow, red, and blue. For a diversion, I threw in pink.

The firm's original idea had been for the shelves to stretch from one end of the office to the other. They certainly would have housed more books, but twenty uninterrupted feet of shelving seemed oppressive. I suggested we break up the bookcase by leaving a large space in the middle for art. I had just the picture: Andy's **Superman** was once again enshrined in a place of honor. As I said, the two polestars of my office decor were Gerrit Rietveld's 1918 chairs and Andy Warhol's 1981 **Superman**. They seemed to me in perfect balance: the Rietveld chair, a functional object but a three-dimensional abstraction; the Warhol, a two-dimensional illusion of a three-dimensional reality. That is, if you believe, as I do, that Superman is real.

With windows on two sides and the Warhol and bookshelves on the third, you would think there was little room left for art. But I was undaunted. In addition to the fourth wall, I considered everything fair game: closet doors, structural piers, the tops of radiators.

There's a lot going on in my office: primary colors,

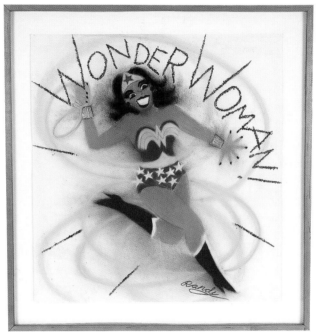

Randy Stevens's spirited rendition of Wonder Woman wrapped in her lasso's golden skeins.

lamps in the shape of televisions and mobile homes, superhero figurines, 1960s telephones, 1930s kindergarten toys, a family of Mr. Potato Heads squatting on my desk. To contain the busyness, some strong graphic elements were needed. The most significant of these was a huge photograph by Sandy Skoglund called **The Green House**, a remarkable surreal work in which countless purple and green dogs inhabit a domestic interior where everything—the furniture, the floors, the ceiling, the walls—is covered in a green material that resembles unkempt grass. There is so much to see in this picture, and because of its complexity and sense of unreality, many people assume it's a painting. The fact that it's an unmanipulated photograph gives it added strength.

I love Sandy's work and never tire of looking at it. Each time I glance up from my desk at **The Green House**, I have the sense of discovering something new. The picture is weirdly provocative—pleasurable and disconcerting at the same time. But there is another reason that Sandy's photograph is important to me. It's easy when you're in a field to develop a kind of industry myopia. As much as I love them, I didn't want my office to relate solely to comic books.

Years ago, the **Village Voice** ran a terrific ad campaign with drawings by Tomi Ungerer. The headline read: "Expect the Unexpected." What challenges us, what makes us grow, are the surprises, not what we already know. The connections may not be obvious, but every life experience is a resource. The unexpected assaults our preconceptions and, if we're willing, leads us into uncharted territory. Sandy's vivid, beautiful, troubling photograph does just that.

Other, much smaller pictures in my office also have little to do with comic books. But with Andy Warhol's **Superman** in such a prominent position, I had to make sure that Batman and Wonder Woman were represented as well. Superman may have launched the comic-book industry on his powerful shoulders, but Wonder Woman and Batman are equally significant icons and, along with the Man of Steel, the only characters who have been published consecutively since their inception over sixty years ago.

Sometime in 1980 I stopped by a gallery on Fifty-seventh Street and saw the work of a young woman, Randy Stevens. The smaller pictures were colorful pastel scenes, full of attitude and social commentary. They looked like punk **New Yorker** cartoons—smart, sassy, and insouciant. In addition, they were remarkably affordable, even for someone with my limited funds. Overcome by their low price, I immediately bought four.

In my old office I'd installed a low rail, like an easel lip, so that I could lean pictures up against the wall without formally hanging them. I put Randy's work there, and it always gave me pleasure. Her pas-

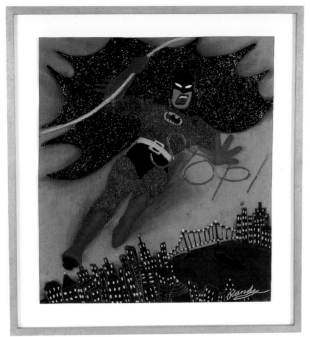
Batman—The Caped Crusader—by Randy Stevens, swinging over a glittering Gotham.

tels had a freshness and humor that seemed perpetual.

When I decided to add Wonder Woman to my office, I thought of Randy. I could have enlarged one of our classic Wonder Woman covers, but our halls are lined with oversize art from our comics. What I wanted to see instead was a view of Wonder Woman from someone outside the industry. I wanted to be surprised.

I spoke to Jill Kornblee, who was Randy's dealer in New York, and asked if Randy would be willing to take on a commission: creating her version of Wonder Woman. Jill consulted with Randy, and the answer was yes. We agreed on a price, and I once again adopted my Zen attitude toward waiting. What finally arrived was an exuberant Amazon princess against a lively yellow ground. Was she beautiful? Not exactly. But her eyes flashed, her mouth was wide, and she twirled her golden lasso with abandon.

I waited, with a substantially diminished Zen attitude, for the reaction of people at DC. Ever since Superman was first published, in 1938, there has been a consistent thrust in comics not only to master perspective and turn a figure in space but to articulate that figure with both balance and proportion. These are Renaissance ideals, and comic-book artists, four hundred years later, strived to achieve them. How would they respond to a Wonder Woman with an overlarge head, a short torso, and stubby legs?

The response was better than I thought. No one genuflected. But there was a clear respect for the fact that Randy had managed to capture Wonder Woman's spirit despite her funny, compact body. She succeeded in this because Wonder Woman's face was full of character and warmth. In addition, Randy caught Wonder Woman's lucent vitality, wrapping golden skeins around her as though heroine and lasso were one, a whirling dervish, a radiant force of light and truth.

Some time later, I inquired whether Randy would be willing to create her version of Batman. Once again the answer was yes, and the result was both pure Randy and pure Caped Crusader. In contrast to the vibrant Wonder Woman, and in keeping with Batman's Dark Knight persona, Randy drew him swinging from his bat rope against a blackened sky. Beneath him the nighttime city gleams, its windows shining with glitter. Like Wonder Woman, this is no idealized superhero. His body, too, is clunky. But his athleticism and fierceness are never in doubt. The picture is all grays and blacks, but four vermilion letters snap through it like a whip: STOP! And whomever has been targeted by Batman's wrath, we know they have done just that.

Interestingly, Randy's **Wonder Woman** had earned respect from the DC staff. But her **Batman** was different; it provoked admiration. The reaction surprised me, because I thought Batman was sacrosanct. But art has a power of its own, and you can never be sure how people will respond.

Solid Geometry

It seems to me that for a space to feel truly animated, it has to be imagined as a total environment. Art on the walls is not sufficient. That's what you expect in galleries and museums. And while the art in these institutions might be powerful and beautifully displayed, it's rare that one would speak of the spaces themselves as inviting. Although there may be other exceptions, only one comes immediately to mind.

When I was twelve years old, my family moved to Washington, D.C. Of all the wonderful museums there, my favorite was the Phillips Collection. Mr. and Mrs. Phillips were passionate collectors who, even when they were living, turned their mansion into a museum for the public. The large paneled hall on the first floor had a grand piano, and every week on Sunday afternoons, concerts would be held there. These were intimate events. Although they were open to anyone, you nonetheless had the feeling of being personally invited into someone's home.

The concerts emphasized that the Phillips Collection was still a house, and the art in it a matter of individual taste. But the Phillipses' sensibility was manifest in other ways. One small room contained a magnificent Degas: dancers in blue tutus against a brilliant orange field. This same room had other paintings on the walls, but the Degas was clearly the centerpiece. In quiet tribute, the windows were draped in a subtle salmon fabric, the delicate Duncan Phyfe sofa covered in satin, striped orange and blue. In an unobtrusive way, the room was decorated. The Phillipses had created something more than a museum. Once again, they were inviting you into their home, this time into a sitting room.

A modern wing had been added to the original Phillips mansion, and here too there was a special room, a space more perhaps for meditation than contemplation. The light was dim, as in an inner sanctum. Carpeting added to the hush. Classic modern seating —was it Mies van der Rohe or Marcel Breuer?— offered spare lines but comfort. The decor of this room, and it was decorated, was muted and discreet, with a single purpose. On all four walls were masterworks by the abstract expressionist Mark Rothko.

Rothko had divided each painting into a few rectangles and squares of brushed color that filled the canvas nearly to its edge. Other than the perimeter of the canvas, there are no hard lines in the internal geometry of these pictures. The colors, whether somber or bright, pulse against each other, and their rhythms create a vibrational field that seems to flow out from the canvas just as sound waves emanate from their point of origin. The Rothkos are incredibly beautiful, and critics have reached for words like spiritual to describe them. There is no doubt that, like a tuning fork, they strike notes within us, deep and unnamable. As with other spaces in the Phillips, the Rothko room was designed for a function that went beyond the surveying of art. It was the museum's chapel.

What does this all have to do with an office or a home? The Phillips Collection taught me the pleasure of a totally conceived creative space, of a human and humane artistic environment. That lesson has stayed with me. I believe art occurs in the interior space as much as it does on the periphery. That is how I look at functional objects like furniture and rugs, and at nonfunctional ones, like the large red display cabinet you see as soon as you walk through my office door. It has three glass shelves fitted against a mirrored back so that everything in it seems to sparkle. And it's in the shape of an oversize string bass.

I found the bass some years ago at the prestigious fall folk art show on the New York piers, in the booth of Kelter-Malcé, who bring together quality and quirkiness in an appealing blend. I've known Jolie Kelter and Michael Malcé since my twenties, when I began collecting quilts. They're a great couple with total enthusiasm for what they do, and they're more than happy to share it. I thought the bass, which was actually one of a pair, was spectacular. It was, however, painted white.

"The bass is fabulous, isn't it?" Jolie asked.

"I love it. Except for the white. It isn't strong enough. But it's a piece of folk art. I wouldn't want to change the original."

"Jenette," Michael whispered conspiratorially, "trust me. The bass has already been painted at least five times."

"Oh, well, in that case." And I took it.

As you have already gleaned, I immediately got rid of the white and painted it bright red. Or, that is, Steve Kursh, the Man of a Thousand Talents, did. We kept the neck of the bass black and the ornamentation gold, although Steve repainted them too, so that they would match the luster of the body.

Steve did the work in his loft. When he delivered the bass, he had added a little fillip, a spontaneous flourish that was his way of gift-wrapping the case. Months before, Steve and I had gone shopping for armloads of fake flowers to wind throughout my guest house in the country. One of them, a slender strand of miniature pink roses, had found its way into Steve's home. Now it was twisted around the neck of the bass, a grace note that hinted at sweet, sprightly music from this sonorous instrument. I don't think Steve intended for me to keep the flowers there. But I have, loving this visual gesture that is half bonbon, half bon mot.

Things Change

In time we moved again, and although I tried to re-create my office as though I were installing a model room at the Met, I lost some things and gained others. Jody Harrow's dance-step rug had suffered too much abuse from thousands of feet bringing the grime of the city indoors. Even so, it was hard to imagine my office without it. But Jody had created a Superman rug for the Warner Bros. stores, and I bought one of them to go in front of the couch. Superman is invulnerable to practically everything. We'll see how he does against dirt.

There are new knickknacks, new tableaux (tiny figures of the Olympic "Dream Team" surrounding a

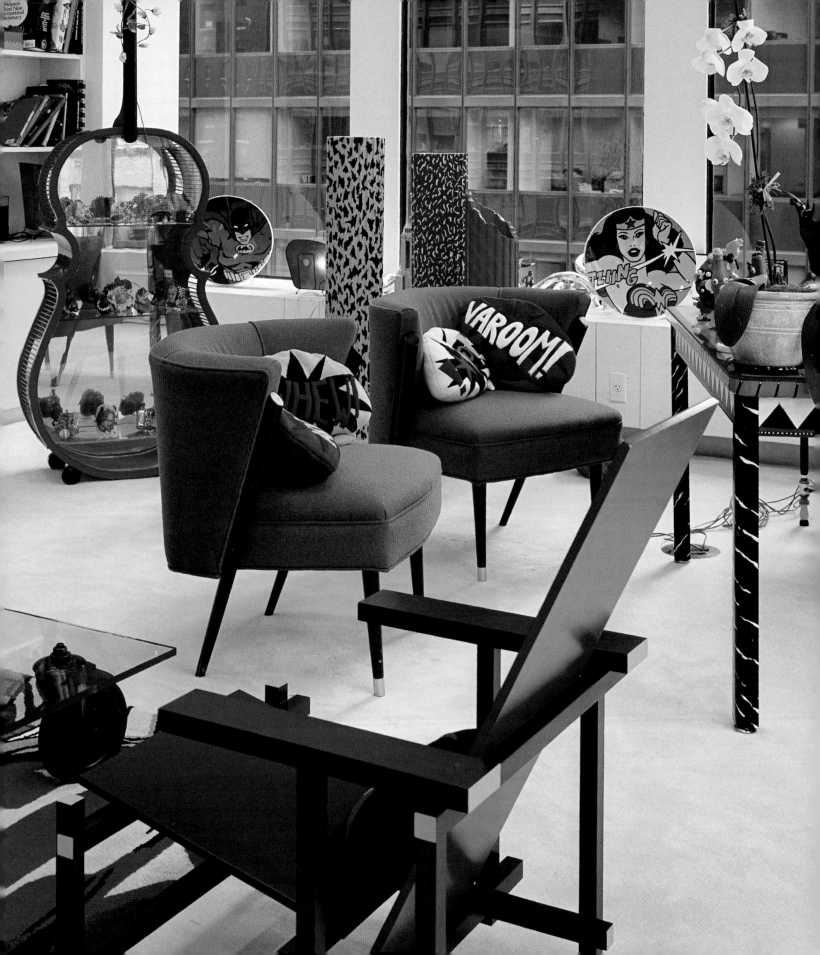

signed Atlanta Hawks basketball, a pileup of minia-ture model cars). The shades are rice-paper-edged in four bright patterns that pick up the colors in the room. A Swid Powell plate with the red AIDS ribbon hangs by the door, a note of seriousness, a gentle reminder. Behind the door is a mirror by the Italian designer Massimo Iosa Ghini, printed so that the reflective space is in the shape of a dialogue balloon,

that tailed bubble that indicates speech in comic books. Some things are just too perfect.

When people come into my office, their eyes widen. Anna Ng, my assistant, gets requests for viewings from out-of-town visitors, which she graciously tries to accommodate. Sometimes I think I'm on the Big Apple Tour. But one thing is consistent. Almost every-body asks, "How do you ever get any work done here?"

Lessons Learned Along the Way

1. In case there was any doubt, the Rolling Stones drove home what subliminally we already knew: you can't always get what you want. But by turning yourself into a wirehaired terrier, you vastly increase your odds of getting satisfaction. I had seen Tom Miller's furniture on the other side of the country. But even though I would gladly have shipped one of his hand-painted desks to New York, there was none to be had. Rather than give up, I tracked Tom down in Baltimore, pressing my case by visiting him in person. The effort was worth it. In my office, Tom's gleaming desk is the most beautiful piece of furniture. When you set your heart and sights on something, doggedness is your best friend in getting it.

2. New pieces and new designers come on the scene all the time. If you're looking for something original, or for an artist who can create an item just for you, it's important to keep up. The best way to do this is to read everything you can get your hands on. The Home sec-tion of the Thursday **New York Times** features new finds. So do the shelter magazines. For a comprehensive annual survey, Abbeville Press publishes the **International Design Yearbook.**

3. Whenever possible, try to seek out the artist or designer behind the work you love. Often this endeavor will simply be a courtesy, a direct way of expressing

Unattributed but stylish 1950s chairs in front of a hand-painted desk by Tom Miller.

your appreciation. But sometimes a real connection will be made, and it is rewarding to know a creator, and support her in whatever ways you can. In addition, the artists with whom you develop a personal relationship can be your best collaborators.

4. An object's interest depends not upon size, but on conception and execution. So it wouldn't be surprising if one day you find yourself with a plethora of small, fascinating items that you want to display. This poses a challenge for any interior. If you place a lot of little pieces in one room, they will tend to make it look busy, even cluttered. To counterbalance your smaller objects, add large, strong, graphic elements. They will act as respites and anchor any number of small-scale items.

5. By creating tableaux, you can make your collections of small-scale objects more important and fun. I had bought Franklin Mint's miniature editions of 1950s and 1960s automobiles. But despite the beautiful detailing of the cars, they were too tiny just to line up on a coun-tertop. However, when turned into a full-scale pileup, doors flung open, vehicles overturned, they became a focal point, eliciting the uneasy laughter that comes with black humor. Similarly, by themselves, my miniature plastic versions of the Olympic Dream Team would have seemed puny and cheap. But by placing the figures around a towering regulation basketball, they became larger and more serious than the parts: an installation that comments on how large sports loom in our lives.

5.

Paradise Found:

A Country House Overlooking a Lake

A view looking across the lake at my vacation home nestled in the trees.

My decision to buy my house in the country was impulsive. All of the intelligent, adult criteria one is supposed to bring to bear on major purchases like this were conspicuously absent from my thinking. I failed to factor in those things that sane people care about: real estate taxes, water supply, the value of surrounding homes, the driving distance from New York. Instead, it happened like this.

I have a close friend, Wendy Gell, who works in many art forms but is best known for her lavish and highly personal jewelry designs. Although Wendy makes rings and earrings, necklaces, pins, and even tiaras, I like her own invention, the "wristie," most of all. The wristie is a metal cuff—it might be one inch wide or as much as three or four—encrusted with glistening stones, ethnic arti- facts, fake pearls, ropes of silver and gold, pop culture icons, chunks of turquoise, rhinestones, tiles, flowers, beach glass, even bark from trees. The list is endless. Wendy fuses some combination of these elements together on her tiny metal canvas, wielding her glue gun like a latter-day Annie Oakley as she brings to bear her unique sense of artistry, discipline, and balance.

When I first met Wendy, she had her showroom and studio in Manhattan. I would come over after work, and eventually we started to make wristies together. The Italian restaurant across the street would send up food, and we'd make dinner look far more sumptuous than it actually was by setting the table with glasses and candlesticks shining with Wendy's trademark baubles and jewels. Thoroughly full and full of ideas, we'd then storm the workshop and seize the glue guns.

A Trial Summer in a Tiny Lakeside Cottage

One night, before the creative process consumed us, Wendy mentioned that she and her husband, Hadley, were having financial troubles.

"I really don't want to," she lamented, "but I guess we're going to have to rent Clara's House."

Clara's House, Wendy explained, was one of two small cottages that she and Hadley had bought for investment purposes on the lake where they kept a weekend home. The Rock House had a tenant. But Clara's House was Wendy's private retreat. She hated to think of someone else inhabiting it.

This was April, and summer was barely six weeks away. "Well, I'll rent it," I said.

"Jenette," Wendy counseled, "don't you think you should come up and see the house first?" A valid point. I accepted Wendy's offer of staying at Clara's House for a weekend to see if I really did want to spend the summer there.

There were obstacles. I had a boyfriend who was loath to leave the city for almost any reason. I had to convince him that we should drive to Connecticut (hard, but not impossible) and check out Clara's House (impossible, but there are miracles), with an eye to going up there for most weekends. To my amazement, he agreed, at least to part one. We rented a car and found ourselves two hours later in a little cottage on a lake that had somehow eluded cartographers. My boyfriend was tall and so am I. Clara's House, with its low ceilings and tiny rooms, was clearly built for people under five-foot-two, cer- tainly not for us. Perhaps it was something we ate. But we decided to take the house.

It was that summer that convinced me. I loved the lake, which turned myriad colors as the sun rose higher and higher in the sky. I loved its mystery at night with the ache of cars' headlights that briefly

In Your Space: **Personalizing Your Home and Office**

flashed in the darkness on the road across the way and then were gone, their red taillights streaming out of sight. I wanted a house of my own.

When I mentioned this to Wendy, she was thrilled. "It's not on the market yet, but our neighbor two doors down is going to sell his home. This is so great! We'll get him on the phone."

The neighbor was actually in Florida, but Hadley had his number, and we placed the call from Wendy's house. Yes, he wanted to sell. And I was welcome to go inside. Wendy and Hadley could get me the key.

On the next day, I was there. The house was modest and undistinguished but well kept. It felt like a 1950s notion of a lakeside cottage: homes close on either side, lots of interior wood, small rooms that were meant to be cozy. The windows facing the lake were small, too, with slats of glass that let in the air but prevented an unobstructed water view. It was hard to know how to open up the space

Against the bright yellow siding, two plastic "terra-cotta" chairs from Spain and Richard Schultz's classic garden table.

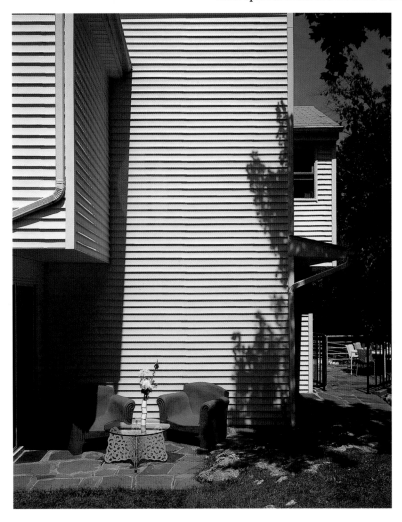

without spending a great deal of money, and the asking price was already steep because the house was in good condition and had beautiful lakefront property.

I wasn't certain. What one person might have seen as warm and woodsy I saw as dark and cramped. Yet I didn't have the money both to buy the property and do a massive renovation. There was another house on the lake for sale. I needed to see it.

The good news: The second house was considerably cheaper than the first. And the bad: It was an unmitigated wreck. The house had been on the market for a year, and I could see why. A handyman's nightmare, it didn't even meet the definition of a "fixer-upper." There was only one house worth buying, and it was the one near Wendy.

I was in the early stages of negotiation for it when Wendy phoned. There was panic in her voice, and I thought she'd been crying.

"Wendy, what's wrong?"

"Well, it's the house. I mean, I want you up at the lake, but this house, it's just so close to mine. You know, the lake is my refuge. I come up here to get away from my job. And I can see it now. I'll be out on my deck and I'll look over and there you'll be out on your deck and you'll have a wistful expression on your face, wanting to make wristies. Because that's fun for you, that's relaxation. But I won't want to because I make wristies at work. But then I'll feel guilty."

I could hear the panic rising.

"Wendy, Wendy. Don't worry. I won't buy it. No house is more important than our friendship." And that was that. Only, where was I going to live?

Can This House Be Saved?

It was actually Wendy who suggested I look again at the disaster house, this time with an architect and a contractor in tow. I was dubious, but the only alternative was to wait—how long? months? years?—for a new house on the lake to come up. The prospects were bleak. Desperate, I called two people who had worked on Wendy's house, Arthur Zweck-Bronner, an interior architect, and Phil Hayes, a local contractor.

Not long after, Phil and Arthur and I met to tour the house that nobody wanted. It seemed to me it was hopeless, and Phil shared my glumness. But Arthur was unflaggingly optimistic, and Phil began to perk up. Maybe the house could be salvaged after all.

We went round and round. I knew what I wanted: light, space, air, and a house that opened up to nature while still feeling sufficiently enclosed for the fall and winter months. Despite the honeycomb of low-ceilinged, dark little rooms, despite the spit and baling wire that barely held the house together, Arthur said we could achieve my goals and mapped out a general plan. Could it work? I didn't know. But what options did I have? Ultimately, it came down to a leap of faith. I closed my eyes, held my breath, and jumped.

Once again I began negotiations, this time on the disaster house on the hill. It was interesting how they proceeded. Beauty is unquestionably in the eye of the beholder. The house that I saw as ramshackle and desperate, the owner, who was a photographer, genuinely loved. But there could be no argument about its extraordinary site. The house sat high on a rocky promontory, apart from all the other homes save for a small, rundown shack to one side that shared its majestic views. If you stood on the ridge, you could see left down the length of the lake where the sun rose in the morning. Across the water was a small mountain covered with trees. To the right was the mouth of the lake, which bled into acres of blurred woods and, more distantly, soft mountains where the sun set. Oddly, the house had only one large window facing the lake, and it was sealed, permitting just a snapshot of this startling panoramic sweep. I looked forward to a time when the house was mine and I could break it wide open, letting the outside world flood in with a beauty so immense it stopped your heart.

Buttressed by my stalwart financial adviser and counselor, Tom Ruta, and my vision of a home that embraced the vista of the lake, I was able to succeed in my negotiations. The price was a little more than I would have liked to pay, and a little less than the owner would have liked to receive, but neither of us was unhappy.

We met for the closing in my lawyer's office in a seventeenth-century white frame house on the village green, a far cry from the glass-and-steel caverns where so much business is transacted in New York. Life in the country has an incomparable rhythm of its own.

Not long after the closing, I went to Europe for the Christmas holidays. I couldn't help phoning my office—it's in my DNA—but in retrospect, I shouldn't have been so inquisitive. My assistant told me that the pipes had burst, a mere two weeks after I'd bought my first house. Without even applying, I'd been initiated into that fairly large and endlessly beleaguered group: Homeowners of America. Should I laugh or should I cry? I decided to laugh. I'd bought a disaster. The house was a total gut anyway.

The Best-Laid Plans . . .

When I returned from vacation, Arthur and Phil and I began our talks in earnest. My sense of the house was quite clear, and Arthur and Phil were wonderful collaborators, often expanding or improving on my ideas. I learned from Phil that the town zoning laws required that whatever we did had to stay within the "footprint" of the original house. We were not permitted to increase the perimeter of the house, and therefore its square footage. In fact, we couldn't even

add another bathroom without also enlarging the septic system, a near impossibility for a house built on rock so solid and immense that you could rappel off the cliffs in back.

The house was two stories, but the footprint itself was relatively small, probably no more than 800 square feet. The only way to create a flow of space and the impression of expanse was to open up the downstairs into one giant room that would accommodate cooking, dining, and entertaining. There would be just two enclosed spaces: a closet for storage, and a small guest bathroom with a laundry room tucked neatly inside. Upstairs would be two substantial bedrooms, sizable closets, and a large, sybaritic master bath.

There were countless more things on the list. Arthur was busy drafting his first set of blueprints, trying to incorporate them all, when Phil weighed in with a bombshell. No matter how he tore apart the house, there was no way he could get the ceilings an inch or two above seven feet. I was stunned. It was one thing to spend a summer in Clara's tiny house. It was quite another to rebuild a house and still have ceilings that would shave an inch off Patrick Ewing's hair. The alternative was to knock it down and truly begin from scratch.

We were halted in our tracks. Arthur put down his blue pencil, and I mentally filed away my ideas. Only Phil was active, trying to estimate the cost of tearing down the house and building a new one. In this time of disappointment, the guest house was our salvation. I had wanted to build it while the main house was under construction so that I'd still have a place to stay while work was going on. Now it became our sole focus.

Weeks went by, and Phil came back with an initial report. Because the house was on a ridge above a forest that marched down to the lake, it could not be razed wholesale. Instead, the house would have to be dismantled piece by piece, a lengthy and expensive process. The cost? Thirty thousand dollars, if all went smoothly, which even your certified dingbat knows never, ever does.

I was in a quandary. On the one hand, I felt I couldn't live with seven-foot ceilings. Yet somehow, strangely, even I couldn't seem to stomach spending $30,000 on something that would vanish as the last Dumpster rolled down the hill. Unable to make a decision, I stalled. The weeks stretched into months. We worked on the guest house while I let the battle fight itself out on more subterranean levels. Finally it surfaced. I asked Arthur and Phil to walk with me up to the main house.

"Phil, can you do any better than seven-foot-two?"

"Jenette, you know I'll do everything in my power. But I can't promise. Right now, seven-two looks like the best we can hope for."

"Arthur, tell me what you really truly think. If we emphasize the verticals everywhere, if we surround the bottom floor with sliding glass doors, do you believe the effect will be open enough and high enough to compensate for the low ceiling?"

"Yes, if we do that, I believe no one will ever notice."

"All right, then, let's get started."

The relief and the hope were palpable. And we never looked back.

Back on Track

Arthur picked up his blue pencil; I grabbed my filed ideas from the shelf. The creativity that had been suppressed so long now erupted like a geyser. The open plan and sliding doors were givens, but new notions flew fast and furiously. The house had been heated by wood-burning stoves on each floor. Clearly, these had to go in favor of zoned central heating. But how could I have a country house without a fireplace? Certainly there had to be one centered at the far end of the living area, an organizing focal point,

an expression of literal warmth and the warmth of conviviality. There wasn't one, of course. We would have to build it.

The cramped spiral staircase that led from the living space to the floor above had two serious problems. First, it was hard to negotiate. And, second, although small, it took up too much room. It was here, I think, that Arthur made his greatest contribution. He suggested a stair tower that went only slightly beyond the footprint of the house and therefore was legitimated by the zoning board. In one masterful stroke, Arthur's stair tower accomplished several wonderful things. First, it took the staircase out of the living area so that the space was now wide open. Second, it provided a strong architectural element to a house that had had no identifiable form. Third, it created a beautifully lit interior space with high, enormous walls for hanging art. The stair tower was a vertical gallery.

There was a geometry to the tower. The roof itself was peaked, a triangle at the top of the structure. Just below it were two large round windows, one on the north side, one on the south. Below the large round window on the front of the house was an even larger square one. Triangle, circle, square—the stair tower descended with mathematical precision.

I had put panes in the guest-house windows to give it the charm of a cottage. Arthur believed we should follow suit in the stair tower, although why, I'm not sure, perhaps to establish a visual relationship between the two homes. Whatever the reason, I acceded without enthusiasm. My heart wasn't in it, but I caved with little more than a murmur.

A Cautionary Note:

Agreeing to something halfheartedly is never wise. You might be doing it for a host of seemingly good reasons, like being supportive of another person's input, or for a shamelessly pathetic one—because it's the path of least resistance. The rationale doesn't matter. A halfhearted resolution almost always means you will have regrets. Needless to say, even though Arthur had ordered the panes for the stair-tower windows and I had paid for them, I never put them in.

We adhered to our plan of a fluid living space on the first floor and two large rooms on the second. Unable to get the height I'd hoped for downstairs, we compensated on the floor above by taking the ceilings all the way up to the peaked roof. Beneath the eaves of the guest house, we had put a small round window, both to let in light and to emphasize the heightened ceiling as an architectural element. We did the same thing here, although with a much larger window, in the master bedroom. It, too, let in light and served as an architectural element. I always thought I would paint a giant eye in the window and let the clouds outdoors pass behind it, an homage to Magritte's classic surrealist painting. Although this was my own idea, and I was in love with it for quite some time, it went the way of the windowpanes Arthur had wanted so much. The clouds still pass behind the window, but the surprise of the eye is not there. In the end, simple was better, especially in a house surrounded by nature. Sometimes you can try too hard.

I feel the same way about the windowpanes. Lying in my bed I can see out the door of my room to the square window in the middle of the tower. I have watched the stark branches of winter trace a dark pattern across the glass. I have seen it suffused with green in the summer and explode with color in the fall. I have watched snow pelt the surface with such ferocity that the window became a solid square of white. And I have seen it replaced minutes later by an exalted sky, blue and struck by light.

Yet another educational moment: in everything

you do, you have to be willing to edit. Sometime in the 1960s, the minimalist art movement proclaimed, "Less is more." Twenty years later the architect Vincent Scully shot back, "Less is a bore." I tend to side with Vincent Scully. Nonetheless, a glut of ideas or objects can obscure what is best in a project. Letting go of them, no matter how good they are or how attached to them you are, is essential to the creative process. Interestingly, it's rare that ideas disappear altogether. It may be months, it may be years, but they have a way of resurfacing—usually in mutated form, but resurfacing nonetheless.

We turned to other ways of opening up the house. The entire south side faced the lake, affording incredible views no matter which way you looked. On the lower floor, where the ceiling height was a problem, I was especially committed to glass doors. But I wanted them on the upper floor, too. I had always loved European rooms where majestic doors open onto tiny balconies. Although sliding glass doors have a much more modern look, the principle is the same. No matter what room I was in, I wanted to be able not just to observe the view but to enter it. To achieve this, my plan was to build small balconies off every doorway.

Arthur, however, worried that balconies on the top floor would cast shadows on the deck below, where the most active socializing would take place. I was unconcerned. The upper decks would be shallow, just wide enough for a chair or two. Their real function was to give everyone a private opening onto the vista of the lake.

In the end, as it turned out, Arthur was right. The upper balconies did cast shadows. But they were small, and welcome. None of us had anticipated how hot and strong the sun was on the lakeside, even in the non-summer months. It was good to have pockets of shade to retreat to, and these were supplied quite accidentally by the balconies above.

The process of creativity involves so many variables that it is unpredictable, and for that reason constantly engaging. When I graduated from college and had a fellowship at the Museum of Modern Art, I became friends with the photographer Garry Winogrand. More than anything, it was a mentor-student relationship; Garry was so blunt and so smart, and I was so eager to learn. He was often called a "street photographer," someone who had the quickness to interact with the human parade as it unfolded around him, extracting the most telling moments of form and commentary from a swirl of detail and gestures.

I asked Garry about printing his own work. "If I knew what the pictures looked like," he said, "I wouldn't bother. But I do it because I know I'll be surprised. Some things take place in the darkroom that you didn't account for when you took the shot. You never know what they'll be. That's what keeps it interesting."

No matter how much work it might be, creativity is never boring. When it becomes dull, you've probably slipped out of invention into formula, often without even knowing it. But creativity, because it surprises you, is a stimulant, and the most gratifying rewards are often the unexpected ones. Garry had taught me an important principle, and when I sit in the cool shadows cast by the balconies above, I think of him.

A House of a Different Color

I knew not only that I wanted decks leading out of each room but also that they would have curved metal railings, the sort that one finds on ships. Now it was a question of colors. The house for the most part was white. I decided on yellow for the lakeside railings off the top floor, and red for the larger ones below. Yellow expands and floats; the more intense

red beneath would both anchor the upper railings and serve as a counterpoint.

Off my bedroom, above the screened porch, was a large square deck, and here, as with the lower lakeside railings, I again opted for red. The parallel railings beneath them I painted a bright cobalt blue that had more weight than the red, just as the red had more weight than the yellow. Although I hadn't planned on any additional railings other than those following the stone steps up to the house, the local building code intervened. Despite a good amount of land that fronted right on the lake, I had decided to build a swimming pool. A pool meant many things, but it also meant more railings, a safeguard to protect young children who might somehow wander onto the property. I was forced to put up railings at entry points to the pool area, most of which I painted black. But there were also accents of red and yellow to keep things lively and extend the colors I already had.

The pool, like the house, was high up on solid rock. And it was small. The town code required railings all around it, which constricted the already limited space, stealing the sense of freedom of standing on the pool deck, surrounded by treetops on all sides. It was hard to imagine any color I could paint them that wouldn't make it worse.

I considered yellow, because of its light, expansive qualities. But yellow is also very vivid and can be quite demanding. In this particular instance, it had the additional problem of facing a background of dense green leaves. I usually think that yellow sparks the best in other colors, but although it brightens green, it also brings out its acidity. The rails around the pool needed to be softer so that the surrounding trees would be muted and calming, the leaves forming a protective glen. What were the alternatives? White I felt was stark; light blue, always beautiful against green, too repetitive, when the pool and concrete deck were shades of blue as well. The only answer seemed to be pink. And pink it was.

Phil had suggested vinyl siding for the house, and this seemed like an excellent idea. Although certainly not luxurious, it was eminently practical. Vinyl requires no painting, only periodic cleaning, accomplished easily by hosing with pressurized water. The house would be white, a crisp, clean canvas against which the colored rails could sparkle. But the stair tower, I felt, had to be sheathed in a color of its own. It was, as I have said, the one truly strong architectural element in the house that lifted it out of the mundane and gave it something even more than distinction—a commanding presence as it stood high on the rocky bluffs.

Arthur agreed that the stair tower should have a color of its own, but for him the color was gray. But to me, it felt like an architect's choice, somehow both modernist and safe. I wanted a color that, in the jargon of design, was postmodern, a color that was definitely not safe, but strong and vibrant to set the tone for the house. My choice was a bold, sunny yellow. Arthur sighed, and Phil gave me a look that I'd come to know well. Not impolite, simply one that registered that I'd once again gone off the deep end.

Nonetheless, Phil was a trouper, and dutifully set out to find bright yellow siding. The news from the front was not good. Apparently there was little if any demand for siding in a clear, strong yellow. After an extensive search, Phil came up with a weak-kneed pastel. I was disheartened. It was about as bland as yellow can get.

At this turn of events, Arthur brightened, beginning to feel that gray was a shoo-in. But gray for me was still out of the question. What, then? Light blue? (All vinyl colors, I'd now learned, were going to be light.) I couldn't even go there. Once again, I considered the lame yellow samples that Phil had brought back.

I try not to let diminished expectations become a habit, but sometimes you have to settle for less. Looking at the yellow samples, I decided this was one of them.

When the siding went up, it really wasn't so bad. I certainly would have preferred a brighter yellow, but this worked nonetheless. While strengthening the stair tower, it also engaged the colored railings and integrated them with the rest of the house.

I never thought the colored railings were very radical. But Phil told me that people, spying them from the far side of the lake, would try to find the hidden path to my house just to check them out, the equivalent, in construction terms, of a UFO sighting. Yet while others saw the railings as an unexplained phenomenon, I knew they were rooted in something classic and historic, the same 1918 Gerrit Rietveld chair that later inspired my office. The Rietveld chair, constructed in red, yellow, black, and blue, had clearly lodged itself in my psyche, an endless source of pleasure and inspiration. With my office, the inspiration had been conscious. Here, with the railings, I had felt that every color choice was individual and autonomous. Yet looking at them, I realize how much of my decision making had been predetermined by the strong image of an object I'd loved and internalized many years ago.

When City Folk Head for the Country

My neighbors were endlessly perplexed and amused by the goings-on at my house. When they heard the rumor that I was putting in central air-conditioning, the idea entertained them immensely. In a house on a lake surrounded by trees and just fifteen minutes from the shore, breezes abounded and temperatures were cool. No one had central air. Why would you when you

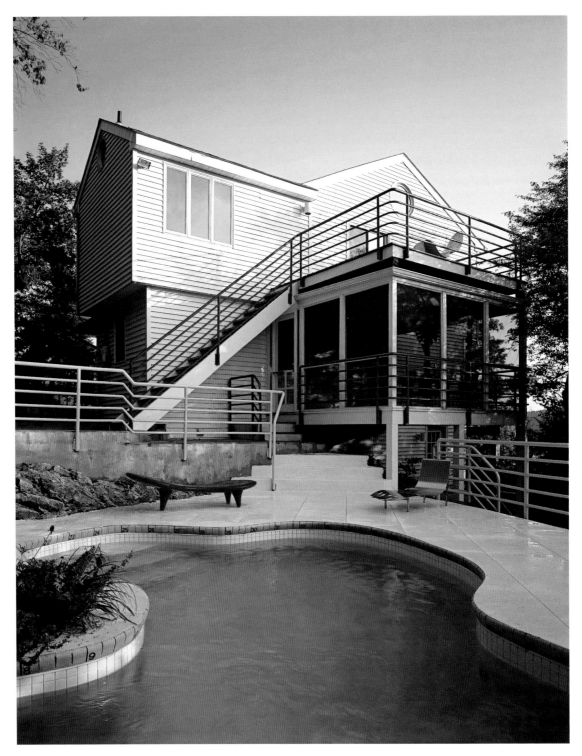

Tale of the tape: Chill Hill's small but welcome swimming pool, fifty-eight feet in perimeter.

In Your Space: **Personalizing Your Home and Office**

could open your windows to the fresh outdoors? For those one or two stifling summer nights, inexpensive electric fans took off the edge. Only a crazy city person—a New Yorker, of course—would go to such ludicrous and costly extremes as building a housewide air-conditioning system.

Most of this talk took place behind my back. But a few people did manage to broach the subject with me and still keep a straight face.

"Jenette, you really don't need central air. This is the country. Even during the day it's not too hot, and at night the temperature drops. You're on a lake. Why would you waste your money on something you'll almost never use?"

Now, it's true, I had spent a summer at the lake in Clara's House, which was not only tiny but devoid of all amenities as well. And I had been comfortable. But despite the naysayers, some of whom genuinely had my interests at heart, I felt this situation was different. For one thing, Clara's House, like almost every other on the lake, was close to the water and tucked away among trees where breezes and shade were common. Although my house, too, was nestled in the woods, it still rose above them, and sun poured into the windows from morning until night. I had more lakefront than most, but it glistened far below.

This was my very first house, and because I was gutting it and virtually starting from scratch, it reflected me in deeply personal ways. Why not be totally comfortable in the house? Why suffer through those dog days of summer when the air is so heavy and still that you can barely breathe indoors, when sleeping at night is a pipe dream? And although I had no intention of selling the house, I knew that life has a habit of intervening, and the best-laid plans of us mice often go awry. Perhaps central air would add to the resale value, should it come to that.

So air-conditioning became a feature of the house as my neighbors shook their heads. But they did so not nearly as hard or with such unbridled glee as when rumors reached them about the pool.

Jenette's Folly: The World's Smallest and Most Expensive Swimming Pool

As I've mentioned, my house stands high on a rocky promontory, separate from the other homes surrounding the lake. The site is quite extraordinary: from the front, primal, raw, and sculptural. The top of the rocks, where the house sits, is surprisingly flat. On the far side of the house, below the living room deck, the landscape plunges in a dizzying drop. Looking up through the trees at the house, you see only a sheer face of stone, massive and impregnable. And it was here, on rock as stubborn and dense as a fortress, that I elected to build a pool.

My waterfront is beautiful. It follows the curve of the mouth of the lake so that, from a deck Phil fashioned there, one can see its entire expanse. Minute by minute the lake changes. Clouds and sun stir its secret colors. Shouts of children echo from a distant beach, ducks paddle by, fishermen move their boats, drop their lines, and wait. Somewhere downshore a young girl practices the violin, unseen laughter shakes the trees, the splash of a swimmer ripples the water. You can sit on the deck for hours feeling the light touch of the lake and its activity and the deeper touch of your own peacefulness.

Why, then, a pool, when the lake offers so much? Aside from my penchant for warm water, in truth, getting to the lake from the house is a major commitment. The price for privacy and incomparable views is a steep and lengthy trek through the forest. It's not treacherous or particularly demanding—there are stairs all the way down—but some planning is in order if you intend to spend time on the lake. What do you need? Sunglasses? Towels? Books? Something to drink? I wanted to have a more spontaneous option, a body of water, albeit quite a small one, right outside my door. And the pool was it.

The pool I imagined was not rectangular in shape but organic, as though nature, not human beings, might have created it. And with this idea of a pool found in nature, I imagined, too, a waterfall. Arthur drew up sketches while Phil surveyed the site. There were two major problems. Considering the available flat land, the pool would have to be quite small. And then, because the land was on solid rock, we would have to dynamite.

In the end we dynamited not once but twice. The house was nearly finished when the explosives carved a crater in the stone. To this day, I'm amazed that the house didn't crumble and fall off the cliff.

But miracles do happen. The house remained intact, and the shell for the pool was formed. There were no angles, only curves, and I was happy. Arthur created the waterfall from piled rocks, so you could sit in the pool's shallow end and feel its welcome pressure on your back. On the far side, the pool was a respectable five feet deep. And it was heated for comfort and lighted for swimming at night. But the pool was small. At its longest diameter, it measured about eighteen feet across.

Looking out from the pool to the trees, with Marc Newson's red lounges and Nicola's stainless steel foot chaise.

Still, I loved my little swimming pool. We painted the interior aqua and stained the concrete deck around it a lighter shade of blue to give the illusion that the pool was actually much larger than it was. The idea came to me, probably in a fever dream, that it would be fun to play with the pool's dimensions. It might be only eighteen feet across, but it was fifty-eight feet in perimeter. I decided to paint a bright yellow tape measure around the edge.

Lloyd Schwan, my wonderfully artistic neighbor and good friend, always debated every creative notion that I had. It had become a ritual, and he was totally opposed to this idea. So I took paper and markers and did a partial life-size mock-up. It looked great to me. Lloyd harrumphed as loudly as he could, but, undaunted, I cheerfully went ahead.

You might wonder that I was so determined to have a naturalistic pool and then totally contravene it with the tape measure. I think a lot of my decisions encapsulate an aesthetic tension—the natural and the artificial, the classic and the kitsch, the historical and the very modern. There are beautiful spaces that stay within one theme, but I seem to enjoy the interest that lies at the intersection of dichotomies.

The pool turned out to be everything I hoped for. Whether through the screen door, the front door, or down the steps outside my bedroom's sliding doors, access to it was just footsteps away. Hot? You could jump in and jump out refreshed. Tired? You could sit on the steps in the shallow end, or under the waterfall, with its pressure massage. Ambitious? You could spend hours in the pool, paddling, floating, playing, even attempting micro-laps across the eighteen feet. The pool was a folly, but in the best sense of the word. My brother came up, took in the pool's small size and unusual shape. "I think you should put up a sign," he observed good-naturedly. "Stay in your own lap lane."

Full Circle

When the house was finally finished, there was one very special surprise. Somehow, using all his ingenuity, Phil had managed to raise the first-floor ceiling to close to eight feet. I had been prepared for much less. The additional height only added to the sense of lightness and spaciousness I had wanted so much.

Guilford is a charming town, and I enjoyed my forays into it to buy groceries or visit the stores around the village green. But for the most part, I stayed home. Why leave when I had such welcoming space, when I had decks and a pool, woods and the lake? There was

so much to enjoy and so much ease in enjoying it. The name for the house came readily: Chill Hill.

"I understand the 'hill' part," said my father, "but why the 'chill'?"

"Well, Papa, you see, the word 'chill' also means to relax, hang out, bliss out . . ."

"Oh, I get it. Chill Hill."

It's great to have had such a supportive dad.

Wendy, although now divorced, continues to live on the lake. Sometimes I drop over to her house, or she comes up to mine. I'd been at Chill Hill about two years when Wendy stopped by in a confessional mood.

"You know, Jenette, I am such a dope. You wanted that house next to me, and I stopped you from buying it because I was afraid you'd be too close to me and I wouldn't have privacy. So I forced you to buy a house you didn't want, and now I hardly ever see you, and I realize what a complete and total fool I was. I'm sorry, I'm really sorry."

"Wendy, please, don't apologize. You did me an enormous favor. I would never have been anywhere near as happy in the other house. I love this place, love it with all my heart. And I owe it to you."

Which all goes to show, life moves in strange and mysterious ways.

Lessons Learned Along the Way

1. Despite the fact that I love my country house, there are many questions that I regret never having asked: What were the real estate taxes? The zoning laws? The resale values of homes in the area? The taxes, it turned out, were reasonable. But the zoning laws have frustrated my ability to make additions to my property. And it seems that resale values are fairly flat. New Yorkers have not yet targeted my community for summer and weekend homes. And while, as a result, the town retains its charm, there is no real estate boom to drive

the prices up should I choose to sell. If I'd done my homework, would I have opted for another place? Who can say. But when you make a considered decision in full command of the facts, you never have to look back.

2. Just as you should be fully informed before making the decision to buy a house, so too should you know as much as possible about your architect and contractor. Ask to see examples of other homes they've built, and get names of their clients you can speak to. It's also important that your contractor lives nearby so that he not only knows the local codes and regulations, but is also familiar with how the town administration works. Hopefully, he's built some solid relationships there, and can expedite the often protracted process of approvals.

3. When building, or rebuilding, your dream home, it is natural to want perfection. But perfection is elusive, and there are times you have to compromise. When you do, it's important to find a way to work with the compromise, so that it seems like less of a concession. I was crushed when my contractor said I would have to settle for seven-foot-plus ceilings on the lower floor. But I mitigated the closed-in effect by painting the walls and ceilings white, and surrounding the space with sliding glass doors that opened onto large vistas. Wherever I could, I emphasized the vertical dimensions of the room. No, it wasn't perfect, but nobody noticed, and soon the ceiling height wasn't an issue, even for me.

4. Creativity is a labor of love, and there is no way to avoid the hard work it entails. But the toil is worth it, not just for the glorious results but for the incredible rush that accompanies the process. If the creative process fails to excite you, if you experience only the labor and none of the love, then you're probably going at it the wrong way. Here are certain creativity don'ts: don't try too hard, don't intellectualize, don't overanalyze. And here are certain creativity dos: define the problem, then forget about it. If you're struggling, stop, and do something else. Look at pictures, magazines, illustrated books. Go to the movies. See some art. Sleep on it. The solution will come and, with it, the joy.

Chill Hill at night, high above the rest of the world.

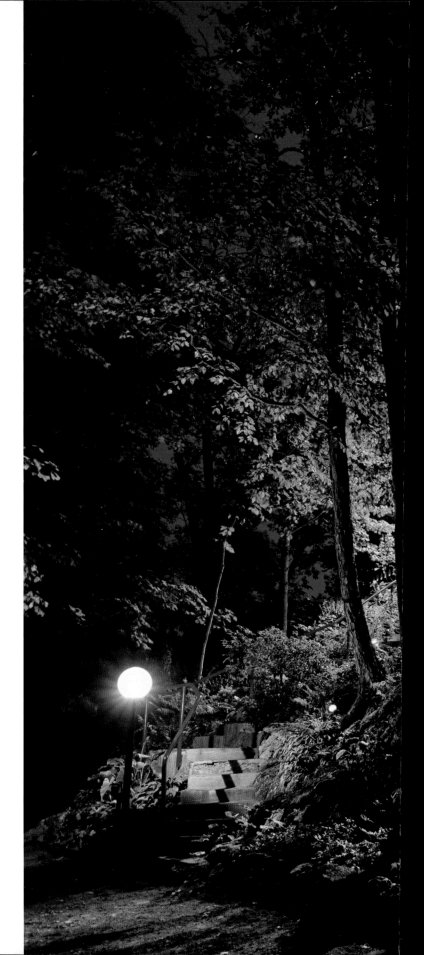

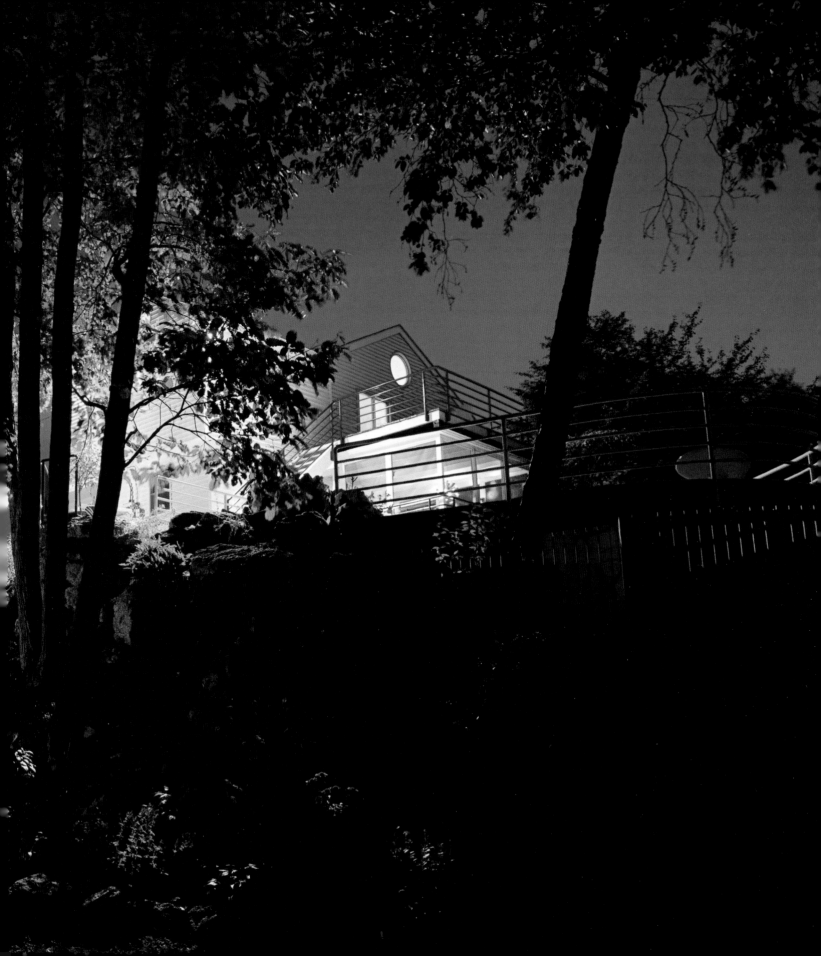

6.

My Secret Garden:

The Guest House

The guest cottage's virtual garden bed, with fake flowers woven through the trelliswork.

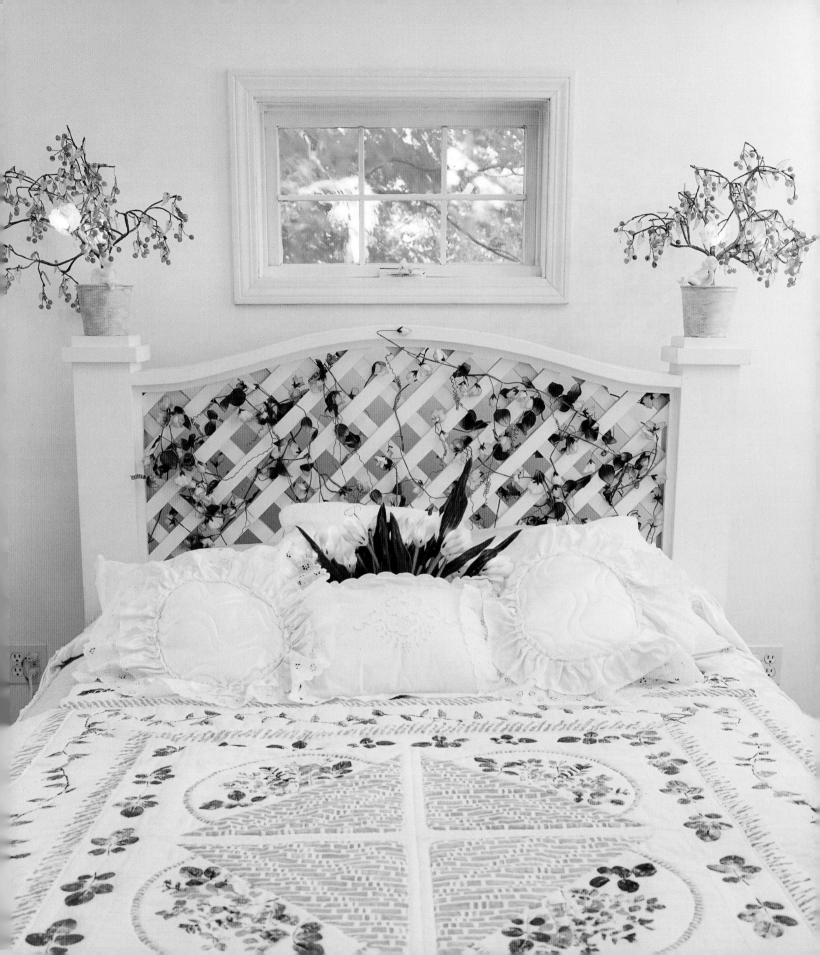

At the foot of my lakefront property, below the stairs that lead up the craggy rocks to the main house, was a small outbuilding that the former owner had used as his photographic studio. Like the main house, it had a picture window that didn't open, impossibly low ceilings, and no plumbing. But it did have electricity, and that gave me an idea. If I added plumbing, it could serve as a guest house for my friends. And if I started work on it right away, then I would have a place to stay while the main house was still under construction. This is not to say that the little building didn't have to be entirely rebuilt. But it was little. And although cheaply made, it was also an empty shell, allowing for a relatively rapid renovation. I could be happily entrenched in the guest cottage long before the main house was finished.

Because the house was small, I wanted everything white, even the floor, so that the area would look larger, and always clean and fresh. With my interior architect, Arthur Zweck-Bronner, and my contractor, Phil Hayes, I decided to knock out the low ceiling and extend the new one to the roof. This immediately gave space, light, and character to what was otherwise a plain white box. Beams, of course, were necessary to support the roof, but I made special use of them when it came to decorating. We all agreed there should be a window at the peak of the cathedral ceiling. I actually argued for two that would follow the geometry of the roofline, but Phil and Arthur made a more persuasive case for a small round one, and I agreed. The round window, with variations, became a motif not just for the guest house, but for the main house as well.

In addition to the decorative round window, it was necessary to have windows that opened. To save money, Phil used the frame of the picture window to create two standard windows side by side. He cut a window into one wall of the main room, and a small window across from it above where the bed would go. And he also cut another standard window into what would become the bathroom. With windows on three sides and the screened door on the fourth, the guest house now had good cross-ventilation, sparing it the need for air-conditioning.

I wanted the windows to have panes, because I was beginning to conceive of the guest house as a cottage and, ultimately, an indoor-outdoor garden. Panes, I knew, would give the cottage a more charming look in contrast to the modern spatial relationships of the main house. Again, to save money, we opted for snap-on wood strips that gave the illusion of real panes without the expense.

Because it was important to me that the guest house be self-contained, Arthur designed a miniature kitchen with cabinets, a two-burner hot plate, a microwave, a small refrigerator, and a tiny sink. I didn't want the television to take away from the effect of the cottage, so Arthur responded with a diagonal shelf in the high corner of the kitchen area. The television was now out of the way but easily watched from bed. We put in a bathroom that, like everything else in the house, was totally white. Across from it we built a large two-door closet with ample room not just for clothes but for suitcases, cleaning implements, and even some storage.

A Candlelit Retreat

As I mentioned, I saw this little house from the beginning as a cottage, not a separate, modern annex to the main dwelling. In keeping with my concept of it as an interior garden—and ultimately defining this motif—I bought a pair of five-foot-tall curvilinear sconces from Suzanne Lipschitz of Second Hand Rose, who had purchased them from a Miami Beach hotel. They were among the many unpredictable artifacts one could find in her vast cavern, then located on Manhattan's Lafayette Street. When I saw them, I knew they had a home. The sconces sprouted metal leaves painted in shades of pale pink and green. But what mesmerized me was that each sconce held sixteen long, electrified candles staggered from top to bottom within the curves and the pastoral, if frankly fake, foliage. I placed a sconce on either side of the rear double window, so that the first thing you'd see upon entering the house would be a room transformed by candlelight glowing in a spray of softly colored leaves.

To me the sconces were perfect. They had graceful curving lines that offset the building's tight geometry, and they established the tone of a magical garden. I could not have imagined a better starting point. Several months passed; then, one day, Phil and I were in the cottage, which now threatened to be a finished work. "You know," said Phil, looking with admiration around the little house, "when you first put up those sconces, Arthur and I thought you were out of your mind."

Phil's comment made me laugh. I had been so committed to the sconces, so sure they were perfect, that I never even entertained the idea that someone might not share my enthusiasm. Later I said to my boyfriend of the time, "You know, Phil and Arthur thought I'd really lost it when I put the sconces up." He looked at me deadpan—his natural mode of expression—and replied, "They weren't the only ones."

Whether myopia is a blessing or a curse can be debated long into the night. I believe it is both. But in the case of the guest-house sconces, it turned out to be a blessing. Every once in a while, you get to be muleheaded and right at the same time.

A New Spin on Garden Furniture

With leaves and candles on the wall, everything else flowed naturally. To continue the garden theme, I wanted a bed made out of trelliswork, with fake flowers woven through the headboard and ivy through the footboard. Since there's not a dexterous bone in my body, this meant a call to my friend Steve Kursh, an artist who can build anything. We talked the concept through, and Steve began to make preliminary drawings. Although my own first sketch had called for a straight headboard, Steve tried curving it between the posts. His suggestion was a good one, giving the bed more importance and more scale. I had asked Steve to make the bottom bedposts hollow so that they could hold real plants whose leaves would mingle with those from the artificial vines. He improved on the idea by lining the posts with copper so that I could water the plants in place.

We were both enormously happy and ready to start when Arthur eyeballed the finished drawing and offered a significant modification. "Lower the footboard," he said. "The room is small, and a low footboard will keep it more open." Arthur was right, and we made the adjustment.

If myopia can be a blessing or a curse, then the same can be said of entertaining other people's suggestions. Give too much weight to what others think, and you're in danger of losing your own point of view. But many times the best advice comes unsolicited, and even from the most unlikely sources.

What can you do? Listen, then balance the suggestion against your own instincts. If the advice feels right, go with it. But make sure that your response comes out of self-confidence, not insecurity. When you're confident about your own sensibilities, only a good idea from someone else rings true. When you're insecure, all ideas seem to have merit. Follow what you believe unless another notion is irrefutably better.

While Steve was building the bed, the concept for the bureau occurred to me. It was original but incredibly simple, and extended the garden theme.

In seconds, I was on the phone to Steve. "Let's buy an old chest of drawers—straight lines, no frills—paint it white, and surround it with a picket fence. Then we can buy fake flowers and plant them between the slats."

Steve loved the idea. It would be inexpensive and easy to build but still fresh and witty, and possibly even beautiful. He promised to get on it right away.

With the bureau taken care of, I addressed the question of table and chairs. Some months before, with the porch on the main house in mind, I had bought an antique garden set made of metal strips woven to look like basketry. I actually thought the table and four chairs were lovely, but they brought only derision from two of my design friends, the dealer Jim Walrod and artist Alex Locadia. "Kahn," Jim remonstrated, while Alex nodded in hearty agreement, "this does not go with all the modern things you've bought."

As time passed, I began to believe they were right that the table was too old-fashioned for the main house. Not wanting to admit defeat, I considered it for the cottage, but it was too large. The only recourse was to sell it, so I showed photographs of it to Suzanne Lipschitz, from whom I'd bought the sconces. Suzanne managed to restore my flagging spirits.

"What a great set!" she exclaimed. "I'll take it."

The deal was done when I noticed a smaller garden suite in the Suzanne's Lafayette Street store. It was graceful and light in appearance, with curving lines and padded pink cushions on the seats and backs of the chairs. It had the right measurements for the guest house, and its airiness meant that it wouldn't overwhelm the small cottage. I bought it, and soon it was in place, looking as though it had always belonged there.

The guest-house interior, pristine white with a floral theme.

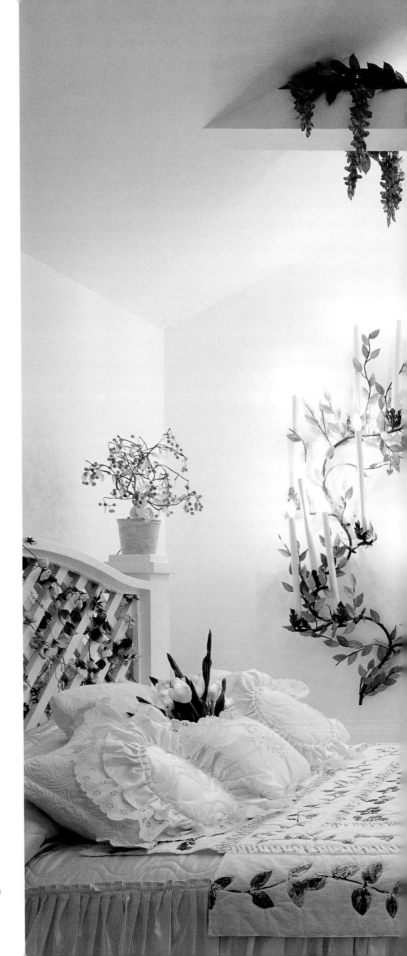

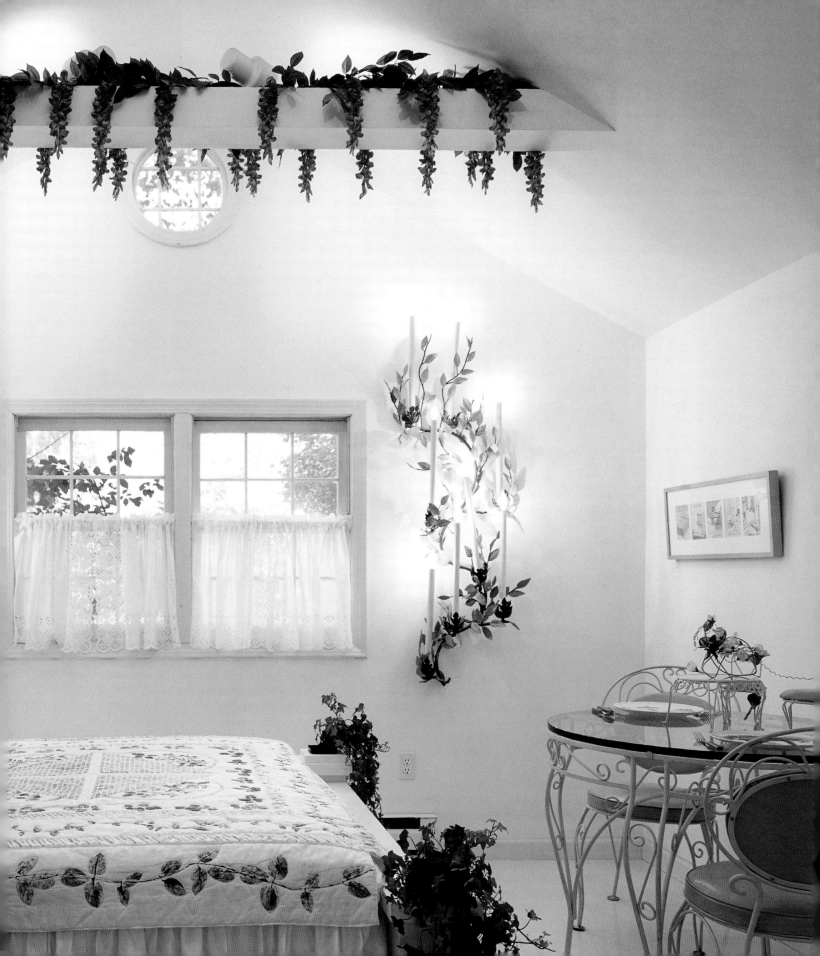

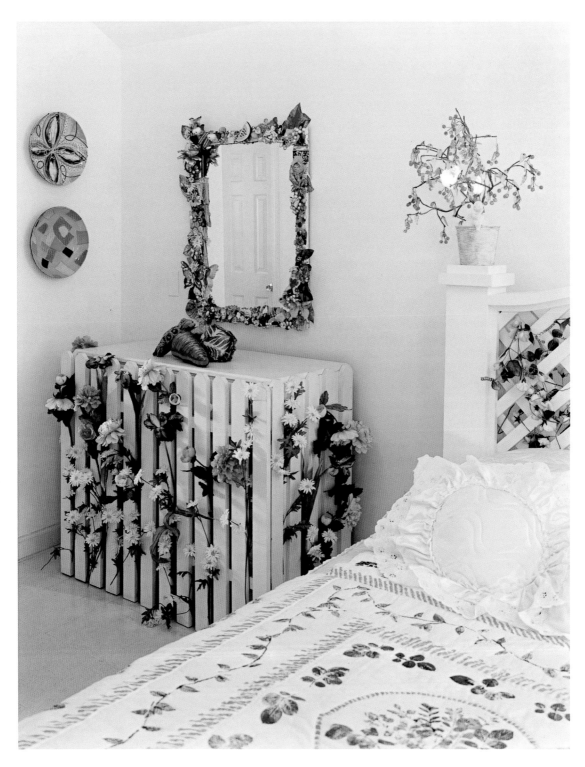

Beneath Wendy Gell's garden-fantasy mirror, a bureau is secreted behind a picket fence.

In Your Space: Personalizing Your Home and Office

Some speak of fate, others of science, and others call it just dumb luck. But there is no doubt that life holds many mysteries: patterns, simultaneity, circles within circles, remarkable connections. Many things occurred as I worked on the house that seemed almost destined, some of them large and others exceedingly small. But no matter the origin of these incidents or their scale, they always added to my sense of pleasure and wonderment.

One of the small but meaningful connections related to the guest-house table and chairs. I was wending my way through endless aisles of furniture, objects, and collectibles at a giant pier show in New York. Although not particularly interested in dolls, I was stopped by a miniature table and chairs that had clearly been made for them. The set was fashioned of metal, with curved and graceful lines like those in the full-size table in the cottage. Although they were a dark red instead of pink, these chairs—like the guest-house chairs—had cushions on them, too.

The similarities were insistent. I bought the doll's set, asked Steve to paint the cushions pink, and placed the small table and chairs in the middle of the large table as a centerpiece. It had a festive, wedding-cake quality, but there was a visual slyness to it too, with the doll's set perched on the full-size set, mimicking real life.

The Mad Fake-Flower Shopping Spree

What is a garden without flowers, even if that garden is totally indoors? The time had come to make the guest house bloom.

Steve did the initial research, plying his way through stores in New York's flower district. Scattered among the purveyors of live and breathing plants were those who specialized in fake flora, from the patently plastic to naturalistic silk. When

Steve found the optimum garden variety store, he called me and we set a date. On a swelteringly hot summer's day, when flower lovers should have been outdoors watering their perennials, we found ourselves in a basement on Ninth Avenue, pawing through bins of fake flowers.

It was amazing how beautiful they were. I was looking for small pink flowers for the headboard of the bed, ivy for the footboard, and tall flowers like irises to plant in the spaces of the picket fence. Despite my love of primaries, I chose a palette of pinks, whites, lavenders, and green that would complement the floral sconces and create a gentle space as surprising and peaceful as a hidden copse of trees. Knowing the colors I was looking for, Steve pulled out an incredible cluster of wisteria.

"Oh, it's beautiful! But where can it go?" We looked at each other, and the answer floated through the ether. The wisteria could cover the two support beams and hang down from them like a canopy. It was one of the great inspirations for the guest house that could only have occurred in that flower-shop basement.

When we finally left the store, the trunk of the car was filled and our arms were still heavy with flowers. You would have thought we were making a float for the Rose Bowl Parade.

More Circles within Circles

The flowers were now woven through the bed frame, hanging from the rafters, and climbing up the picket fence. They wound around the sconces on either side of the window and sprouted from below the table, where I found a metal ring to thrust them in. The house was coming together. But I wondered what was going to go on the bed, a surface of huge importance, considering its relation to the size of the room. I knew that the sheets, pillowcases, and pillow shams would be white and edged in lace, but I had no idea how to cover the top of the bed.

I remembered a quilt I had commissioned a very long time ago from Margot Strand Jensen, whose work was published in Dutton's annual quilt calendar, edited by Cyril Nelson. The calendar is a beautiful sourcebook for quilts in particular and visual imagery in general. It features a photograph of a single quilt on each facing page, most of them antique but some by contemporary artists. The quilts are alternately bold, original, historic, figurative, graphic, abstract, anecdotal, intricate, and personal. I have referred to the calendars again and again, both for pleasure and for creative stimulus.

In one of these calendars I found Jensen's wonderful contemporary quilt. The fabric was stitched, but the pattern, rather than pieced together or appliquéd, was painted with a garden motif in shades of green, ocher, and brown. Somewhere on the page, along with the artist's name and the dimensions of the quilt, were the words "Denver, Colorado."

Although I had no space for the quilt, I still found myself dialing Directory Assistance for Margot's number in Denver. The quilt in the calendar, she told me, once I reached her, was unavailable. But she did have an idea for another one in the same spirit. I told her to go ahead. A little while later, Margot called to ask whether I would have a problem if she omitted the squares in the corners, a common practice when a quilt was meant for a four-poster bed. Margot was interested not in the pragmatism of this configuration but in its shape. I didn't have a four-poster bed and doubted there was one in my future. But, certain that I would only display this quilt on a wall, I agreed.

The quilt arrived some months later. It was truly original and truly beautiful. I had no space to showcase it, but, believing someday I would, I folded it with care and put it gently away for that time.

Now, with the expanse of bed staring at me in the guest house, I thought of Margot's quilt. But the quilt had two problems. First, it was too small; it would barely cover the top of the queen-size bed. Secondly, it lacked its four corners. The only solution I could think of was to call Margot and ask if she would fill in the missing squares and enlarge the quilt by adding a second border.

But Margot Strand Jensen, as it turned out, no longer lived in Denver. The trail was cold. I had no leads, but, like Lew Archer in Ross Macdonald's dynastic mysteries, I tried to create them from the few fragments of history I had. I contacted Cy Nelson, who was still editing the annual quilt calendar. Dead end. I tried the American Craft Museum, which tries to keep a comprehensive list of artists. I spoke to people I knew: dealers, designers, other quilt makers. Sometimes I'd get a new phone number that would lead to another, then another and another.

It took months, but eventually I found Margot again. She remembered the quilt, but her work, she said, was now totally different. Would she consider adding to my quilt? Yes, but she'd have to figure out the cost. Margot's estimate, when it arrived, took my breath away. Her price for the addition was many times that of the original quilt. I couldn't afford to proceed. I had brought the quilt with me to Connecticut, but by now I was soured on its prospects. Not only wasn't it big enough, and lacking the necessary corners, but I'd also convinced myself that the yellow ocher in it would clash with the other colors I'd been using.

In the cottage, I related to Steve the protracted saga of the quilt. "You see what I mean," I concluded, spreading it out with all of its painterly beauty and all of the limitations I'd seen months before. But now that the quilt was again unfurled, I was stunned. "You know, it looks great. Even the yellow ocher works. What was I thinking of?"

This phenomenon, although seemingly inexplicable, is not uncommon. There are many times that you revisit something you didn't like, and now you see it differently. Suddenly it is wonderful. Why didn't you notice before? The converse can be just as true, of course. The reason? Who knows. Perhaps the context is different. Maybe your needs have changed, or you have changed. I have always believed there is no idea, no matter how thoroughly trashed, that cannot be recycled. This is a critical concept, and is just as true even if you've been the one to trash it.

A Cup of Sugar, a Dash of Black Humor

I began with lace-edged pillows on the bed, which over the years have grown into an abundance of different shapes and materials. In Paris I found pink plastic tulips with tiny bulbs that give a warm and inviting glow when they're plugged in. If guests are coming for the first time, I try to race down to the cottage to make certain each side of the bed is lit by these radiantly fake bouquets.

In Modern Age, another design store on Lafayette Street, I found a set of plates by the late Italian artist Piero Fornasetti, who throughout his life drew heavily on both surrealism and trompe l'oeil. I've never been a huge Fornasetti fan—for all

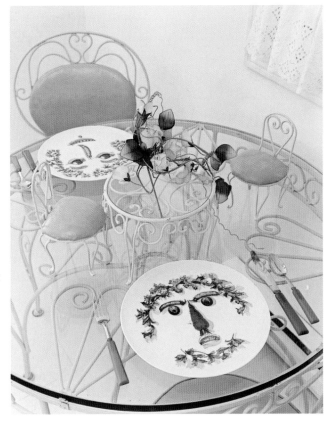

Taking the edge off the sweetness with Piero Fornasetti's grumpy vegetable plate.

its dexterity, there is something a little mechanical and cold in most of his work—but there are still some individual pieces that I like.

Sometimes context increases your appreciation. And that was the case with these Fornasetti dishes. They were decorated with vegetables—lettuce, carrots, radishes, onions, peas. But despite this wholesome imagery, they were anything but your classically pretty garden plates. Quite the contrary. The vegetables were arranged on each dish to form a face. One visage was ingenuous, another frowning, and another downright crabby. All were seductively weird.

I bought the plates and set the table with two of them, flanked by green-handled Bakelite silverware from the 1940s. The guest house had been getting a little too treacly, with all those flowers and pastels. I had to bring in some counterpoint and substance. The plates certainly weren't substantive, but their disconcerting imagery unquestionably struck a different note.

In the same vein, I assembled five watercolors by Steven Guarnaccia, a witty illustrator whose work I discovered in **Metropolitan Home** magazine. Every month Steve created a cartoon having to do in some offbeat way with home decor. Each was a visual play on words, ranging from the sweeter "Garden Bed," composed entirely of flowers, to the more macabre "Armoire," a chest that opened to display a number of disembodied arms hanging from a rod. Although every picture was individual, they had a united palette of pastels.

Steve confirmed that he'd be willing to sell his work. The first illustration in which I was interested was gone, but he had many others from the **Met Home** series. The pictures were small, so I chose five that I could frame together to give them more weight. On the surface, Steve's watercolors seemed a charming addition to the cottage, extending the existing palette of pink, lavender, and green to include soft yellow, an accent of red, a thin black line. But closer inspection always revealed wit, and often a hint of black humor. Just when you thought it was too saccharine to go into the guest house, touches like these redeemed it.

Details of Delight

From two wonderful artists in Maine, Brenda White and Jesse Rhodes, I bought a heavy ceramic charger with an impish Bugs Bunny painted in graphic black strokes on a lavender ground. I placed it on top of the kitchen cabinets, so if you happened to look up, you would chuckle with surprise. It was also a way of offsetting the guest house's one unfortunate but essential anomaly, the television set.

In an antiques market I found two timeworn cloth cabbages. When you squeezed them, they collapsed. It turned out they were magicians' props from the turn of the century. I put them on top of the bureau. Later I added a needlepoint pillow in the shape of a carrot. The room needed a little more color. Because it needed something serious as well, I hung a photograph by Jan Groover, a still life of green leaves against a pink field with the glinting reflections of a silver knife. Though at first glance Jan's photo seems simply decorative, it is a strong

picture, worthy of close scrutiny and frequent revisiting. Its depth gives the guest house integrity.

My friend Wendy Gell, who also lives on the lake, had at first protested that she didn't want to work in the country. But that was a momentary phase. The truth was, we still loved to make "wristies" together, and she was thrilled when I suggested that we collaborate on a mirror for the guest house. I'd found two clocks that I wanted to use, made of flexible material in the shape of lily pads; each one had a tiny frog on it. I imagined placing them diagonally opposite each other on the corners of the mirror. I also wanted to mass seed packs up the side.

"Seed packs?!" Wendy, the Queen of Gleam, had trouble with these humble packets. But she swallowed her dismay with grace and acceded in spite of her natural inclinations.

Ever the eclectic collector, I owned a number of salt and pepper shakers with fruit and vegetable themes. I suggested we layer the bottom of the frame with these. The other two sides of the frame should, I mentioned, be simple, covered with something fresh and unassuming, like beach glass. I went over to Wendy's house and delivered my stash: seed packs, salt and pepper shakers, and lily-pad clocks. Usually Wendy and I sit together and work out where to place the objects, but it was late, and that could wait for another day.

The next morning, Wendy called me. "Jenette, those pieces were so great, I stayed up all night and worked on the mirror. I hope you like what I've done."

Oh-oh. Anything was possible. Sometimes when Wendy does something for me on her own, I think it is sheer genius. And then there are the other times.

I whizzed over to Wendy's for the unveiling. Just as we'd discussed, the lily-pad clocks were on the diagonal, the seed packs were glued to one side, and there were salt and pepper shakers on the bottom. But there were also salt and pepper shakers on the top and on the other side, along with jewels, glass flowers, and a profusion of gleaming adornments. Simplicity is not a word in Wendy's vocabulary. The mirror was not what I had first imagined, or what I had hoped for. It had become Wendy's mirror as much as it was mine, and that would take some adjusting to. Rather than subtract, which at this point was hard to do, I added, trying to pull a sense of overall symmetry from the sum of many, many parts. But there was no denying that the mirror, even as it burst with more objects than one could count, had an aesthetic of its own. We hung it over the bureau, a celebration of creative exuberance. Even though the mirror I'd envisioned was infinitely more restrained, I am tempted whenever I look at this one to take it down and add just a little more.

Looking Back

The guest house was more or less complete, and I loved it. What was once a modest, unassuming structure was now a fully imagined space. I carried its imprint everywhere I went and continued to embellish it—eyelet curtains, white towels with embroidered lilies of the valley, a pink water-lily candle that could float in the tub.

Many months before, Steve Kursh had observed, "It's getting awfully girlie, isn't it?" I immediately took offense. He must have hit a nerve. I wanted to disown the notion that there was anything gender-based in my garden fantasy. Yet beneath my protests, I secretly wondered whether Steve was right. The guest house really is pretty, and if not exactly "girlie," it's undeniably romantic. Nonetheless, as the years have passed, I've observed that while women like the cottage, men appear to love it. If I have company, my male guests always try to co-opt it. One of my friends asked if he could honeymoon there and, months later, actually did. Joseph Campbell, were he alive, could have had a field day, but some things seem better unexplained.

Lessons Learned Along the Way

1. Many modern interiors tend to be boxy, without any details to distinguish them. How do you make them more inviting? While you can't go against a room's geometry, you can soften it with curves. In my guest house, the rounded headboard, the curvilinear sconces, the round window, and the circular table mitigated its Spartan quality. If a room is severe, you can give it charm by adding such details as moldings and windowpanes. And atmospheric lighting can blur hard lines.

2. What can you do with a small space to make it look more expansive? The most tried-and-true solution is to paint everything white. For the guest house, I even added white flooring so that the entire interior looked airy and fresh. A cautionary note: all white can look sterile. Splashes of color are one antidote, as are imaginative touches, and compelling objects and art.

3. Sometimes you know in advance your theme for a room. At other times, the concept takes longer to develop. But once it's established, filling in the details comes easily. As long as you hold onto your guiding concept, you will find the right accessories everywhere you go. Your clarity of vision will enable you to discover treasures even in the most unlikely places.

4. A unified room is harmonious, but you don't want it to be homogeneous. If a theme is starting to feel predictable, you need to add some contrarian notes. Shake things up. A piece of serious art never hurts a lighthearted room, and neither does a bit of black humor.

7.

Chill Hill:

Wild and Witty in the Woods

Opposite: Night has fallen, but the screened porch is alive with light.

Pages 110–111: On the left Jan Groover's subdued and rich still life adds ballast to the living area's wit and vibrant colors.

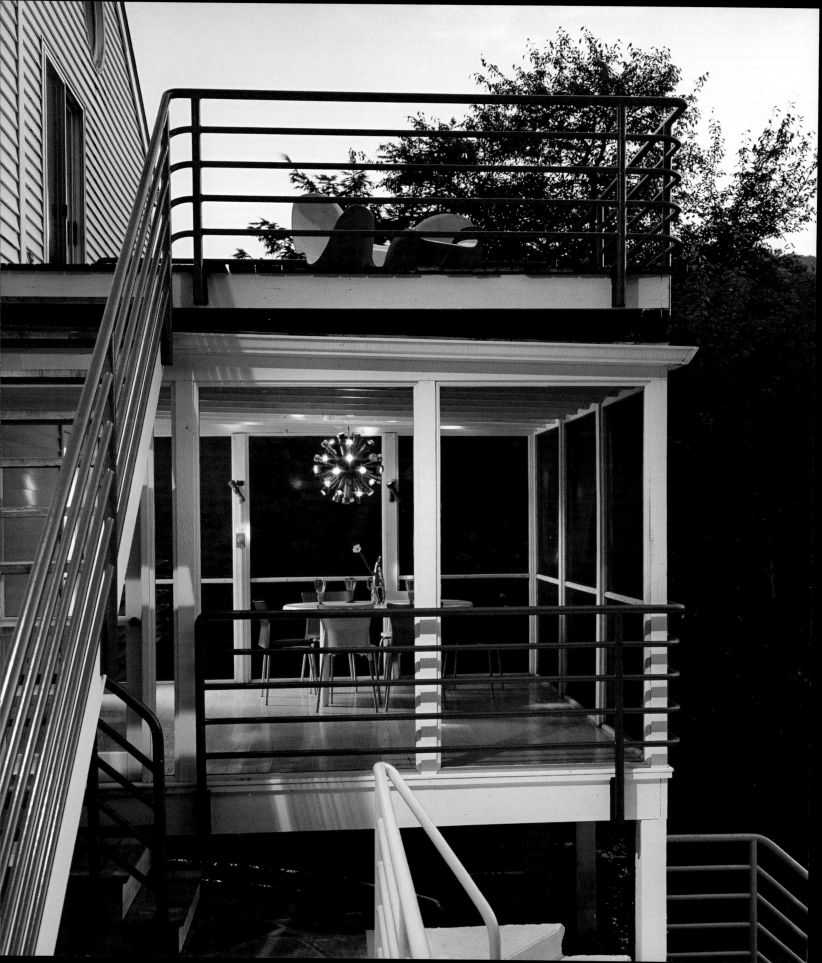

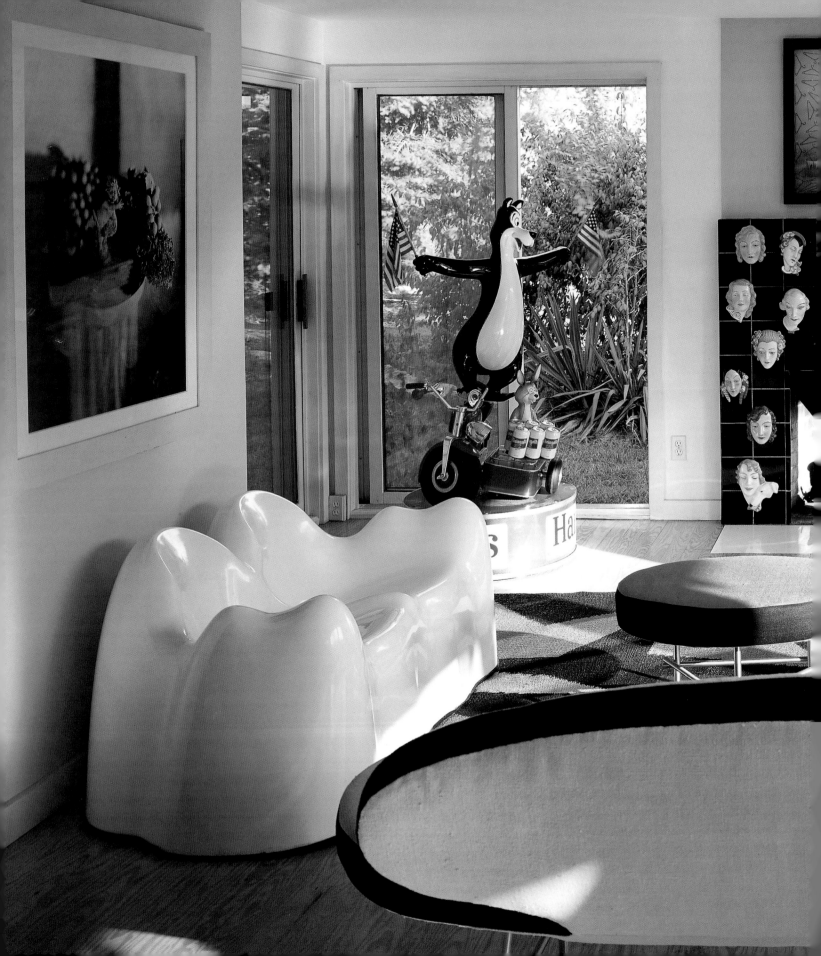

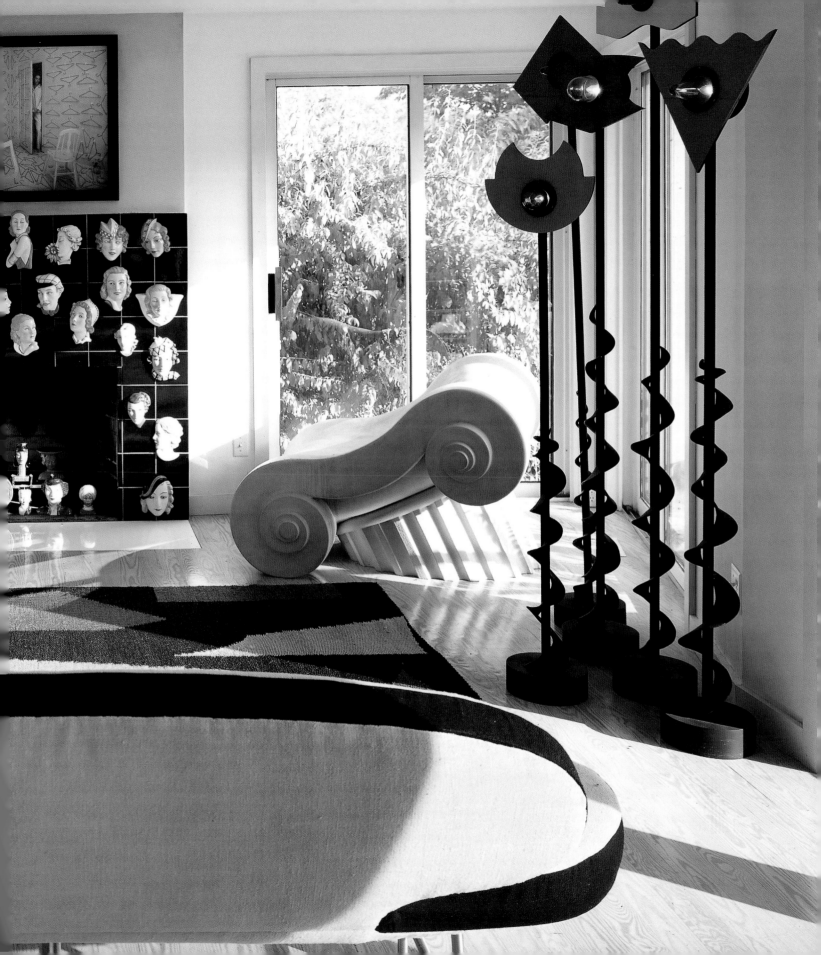

It was May, and the renovation of the main house was almost finished. But before I could bring any furniture inside, I had one more issue to address. The floors in the house were pine, with an active pattern to the grain. I liked the way they looked and knew that with a light coat of polyurethane they would work well on the second floor, with its high cathedral ceilings and large expanses of white. But I had other feelings about how to treat the wood on the entry-level floor.

To maximize the sense of space, I had chosen an open plan of the sort that is common in urban lofts. The floors in them are almost always plain polyurethaned wood, and individual areas are subtly parsed by the placement of seating and rugs, by a bookcase, a kitchen island, or a dining room table and chairs. While this aesthetic has been very much in vogue for over thirty years, I didn't feel it was exactly right for Chill Hill. Something inside me wanted to unify the space and make it all of a piece. And the way to do this, it seemed, was to avoid the effect of natural wood, which by its very nature looks standard-issue, not like a purposeful choice. If I wanted anything, it was that the designs in my open plan look purposeful. The solution, I concluded, was to stain the floor pink.

Pink? Why pink? Well, if the floor was going to be a color, I had very few options. The stain had to be light, because it was important to keep the space as airy as possible. It's hard to accuse white or cream of being too dark, but neither makes much of a statement. Blue was too cool. Yellow? Yes, yellow was a possibility. It is visually and emotionally sunny, and has a catalytic effect on any hues nearby. But I wasn't sure I wanted such an expanse of warm color in a house facing a lake that constantly reflects the bright light of the sky. The overall effect, although welcoming, would have been intense, and I thought the house should be a refuge from the blazing sun outside. So what was left? Pink. Not a bluish pink, but one mixed with yellow to make it more radiant and inviting.

Not long after the floor was finished, my father visited me in New York. "Why don't we go to Connecticut and check out the house?" I suggested. "It's only two hours away, and I'd love you to see it."

My dad, who always was willing to go on adventures with me no matter where they might take him or whom he might meet, readily acceded. He had had reservations when I told him I wanted to buy the house. "You're a city girl," he protested. But now that I had purchased it, he wanted to be as supportive as possible. So although he seemed a little taken aback by the multicolored railings, he busied himself finding the positive—praising the rusticity of the site, the way the house stood high on the rocky promontory, and the spectacular views of the lake. But when we entered the house, even my dad couldn't keep his composure.

"A pink floor?! What in the world ever made you think of a pink floor?"

"You don't like it?" I asked, suddenly eight again.

"Oh, no, no. I didn't say that. It's—uh—unusual. Yes—uh—very unusual."

Although momentarily crushed, my spirits rebounded, and my father, ever sweet-natured, spent the rest of our visit chatting cheerily about the house, which he really did seem to like. My father respected my privacy. But he also delighted in regaling his companions in Washington, where he lived, with stories of my exploits. The truth is, he was proud of me, and you didn't have to twist his arm to get him to talk about his daughter. So when I visited him, I wasn't at all surprised that his friends came up to me and said, "Oh, Nettie, we heard about your wonderful house on the lake!" I was pleased—the report from the front had been good—and listened politely to one or two more complimentary sentences. And just as I was thinking, Thank you, that's so nice, I think I'll move on now, they'd hit me with: "Oh, and we heard about your pink floor!!"

Nonetheless, I loved it, and couldn't wait to add the furniture.

Furnishing: Inside and Out

Not surprisingly, I already had a number of pieces ready to cart through the doors. In my quest for

Chill Hill from the west, with red railings leading off the master bedroom deck directly to the pool below.

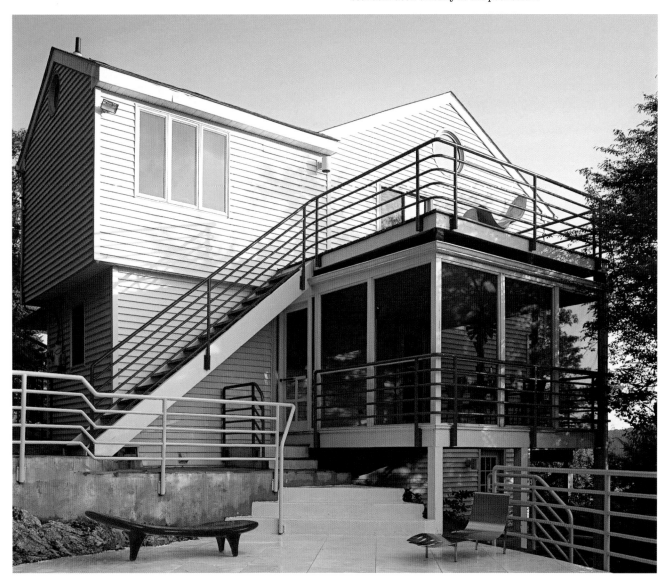

1960s icons for my apartment at the Century, I'd also bought more than I needed in anticipation of the day when the house at Chill Hill was built. Among these were the Wendell Castle love seat and Molar chairs, and the black sisal rug with an artist's distribution of color and geometry. There was Gae Aulenti's King Sun lamp, with its heavy orange base and large Plexiglas half-moons. And there was the fallen foam Greek capital designed by Studio 65 and manufactured by Gufram.

These objects represented my first roundups. But because the house took nearly a year and a half to gut and rebuild, I had ample time to do infinitely greater damage. One of the first items I bought was for the lakeside deck, which was accessible through sliding glass doors on the lower floor. Spacious, curved, and surrounded by bright red railings, it was designed to be an extension of the living and dining areas. Because it looked out on the treetops and the water below, it added not just square footage but also an unconstrained sense of openness. With the thought of connecting life on one side of the glass with that on the other, I purchased a very swank termite, spiffy in white gloves, spats, and a white top hat. Bug or no bug, if there was a party going on inside, he was dressed and ready to revel. I placed him on the deck, his face pressed up

The living room deck, with a Wendell Castle Molar chair and a denizen of nature eager to come inside.

against the see-through door, to indicate just how close we are to nature and nature is to us.

When it came to other objects, my friends and weekend neighbors Lyn Godley and Lloyd Schwan were perhaps the largest contributors. Among their signature pieces was a storage unit Lloyd had designed called the Checker cabinet, made of wood that curved into a long, horizontal ellipse. Lloyd had fashioned a shape that felt fresh, but the true excitement lay in its façade. It was broken into seventeen skewed squares—trapezoids, really—every one a different color. Lloyd had spent weeks choosing and refining each hue and shade, and it showed. The combination was utterly arresting, so personal and so unique. At the center of each square was a knob, so that the cabinet seemed as though it were comprised of seventeen separate drawers. But this was only an illusion. The cabinet was composed of drawers, but not nearly as many as there were squares with knobs. Sometimes you'd grab a pull, and a single square would open. But the drawer that opened could just as easily be two squares wide, or three. The Checker cabinet was an extraordinary work, not just because it played with color and form in new and inventive ways but also because it played with anyone who tried to open it.

In Your Space: Personalizing Your Home and Office

I wanted to use the Checker cabinet more or less as a sideboard. I say more or less because Lloyd, in an act of artistic rebellion, had purposely curved the top so that it was impossible to put anything on it. He wanted the Checker cabinet to stand on its own, even when it was out of his possession. No overeager owner was going to sully his handiwork by deciding it would look much better with a vase on top. For me that wasn't a problem. In fact, I liked Lloyd's wily efforts to protect his design. But what did pose a problem were the multiple drawers. Although I could use some of them to store silverware, I badly needed shelves on which to hold plates. Luckily, Lloyd was totally accommodating. He altered his design so that six squares in the center of the cabinet were devoted to drawers, but the ones on either side of it defied their visual appearance and formed two solid doors. When the doors swung open, they revealed the wooden shelves I'd asked Lloyd for.

In addition to the Checker cabinet, I also asked Lloyd to design a couch. "It has to be comfortable," I advised. "Everyone is complaining that I have no comfortable furniture."

Lloyd happily acceded. Comfort would not be an issue. He dropped by one day with a number of drawings, and I chose a sketch that, like the Checker cabinet, was based on ellipses, one for the seat of the sofa, one for the back. I accepted on faith that it would be comfortable, but began to wonder just how much you could really kick back when your feet had no place to go but the floor.

"Lloyd? Why don't we make an ottoman in front of the couch so you can put your feet up if you want? Or not just one ottoman but two? Maybe they could even be puzzle pieces so that you could connect them if you're feeling cozy with the person next to you. But if you're sharing the couch and don't want to be that close, you could take the two pieces apart and each person could have his or her own footrest."

So Lloyd came up with two separate pieces that echoed the sofa's shape. They didn't interlock, as I had suggested, but they looked better this way, and ultimately they didn't need to. Since they were light and easy to move, you could place the ottomans right next to each other, or as far apart as you liked.

"You pick the colors," said Lloyd. And I did. Yellow edged with black for the sofa, fuchsia for one ottoman, kelly green for the other, and both edged with black like the couch. Lloyd also made a small table on which to place the Gae Aulenti King Sun lamp. I wanted it to sit next to the couch, and this time Lloyd chose the colors—a soft purple for the legs, a medium green for the top.

Meanwhile, Lyn was busy at work on a collection of lights that she was going to show along with Lloyd's furniture at the American arm of a French gallery called Neotu. They were in metal, many with thin strands that spiraled and looped, catching the light. I thought her designs were wonderful, and there was one that I felt would work over the dining table at Chill Hill. It had a central stem that ended in an upturned bowl. The bulb was secreted inside, but its light illuminated not just the surrounding area but a tangled skein of metal tubing that cascaded down from the canopy. I asked Lyn if she would make a second version for me, but in color rather than the unpainted metal she had planned for the exhibit.

"I'll make this one in color for you, sweetie," said Lyn. "As long as you allow me to show it at Neotu."

"Of course you can! Oh, this is great!! What colors shall we make it in?" I wasn't actively thinking about Lloyd's sofa and ottomans, but subliminally they had to have played a role. "Hmmm-m,"

I pondered as though I were coming up with this combination for the very first time. "I think I'd like green for the small canopy and green for the bowl. A deep pink, a fuchsia, really, for the stem, and for the little ball at the bottom of the bowl. And yellow for all the wires." Lyn was fine with my choices, and the light went to Neotu, where it looked like a million bucks in all its bright-hued glory. It was only when it was installed at Chill Hill that I noticed how neatly it echoed the colors I'd picked for Lloyd's sofa and ottomans, just ten feet away. What usually seems like a wonderful coincidence is more often than not the result of a thoughtful, if unconscious, subterranean plan.

I'm sure Lyn's lamp had a name when it hung at the gallery above Lloyd's furniture and next to her other work. But if so, none of us remembered. Looking at the green bowl and the tangled yellow strands glowing even brighter from the hidden light, the new title was inevitable. We all called it the Spaghetti lamp or, depending upon how cosmopolitan we were feeling at the moment, the Pasta lamp.

Dining In

The table below the Spaghetti lamp was a collaboration between me and my friend Alex Locadia, who had designed the fabulous Catwoman chaise. When I was in the first heat of collecting 1960s furniture, I'd bought from Jim Walrod five lights in the shape of giant pills. Italian, by Cesare Casati and Emanuele Ponzio, they looked like capsules you'd find in your medicine chest, with one half in color, one half in white. The Pill lamps were weighted on the bottom so that you could put them at any angle. I loved them. Playful and elegant, and like so much European design of that time, they represented the best of three-dimensional pop art. Although I could have scattered them throughout a room, or arranged

all five in a sculptural cluster, I believed there had to be an even more interesting solution that still wouldn't dilute their integrity.

The Pill lamps are tall, and light emanates through the clear white plastic at the top. I began to think how great it would be to have a table that was illuminated not from overhead but, in a far less traditional way, from below. The Pill lamps were sufficiently substantial to hold their own even beneath eye level. Yet they were just narrow enough that you could place five in a row under a table-top. Excited, I raced for a felt-tip pen and made a drawing. Although I was to repeat this sketch many times, it was always the same. My straight lines veered, my ellipses looked like Luther Vandross before dieting, and I'd clearly invented an entirely new form of perspective. But nonetheless my original effort had nailed the design.

There are few better poster children than myself for the fact that you needn't know how to draw to conceptualize visual ideas or to communicate them to other people far better equipped to realize them. With my pen and college-ruled, single-subject note-book, I have demonstrated this maxim over and over. As long as there is dexterity in your brain, it doesn't really matter how much or how little there is in your body.

My design was actually quite simple. It showed a table made of Plexiglas, held up by two recessed rectangular columns. Between these supports was a shelf, raised several inches above the floor. I sketched the Pill lamps on it, two with yellow bases, one with red, one with blue, and one with green. Then, on each of the columns, I drew a large, open elliptical space. I wanted to take advantage of the fact that the Pill lamps could be set at any angle. If the supports were solid plastic, then the lights could tilt only slightly in the allotted space. But elliptical holes in the supports would make it possible to push

In Your Space: **Personalizing Your Home and Office**

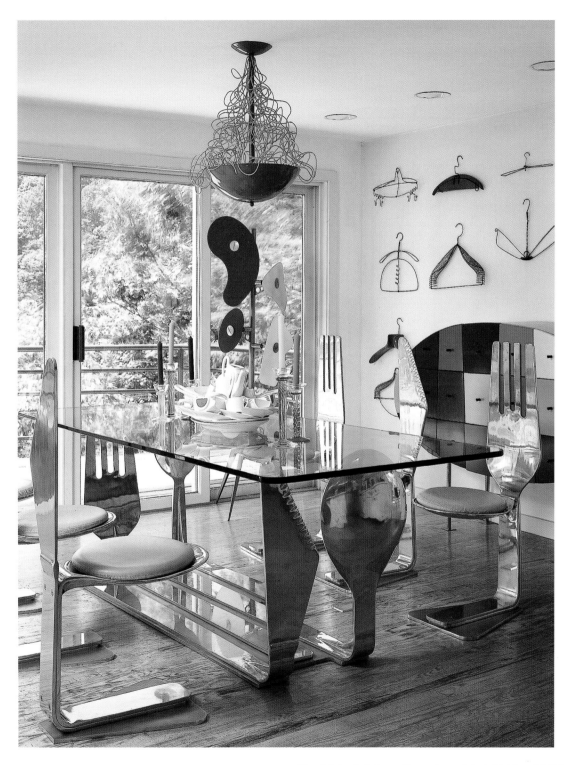

Yonel Lebovici's inventive and magisterial table establishes
the dining area.

Chill Hill: Wild and Witty in the Woods

the lamps through them, breaking the implicit borders and opening up the structure of the table.

I took my drawing to Alex, who loved it. "We can definitely make this," he said, already eager to get started. I wanted the top of the table to be yellow, and Alex said, fine, we would just have to sandwich the plastic between two layers of glass. We looked at color samples for the rectangular supports and chose a soft blue for one, a medium pink for the other. When Alex completed the table, I was amazed. His innate sense of form, his meticulous attention to the smallest element, had taken my design to a whole new level. Someone else, given my drawing—which, after all, was not a detailed rendering, with every measurement and material specified down to the last bolt—would have delivered a table that had the surface effect but not the true substance. Luckily, Alex is a wonderful artist, and he had turned my idea into a work of art.

The Pill lamp table was installed four feet in front of Lloyd's Checker cabinet and under Lyn's Spaghetti lamp. Five years later I replaced it with a second table, not for lack of loving it, but because there was another artwork I felt I couldn't live without. The Pill lamp table was a rare event—a joyous, perfect collaboration—and it made the dining area come alive. I disassembled the structure and saved both it and the lights for the day I'd have another space to put them together again.

There were only two more additions to the dining area. One I bought several years after I moved in. A standing lamp called the Orbital, it had large, organically shaped glass panes in clear and vivid colors. In the daytime it was vibrant, but nothing compared to how it looked at night, when hidden bulbs made the colors glow like latter-day stained glass. When early on I'd decided that the floor should be pink, it was to unify the open plan. Many of my succeeding choices were influenced at least in part by this idea. If there were curvilinear forms and splashes of color in every area, then the entire first floor would work as a whole. Most of the furniture topped out at mid-height. So objects like the Orbital lamp were significant, carrying the shapes and the colors upward toward the ceiling.

Hang Time

The second addition followed a pattern I'd unwittingly established years before. As with so many items, this was something I saw and loved, and having no place for it, bought and squirreled away for when I did. These were hangers, wild, inventive, sculptural hangers, all manufactured between 1890 and 1910, although they could not have looked more modern. In fact, had I not known otherwise, it was easy to think that Alexander Calder in his spare time had fashioned them with pliers and wire, as he did so many other household objects. I first learned about the hangers in an article in the **New York Times** reviewing an exhibition of them at Ricco/Maresca, a gallery best known for its quality folk art. The hangers, perhaps seventy-five in all, had been assembled by a dealer, Harris Diamant, over the course of a decade.

In the world of collectors and collectibles, there are also pickers and dealers. Pickers are the people who scour the countryside, hitting everything from estate sales to tag sales trying to find the gold amid the dross. Sometimes they've been given a particular assignment—like finding an Eames chair with the original leather in brown rather than the more commonplace black. But more often they're on their own, doing the legwork, using their judgment, and returning to urban hubs where their potential buyers do business—the retailers and dealers with their own clienteles. Needless to say, with the burgeoning number of pickers, many dealers have become slack, rarely venturing beyond flea markets and shows in their own immediate areas. Pickers are hungry, while the new breed of dealer tends not to be. It is so much easier to cultivate a string of contacts out in the field, stay in one place, and let the pickers come to you.

But despite this changing landscape, a few dealers still have a passion and an instinct for finding the new new thing, or perhaps more accurately, the new old thing. I know only a handful of people like this. One is Suzanne Lipschitz, a pioneer in, among many things, Art Deco design, period wallpapers and linoleum, and classic wicker furniture. Another is John Sideli, who, well ahead of most everyone else, saw the beauty of Bakelite radios and assembled a collection to showcase their formal invention and breathtaking colors. Dennis Bozes and Dennis Clark of Off the Wall in Los Angeles are always finding new treasures, from streamlined Deco trains to Baranger motion displays designed for the

Turn-of-the-century hangers frame Godley-Schwan's Checker cabinet.

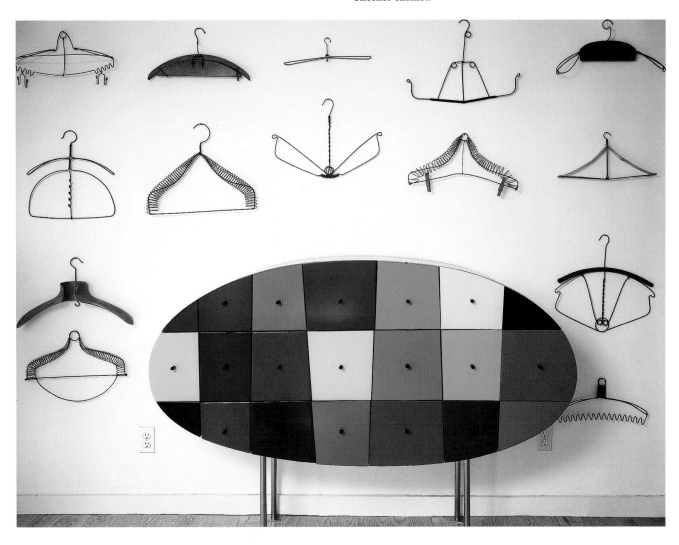

Chill Hill: Wild and Witty in the Woods

windows of jewelry stores. New York's Norman Brosterman has made a career of mining fascinating areas of personal interest, from architectural building blocks to kindergarten toys to dazzling futuristic illustrations. And here was Harris, a folk-art dealer who, in rummaging through some of the country's biggest flea markets, had spotted these astonishing hangers and spent ten years culling the very best examples.

As soon as I could, I was down at Ricco/Maresca to see them. The write-up in the **Times** had been glowing, and I was sure that if the hangers hadn't been sold before the article appeared, by now there would not be a single one left. The article had, in fact, generated a great amount of interest, and many people had already flocked to the gallery to view the installation. But there had been no takers. Why? I couldn't fathom the answer. But there were reasons. First, Harris wanted to sell the collection as a whole, and he was asking a great deal of money for it. You could purchase a serious painting for the same amount. Secondly, a buyer would have to be convinced that these utilitarian wire objects were art. Although they were functional and created anonymously, many art objects fall into this category; but these hangers were also manufactured. This removed them one step further from more stringent definitions of art. And if one doubted that the hangers were art, it was a large leap to believe that they might suddenly be on a list of top collectibles.

Enter the pushover. If the hangers did not meet others' definitions of art, they met mine. And the price? Well, there was no way I could afford the whole collection, nor did I have the space for it. But fate moves in mysterious ways. Harris happened to be at Ricco/Maresca when I came by. He was not someone I knew well, but years before, when I had absolutely no money, he had allowed me to purchase from him a great piece of folk art by paying for it in tiny monthly increments over a year. It was an overwhelmingly generous arrangement, and I had never forgotten Harris's kindness. Now we were in the gallery, and Harris could see how enthralled I was with the hangers.

"But, Harris, seventy-some hangers? I don't have the room. And I don't have that kind of money."

This was toward the end of the show, and Harris had probably concluded that his dream of moving the hangers en masse was not going to happen.

"I'll tell you what," he suggested. "I'd be willing to break up the collection and let you buy a fourth of it."

Well, that was tempting. But Harris's price for a quarter of the hangers was still pretty staggering. I found myself in a moral quandary. There was no market value for the hangers. They could have been priced at $300 as easily as at $10—or, more importantly, vice versa. The show was about to close, and there was no other buyer in sight. It seemed certain that I could get the hangers for a great deal less. On the other hand, I knew that Harris was struggling to make ends meet. I didn't have the heart to negotiate, even when I felt the hangers were overpriced, even when I knew I had the leverage. And I admitted as much to Harris.

He looked like a load had lifted. Yes, clearly he needed the money. But he was not unappreciative.

"Look, I won't divide the hangers into fourths the way I normally would, mixing a few of the very best with others that are not at the same level. I'll let you choose whatever hangers you want. And once you get them home, if there are some hangers you think aren't wearing well, well, you can bring them back and exchange them for any others you'd like."

And that is how I came to buy the hangers. Were they worth it? In terms of cost, no. I thought they were overpriced then, and I still do now. But are they fabulous and original? Do I love them? Yes, yes, yes. And had it not been for Harris's unique perspective and his decade-long search, I would never have come across them. It's hard to put a price on someone else's vision, especially when it makes your own world that much richer.

Tableware

So that was more or less it for the dining area: the Pill lamp table, the Orbital lamp, the Checker cabinet, and the hangers above it. Later on, when I had the chance to buy Yonel Lebovici's spectacular steel table, whose base and chairs are shaped like forks and spoons and knives, I couldn't resist. Yonel, who lived and worked in Paris, had made the safety-pin lamp in my living room, and I was an enormous fan of his work. The dining set, I was told, had been commissioned from him in the 1980s by the inventor of the bar code. Yonel had made a second set for himself, and one night in Paris I shared a raucously cheerful meal at it with Yonel and his ebullient wife, his two warm sons and their equally lovely girlfriends. There was apparently a third set that Yonel had started work on and then stopped midway. The tables and chairs and the tall spoon lamp were pinnacles of workmanship and tremendously labor-intensive. The set would have had to command a very high price, and Yonel could not be certain that his efforts would ever find a buyer.

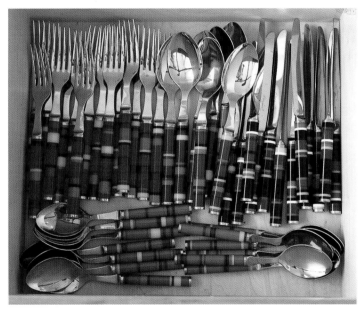
A drawerful of Guy de Rougement's silverware with multicolor acrylic handles, just a fraction of the monumental set.

Yonel was right. Only a tiny number of modern design collectors would commit to such a serious expenditure. He put a halt to his exertions and moved on to more salable pieces. But Michael Ralphs, a young British dealer who had heard of my collecting, thought he might broker the perfect transaction. He believed I would be that one person who was willing to make the purchase, and once he'd ascertained that that was true, he persuaded Yonel to complete the set. Convincing me was a piece of cake. The table was one of the most beautiful objects I'd ever seen. That I would be able to own it? The thought was overwhelming. So I wired half the price to a European bank and made a point of visiting Yonel on my next trip to France.

Yonel was still working on the table when I arrived, but already it looked magnificent. Despite the fact that neither of us spoke the other's language, we immediately hit it off, finding a legion of nonverbal ways to communicate. One visit led to another and another, and to that glorious dinner at the Lebovici home. These were special encounters. But there came a time when Yonel moved me beyond words. Like most designers, he saved every one of his maquettes, the small-scale models artists use to guide them as they work. I was getting ready to go home, and Yonel wanted to make sure that I did not return empty-handed. He pressed on me a present, the maquette of the table and chairs. Today, this most personal of gifts sits on the fireplace mantel in my bedroom, a constant and poignant reminder—Yonel died several years later, while still in his early sixties—of a man full of life and full of heart.

Setting the Table

Design, of course, comes in many forms, and I would be remiss in leaving the dining area if I didn't at least briefly mention the plates and silverware. Although it is infinitely smaller in physical scale, I have always felt that what you eat with is as important as the chairs you pull up to the table or the table itself. They all deepen your pleasure, just as a chef's artful presentation of food on a plate adds a dimension of wonder and delight to the dining experience. Up at Chill Hill, the silverware is the star.

I bought two very different sets of utensils, although both were distinguished by their use of vivid color. The first, so comprehensive that it included fish knives and forks for twelve, was by the French artist Guy de Rougemont. Each handle was made of multicolored acrylic bands. The knives were black, highlighted by stripes of yellow, turquoise, red, and white; the spoons were red with stripes of turquoise and yellow; the forks orange, with similarly contrasting bands; the fish set white with green and yellow stripes. This in itself was an exciting innovation. But what made the set all the more remarkable was that no two implements were exactly alike, even within the same subset. The colors on the knives were identical, but their distribution was different on every one. The de Rougement silverware was produced in a signed and numbered edition, and it was expensive. But it was as much a work of art as any print or sculpture multiple. I paid the price with no regrets.

The second set I bought was handmade by an artist named Mardi-Jo Cohen. I had popped into the Park Avenue armory in New York to check out a show devoted entirely to crafts. No matter where I looked, I saw nothing of interest to me. Crafts are an ambiguous area of expression. The vast majority of things one comes across, even in so-called juried shows, tends to be pedestrian. For whatever reasons, few people in the field have the necessary imagination or vision to raise their work from the realm of handcraft to that of art.

The armory show did nothing to prove otherwise. I cruised the aisles like Wile E. Coyote's neme-

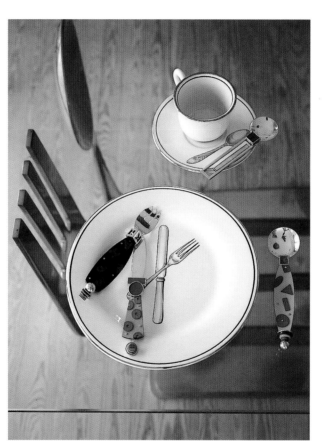

Another take on table settings: Mardi-Jo Cohen's graphic handmade utensils toying with the black-and-white designs on the plates.

sis, believing that the only merciful antidote to having paid admission to this mundane exhibit was to depart as quickly as possible. Just yards away from freedom, I hit the final booth. And I stopped. Because here was silverwork that looked like nothing else. It was creative and colorful, modern and fun. Suddenly no longer in a rush, I waited patiently for the owner to become available. And when she did, I introduced myself and met Mardi-Jo.

"Would you be willing to make a set of silverware for me?" I queried. "Silver for eight?"

"Sure. I've done sets before. But if you want it soon, forget it. I've got so many orders to fill, it will take months, maybe even a year."

"Oh, that's okay. I've got time. I'd just like every piece to be different."

"You mean every place setting?" Mardi-Jo inquired, more a confirmation than a question. She was unable to conceive that anyone would want something more radical than that.

"No, I want every piece to be different—every knife, every fork, every spoon. Your style is so strong that I'm sure they'll all work together."

"Wow, I don't know. I mean, that is a huge amount of work. I don't have any idea when I could have it done." When I pressed her, she conceded that it might be possible, and we left it at that.

Mardi-Jo lived in Philadelphia, but she called me one day when she was coming to New York to see if she could bring some sketches to my office. Of course! So Mardi-Jo arrived, and we spread them all out on the floor so that we could judge them not just individually but as a group. I edited them, expressed my preferences, and praised the best of the designs, which truly were exceptional. Mardi-Jo went back to the drawing board and returned a month later with a revised set of sketches. This time there was almost nothing to say except that everything looked wonderful. And although, as Mardi-Jo

had predicted, I did wait close to a year, the results made it all worthwhile. Mardi-Jo had outdone herself, improving even on the drawings we'd agreed upon. Every single piece was a work of art, and she had kept me in mind the whole time, personalizing individual elements so that, for instance, a jumble of letters on the handle of a fork managed to spell out my name.

Several months later, I was on the phone with her. "You know, Mardi-Jo," I said. "I just realized we only made knives and forks and soup spoons. I totally forgot about teaspoons."

"Jenette, don't even go there. I'm very happy that you love the silverware. But don't ask me to do anything else for a long, long time."

As a foil to these two vibrant sets of silverware, I chose black-and-white plates from Wolfman-Gold & Good, a SoHo store no longer in business. Wolfman-Gold is not a shop I ordinarily would have frequented. Almost all of its china was entirely white and, from my perspective, undistinguished. But once again I was indebted to the **New York Times**. In a small area of the Home section, it alerted its readers to four or five new and noteworthy objects. One of these was a white plate from Wolfman-Gold with a Renaissance etching of a black knife and fork in the center. It had an appealing, slightly pop vibe, but it was the imagery that mattered to me most. I trooped downtown to investigate, where I discovered that the china was even more special, because each size of plate in the collection had a different utensil on it. For my purposes, I could not have imagined anything better. The plates showed two-dimensional renderings of classic silverware, black and white and frozen in place. In juxtaposition, I had Mardi-Jo Cohen's and Guy de Rougemont's three-dimensional silverware—animated, modern, and in vibrant, living color. Although the plates and utensils were contemporary and had

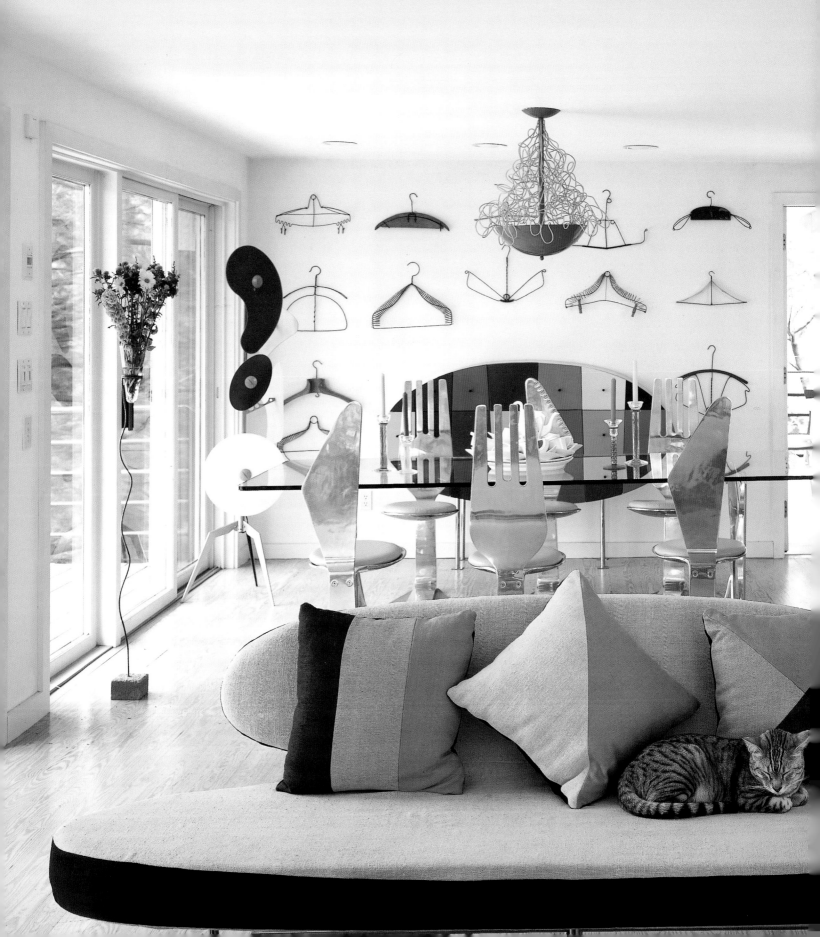

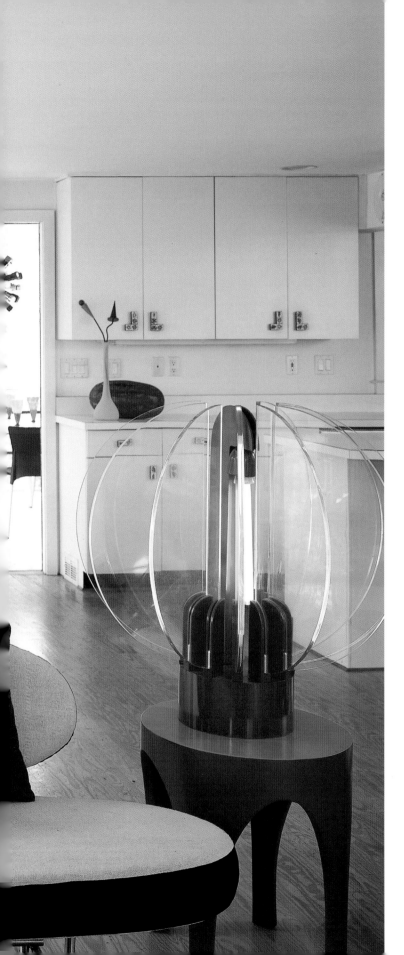

been made at about the same time, they seemed to hint at an historical evolution, a transition similar to that from black-and-white still photography to Kodacolor films. Sometimes you find just what you need in the most unexpected places.

Beyond the Dining Area

Dividing the dining section from that of the living area was Lloyd's yellow couch. Unlike many sofas, which look good only head-on, the shape of Lloyd's was so beautiful that one could place its rear side toward people at the dining table, and they would see not only a bolt of bright color but a sculptural form. In this way the couch was able to separate the areas of living and dining without appearing to turn its back on either one.

In front of the couch and the ottomans I placed the black sisal rug, with its varied and colorful shapes. To the left, against an extended pier, went the white Wendell Castle love seat. In the far right corner I placed the foam Greek capital, making sure it was on the diagonal to highlight its sweeping scrolled profile. Near the glass wall perpendicular to it were five standing lamps of different heights, each one on a black pole with a corkscrew bottom topped by a metal flag. With their different colors and geometric shapes, they looked like signal lights. They had been inspired by a stamp-size photo I'd seen in a French design magazine, in a section on current exhibits and shows. The short article next to it identified these sculptures as the work of the Greek artist Takis, who lived and worked in Paris.

It was difficult to tell much about them, but I had the feeling that they had lights in the center. I already owned several Takis lamps and loved them.

Lloyd Schwan promised that the couch would be comfortable, and my cat Fusion proves he succeeded.

Chill Hill: Wild and Witty in the Woods

These, I thought, would look great at Chill Hill. So the next day I was on the phone to France, one hand on the headset, the other on my checks. But assuming I hadn't completely bollixed the conversion of metrics and francs, these sculptures were not going to work. Each one was over fifteen feet tall and cost $70,000 or more. They seemed more appropriate for public spaces than for a home, and if one was far beyond my price range, five would have plummeted me to the depths of the money pit.

Nonetheless, I kept thinking about how great they looked, and wondered if it might be possible to find someone who could make a smaller, more affordable version. Luckily, at this very instant, I read a brief magazine account about a man who could supposedly reproduce anything from a gilded Louis XVI desk to lavish Art Deco chairs. Naturally, I sped to the phone to try to engage his services. I don't really remember our conversation, and worse, I don't even remember his number or name, having made the fatal error of failing to file this information away for when necessity would surely strike again. What I do recall is that he was too busy to make the lamps, but kindly recommended a woman he felt was just right for the job.

I am chagrined that I neglected to file away her name and number, too, because she deserves credit for taking the project on and producing wonderful results. Together we decided on the colors and shapes of the metal flags atop the poles and colors for the blown-glass noses in their centers that would house the bulbs. She knew a metalworker with a foundry who was able to forge the components, and when they were assembled, I could not have been happier. Like the Orbital lamp in the dining area, these lights added color and interest where they were especially needed, well above one's line of sight. For a space with lower-than-usual ceilings, they emphasized the room's vertical dimension and gave it the illusion of greater height.

A Bear Comes to Visit

In the far corner of the room, to the left of the fireplace, I put one of my favorite advertising icons. Three-dimensional and full of warm good humor, it was for Hamm's Beer. While our national parks have long had a rather stern Smokey the Bear letting each of us know that we can prevent forest fires, Hamm's has had its very own bear, too, but a bear of decidedly different demeanor. Black, with a white stomach, a cheerful expression, and a bulbous nose, he is a kindly bear, lovable and ebullient.

In the 1960s, Hamm's made a number of large-scale motion displays featuring its woodland mascot. I bought two of them in Off the Wall, my favorite L.A. store, one for the main house at Chill Hill and one for the future. The first display shows our buoyant bear standing on a red motorcycle on a circular pedestal base. His arms are outstretched, each paw holding what most likely was an advertising sign when this bear was first made. In the sidecar next to him is one of his forest buddies (he had at least five that hung out with him in various combinations) a small brown rabbit. There is just enough extra room in the sidecar for a six-pack of Hamm's beer. With the flick of a switch on the base, motorcycle, bear, and bunny revolve, revealing a license plate on the car numbered 1965. It marks, if anyone was curious, the year in which the motion display was made.

The bear added a joyous and fanciful note to the downstairs, which might have seemed slightly out of place in a city home but felt just right in the country. It was a theme I continued throughout the open plan. Across a ceiling support that separated the dining and living sections from the kitchen area and entranceway, I incorporated a number of other playful elements. At the design store of the Museum of Modern Art, I found a stack of white plates by Jean Cocteau first issued in 1959. On each one was a drawing of a cat. Slightly off-kilter, with eyes turned upward toward an invisible owner, they had an endearing, whimsical quality. At the same MoMA store I also found a cache of Keith Haring pull toys licensed by his estate after his death. Red, with yellow bases and framed by thick black lines, these were Keith's famous barking dogs. I loved them, both the plates and the toys, and couldn't resist their inevitable natural order: cat, dog, cat, dog, cat, dog—fifteen in all on the beam, enlivening what could have been an inelegant structural support but was now an animated part of the room. As always, Lloyd was an invaluable contributor. When I told him the idea, he fashioned small, plinthlike shelves with rounded edges on which to mount the dogs. They made the display graceful in a way that a long, uninterrupted shelf never could have been.

Clearly, the Hamm's bear, the Cocteau cats, and the Haring dogs gave a lighthearted feel to the space. And this was continued in the fireplace surround, which despite our many collaborations, became a point of royal contention between Lloyd and me. When I bought the house, there was no fireplace, and it was something I wanted very much. This was not simply for the pleasure of having chestnuts roasting on an open fire, but also because the room needed a primary focal point.

Facing My First Fireplace

Whenever I'm in London, I try to visit Beverley, who once had an antiques stall at Alfie's Market on Church Street but now has a shop of her own right across the way. Although Beverley specializes in Clarice Cliff pottery, which I had once collected, she always has many other wonderful things—Susie Cooper tea sets, exquisitely detailed Goldscheider ceramic figurines, teapots in the shapes of racing cars, airplanes, and tanks. Always interested in

planes, trains, and automobiles, I'd occasionally buy these fanciful dispensers of tea. But what I began to purchase from Beverley in earnest were faces of women made in the 1930s and '40s in England, Austria, and Czechoslovakia.

Often based loosely on movie stars, these faces were designed for decorative purposes, with indentations on the backs so that they could be hung on walls. I liked them for the particularity of their features, the tilt of a beret on a head, the stylish wave of scarf, a greyhound's head next to its owner's, a band of bracelets around an upper arm. Without knowing what I would do with them, I over time built up a sizable collection of heads. Among these ceramic masks it was rare to find the visage of a man. Once Beverley offered me a face said to be Bing Crosby, another time one thought to be Fred Astaire. They seemed less interesting to me than their female counterparts, and I therefore let them go. When just a few days later I had second thoughts, they'd been sold. My failure to buy at least one of these male heads was something I came to regret—but that was later. At this moment in time I had a raw stucco fireplace. Built as part of the renovation of the house, it was crude and unfinished, waiting for a concept. Eventually I thought of my several cartons of ceramic masks.

"All right," I said to Lloyd when he'd wandered over to my house one Saturday morning. "I've got it. I'll ask Phil to cover the stucco in a grid of large black tiles, and then I'll hang the heads on top of it."

"You can't be serious."

"Why not?"

"Why not? Because they are so kitsch. You have to do something modern and elegant."

"I like them. And I think they'll look great."

"No, no, no. They are wrong. You've got to think of something else."

Well, that was a setback. I respected Lloyd's judgment, so I put the project on hold, as he had urged, to consider other possibilities. But as much as I tried to be open-minded, I kept coming back to the masks on the black tile squares. Yes, Lloyd was right, there was something kitsch about the ceramic heads. In fact, because of this quality, I often wondered how people had displayed them when they first came out. Did they place one or two on a foyer wall, or hang a series of them going up the stairs, or put several over the night tables by the bed? I couldn't imagine doing any of these things. All of these usages seemed corny. But the idea of massing them together on a geometric grid was interesting to me. Despite my sentiment, Lloyd and I were proof that one person's notion of interesting was another's sense of banal. Lloyd still hated the idea, and his protests continued unabated. I ran the concept by another one of my collaborators and friends, Steve Kursh.

"I like it," he said.

"Lloyd hates it," I replied.

"Maybe he just needs to see what it would look like," Steve volunteered. And with his computer and some versatile software, he printed out a reasonable facsimile of the heads on a black tile fireplace. Needless to say, Lloyd was unmoved. But Steve's mock-up clinched it for me, and I asked Phil to lay in the tile grid while I organized the heads in a pattern to go on top of it.

It was at this point that I wished I had Bing Crosby or Fred Astaire. The layout seemed to need at least one male head to offset these countless women's faces. While the work on the fireplace was nearing completion, my friends Fab Five Freddy and Seymour Stein came up for an overnight visit. We arrived at my house after I nearly killed the three of us by crossing the railroad tracks at a decidedly inopportune moment (I had just gotten my license and was still dangerous when parked). Once Seymour

and Freddy had recovered sufficiently to walk without their legs buckling, they began to look around.

"Oh, my goodness!" Seymour exclaimed, taking in the fireplace. "I have those exact same heads."

What Seymour really meant was that he had those exact same heads and at least several hundred more. Seymour, the founder and head of Sire Records and one of the best music men in the business, is a crazed and compulsive collector. If he takes vacations, it is to go to the multi-acre Brimfield antiques shows that are staged three times a summer in Massachusetts, or to the Atlantic City show in March, or to every single show on the West Side Highway piers. He too frequents Alfie's and Beverley's, and he knows the schedule of every flea market in Europe. Seymour has warehouses full of the pieces he's purchased over the years and now employs a curator to help him make sense of what he's bought.

"Did you get most of yours from Beverley?" I asked.

"Oh, yes, quite a lot of them."

"You know, she offered me the Bing Crosby and the Fred Astaire, and like a dope I turned them both down. I call periodically, but she hasn't had them again."

The next day was beautiful, and since everyone had survived my driving without loss of life or limb, we ended the visit on a positive note. About a week later, I received a small, nondescript package at work. It had been messengered from Seymour's office to mine, and since there were no outward clues as to what it might be, I opened it with extreme curiosity. There inside the plain brown wrapping was the most thoughtful and unexpected of presents. Seymour had sent me the Bing Crosby head, complete with sporting cap and pipe. It was such a generous, perfect gift, and I was overwhelmed. When I returned to Chill Hill, I positioned Bing on the fireplace just slightly right of center. In this whirl of glamorous women's faces—hard, haughty, wide-eyed, perky, piquant, exotic, and romantic—he was the anomaly that gave every other head a little more meaning, a little more depth. Although I'd placed an aristocratic redhead directly in the center of the top row, her cool countenance extending past the uppermost border of tiles to break the constraints of the grid, the Crosby face was the emotional focal point. Seymour's warmhearted present had made the fireplace that much better.

So did Lloyd come around in the end? Did he finally like the fireplace despite his vociferous campaigns to block it? I don't think he ever got that far. But it was clear that he no longer hated it, and that in itself was a victory.

Adding Some Serious Themes

As I've said, there were many playful touches in the room, and they continued into the kitchen area and up the staircase, which was also part of the open plan. I loved these elements. They made the house sunny and cheerful, welcoming and fun. But I also believe that every space should evoke a number of different feelings. And while I like to use primary colors, and relish humor and unexpected quirks, they are always offset by strong, serious passages.

Over the Wendell Castle love seat I hung a photograph by Jan Groover. A subdued and lovely still life, it shows a three-dimensional cherublike figure in the style of ancient Greek sculpture. Although

small, the figure is animated. His hair is a wind-blown swirl of curls, and his mouth is open wide, as though he is calling out to someone far away. His body is a torque of energy, his back slanted forward as though he's racing with the wind. In his left hand he holds a sphere. His right arm, stretched out across his body, gesticulates with a sense of urgency.

The cherub stands on a small pedestal in a faded wooden crate that is propped up from behind to bring it closer to the picture plane. To his left is a mass of blurred white ovoids limned by lavenders and grays.

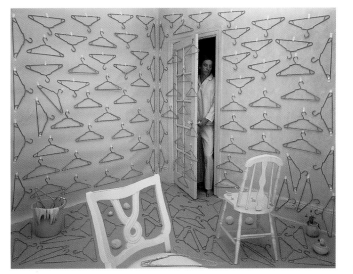

Sandy Skoglund's photograph **Hangers** echoes the wire hangers on the opposite wall.

To his right is a cluster of what might be grapes, exquisitely pale, with only the coolest touches of gray and green. Under it, casting a shadow over the crate, is an organic form, a tightly bunched tangle of skeins that resembles a piece of coral dredged from the sea. These classical props seem assembled for students to draw in an antiquated art class. But that is only an illusion. Nothing is quite what it appears in Jan Groover's photograph. The depleted colors, the seemingly commonplace forms that are anything but, undo our expectations and give us instead a complex image steeped in mystery. It is a beautiful picture, and a powerful one.

In addition to the Groover photo, I hung one by Sandy Skoglund over the fireplace in the living area. It was called **Hangers**, and I had loved it from the moment I first saw it at a benefit auction for AIDS. Sandy is renowned for her installations of skewed domestic landscapes. These environments are artworks in their own right, but Sandy receives far greater acclaim for the photographs she takes of them, and the single, perfect image she selects that crystallizes each installation at its best.

Hangers is one of Sandy's earliest works, when she was using found objects rather than sculpting many of the elements herself. A door opens partway into a room, and in it a man in yellow pajamas tentatively stands, his hand on a yellow doorknob. The walls of the room are yellow, the floor pink. There are two yellow chairs in the space, one facing the man directly, the other turned in the opposite direction, its back aligned with the far left wall. They are placemarks, giving structure and dimension to the room. But what makes this environment both so weird and so engrossing is that there are hangers everywhere. Over 130 in all, the blue hangers become triangles that trisect the space, forming a floor-to-ceiling pattern reminiscent of some of Matisse's most seminal paintings. There is an elegance to how the hangers are organized—one sees the precision of their layout through the negative spaces of a straight-backed chair—and a sense of humor, too. Three peer out of a yellow scrub bucket draped with yellow latex gloves; another sits face forward on the seat of a chair, leading the viewer directly into the picture.

The photograph works on many levels—it is arresting and formally complex, disturbing and beautiful. Centrally placed over the fireplace, it was the keystone that united the different parts of the open plan. Yet Lloyd felt I could make it appear even more important. Despite the colorful spatters throughout the downstairs space, Lloyd suggested I add a block of solid color to the wall on which I'd hung **Hangers** and another to the pier behind the Jan Groover. I was a little dubious at first. But Lloyd made a comment that I never forgot. "You can always repaint," he said. If he was right, how dras-

tic could any decision be? There are times when you have to implement a concept to see if it works. And, if it doesn't, you can, as Lloyd said, always change your mind and repaint.

And repaint I did. **Hangers** is primarily yellow, blue, and pink, and I felt that only some shade of one of these three colors would work on the wall behind it. I selected pink. Blue is cold and contracts, which would make the fireplace wall seem smaller and less inviting. Yellow, I thought, was too insistent. So pink was the choice: soft, but still expansive. However, when the coat of paint dried and Sandy's picture went back on the wall, it seemed that the hue I'd chosen was too close to the pink in the photograph, diluting its self-containment despite the thick black frame around it.

I struggled to find another shade that would neither fight the pink in the photo nor extend it. I worked—as I do in selecting almost all paints—from a Pantone book that held myriad colors in small, die-cut stamps that could be torn out for maximum flexibility. Although few volumes are as useful as the Pantone book, there is a significant downside. Pantone colors represent printing inks and therefore can't be replicated by the computer analysis now commonly used in paint and hardware stores. To achieve the color of your choice, you have to rely not on technology but on good old-fashioned judgment.

Nonetheless, the Pantone book did yield a pink we were able to approximate, and Sandy, up for a day and assessing the result of "Pink Paint, the Sequel," voiced to my delight that it was the only possible choice. Lloyd had taught me an invaluable lesson that has stayed with me not just in design but in every aspect of life. Never be afraid to try something. You can always repaint.

As hard as this might be to believe, it didn't immediately occur to me that there was any connection between the blue hangers in Sandy's photograph and the hundred-year-old wire hangers on the opposite wall. I had bought each out of love, and hung them for the same reason. Yet when both were up and I started to spend weekends at Chill Hill, it was impossible to ignore the serendipitous relationship between them: two musical scores with nearly the same notes in counterpoint and opposition, forging a melodic dialogue of images, textures, and shapes.

Years ago Marcel Duchamp, the radical artist and theoretician, postulated what he called the Artistic Coefficient. According to Duchamp, every creative work is the result of all the things an artist intended to express but in the end somehow aren't

there, and all the things he never consciously thought of but emerge in the piece nonetheless. Looking at the hangers on either end of the living space, filling the room with a rhythm and life of their own, I knew Duchamp was right.

Cooking with Gas: A Spunky White Kitchen

In contrast to the multiple bright colors in the living room and dining areas, I chose to make the kitchen section white. Had I been constantly on-site when the house was being gutted and rebuilt, I probably would have been hanging on Phil's shoulder while

The kitchen area, with Keith Haring dogs chasing Jean Cocteau cats and Haring dominoes as doorpulls.

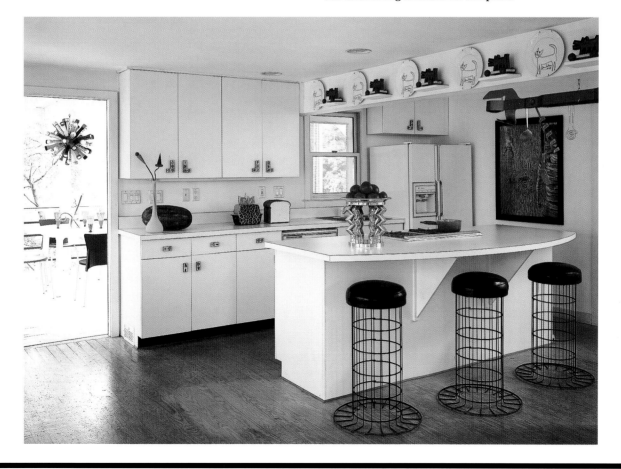

he ordered fixtures, happily paying a premium to get primary accents for objects like the faucets and spigot for the sink. However, I was in New York for most of the construction period, and Phil installed a kitchen that was 98 percent what I wanted: crisp and clean and subordinate to the other two sections of the open plan.

Despite the completeness of the kitchen, Phil did not choose any door pulls for the cabinets, wisely intuiting that I would want to decide on them myself. However, when I conducted a superficial search of manufactured handles, none of them seemed to have the invention or spunk I was looking for. Rather than purchase something I would live to regret, I decided to focus on other issues and let the door-pull question rest for a while.

A while, however, turned into months, and the lack of door pulls was a source of enormous frustration to friends who had to use ingenious methods to open cabinets and drawers. Despite mounting peer pressure, I was unflappable. "I'm not going to install any handles until they're exactly the ones I want," I would say. "And how long are you willing to wait for them?" the naysayers sneered. "As long as it takes," I'd declare, with just enough stubbornness to call off the dogs.

At the Museum of Modern Art Design Store, I always gravitate to the children's area, where you find some of the most appealing and sophisticated objects. On one of my forays I spotted a box of Keith Haring dominoes that, like the barking dogs, had been licensed by his estate. They were lively, colorful, and hip, and a wonderful way, I thought, for kids to enjoy modern art.

My next-door neighbors, Lyn and Lloyd, had two young boys, so I purchased a set for them. But something impelled me to buy two more sets for myself. I could sense a tingle somewhere in the back of my mind that said the dominoes would inspire me if I brought them into the house. I gave Wolfgang and Otto their set and placed my two boxes—open— on the kitchen counter at Chill Hill.

True Confessions

I have a terrible habit of waking up in the middle of the night and raiding the refrigerator. Different ideas come to me at that time, and lost in my thoughts, I polish off the cookies or the ice cream without even noticing. So there I am at 4:00 A.M., musing and munching and spreading the Keith Haring dominoes in patterns on my countertop. As I look at them with their neon hues and signature imagery, and then up to the solid white kitchen cabinets, bare of anything, even handles, I realize that the dominoes would make great door pulls, echoing the humorous style of the barking dogs and drawing color from the living area into the kitchen. The solution at last! I couldn't wait for Lloyd to come loping over the next morning so I could share my discovery.

Lloyd loved the idea, mounting the dominoes so they could be used as pulls, while painting black on the sides to pop the pigments on the surface. He left the arrangement of the dominoes up to me, one of those tasks that can drive even the sanest of people gaga, especially if you're as obsessed as I am with color and design. I won't bore you with the process, but I did come up with an installation that took both pattern and palette into full account, while still following the logic of how dominoes fit together. Despite the immense amount of thought I put into this, I have to admit that another person could probably have arranged the pieces randomly, and they would have looked just as good.

With the exception of the door pulls and a giant can opener that hung from the ceiling over the countertop, the kitchen was relatively simple and subdued. The only other additions that helped to give it some character and punch were three black wire Verner Panton bar stools and another photograph by Sandy Skoglund, entitled **Body Limits**. As with all of Sandy's work, the immediate impression is simultaneously arresting and diverting. The picture is pared down to a minimum of elements—two mannequins, one male, one female—and a chair on the diagonal between them. As with **Hangers**, the wall and floor are covered with an overall pattern, but in **Body Limits**, made thirteen years later in 1992, the design is so tightly meshed that it is hard to notice where one begins and the other leaves off. The surface of narrow brown and cream vertical striations makes one think of bamboo, and the whole effect is primitive, even tribal. Only when one looks closely at the image does one realize that the material is not bamboo at all—in fact, not anything close. It is bacon.

I had bought the photograph as soon as it arrived in Janet Borden's gallery. Only a few days later, my father came to town. "How would you like to go to SoHo?" I asked. "We can go see Ron and Frayda and drop by Exit Art and visit Janet." My father, as always, was game, and we hopped in a cab to make the downtown rounds. At Janet's I was eager to share my latest acquisition, so she brought **Body Limits** out from the back room so my dad could see it, too.

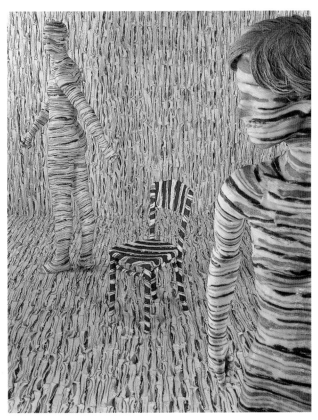

Sandy Skoglund's **Body Limits**, where everything is covered with strips of uncooked bacon.

"What do you think?" I asked Papa, thrilled that he was so ready to share my enthusiasms.

"Hmm—mm. It's interesting. Yes, very interesting." He paused, then shot the photograph a penetrating look. "Wait. What's that? Is that bacon? What's a Jewish girl like you doing with a picture covered in bacon?"

I guess I neglected to mention that my father was a rabbi. A rabbi who looked like every priest in every Boys Town movie, but a rabbi nonetheless.

"Oh, Papa," I quickly replied. "I don't think it's bacon. I think it's really Kosher Beef-Frye."

"Right," said my dad, his deadpan expression betrayed by small smile lines around his mouth. "Kosher Beef-Frye. Yes, Kosher Beef-Frye. It's definitely Kosher Beef-Frye."

Several months later the picture was installed in the kitchen at Chill Hill, and I was hosting yet another in an ongoing series of Usual Suspects Annual Collaborative Thanksgiving Dinners. My father had driven up with me the night before, so he was there to greet my friends when they arrived. Because Chill Hill was still a work in progress, everyone who walked through the door would tour the house to see what was new. Eventually they'd focus on Sandy's **Body Limits**, tucked in the kitchen corner perpendicular to the refrigerator.

"Wow, that's an interesting photograph! What exactly is it? Wait! It's bacon. What's a rabbi's daughter doing with a picture covered in bacon?"

"Oh, it's not bacon," my father, who was in earshot, cheerfully interjected. "It's Beef-Frye. You know, Kosher Beef-Frye."

Porches Need Furniture Too

Just off the kitchen and leading out to the swimming pool is a screened-in porch. Although it was outside, I wanted it to connect to the first floor of the house because one could see it through a glass door. Accordingly, I had the floor painted pink, a bubblegum pink somewhat deeper than the interior stain, and opaque rather than translucent. In Europe I found one of my all-time favorite pieces of furniture, the Elephant chair by Rancillac. A solid but amazingly buoyant piece of fiberglass, its upper section was shaped like the wings of a giant butterfly. The wings tapered down to the seat, and from the seat extended a long and narrow footrest. It was called the Elephant chair for good reason. One could easily imagine that what looked like butterfly wings were instead the floppy ears of a pachyderm, and the footrest its trunk. The fiberglass structure was inserted with bolts into a heavy black metal base so that it was possible to sit in the chair and rock back and forth. Although the Elephant chair came in a handful of colors, even gray, which would have emphasized all the more its animalistic qualities, I wanted a yellow one, and I found it. I placed it in the far corner of the porch, allowing, despite its elephantine size, room for an outdoor table and chairs.

For a table I purchased one of those incredibly inexpensive white plastic ones you find in Kmarts and Wal-Marts or, as I did, in the now-defunct Bradlee's. I don't think I paid more than $30 for it,

if that, and it's lasted forever. To make up for the conventional nature of the table, I surrounded it with six chairs in a rainbow of interesting hues by the Italian designer Massimo Iosa Ghini. They looked terrific, but lacked the life span of my storable, washable, fabulous cheapo table. When it was clear that I could not eke out another summer from my haute but fast-disintegrating Iosa Ghini chairs, I nabbed my friend Greg Garry to accompany me downtown to Moss to find some equally good-looking replacements. Moss is a terrific SoHo store, full of cutting-edge design, and I have bought many wonderful things from it. But one doesn't go there looking for bargains. Greg and I found some chairs that had good lines and possibilities, but their colors were paler than I would have liked, and they were, as one would expect, fairly costly.

"You know, sweetheart," said Greg, staying my hand before I totally succumbed, "six of these chairs are going to cost a lot of money. Before you spring for them, maybe you should look at a catalogue I get. It's called **Design within Reach**, and although you're not going to find anything in it as high-style as these, you'll still find a lot of attractive design at really affordable prices."

Greg is the photo editor at **Homestyle Magazine** and a veritable fount of resources. I took his advice, stuffed my credit cards back in my purse, and put the chairs at Moss on hold. The next day, the catalogue was on my desk. Good friend that he is, Greg had sent it over right away. And he was right. There were a number of appealing modern pieces that one could buy without having to win the lottery. And there in the pages of **Design within Reach** was a group of chairs that looked like they'd do the trick. They didn't come in a large range of colors, but those that were available were deep-toned and rich, and you couldn't beat the price. Six of them together cost less than a single chair at Moss. I placed my order, and the chairs—two yellow, two red, a blue, and a black—were delivered in no time flat.

A Bright Idea Gets Moved from the Lake to the Porch

The lake below Chill Hill is the true center of activity for those of us lucky to have property that borders it. Almost every house that circles it is only steps away from the water, and adults and children alike mingle at its edges for swimming or boating, or simply to enjoy its limpid beauty. Many people have built decks on the lake, and some have even added gazebos next to them. My friend Wendy is one of them, and her gazebo is an extension of her artistry, draped with silk scarves she's designed, and studded with candles and glittering stones. I've always loved sitting in Wendy's floating world, and I assumed that once I'd completed the reconstruction of the main house, I'd build a gazebo too.

While work was continuing on top of the hill, I tried to imagine what my version of a gazebo would look like. One of the pleasures of having a folly on the lake is to sit on the water's surface as the sun goes down, watching the heavens turn from gold to darkest blue, then tracking the stars as they begin to silver the sky. It is possible to stay there for hours, cosseted by the sensual lake sounds and the indigo of the night. Although one would hesitate to break this mood, I still wondered what it would be like to have a lamp in the gazebo so that one could dine there with friends, talk and laugh, and see their features glowing in the blackness, intimate, like faces around a campfire.

Surely a lamp would require electricity, and although I didn't run the notion by Phil, I assumed that bringing current down to the lake would be a daunting and expensive task. So other than kerosene lamps and candles, was anything else pos-

sible? I've often found that when my options are most limited, I am at my most creative. I narrowed the problem down to its tightest parameters: what kind of lamp could I conceive that wouldn't require electricity? I tried to think if any lights existed that didn't work on electrical current. And, of course! The answer was so obvious: flashlights!

And so I began to dream up a chandelier made entirely of flashlights. I conceived it as a starburst with different-colored flashlights jutting out in all directions. I could also make flashlight sconces so that I could have direct light from the chandelier overhead or indirect light from the sconces mounted to the gazebo walls. There were drawbacks, of course. I'd regularly have to change the batteries and bulbs as they burned out. But still, it was worth it. I got together with Lyn Godley, "Girl Electrician," and showed her my sketch. "Sure, we can do it," she said. And we were off and running.

I bought every flashlight I could find: pink ones, yellow ones, green ones, orange ones, black ones, red ones, and blue. Lyn suggested that we purchase metal ones as well, something I wouldn't have thought of, to intersperse among the others to add sparkle and shine. Years ago, before tools started to be housed in plastic, metal flashlights were the only ones available. Now they were hard to find, but somewhere in the wilds of Ohio, Lyn was able to locate a supply center that still carried them, and ordered a dozen or so to round out the chandelier.

Given both Lyn's schedule and mine, a year passed, and by now I realized that as much as I loved my lakefront and the dock I had built on the water, I spent infinitely more time at the pool by my house or on its decks and patios. Creating a gazebo was no longer a priority. What mattered most now were the indoor-outdoor living spaces around the house. The screened porch had furniture, but it had no lighting.

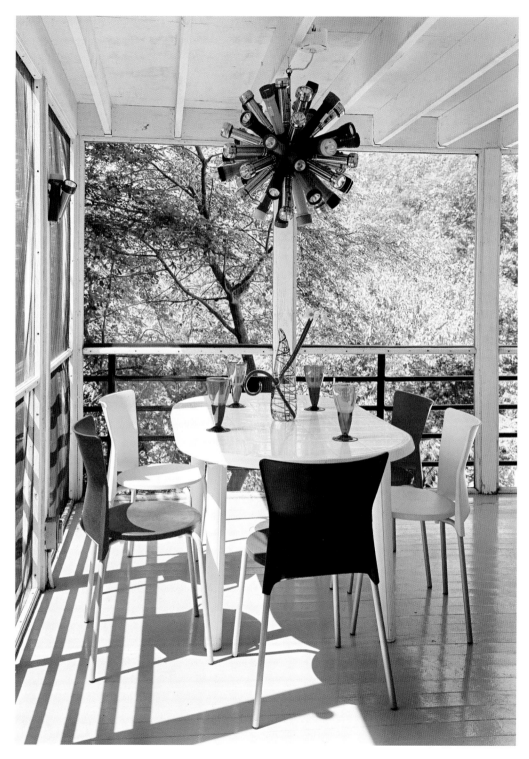

A pink floor and a flashlight chandelier extend the design of the house onto the screened porch.

In Your Space: Personalizing Your Home and Office

Why not move the concept of the flashlight lamp and sconces from the imaginary gazebo by the lake up the hill to where they were needed most, the porch?

"Now that's a great idea," Lyn agreed. "And this way I can electrify the lamp so you don't have to worry about changing batteries and bulbs." You can see why I've dubbed her Girl Electrician, which is not to minimize Lyn's skills as an artist and designer. Aside from decoding the complexities of wiring each torch and then connecting them together so that every one would light with a single switch, Lyn played with the components and made them even more interesting. Since flashlight tops screw off from their stems, she mixed and matched colors, moving a yellow top from one and putting it on a pink base, taking the same pink base and meshing it with a top of solid blue. It was a simple but ingenious idea, and gave the lamp more character.

The silver flashlights were another ingenious addition, but they failed to have such felicitous results. There is a reason that plastic housing has become so popular. Over time the silver rusted, inside and out. Eventually the lamp had to go back to Lyn's for a major restoration, which included coating the metal with a transparent sealer to give it longer life. It also became apparent that the chandelier could not weather the abuse of being on the porch year-round. As fall moved in, it would have to be taken down or else bundled in swaddling cloth to protect it from the elements. But these were minor setbacks. The flashlight lamp could not have been more beautiful, and it added luster in more ways than one to our summer evenings on the porch.

Home Is Where the Hearth Is

The places where you live and work reflect not only who you are at the moment but also how you change and grow. As a result, when you think you're finished,

you never really are. It's important to be able to respond to new art and new objects, to add something as large as a picture or as small as a vase, as serious as a Swid Powell plate with the red AIDS ribbon in its center, or as lighthearted as an Alessi devil-shaped can opener with little pointy metal teeth. Sometimes the addition of new discoveries means the subtraction of older ones. It is hard for us humans to let things go, but that is what we sometimes have to do to make room to embrace new people, new vocations, and new ideas. It is this equation of adding and subtracting that keeps us lively and interesting, not just to other people but, most importantly, to ourselves.

However, these transformations, big and small, are usually meant to occur when the basics are complete. One doesn't think of adding a new chair unless the floor's in place, or of changing the pillows on a couch unless you already have a couch that might be refreshed by new cushions. And so, when I talk about never really being finished, it is not intended to excuse or explain why an essential part of the living area was missing for close to eleven years. And what was it? The hearthstone—or its equivalent—in front of the fireplace. How serious was this? Well, it meant that I had a seemingly permanent hole, six feet long, two feet wide, and two inches deep, at one end of the room.

Phil was frustrated that I seemed unmoved in the face of his suggestions. "How about a big slab of marble?" he'd offer. "Or a large stone? Or brick? You really should do something." And although I said no to each of these ideas, I was still sympathetic to Phil's distress. The glaring pit in front of the fireplace made all of his hard work seem incomplete.

I wasn't trying to be difficult. Phil's suggestions were totally sound, and houses continue to be built all the time with similar solutions. Which I suppose

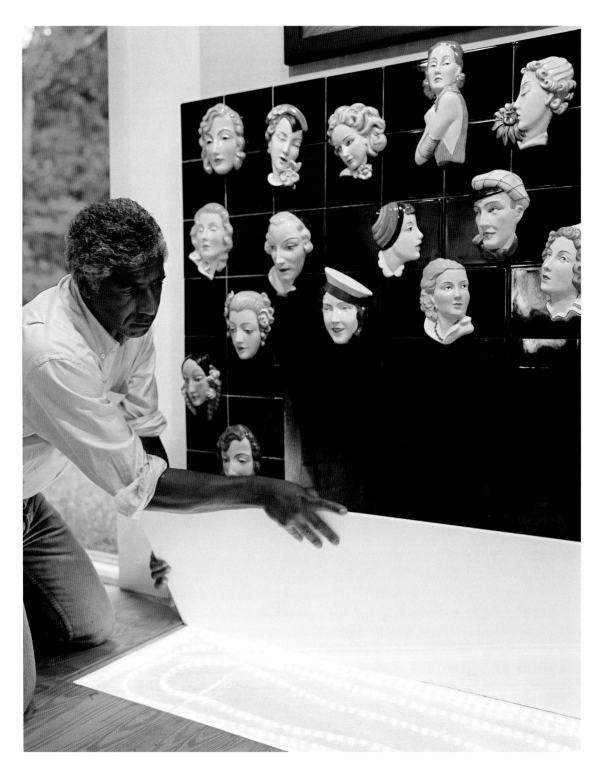

Al Williams, sculptor, chess master, and preeminent problem solver, realizes my vision of a luminous hearth.

In Your Space: Personalizing Your Home and Office

was where the problem lay. Phil's ideas for the hearth weren't bad—quite the contrary—but they were conventional, and I wanted something that wasn't. Needless to say, if you constantly spurn others' ideas but have none of your own, then you are simply a crabby and unreasonable curmudgeon. But I did, in fact, have a very definite concept for the hearth. The trouble was, I couldn't find anyone to execute it.

This idea to which I was so wedded was quite simple. I wanted to place a large sheet of milk glass in the hearth, flush with the floor, under which would be lights. When you flicked a switch, the fireplace would have a buttery, warm glow whether logs were burning in it or not. I ran the concept by Lloyd, who was always so willing to help me out. He liked the notion, but this once—it is the only time I can remember—he seemed uninterested in participating.

In the sixth year after the house was re-built, I thought my waiting had come to an end. I'd met Al Williams, who, like Steve Kursh and Lloyd, is an artist, a problem solver, and a man who can build anything. Al became my contractor on the house I was to buy in Harlem, and it seemed there was nothing he couldn't do. Although the Harlem house consumed nearly all of Al's efforts, there were occasional downtimes when he needed other work and I needed other work done, especially at Chill Hill, where the age of the house was beginning to show. Al came up, installed track lights, and hung some pictures, but for the most part he spent his time there painting, inside and out.

"Al, how about the fireplace? Let me tell you my idea."

He listened, but rather impatiently, and raised, as is his wont, as many obstacles as he could think of. Chill Hill was covered with other people's imprints. The house in Harlem had Al written all over it, in every room, on every floor. I could see

that, despite my imprecations, Al was not going to jump in and build the hearth. Nonetheless, I refused to fold. It was more and more apparent that I was off my rocker, but if I'd waited six years, what was a few years more? And this time the waiting finally paid off. In the summer of 2001, as the renovation of the Harlem kitchen got put off to the fall, Al began to come up once again to Chill Hill to work on the house. And this time he took ownership, making major contributions, like turning the stair tower's uneventful yellow siding into the sunny hue I'd wanted all along. This vast improvement was also a benefit of the passage of time; not until the mid-1990s was a paint developed that could cover vinyl siding while withstanding the yearly wear of the outdoors. And it wasn't until this same summer that I learned of its existence.

Now when I mentioned the question of the hearth, Al was ready. All of the obstacles he'd raised years before were still valid. The glass would have to be supported so that it wouldn't crack underfoot. The lights could not be too intense, and they required air so that they wouldn't overheat. Al would also have to find a way to diffuse the light so that the glass had an overall glow. Otherwise you would see the bulbs, defeating the whole purpose of the installation.

It was clearly going to be a challenge to create the hearth as I had conceived it so many years before. But now that Al was into it, he had ideas. His first thought was to fill the pit with concrete—thus providing the necessary support for the glass—and place the bulbs inside. We stopped at a store in Guilford called Affordable Lighting, where we could survey the range of possible lights. Al had initially thought of using fluorescent bulbs, which remain much cooler than incandescent ones. But when we checked them out at the lighting store, it seemed they wouldn't give us the diffused light we needed. However, off to one side we spied what are called rope lights, extended plastic tubes that house low-intensity bulbs at two-inch intervals. Rope lights have several advantages. The casing is flexible, so you can arrange the tubes in any pattern you want. In addition, while the low-intensity bulbs have a soft glow, their light is diffracted all the more by the plastic housing.

Perry, who with his wife, Barbara Maresca, owns Affordable Lighting, asked us what we wanted the rope light for. I drew a quick sketch of the hearth on the back of a radio-car voucher, and he got it right away. "There's a restaurant in town called Esteva," Perry said. "I sold them rope light so that they could do something similar. They have a long bar there, it might be made of alabaster, and Steve, the owner, wanted the whole area to glow. The rope light really worked. You might want to go see it."

Esteva was just minutes away on the Guilford Green, and Al and I quickly drove into town. Esteva is an upscale restaurant, and Al and I, both working, looked like total slobs. Did we dare go in? Uncertain, we hovered at the door, until a gregarious young hostess beckoned us inside.

"Are you sure it's okay?" we asked. "Perry at Affordable Lighting told us about your bar, and we wanted to take a look, but we know we're not properly dressed."

"Oh, it's no problem at all," said Heather, who, it turned out, was the owner's stepdaughter. "How great that Perry sent you over. Here, let me turn on the bar for you."

We didn't want alabaster or the pale marble from which the bar was actually made, but the effect was there. Much heartened, we bought the rope light and the concrete, and Al began his experiment. However, experiments are just that, experiments. When the dense and dark concrete surrounded the plastic rope, the light no longer had the space it needed to diffuse. Al had to dig out the filling and start again from scratch.

"I have another idea," said Al. "I think if I pour clear resin into the pit and embed the rope in it, then there'd be enough support for the glass, and enough transparency in the material to diffract the light."

This time Al conducted the experiment back in his loft in New York. The model he made was small, but we were optimistic. It looked like Al was on the right track. Back up in the country, he expanded his trial to full size. He poured resin into the open hearth, looped the rope light through it, let the resin harden, and added more. Now for the final test. Al placed the milk glass on top of the resin, flicked the switch he'd installed when he'd wired the lights, and, yes! it worked! The hearth, elegant, modern, and unadorned, was suffused year-round with creamy light, the stuff of which dreams are made.

Eleven years? Only an obsessed maniac would wait eleven years. I can't in good conscience recommend that anyone else do anything close. But, oh, how I loved my hearth!

Lessons Learned Along the Way

1. Many design decisions are active ones, conscious, considered choices. But there are others that happen subliminally, and they can be among your best ideas. Whatever name you give this unconscious process, don't be afraid to trust it. It is often your most creative resource.

2. It would be great to be able to have the talent to draw. It would be even better to be able to build something you've designed. While not all of us are gifted with these abilities, this lack should not impede you from personalizing your space. As long as you have passions, interests, and ideas, you can design your own interiors. Most of the time, you can find the things you want, making them even more interesting by the way that you arrange them. For the items you need to have made, you can hire artists and craftsmen to build them for you.

3. Dealers can be among your best resources in uncovering unusual treasures. While you might pound the pavements on weekends or go online at night to visit eBay, most likely you have a day job that consumes the greater part of your life. But for dealers, the search for rarities is a full-time occupation. Good ones have their own vast networks and, given a specific request, can often deliver exactly what you want. The truly enterprising ones will keep you in mind and contact you when something special comes along. To make sure you're at the top of their list, call your favorite dealers periodically, let them know the kinds of things you're looking for, and ask if they have anything you might like. If not, ask them to let you know when they do.

4. I love museum stores. They are a terrific resource for interesting objects and good design at fairly reasonable prices. Most major museums have a retail component, and some of them publish catalogs of their offerings. Don't forget to canvass the children's section. You can find truly inventive objects there to spark any adult décor. If you decide to buy a lot of modestly priced items, or one expensive one, you might consider becoming a museum member before making your purchase. A membership almost always entitles you to a 10 percent discount. Do the math. It's often worth it, especially if you think you'll strike again during the course of the year.

5. "You can always repaint." My friend and designer Lloyd Schwan first said that when I had doubts about adding color to two large piers in the living room area of Chill Hill. It is a maxim I have lived by ever since. Don't be afraid to try something that you're not certain about. It might be the perfect solution. And if it's not, you can always repaint or reupholster, reconceive, or redesign. Yes, you'll have lost some time and money, but that's part of the creative process. If you don't take risks, you'll never know what successes you might have.

8.

The Second Story:

Technology Themes and Sexy Dreams

The guest room-cum-media room, where a tower of
technology rises near Gaetano Pesce's voluptuous chair.

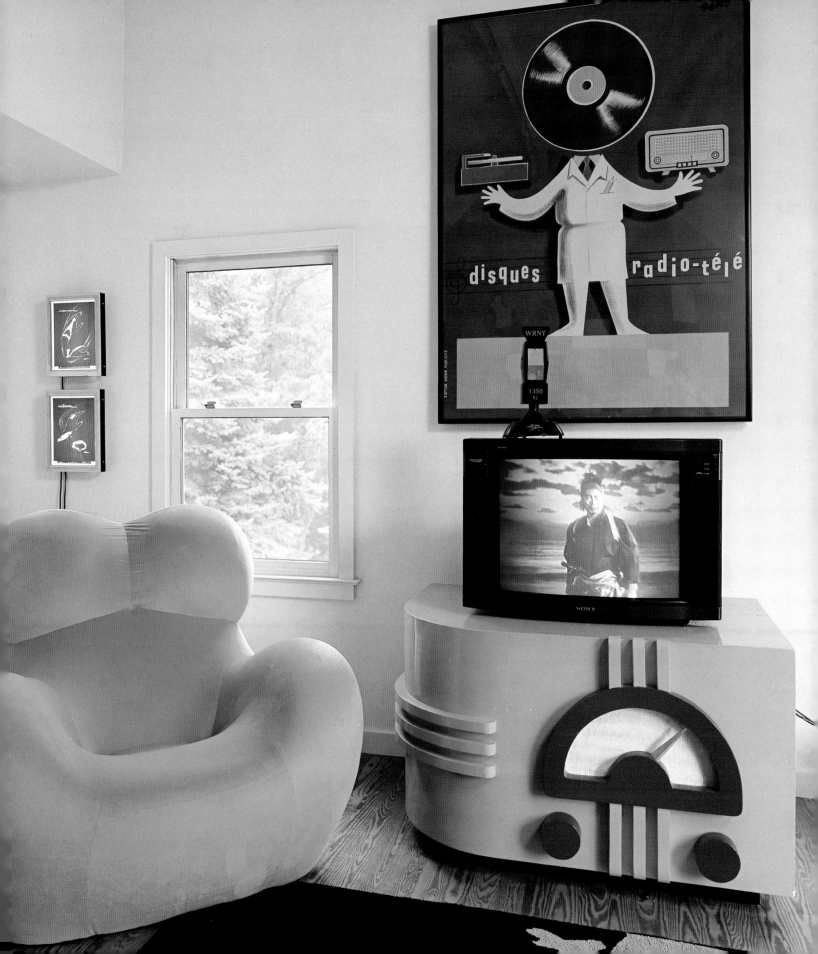

s I've said before, perhaps Arthur's most valuable contribution to the design of Chill Hill was the stair tower, which rises out of the massive rocks like the turret of a modern-day castle.

High Art

Not only did the stair tower's architectural form add style and panache to what otherwise would have been a modest dwelling (although the multicolored railings did their part too), but it also gave me a large vertical arena in which to hang art. The stairs led from the first story to the second, ascending from left to right to a landing, then turning and continuing to the upper floor, where L-shaped white railings formed a balcony. As always, I mixed the playful with the serious, and the interior of the tower became an extraordinary space, as challenging as it was colorful.

For years I had collected what are often called silent butlers, painted wood figures standing at attention with trays in their hands. Although these objects were made as early as the beginning of the twentieth century, probably the greatest numbers were made in the 1930s. There was a reason for this, of course. Millions of people were unemployed, and with time on their hands, many retreated to their workshops to while away the hours. When they emerged, it was with everything from the most mundane to the truly imaginative, from stools and cutting boards to Scrabble and Monopoly, both inventions of the Depression years.

Just as Monopoly's popularity depended so greatly on the compensating fantasies that accompany hard times, so did that of silent butlers. Standing patiently without complaint, they held

shelves for drinks, or metal containers poised for the flick of an ash. And these retainers, whose mission was only to serve and wait, ran the gamut: French maids, stiff valets, voluptuous bathing beauties, cartoon characters, even the occasional bulldog or cat. I loved the whimsical nature of these figures and their endless variety. Now it seemed that nothing could better accentuate the staircase than a parade of them marching up the steps.

As you moved up the stair tower, there was artwork on each of its three sides, and finally one large photograph at the landing behind the railing at the top of the stairs, a beautiful Tina Barney called **Jill and Polly in the Bathroom**. The picture could have just as easily been titled **Pretty in Pink** because it shows both Tina's sister and her niece wrapped in pink bathrobes in the pink bathroom of their Hampton home. The tiles to the right are pale pink, and the deeper pink curtains on the shower and window are reminiscent of the floral-printed chintzes one finds in English country homes. A dish on the counter is floral-patterned, too, and strewn about the sink is an array of pink Elizabeth Arden beauty aids, the cosmetics line of choice for generations of gentility. While the photograph is an astute social observation of a class-based life, the picture is formally fascinating, making it a classic of modern photographic images.

Jill stands between the sink and the window, her face in three-quarter view, her right hand on her hip, her left hand pulling back a panel of the curtain. We see Jill again in the mirrored wall behind her, the sharp crook of her elbow more visible now, her face, seen in profile, more angular too. We catch only a fleeting second glimpse of her daughter Polly—her right hand, a sliver of her robe, a fraction of her thick black hair falling to her shoulder. Beneath the window is an old-fashioned radiator, white, with vertical pipes. And as Jill holds back the curtain, we see through

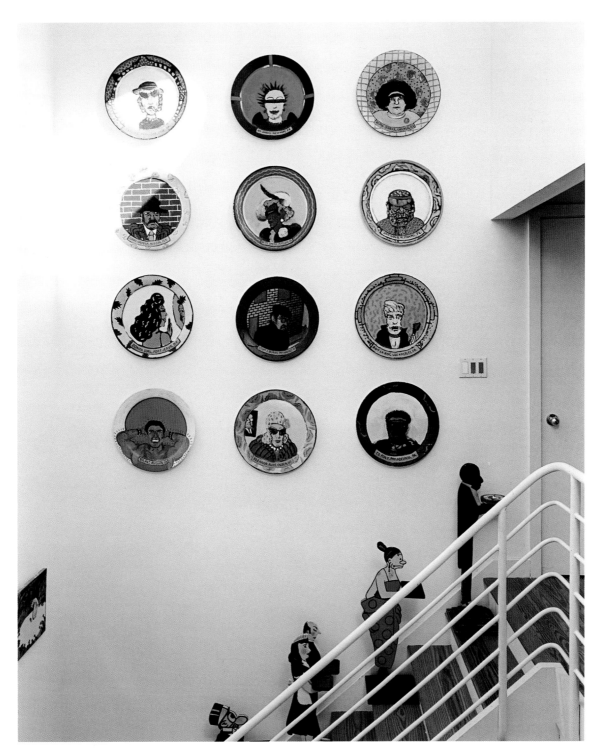

Seymour Chwast's imaginary portraits of quirky Americans gaze down at the silent butlers on the stairs to the second floor .

The Second Story: Technology Themes and Sexy Dreams

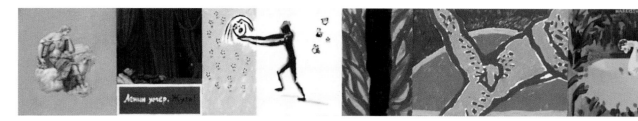

In the stair tower, a powerful horizontal painting by Komar and Melamid.

the window its reprise, a white picket fence along with something anomalous, suburban, and mundane, a plain wooden doghouse.

Across from Tina's photo and halfway up the landing is a painting, **Air, Fire and Water**, by Russian émigrés Komar and Melamid. Long, narrow, and horizontal, composed of seven individual parts, it is a visually inventive meditation on the history of society and art. The picture begins on the left with the image of a Greek woman, rendered meticulously in an academic style. Every fold in her ancient dress is realized, and she floats contemplatively, a swan at her side, against a gray-blue field. Skipping centuries ahead, the next panel seems at first like a small Renaissance painting saturated in dark reds, the sort of picture Raphael might have made, of a formidable, aging pope, his young sycophants plotting behind his back. But looking closely at this painting, we see that the potent leader lying on his deathbed is none other than Lenin, and it is Stalin, only partially concealed behind the curtains with a chalice in hand—to toast the passing of his one impediment to power?—darkly ready to take center stage.

The imagery on the two panels that follow overlaps, and the art styles change again. In contrast to the brooding crimsons of Stalin watching the death of Lenin, the panel beside it is bright yellow and dotted with casually painted blue flowers. At its right,

on a white field and crossing onto the yellow area, is a quickly brushed black figure triumphantly presenting a decapitated head. Its body looks slightly more male than female, but the figure still brings to mind familiar personae of history and myth—Judith and Holofernes, Salome and Saint John the Baptist. The counterpoints in these two panels are odd and disturbing—the sunny yellow, the offhanded blue flowers, stickers of jolly pandas pressed against the white, and the brutal image of someone holding high a severed head. Jutting out from the center panel is a charred and blackened piece of wood against a ground of turbulent flames. It adds literal sculptural depth to the work, and metaphorical depth as well. What exactly does it represent? The fiery furnace, the Inquisitor's stake? These and many others. Looking at it, you feel face to face with thousands of years and thousands of stories of torture and martyrdom.

To its right is a long panel in a raw graffiti style, the torso of a man in acid green outlined in red. The depiction is solely about his maleness, the hair on his chest and legs, his penis lying flaccid across his thigh. Finally, this Komar and Melamid painting, which began with a Greek reference—and a myth? is she Leda?—ends with another one. In a pond surrounded by greenery stands a modern-day Narcissus, his head bent over in total adoration of his rose-tipped appendage, thrusting upward from

In Your Space: Personalizing Your Home and Office

the water. The style is purposefully naïve, although there is nothing naïve in the concept. As we stand directly in front of the reflective pool we realize it is exactly that, a mirrored surface in which we also see ourselves, as inescapably self-involved as the painted figure of Narcissus himself.

Despite its bright colors, it is a deeply serious painting, and I could not contain my excitement when I stumbled on it in a back room of Ron Feldman's gallery. I did not know anything about the painting, or the artists. But I was smitten.

"I love this picture!" I said to Ron. "Tell me about it."

And he did, leaving out the fact, which I was only later to learn, that he had aided Komar and Melamid when they wanted to leave the former Soviet Union and couldn't, and championed them and their work when they finally came to the United States.

"I know I shouldn't even ask," I finally said, "but how much is it?" So Ron told me. And it was, as I expected, well beyond my reach.

"You know," Ron interjected. "I think it's priced too high. The price was right several years ago, but the market's a lot softer now. I'll speak to the guys and suggest that they go down."

A few days later, Ron called. "Okay, this is the price. I told them how much you love the painting and that you weren't a big-time collector with big bucks, but that you had a great eye and great taste and that the painting would have a great home. Oh,

Tina Barney's photograph **Jill and Polly in the Bathroom** greets you at the top of the stairs.

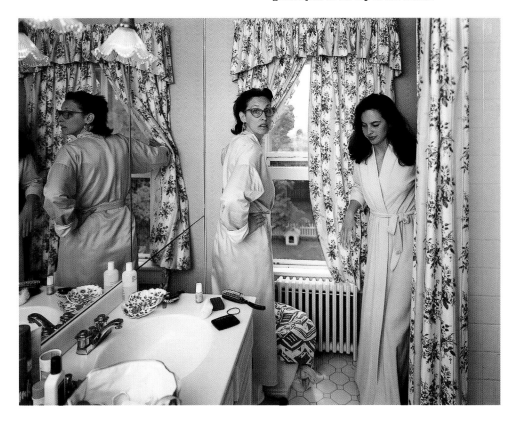

The Second Story: Technology Themes and Sexy Dreams

and we all agreed that you can pay for it over time."

I gasped, a long, sustained gasp that was a combination of amazement and overwhelming gratitude. Ron and Vasily and Alex had together made it possible for me to own an incredible work of art. The picture came up to Chill Hill to be hung on the front wall of the tower so that everyone would see it while going up and down the stairs. And, without seeming too egotistical, I'd like to think that what Ron said to Komar and Melamid was true. Their painting wasn't going to a big collector, but it was going to a small one who cherished it. And it was in good company. Although mounted by itself on one wall, it was surrounded on all sides by wonderful artworks and objects. And it was part of a real home, where it was seen not just by other artists and collectors but by regular people with ordinary jobs who would catch themselves reflected in Narcissus's mirrored pool and laugh with the delight of discovery.

A Perfectly Reasonable Question: Is This a Repeatable Phenomenon?

So how do miracles like this happen? Well, the extraordinary factors that enabled me to purchase the picture would never have converged were it not for Ron Feldman, and there aren't many Ron Feldmans in the world. But while I think that Ron is a truly rare dealer, there are others who value even the smallest collector for her enthusiastic passion for art. Perhaps they won't go to quite the same lengths as Ron, but many of them will make a real effort to work with you.

On the other hand, you have to do your part. You have to look and learn and, first and foremost, open yourself emotionally to connect with what you see. And whatever works you do choose, I believe they should be selected for the purest of reasons—not because you think they're a good investment, not

because the critics are raving or because they might give you status in other people's eyes, but because you deeply, truly love them. A good dealer who esteems these qualities will work hard on your behalf. That doesn't mean he'll be successful—often the artist himself will balk and refuse to alter the price, or insist on full and immediate payment. But just as there are a few Ron Feldmans out there, there are also flexible and egalitarian creators who want to see someone of lesser means own and enjoy their work.

In the stair tower I also displayed the work of the Guerilla Girls, a revolutionary SWAT team who billed themselves as the conscience of the art world. Their identities, hidden under gorilla masks—a broad visual play on their name—they struck under cloak of darkness, papering walls, fences, and construction sites with incisive and challenging posters. These posters, executed most often in black and white, had tremendous graphic strength, but bolder and more potent were the messages. In an art world that was almost exclusively white and male, the Guerilla Girls continuously spotlighted a series of gross inequities. A typical poster reads:

> GUERILLA GIRLS' POP QUIZ
> Q. If February is Black History Month
> and March is Women's History Month,
> What happens the rest of the year?

And upside-down, in boldface type, it says: A. DISCRIMINATION. As powerful as this poster is, many were more so. The Guerilla Girls kept exacting tabs on New York's museums and galleries and at the end of a year would issue a report card. They'd post three columns—the first for the number of one-person shows of white males, the second for the number of one-woman shows, and the third for the number of shows of people of color. And although the city's most prestigious institutions were listed along with its best-regarded galleries, the results were startling and scandalous. In an annual record of the art world's most highly thought of spaces, there would be two one-woman exhibits and only one designated to an artist of color. And while the Guerilla Girls set the moral standard for the art world, shaming it into being more inclusive, they also took on other issues of conscience: homelessness, female mutilation, the federal neglect of impoverished black and Hispanic areas.

But how did I acquire these amazing posters without becoming a guerilla myself, moving at night to where they'd been affixed, a straight-edged razor clutched in my hand to remove one from a wall? Clueless, I posed the question to Jeanette Ingberman, one of my closest friends and the cofounder of Exit Art, one of New York's very few cultural spaces that even years ago would have passed all the Guerilla Girls' tests with flying colors. "I don't know offhand," she replied. "But let me look into it."

A few weeks later, I was down at Exit Art, visiting Jeanette and her partner and husband, the artist Papo Colo.

"Here," said Jeanette as she slid a black portfolio across the table. "This is for you. A present. Just don't ask me how I got it."

I untied the string that held the portfolio together, and there they were, about fifteen Guerilla Girl posters.

"It's not a complete set," Jeanette hastened to add, as though embarrassed that it wasn't. "But some of the classic ones are there. I got them for you because we love you. Now take them and enjoy."

And that is exactly what I did. I framed the posters and chose five of my favorites to stack one on top of the other going up the narrow wall of the stair tower next to the balcony railings.

There was one large wall left in the tower, and incredibly, without even trying, I found just the right thing for it. We all have our nocturnal perambulations of one sort or another. For some it's barhopping or pub-crawling, or after-hours clubs. And for me it's bookstores and magazine stores. I know which are open at least until midnight, and I make a point of detouring to them when I'm wending my way home. It was on one of these diversions that I stopped at Lincoln Plaza News, a minuscule shop on a Broadway block that also boasts an ice cream store and a miniplex devoted to foreign, art, and independent films. Those of us who for years have frequented this tiny space know it as the Magazine Store. And with good reason: every cubic inch from bottom to top is crammed with periodicals in every language and on every subject.

On one of my late-night binges, I decided to explore what was new in the store's graphic design department. Among over forty magazines, one cover shone like no others. Its background was white, and on it were twelve circular paintings depicting a cross-section of Americans: muscle-flexing "Big Al" from Augusta, Georgia, chubby housewife Alma O'Neil of Chicago, Illinois, spike-haired, rouge-lipped Bo Jarris—a transvestite?—from New Hope, Pennsylvania, clandestine Louis J. Burns of Milwaukee, Wisconsin. Each was different, and so was each border. Some were plain, others decorative. But every one of these portraits in the round not only was incisive and distinct but had a painterly looseness and spontaneity. The publication was titled **Creation**, and below it were the words "International Graphic Design, Art & Illustration." I couldn't wait to read it.

But when I crawled onto my bed that night and riffled through the pages, I could not have been more surprised. Despite its English title, I was dismayed to find that the entire text was in Japanese. Luck, however, was on my side. The cover credit was in English. And here I was surprised again, because I realized that I knew the artist, Seymour

Chwast. Yet nothing in these pictures even faintly reminded me of Seymour's work, and I was familiar with a substantial body of his output. In the late 1960s, Seymour, along with Milton Glaser, was one of the founders of the groundbreaking design firm Push Pin Studios. For years his famous illustrated ads—in such publications as **Forbes** and **Capitalist Tool**—had covered the New York landscape. But Seymour's Push Pin work had a purposeful, mechanical precision. Other than a cartoonlike quality that he tightly controlled, nothing in it suggested the joyous abandon of the portraits on the cover of **Creation**.

I longed to know more about the portraits, so I dialed Push Pin Studios and asked to speak to Seymour, whom I had met fleetingly in the 1970s when I first began working with Milton Glaser. I doubted he would remember me, so I reintroduced myself when he answered the phone. Once the connection was made, I raised the subject I'd been dying to ask.

"Seymour, I bought a Japanese design magazine last night because it had the most wonderful circular portraits on the cover. And it turned out that they were by you. I love them. Can you tell me what they are?"

"Well, they're portraits, as you can see. Imaginary people that I dreamed up. They're plates, really, painted on large tin pizza pans that I was able to get. And then they stopped making them. So that's all there are."

"Do you have any of them? Are they available? Would you be willing to sell them?"

"Funny you should ask. They've been gone a long time, traveling on exhibition. But they just came back from Europe yesterday. I haven't even uncrated them yet. And would I be willing to sell them? I hadn't thought about it, but I suppose I would. I think each one should cost—" He named a number I immediately forgot, because I was already on a single-minded race toward the next hurdle.

"Oh, I don't want to buy one or two. I want to buy them all. They look incredible together, and I can't imagine breaking up the set."

"All of them? Well, sure, I guess that's okay. Why don't you come down to Push Pin in the next few days, and I'll unpack them in the meantime."

I couldn't wait. And when I arrived at Push Pin several days later, I was thrilled. The portraits looked even better in person than they had on the cover of **Creation**, and I felt in that moment of seeing them for the first time like the luckiest person on the face of the earth. The plates came up to Chill Hill, where they were hung on the largest wall of the stair tower in four rows of three. Lloyd was my generous installer, and he somehow managed to get all of the portraits up using Velcro and a very tall ladder. And if I felt lucky that day at Push Pin, I felt lucky in a different way when one dislodged from its fittings and crashed to the floor. Thank God Seymour had painted these portraits on tin.

The Guest Room: A Hub of Industry

Directly at the top of the stair tower is the guest room-cum-media room, which became an homage to trains and rocket ships, radios, and robots, a convergence of interests I'd pursued for many years. Something about industrial design fascinated me, perhaps because I was a child of the 1950s, when America's car culture shaped so many of our dreams. In 1957, after driving the same black Chevrolet for eleven years, my father decided to buy a new car, propelling my brother Si and me into a jubilant frenzy. Nothing in our young lives—not Dairy Queen or pinball machines or miniature golf—could possibly be this exciting. Suddenly the two of us were automotive experts, identifying and classifying every new model on the road. We got to weigh in on details like color, although I realize now that when it came to aesthetic choices, it was my mother's vote that counted most. But none of this mattered. My father not only included us, he let us run with the fantasy. And run we did. It was the summer of my first love affair, and the object of my desire was a beautiful hunk of metal.

So deeply felt are our childhood passions that the strongest follow us into adulthood, emotional imprints that seem as personal as DNA. When John Sideli showed me a transparency of his Bakelite radios, it tapped a vein that no Bakelite bracelets or pins, however prized or coveted, could ever hope to mine. The jewelry was decorative, but the radios referenced the same fantasies as cars: industry, technology, power, progress, the future.

When I got divorced, the Bakelite radios of our marriage went to my husband. In the years since my husband and I first bought them, their prices had soared, and it would have cost thousands of dollars to try to reassemble a comparable collection. But there were other radios out there, and no one was paying much attention to them. I began to seek out Crosleys, which were made in the early 1950s.

Radios, robots, and telephones frame the glass doors of the guest room.

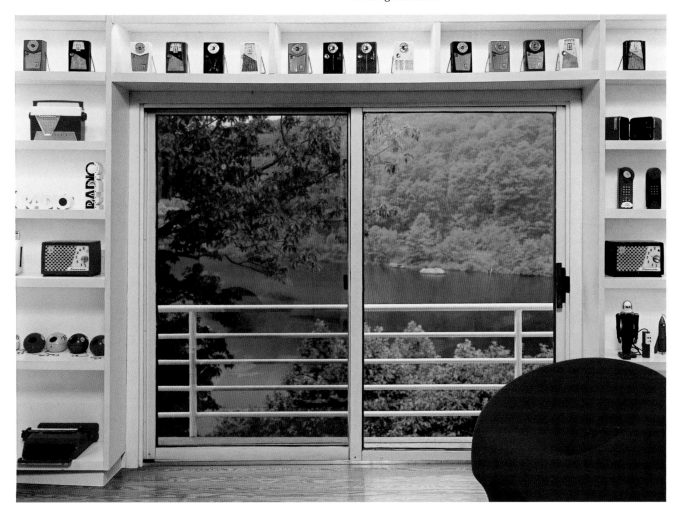

The Second Story: Technology Themes and Sexy Dreams

Constructed from a different kind of plastic, they lacked the gleamingly rich colors of those fashioned from Bakelite, but they had the unmistakable and totally cool look of automotive dashboards. I must have collected well over thirty Crosleys before I realized I had no place to put them.

Because I had been a pioneer in collecting first Bakelite radios and then Crosleys, there was a bonus—dealers knew who I was even before I knew them. The world of collectibles these days is a billion-dollar industry, but it was smaller then, and word spread fast in this odd, obsessive little subculture. For years one of the linchpins of this world has been New York's famous Sunday outdoor flea market at the corner of Twenty-sixth Street and Sixth Avenue. I haunted it regularly, and if I didn't know dealers by name, I was at least familiar with a number of them, and they with me. One day I was taken aside by a person whose first name I did know, Richard, a tall, genial man who presided over a regular stall.

"Look," he said. "I know you're into radios. Well, I have what I think is the next big thing, and it's right up your alley. Transistor radios."

Transistor radios, of course, were the small, even miniature devices made possible by the invention of the transistor in 1948. Perfected by the mid-1950s, the transistor revolutionized the construction of electronic circuits. Although its invention was American, the methodology spread quickly to Japan, and soon tiny Japanese radios dominated the market. Although miniaturization is an aesthetic in its own right, it is not one that per se interests me. I care more about overall design than size, and I said as much to Richard.

"Well, I do have those small transistors you're talking about. But I have some others I think you're going to love. If you're interested, call me, and you can come to my apartment and check them out." And, so saying, he gave me his card and phone number.

Which brings us to Lesson Number 52 from The Innocent Collector's Handbook: no matter how eager you are to get the scoop on the latest collectible, don't go unaccompanied into anyone's home unless you know him extremely well. Most people are what they seem to be, and no harm will come to you. But why take a chance on the small percent who aren't? However, ignoring my own advice, I went alone to Richard's apartment.

I had a lovely visit with him, and finally Richard brought out the radios he wanted me to see. They were Emersons, made in the United States in 1957, and while they were transistors, they had scale, measuring about four inches across and six inches in height. But much more important than the scale was the design. Basically, these were all the same radio, but they abounded in subtle variations that, when you placed them side by side, created a sequence of visual fascination. In addition, each radio embodied not just the sense of an optimistic future but here, in 1957, the year of the launch of **Sputnik**, a romance with the new frontier of outer space. There were sixteen radios in all, and as compelling as each one was on its own, nothing compared to their power as a series. I bought them with pleasure. This time, while the Crosleys still moldered in their cartons, I began to plan how the Emersons would be displayed.

My assiduous search for the Crosleys had not only led me to the Emersons but also sparked a call during this period from Michael Malcé, a dealer, with his wife, Jolie Kelter, from whom I'd bought interesting, offbeat objects and vintage quilts. "Jenette, it's Michael," the voice sounded on the other end of the phone. "I know how you love radios, and I may have just the thing for you. It's a giant radio, the size of a desk. It was a prop made for a precursor to **Saturday Night Live**, a show called **Radio Ranch**. The actors would sit behind it and deliver the news."

"Wow, that sounds great! Can you send me some photographs?"

"Sure. I'll get them up to you right away."

Within hours Michael had the pictures on my desk. And, for a radio girl, the images were enough to fuse my circuits. While not based on any specific design, this television prop was clearly inspired by the Bakelite radios of the 1930s. It had the curved lines of Art Moderne, and its colors brought to mind one of the most popular Fada models of the time— a deep golden yellow with a bright red dial and red knobs. Michael asked only that I give him a quick answer. I presumed that someone had offered him the prop, and he didn't want to spring for it unless he had a buyer in hand. Considering my penchants, this oversize radio, with its tiny but fascinating niche in pop culture history, was too good to pass up. We agreed on a price, and soon this colorful artifact, with its little-known origins (who ever heard of **Radio Ranch**?), was on its way to Connecticut. I already knew where it would go—between the two small windows opposite the couch that was yet to come. Sturdy and large, it would be the perfect table on which to put the TV. There was a certain conceptual appropriateness in this, a miniature tower of entertainment technology, with radio as the foundation, and television, the next evolutionary stage, built on top of it.

A Streamlined Toy Train Inspires an Entire Wall

As any eclectic collector knows, one goes down many tracks at once. So while the radios were a key element in the Chill Hill media room, they were far from the determining factor. Maybe more than anything, what shaped the space, what gave it its atmosphere and magic, was the large, stream-lined 1930s train I purchased at Off the Wall in Los Angeles. Even as I bought it, I knew it would go above the low couch, still to be made, but which would double as a bed. The train, three cars long and originally a dull plum metal, had been replated in silver by the owners of Off the Wall. It's more or less a cardinal rule that one doesn't tamper with vintage objects, for reasons of both accuracy and value, but this was an exception. Only a small number of these trains had been made, and the collectors who coveted them seemed to agree that the silver-plating so enhanced the drop-dead beauty of the design that it would probably cause their price to increase.

I had a minor reason for placing the train over the couch. The windows of the cars lit up, and that made it a perfect nightlight for when the couch converted to a bed. But the major motive was a concept I had for the entire wall. Just as automobiles had fueled my childhood fantasies, so had the incomparable thrill of travel by train. I loved the sleeper cars, with their drawn curtains, the rhythmic sound of metal wheels on track, the private window—mine alone—with its shade that I raised long past midnight to capture snapshot glimpses of the landscape as we raced by. I wanted to re-create the romance of overnight passage by rail, and my streamlined train gave just me the opportunity.

The long wall of the media room was ideal for this. Wide and high, it rose close to sixteen feet at its peak. This expanse permitted me to create a sense of endless sky, for that is how I saw it, airbrushed from dark blue to light blue to pink, and studded with tiny bulbs so that it seemed spangled with stars. In the center of the wall I imagined a map of the United States that would give the impression that the train below it was traversing America at either twilight or dawn.

I made one of my amateurish sketches and knew for sure that I was on the right track. Several years before, I had bought fifty salt and pepper shaker sets that combined in a somewhat herky-jerky way to form the United States, a tour de force in the world of lowbrow collectibles. Every individual state was a salt shaker, and each was paired with a corollary symbol with which to dispense the pepper. Idaho, unsurprisingly, was coupled with a potato, Texas with an oil well, Wisconsin with a slab of cheese. My thought was that this wonderfully eccentric piece of Americana could be installed on the wall as the map.

"Never!" exclaimed a horrified Lloyd, my opinionated weekend neighbor, who as usual had ambled over to my house to discuss art and life before we went shopping for food. "It is so totally tacky. And besides, it's too small for the space."

I had to admit he was right. As crazy and fun as the salt and pepper shakers were, the map they formed was too small. And, more importantly, it had none of the strong graphic quality of the rest of the room. Humbled, I scuttled for alternatives, all of which Lloyd rejected. The wall remained white and bare.

One Saturday morning many months later, Lloyd plopped himself down at my table and opened his sketchbook with a casualness too studied to be innocent. He knew it would take only a nanosecond for my curiosity to get the best of me, and in a flash I was sitting at the table too.

"So what do you have there?" I asked, while simultaneously reaching for his book.

"Oh, just a little drawing I thought you'd like to see."

The little drawing was a map of the United States. But there was something oddly different about it. The perimeter was straight out of a geography book and instantly recognizable. But what had happened

In the guest room, a streamlined train evokes the romance of traversing America at twilight or dawn.

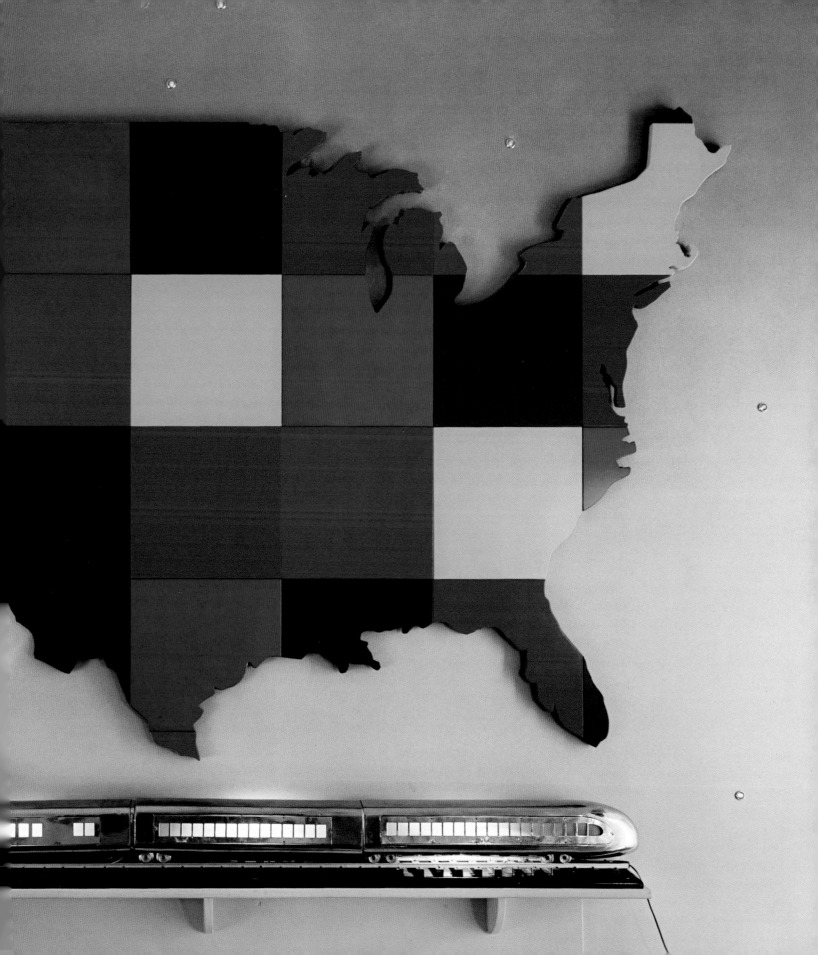

to the states? Lloyd had reduced America's forty-eight contingent states to twenty-eight. And they bore no resemblance to anything I knew; he'd taken the landmass formed by the states' continental outline and imposed on it a rectangular grid.

"I call it the New World Order," said Lloyd. "And they'll be in great colors, of course" (an unnecessary addition—no one was a better colorist than Lloyd).

"New World Order?" I repeated, totally inspired by Lloyd's innovative solution. "Then I want to give the states new names. Let's see. State of the Art, Solid State, State of Confusion, State of Being, State College"—this last one the actual name of the town where I grew up. I soon had a list of over forty possibilities, and it seemed in the heat of the moment like a great idea. Lloyd got into it, too, and we cheerfully debated where the words might go.

Despite our unbounded enthusiasm, it took almost a year before Lloyd cut the twenty-eight states out of wood and painted them. He stored the pieces in a container in my closet, and more months passed. I didn't mind. We all had busy lives and were together in the country only when weekends rolled around. The map wall would get done when it got done.

Meanwhile, Alex Locadia delivered the convertible couch for the media room. It was based on a great Italian design that was still in production but came in only black or red or white. I wanted yellow, and Alex agreed to make it for me. The sofa was composed of two curvilinear pieces, one for the seat, one for the back. Although it wasn't immediately apparent, the back section could easily be lifted off the base and the concave and convex curves interlocked to form one flat and solid surface. Well, not quite solid. The pieces had a tendency to separate unless something bound them together. I found myself giving thanks, as I often do, to those anonymous creators whose inventions simplify our lives in ways we take for granted. Who, for instance,

came up with the contour sheet? Bed making since has never been so easy. It was to the contour sheet and its spin-off, the contour mattress pad, that I owed the passable comfort of my yellow sofa bed.

And then one day not long after that, Lloyd made an announcement.

"Choose a weekend when you're not going to come up. Lyn and I are ready to install the map. And trust me, you don't want to be here. It's not going to be pretty. Just give us a date, and you can come back when it's done."

These were strenuous terms, but something told me I'd be better off leaving them unchallenged. We synchronized our calendars, and on the appointed weekend I stayed in the city while Lyn and Lloyd took over my house. Lloyd was in charge of the painting and installation of the map, while Lyn took over the wiring, scattering bee lights in a pattern that echoed the stars in my crumpled sketch, which now seemed like a remnant from a past life long ago.

When I vacated the house, I had left behind in the media room nothing but an unadorned blank wall. But when the yellow police tape finally came down and I was allowed to return to the scene of the crime, I was staggered. Where once there had been white, now there were only the subtlest gradations of color, merging from blue at the top to the softest pink at the bottom. Studded across this expanse were tiny orange lights that with the flick of a switch glowed like stars in an evening sky. Above the yellow couch, Lloyd had built a shelf painted in the same colors as the rest of the wall, so it was practically invisible. But on it sat three large pieces of track and the gleaming streamlined train. Its windows, opaque but lighted from behind, hinted at tantalizing mysteries—who were these cross-country travelers? — readers? revelers? newlyweds on their honeymoon, families going to visit their cousins in the West, Willy Lomans moving from one stop to the next? And finally, in the middle of it all, the tour de force, the United States, Lloyd's New World Order, the map itself. The wall was so perfect, so complete, that anything else, even the names I'd dreamed up for the states, seemed superfluous. This was a tableau vivant in the truest sense of the phrase. In creating art, Lloyd and Lyn had also created life.

Furniture on the Up and Up

In the year and a half between the conception of the map and its installation, I was busy buying other items for the room—1960s and '70s radios, robots, ray guns and space toys, foam telephones in a rainbow of colors, and Ettore Sottsass's Valentine, his groundbreaking slim red typewriter for Olivetti. All of these, along with the sixteen Emerson transistor radios, went onto the shelves that I'd asked Lloyd to build. They surrounded the sliding doors to the lake, flanking them on both sides and framing them on top. Hidden inside each row of cabinetry were strips of light that at night turned the entire wall into a luminous display of industrial design, split by a breathtaking view of nature.

I needed more furniture, of course. The couch alone wasn't going to do the trick, and as much as I loved its color and its shape, I would be lying if I said it was comfortable. For additional seating I bought two vintage chairs from Gaetano Pesce's classic Up series. There were six variations in all, from a couch to different-shaped chairs, and they were made from foam so compressed that they were packed and sold in large, flat boxes. But, in a miracle of modern science, when you opened the boxes the furniture inflated to full size, defying every law of volume and mass. And unlike the couch, these pieces were comfortable.

The first chair I purchased was called the Donna, or Woman, because the contours of its top were like swollen breasts, its enveloping seat like a womb. Attached to it by a cord was the ottoman, a giant sphere. The other chair I bought was the Uomo, or Man. It, too, had a subtle sexual suggestiveness in its shape, although it was far less massive than the Donna. Both of these chairs started to appear in the late 1990s at auction, the Donna especially commanding record prices. As a result, B&B Italia, the company that originally produced the Up series under the name C&B, reintroduced it at the 2000 Milan Furniture Fair. The pieces, no longer packed in the flat boxes from which they would inflate before your eyes, are still marvels of modern design.

From the Earth to the Stars: A Rug Heightens the Media Room's Themes

In addition to buying more furniture and objects for the media room, I was busily at work on a rug for it as well. Some years before, I had bought a wonderful hooked rug from Jolie and Michael of Kelter-Malcé. Hooked rugs, like quilts, have been part of the American handcraft tradition since the country was settled. Although their creators were also usually anonymous, some of them reached the level of true art, while others simply brought welcome charm, color, and comfort into the home. For the most part, hooked rugs tended to be both rectangular and pictorial. Couples and families, houses and villages, landscapes, flowers, and animals all were among the common subjects, extolling the joys of everyday life.

Yet this rug was neither rectangular nor square, but had its own distinct shape, a shape as innovative as its anomalous content. This rug was a rocket ship. Although it is not surprising that America's infatuation with the space race would be felt in industrial design, the fact that it could have an impact on something as homespun as a hooked rug speaks volumes about the mythic power of this new age. Of course I loved the rug, and as with so many other objects I felt I'd never see again, I bought it without having any place to put it.

But now it seemed perfect for the media room, and I began to design a larger rug around it. I placed the rocket ship in the left-hand corner, with the flames from its engine breaking the geometry of the border as though it were bursting from some launch site into the icy reaches of outer space. The center of the rug described this territory. It was full of radiant stars against a deep blue field, while in the far right corner, diagonally across from the nose of the rocket ship, was a golden Saturn with its seven rings. For the border I chose black, and on each of its four sides I sketched a small house with a chimney, two windows, a bush on one side, a tree on the other. The houses, drained of color by the night sky, were gray, but their windows shone with the yellow light of families awake and filling their homes with ordinary chores and pleasures. I wanted to create a dichotomy that moved between the modest lives of most Americans and the awesome experience allotted to a privileged few.

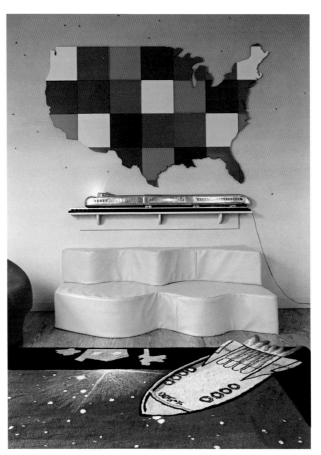

From one corner of the guest-room rug, a rocket ship takes off into outer space.

As always, I called up Jody Harrow, a true artist when it comes to rug design, and whose work I loved. I needed help, and Jody was delighted to collaborate. We soon got together to go over my sketch. I showed her the hooked rug and how I saw it fitting into the larger one. "And, of course," I added, "you'll want to improve on my little houses."

"Oh, no," she replied. "I love them just the way they are. I wouldn't change a thing."

My first reaction was disbelief. I couldn't imagine anyone wanting to retain my paltry efforts at drawing. But maybe in this case their childlike simplicity added a degree of charm, for Jody was genuinely enthusiastic. She left, promising to get immediately to work, and I felt we were off and running. But several weeks later Jody phoned.

"Jenette, I hope this isn't a problem for you, but I've been playing with the rocket-ship rug. And as much as I love the design, I don't think the hooked version is going to fit with the rest of the rug. Everything about it is great—the shape, the color scheme, the portholes on its side. But it's old, and I don't think it can hold its own against the fresh yarns and the deep pile I want to use. Would you mind if I keep everything the same but duplicate it so that the whole rug fits together?"

As attached as I was to my little rocket ship,

I immediately understood what Jody was saying. And besides, it had already done more than its part. By being in my possession, it had inspired the larger rug, which I loved. Who knows what I would have come up with if I hadn't bought the funny homespun rocket?

I encouraged Jody to go ahead, and I could not have been more thrilled when the final rug arrived. There was a romance to it that was both exhilarating and touching. Jody had come up with a way to spray the heavens with starlight, and the rocket ship, powering into the unknown, gave a wondrous credibility to the dream of travel in space. Our little earthbound lives, left behind in the darkness, seemed so small, but they also shone with a bright light, a testament that while one might reach for the stars, one could also find them at home. When the rug was unfurled, it pulled everything in the media room together.

Whatever else I added—Pucci de Rossi's futuristic stalagmites, Alex Locadia's **Star Trek**-inspired Plexiglas case for one of my ray guns, David Levinthal's photograph of a warrior woman defending her stranded rocket ship—simply rounded out the themes that had already been established by the map wall with its streamlined train, by the **Radio Ranch** desk, by the shelves of radios and toys surrounding the sliding doors, and by the large rocket-ship rug. The media room was more or less complete, but there was a bedroom on the other side of it to deal with, and a master bath as well. Of course they were already works in progress, but as always, there was much more to be done.

A Custom but Uncustomary Bed

As usual, I was leafing through the countless design magazines I snag as soon as they hit the newsstands. In one of the few English publications I had

in my stash, I came across two chairs in metal whose openwork backs were individual profiles of a man and woman seemingly engaged in conversation. The heads looked like drawn line art, whimsical and sophisticated in a manner strongly reminiscent of Saul Steinberg's work.

"Aren't these great?" I asked my boyfriend of the time, padding over to him with the open magazine so he could share my enthusiasm.

"They look wildly uncomfortable," he replied, automatically drawing on his limitless supply of skepticism.

"Oh, but I wasn't thinking of chairs. I was thinking of a bed. You know, heads on the headboard, feet on the footboard." It seemed to me like perfect symmetry.

The next step, of course, was to locate the artist. In this case it proved remarkably easy. The magazine had credited him and mentioned that he lived in Los Angeles. And unless this artist, Ries Niemi, had an unpublished number, I had a feeling it wouldn't be too hard to ferret him out from the L.A. directory. After finding Ries, the more difficult hurdle would be convincing him that he wanted to make a bed.

"A bed?" repeated Ries when I got him on the phone. "Well, I've never made a bed, but I guess I could try."

I sent Ries one of my renowned sketches—crude but clear—and the process began.

Ries was a pleasure. He would constantly fax me with updates on his progress. One dispatch informed me that he was making the bed in parts so that I could, for instance, unscrew the footboard and take it off. Ries also faxed me that he had a collection of metal sheets from the 1950s that he wanted to incorporate into the faces to give them more texture and depth. I thought this was a wonderful idea, and told him to go ahead.

Then came our first stumbling block. Ries is

married to a warm and original woman, Sheila Klein, who is an artist herself. Sheila had said she didn't like the feet on the footboard, and Ries concurred. This posed a serious problem. I loved the feet on the footboard, but not wanting to contradict the strong feelings of the artist with whom I was working, I tried to think of what else would satisfy Ries and still make me happy.

As a cat lover I know that animals help create a space as much as the most beautiful piece of furniture or the most treasured painting. More so, in fact, because they bring life and movement and joy into one's home. The great artist Alberto Giacometti understood this. Confronted with the question, If your house were on fire and you could save only one of two things, a Rembrandt or a cat, which would it

In the master bedroom, a bed that's the ultimate in pillow talk.

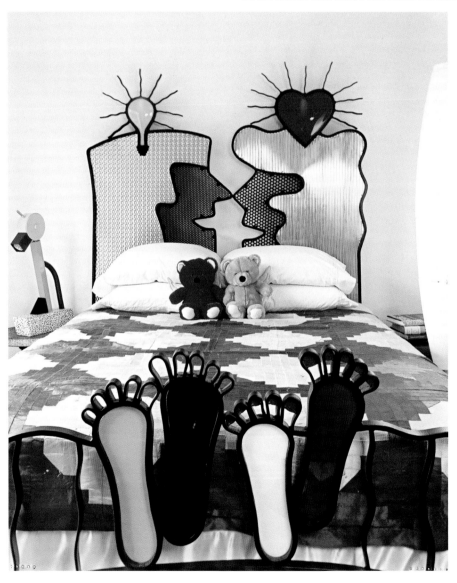

In Your Space: Personalizing Your Home and Office

be? Giacometti replied, without hesitation, "The cat."

As you probably suspected, I sleep with my cats, feeling like one giant feline battery that my smaller companions snuggle up against for warmth. So I faxed Ries a sketch with my cats on the footboard. Not wanting to discriminate, I had drawn all three. For the sake of the design, Ries narrowed them down to one.

I signed off on the drawing, and Ries went to work. Even when we were in foot mode, Ries and I had discussed filling in the metal outlines of the feet with Plexiglas. And so it was, too, in this instance. Ries cut a piece of Plexiglas to fit the shape of the cat, and even painted on it to create the illusion of tiger stripes.

After receiving Ries's photograph of the cat footboard, I gave him a call. "Ries, hi, it's Jenette. Your Nightmare Client from Hell. Uh, Ries. I know you prefer the cat, and you did a really good job, but well, you know, I'm just sort of tied to the feet. So I was wondering, since you made it possible to unscrew the footboard, could you make another one—I'll pay you, of course—with the feet? I hate to ask you to do this, but I know I'd be happier, and I could always interchange the footboards from time to time." I was groping to say something that would salvage Ries's work on the cat.

Ries sounded less than thrilled. But he agreed to make a second footboard with the feet. When I heard from him again, Ries had outdone himself. Along with a photo of the "new" footboard was a note. Ries had found a way to cut out the cat and replace it with the four feet of my original sketch. He sent me samples of Plexiglas as well, but they weren't quite what I had in mind. We agreed that on my next trip to L.A., we'd pick out the plastic together.

It happened that my designer friend Alex Locadia was with me in Los Angeles. Given his own passions, Alex was as eager to see the bed as I. We rode over to Ries and Sheila's for the official viewing. The bed was great, and everyone seemed to love it. But there was still the issue of the Plexiglas in the feet. I had always seen the two feet on the right as the woman's (and therefore asked Ries to paint nail polish on the toes) and the two feet on the left as the man's. Sheila looked at me and at Alex, who is African-American, and mistakenly assumed that we were romantically involved. "How about two white feet and two black feet?" she proposed.

Alex and I were taken aback. "Oh, no, no," we spluttered. "We're just friends." Sheila had made her suggestion in jest. But I heard in her joke the germ of a great idea.

"How about doing multiethnic feet—one black, one yellow, one pink, one brown?" I proposed. And that's what they came to be.

Back home in New York, I received a fax from Ries mentioning that he could also do tables and lighting. Lighting? I was inspired. I immediately sent Ries a sketch with a light bulb over the man's head in blown yellow plastic, and a blown red Plexiglas heart over the woman's. It was as though the man was saying, "I've got an idea," and the woman was responding, "Hmmm. Not bad."

Ries called. "I don't make blown Plexiglas lighting. I don't even know how." It was getting really easy to morph into the Nightmare Client from Hell. "Oh, gee, Ries, I'm sorry. I didn't realize that. I'll try to come up with something else, okay?"

"All right. All right. I'll see if I can figure out how to do it."

The bed finally arrived at Chill Hill. It had heads on the headboard and feet on the footboard, a yellow light bulb and a red heart that lit up above the man and the woman, and yellow, brown, pink, and black Plexiglas feet, which I started to call the United Feet of Benetton. It hadn't been easy getting there, but in the end it was everything I wished for.

Luscious Lips and a Bureau of Easy Virtue

Just as the wire hangers on one wall of the first floor related to the dozens of blue hangers opposite them in Sandy Skoglund's photograph, just as the color scheme I chose for Lloyd's ottomans and couch paralleled the one I selected for Lyn's Spaghetti lamp, it's amazing how much unconscious intelligence occurs without our even noticing. The media room was filled with motifs of industry, transportation, and technology. And in contrast to it in the bedroom, I was unknowingly assembling a room in total counterpoint—a room based not on the manufactured but on the organic, on the human body, on human interactions, and on implicit, very human sexuality. Most of these concepts, of course, were established by the room's largest piece of furniture, the bed. But while Ries was busy building it, I was acquiring other items that expressed different aspects of these themes. I bought every piece simply because I loved it—or so I thought. It was only when they were together in the same space that I realized how clearly they belonged together, and that the choices I believed to be totally spontaneous were anything but that.

Knowing how much I loved Nicola's work (see page 41)—Nicola of my giant yellow living room sofa in the shape of a woman—Jim Walrod had brought me to her studio so that she and I could meet. Nicola was generous and warm and full of joie de vivre. We spent a wonderful afternoon together, diverted only by my furtive glances to absorb whatever work of hers I could without stopping our conversation in its tracks. On one of these visual forays, I spotted Nicola's luscious red lip lamp, made in Paris in the late 1960s. It was an icon of the new pop sensibility permeating European design at that time, and I coveted it, not so much for its place in history but because, when lit, it was so utterly

yummy to look at. I tried not to detour, but I couldn't help myself. There had been twenty-five lip lamps in the original edition. Was this one of them? Was it available, or was it a piece Nicola had chosen to keep for herself?

But Nicola took my enthusiasm cheerfully in stride. This was the last lamp of the lot. Grace Jones had only recently bought the twenty-fourth, seeing in it a candy-apple reflection of her own signature lips. And, yes, Nicola would be willing to sell the last one. I was ecstatic, and now we shifted gears, actively walking around from place to place so that I could see not only the classics for which Nicola was known but also the new things on which she was currently working.

"You know, Jenette," Nicola interjected, "you should really buy the Woman bureau. It's a fabulous piece!"

Nicola was not exaggerating in saying this. The woman bureau, which, like the lip lamp, dated from the late 1960s, was more sculpture than furniture. Well over five feet high, it followed the contours of the female body from its head to the top of its thighs. It had nine drawers—for her nose, eyes, mouth, breasts, upper and lower stomachs, and pubis—and they all opened.

Although I concurred with Nicola that the bureau was fabulous, I explained that all my furniture was in color, and that the plain wood of the cabinet wouldn't work with everything else I owned.

"Wonderful!" shouted Nicola, who tends to speak in exclamation points. "I've always wanted to paint the bureau Yves Klein blue!"

Now, Yves Klein blue is not a color you will find in my beloved Pantone book, or on the innumerable charts that paint companies issue every season with names, like those for lipsticks, dreamed up for their subliminal allure. But anyone who knows contemporary art knows Yves Klein blue. Used like a trade-

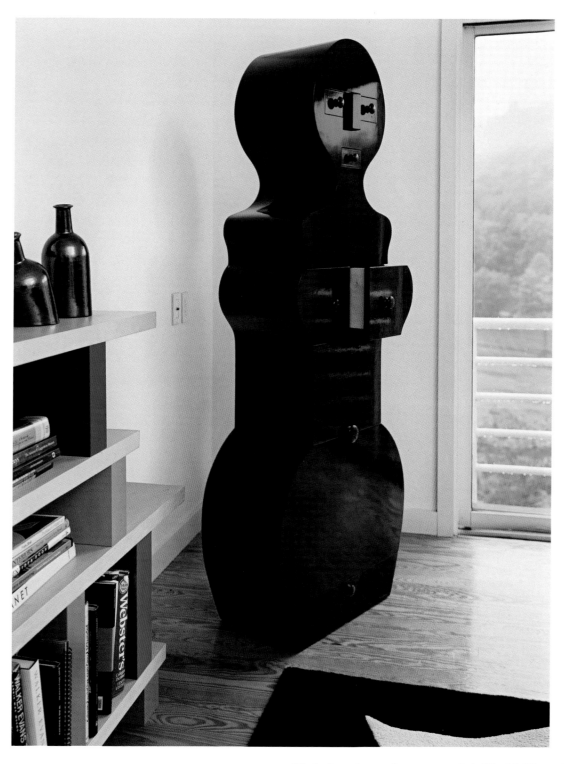

The bedroom's sexy themes resonate in Nicola's Woman bureau,
whose drawers open with ease.

The Second Story: Technology Themes and Sexy Dreams

mark by the famous French painter, it is a vibrant cobalt, as vivid as it is deep.

"Yves Klein blue?" I echoed. "I love Yves Klein blue! Oh, I can't imagine a better color for the bureau!" Clearly I was succumbing to the contagion of exclamation points.

So Nicola sent the bureau out to be painted, and seven coats of lacquer later it came back, showstoppingly beautiful.

"You know," Nicola added as we stood in the glow of the bureau's transformation, "when I made this piece, I named it 'La Femme Commode.'"

I recognize only about a hundred words of French, which I simply rearrange, but now I felt as though I'd been fluent for years. "Ah, yes. 'La Femme Commode!' The woman bureau!"

"Well, yes, of course, it does mean that," Nicola indulgently replied, eschewing the disdain that my pridefulness quite certainly deserved. "But it's a double entendre. 'La Femme Commode' means not just a woman bureau but also a woman of easy virtue. And she definitely is that because all of her drawers open so easily."

Live and learn.

A Bathrobe and Formal Wear

So now the space had a man and a woman snuggled together in bed, a woman of questionable modesty ready to open her drawers if not drop them, and a gleaming pair of firm but pliant lips. And these pieces were all in the bedroom. An accident? I had thought so at the time. But a one-step program in self-awareness would have taught me otherwise.

All the while, I was adding more human elements to the room. They weren't necessarily as explicitly sexual as the bed, the lamp, and the bureau, but at least two of them had a little of that fueled frisson. One was a picture by Jim Dine that I hung on a wall overlooking the bed. Jim Dine, like many artists, over the years visited and revisited a number of the same motifs: hearts, bathrobes, scissors, palettes. So it was not unusual that I would purchase one of his bathrobe images, especially since Dine had donated this particular print to help raise money for the 1991 Democratic presidential campaign and for liberal women candidates, both of which causes I supported. But now, taking it all in, I had to admit that a bathrobe was yet another variation on the bedroom theme, especially since it was titled **Bill Clinton**.

The second piece with an underlying charge was also a picture, this one a large, complex pastel by Randy Stevens, whose work I had discovered years before at Jill Kornblee's gallery on Fifty-seventh Street. Her art was witty and winsome even while it skewered our social lives. I had bought Randy's early work and later commissioned her to create a Wonder Woman and a Batman for my office. But then Jill Kornblee closed her gallery, and I no longer knew how to get in touch with Randy.

Now, as I was decorating the main house at Chill Hill, I was contacted out of the blue by the Newbury Fine Arts Gallery in Boston. It was representing Randy and about to mount a major exhibit of her work. Hoping to expand its client base to ensure the show's success, it was searching for people who had bought Randy's art in the past. It was in this spirit that the gallery sent a letter to inform me about the exhibit and to give me the opportunity to purchase Randy's work in advance. It also included three transparencies, and each picture was extraordinary. As much as I loved Randy's earlier art, she had traversed an incredible distance since I had seen it last. I pored over the images and finally decided that there was one I had to have.

The picture I chose shows a hip and flashy cocktail party filled with moneyed, self-satisfied people and posturing wannabes. A woman in a red-sequined strapless dress, her shoulders draped in ermine, enters with an escort, chattering with the entitlement of the rich and thin. A blond ingenue looks up, eager and expectant, hoping to win approval from the older man she's talking to. A young roué in a gold lamé jacket guzzles his drink while leaning against a wall hung with a generic abstract painting. Another young turk, sporting a sour expression and a trendy pink suit, hugs the perimeter of the party in affected disdain. Meanwhile other males join the fray, as eager as the ingenue, straining to dazzle with their intellect and wit, including several men of color who, suited and suave, have the look of foreign diplomats. It feels like a party on New York's self-conscious Upper East Side.

This work is at once exuberant and merciless. Despite the endless details over which one can linger forever, despite the robust flow of activity, Randy's scalpel is everywhere. It cuts through to the artificial smile, the too-familiar arm, the exaggerated boredom of someone who isn't fitting in. She dissects the human comedy with a breathtaking command of both its sweep and its particularity. And underneath the attitude and affectation, we realize that the picture is also about sex. Because one way or another, everyone at this party is trying to score.

From the Human to the Abstract and Back Again

Not everything in the bedroom had a sexual spin, and what did was lighthearted. And while we humans hogged the limelight, I added other elements simply because they were colorful and interesting, with appealing forms and lines. A small Miró rug from 1947 went on the floor. A lamp in the shape of a yellow cigar stood to one side of the bed. I had seen it in Barcelona in the fall of 1993 and had carried it on the plane back home. I had no idea who the designer or the manufacturer was, but I loved it. As with so much of European design, it was available only on the Continent, so I bought it and carted it through customs. The inconvenience and the import tax were worth it—anonymous or not, the light was terrific, and fit perfectly in my bedroom at Chill Hill. And while I tried not to get too carried away with myself, I did harbor a sneaking sense of personal satisfaction in having the only cigar lamp in America.

That lasted for about six months. Suddenly my favorite design stores were carrying the light and, worse yet, charging only two-thirds what I'd paid for it. Still, while my sense of self lost some of its luster, my light lost none of its sheen. In 1998 it was acquisitioned into the permanent design collection of the Museum of Modern Art, and several years later, when someone showed me an ad for it in **Wallpaper** magazine, I finally learned both who the artist and manufacturer were and even the official title of the lamp. It was called, appropriately, Havana. The light had been designed by Jozeph Forakis in the year that I bought it, 1993, and was still being manufactured by Foscarini. Maybe there was a sexual allusion here that I'd missed. Or maybe an antisexual allusion, because, as Winston Churchill said, "A woman is a woman, but a good cigar is a smoke."

Perhaps everything has a basis in nature. The Foscarini lamp looked like a cigar, the abstract pattern on the Miró rug had surreal shapes that one could easily call biomorphic, and the yellow Masanori Umeda chair I bought from Edra purposely resembled a flower, although it always seemed to me like the pulled-back peel of a banana.

Only the bookcase Lloyd built for the room appeared to lack organic antecedents. If it had any precedent at all, it was Early College Dorm. Remember those primitive shelving units we once made of

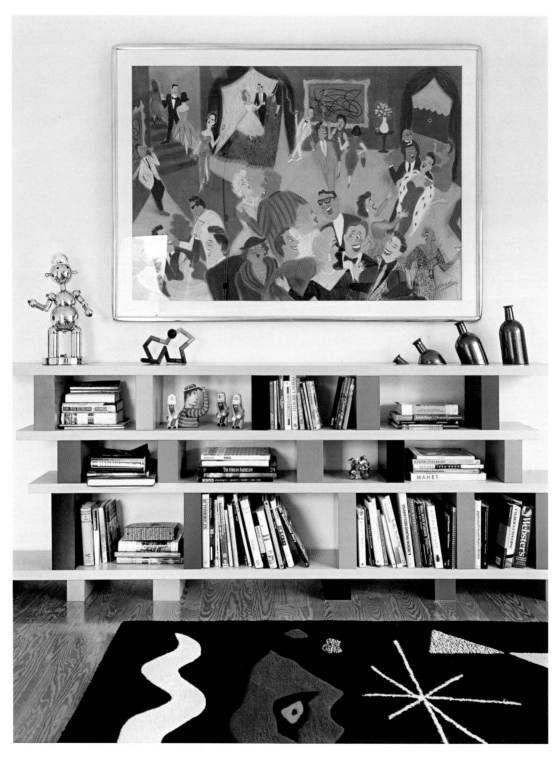

Beneath Randy Stevens's posturing party-goers are Lloyd Schwan's "cinderblock" bookcase and a vintage Miró rug.

In Your Space: Personalizing Your Home and Office

bare wood planks and cinder blocks? Well, this was very much the same idea, except that the planks were polished and polyurethaned, and the blocks were different widths of wood instead of the same-size concrete chunks. And they were painted, of course, in great colors. Lloyd and I had argued over the palette—his approach was too acid for my taste, mine too primary for his. But miraculously, we compromised, and both of us were happy.

Despite these few exceptions, the human element kept returning to the space. I bought a merry, bright, bold chair by Tom Miller, who had made the desk in my office and the telephone table beside it. As always, Tom had taken an old piece of furniture and revitalized it with vibrant colors and imagery. In reds and blacks and yellow, with a sunlit sky floating up the slats of the back, it immediately caught your eye. But it wasn't until you looked down that you laughed. Because there at the end of each leg was a folded sock and a glistening white buck, splayed outward with all the devil-may-care attitude of a man hanging out on the stoop. It was called "On the Sunny Side of the Street," and brought to mind the male conviviality of hot summer days, a gaggle of guys reclining on the steps, joking, jiving, and ogling the passers-by.

The final piece of furniture was a two-sided folding screen by Philippe Starck, made of pear wood, with elegant proportions. I was particularly interested in it because it had nine clear windows, where images could be placed between the glass. When the screen arrived, it came, to my surprise, with a packet of black-and-white photographs taken by Starck himself, including several self-portraits. I'm a fan of Starck's work, but I was not about to turn the screen into a designer shrine. I knew that when it came to choosing the art to place inside the windows, they would reflect my sensibilities, not his. And although I had often waited months, sometimes even

years, to find the exact right thing for the exact right spot, in this instance I was lucky. Because not long after the screen was installed in the bedroom at Chill Hill, I attended an auction at Christie's East.

The auction was a bit of a smorgasbord—a combination of comic-book art, animation cels, and art from **Mad** magazine. I had really dropped by for the fun of it, and didn't bother to register to bid. But as I turned the pages of the catalogue, I saw something I wanted—sixteen paintings of Alfred E. Neuman morphed into famous personas of history. They had been created for a set of stamps bound into **Mad** in the 1970s, and they were hilarious, graphic, and great. There was Alfred as Charlemagne, Alfred as Attila the Hun, Alfred as Toulouse-Lautrec, as Lincoln, as Hitler, as Tojo, as Wild Bill Hickock. Their dimensions were exactly right for the screen. Now I was in a quandary. The auction was in full swing, and it was too late for me to participate. But here, once more, I was fortunate; sitting near me was Scott Dunbier, a friend and comic-art dealer, and he had a plan.

"I know someone who's probably going to be the highest bidder on these," Scott confided. "But he's a dealer and is just going to turn around and resell them. I'll make sure that he sells them to you."

And that is exactly what Scott did. I purchased the Alfreds the next day and transported them to Chill Hill. From the sixteen pictures, I chose my nine favorites, and I had organized them in a pattern to go in the screen when suddenly, after an amazing run of good fortune, I hit what seemed an insurmountable roadblock. The portraits were painted on watercolor board, which was too thick to sandwich between the glass panels of the screen. The Alfreds were not going to work.

Dammit, dammit, dammit. But wait a second. I hadn't worked at DC Comics all these years not to have learned a trick or two. The halls of DC were lined with famous comic-book covers, documenting our rich and varied history. But the covers were neither original nor actual size. They were large color reproductions, and they looked great. I gathered up my Alfreds and brought them back to New York. A few phone calls later, and they were out being copied on quality lightweight paper, thin enough to fit in the windows of the screen and still leave sufficient space for pictures on the other side. And now I had those images too.

While Alfred E. Neuman's Skewed History of the World dominated one side of the Philippe Starck screen, a young black artist, Chuck Frazier, supplied a more serious chronicle on the other. Chuck came to me through one of DC's editors, Andy Helfer, who knew I was keenly interested in the pioneering achievements of African-Americans. Chuck wanted to document some of the most important contributors with a set of commemorative collectors' cards, for which he'd already completed the art. His portraits included scientists, educators, artists, and activists. And although he was no more than twenty-five when he made the pictures, they were beautiful and sophisticated collages of the highlights in his subjects' lives. Unfortunately, Chuck was unable to find a manufacturer for his cards. We were not in that business, but I fell in love with his artwork, and asked if I could buy some of the originals. Chuck agreed, and soon the second side of the screen, which often faced out as the first, was filled with mini-histories of some of our most outstanding Americans—Martin Luther King Jr. and Malcolm X, Paul Robeson, Eubie Blake, Katherine Dunham, Billie Holiday, Fats Waller, Duke Ellington.

The screen completed the anthropological themes of the space, from human comedy to human drama

Mad magazine's Alfred E. Neuman assumes different historic personas while enlivening a Philippe Starck screen.

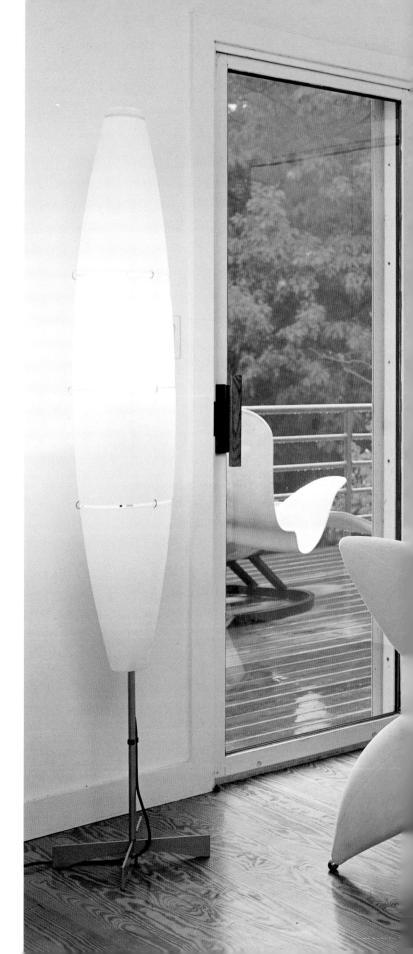

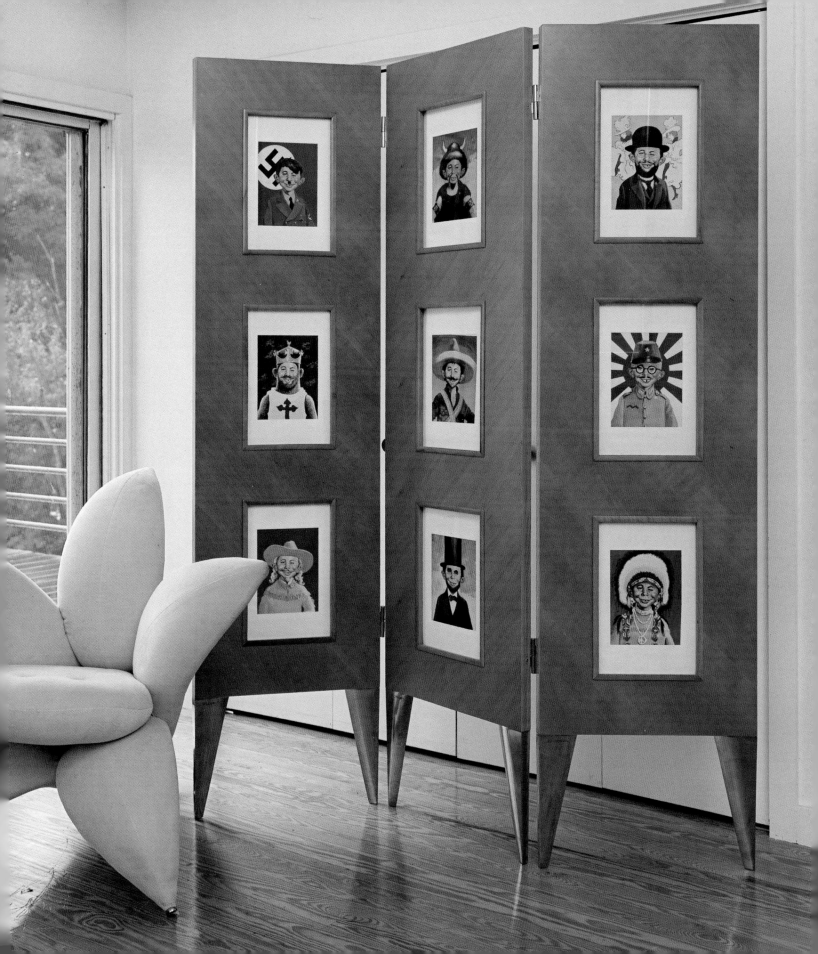

and everything in between. The bedroom objects touched on intimate sex and easy sex, on shallow upper-class mores, and on simple working-class repose, on history, psychology, and laughter. If the media room was about technology, the bedroom was about humanity.

Sink and Swim: The Bathroom

There was only one more thing I wanted on the second floor, a giant, sybaritic bath. Aside from the standard accoutrements—two sinks, storage cabinets, and a toilet—the sine qua non for me was a Jacuzzi big enough that I could turn this way and that, imagining summer or winter that I was, if not exactly swimming, then at least floating in a woodland pool. The location of the bathroom made this fantasy possible. It looked out on one side to the stair tower, but on the other directly toward a blur of hills so dense and deep

A 1960s AT&T seashell phone, the perfect bathroom convenience.

that they seemed to go on forever. I cut a large three-part window to gaze out from, a window different from all the others in the house. The central panel was fixed in place, but the other two opened to all angles to catch the breezes off the lake and trees. Even in the coldest months, it was possible to lie in the Jacuzzi totally surrounded by nature, the crisp

air coming in from the snow-topped hills, the steam rising from my tiny pool in the sky.

I also knew what colors I wanted in the room. The Jacuzzi would be seafoam green, surrounded by a wall of tiled cobalt blue. The sinks and toilet would be white, the floor black, the countertop yellow tile, and the walls leading to the high, peaked ceiling yellow and pink. Phil was about to paint the bathroom when his instincts recoiled in protest. He couldn't believe I wanted all seven colors in this single space. But when I assured him that I did, Phil returned to his labors, and the bathroom turned out just as I'd envisioned it.

The basics in place, I began to add other objects to make the room less ordinary, although Phil clearly believed I had overstepped that boundary long ago. One was Ron Arad's Bookworm, a flexible, plastic shelving unit that I curved over the window next to the sink and looped around the wall. A dark green, it added yet another color to the space. It was probably lucky that Phil wasn't there to see it installed. I filled the Bookworm with the kind of material you can easily dip into, because bathrooms, after all, are second only to libraries as valued reading rooms. I also added an incredible photograph by Neil Winokur that showed simply a full-frontal glass of

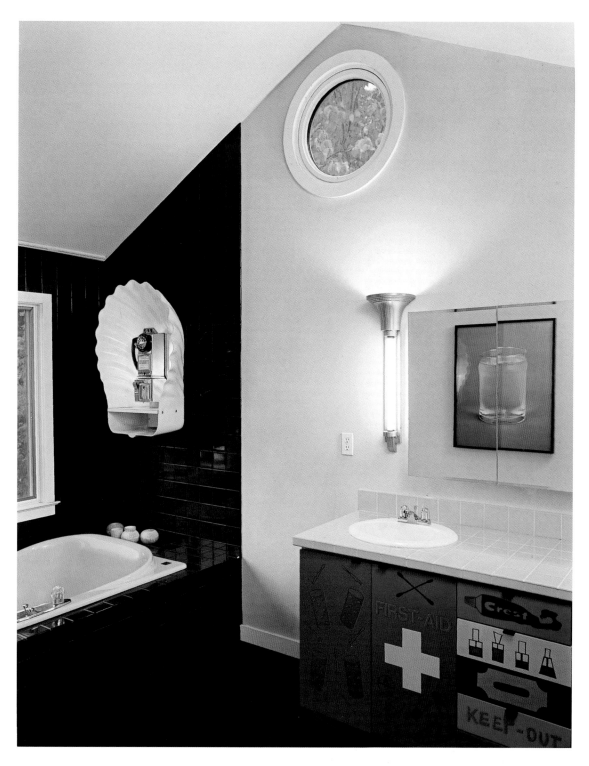

The master bath, with Lloyd Schwan's witty painted cabinets and
Neil Winokur's photograph mirrored in the glass.

The Second Story: Technology Themes and Sexy Dreams

water against a subdued blue field. The image did more than document an ordinary object. Unaltered and unmanipulated, it nonetheless transcended the glass's humble functionality and turned it into something more, something lyrical, something even poetic.

Finally, I added an object I saw in L.A.'s Off the Wall that I couldn't resist—a 1960s AT&T pay telephone fashioned from plastic. The area surrounding the phone was in the shape of a giant shell. On either side at the back of the black phone was a white translucent strip that hid four bulbs in sherbet colors—pink, lime, light blue, and tangerine. At night these colors danced through the shell, filling it with an otherworldly iridescence. The phones had been specifically designed for beach resorts like Atlantic City and Asbury Park. I couldn't imagine anything more ingenious, but they were a complete and total failure. This was a time when Superman still ran into the nearest phone booth, shut the door, and changed his clothes. In this day of cell phones, when hundreds of open-air conversations take place in a single city block, it is almost impossible to comprehend people's reaction to these seaside telephone stalls. But even beach bums stripped down to their bathing suits hated the lack of privacy. Like Superman, they wanted to go

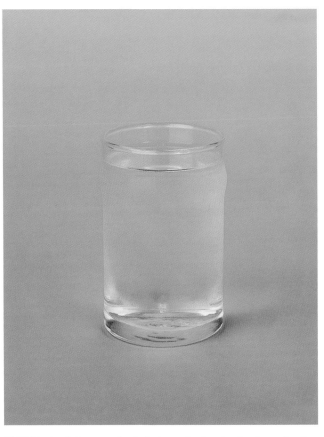

Neil Winokur's transcendent photograph of a simple glass of water.

into a phone booth and close the door, if not to change, then at least to talk where no one could hear what they said.

Failure or not, these phones were beautiful. I bought one, took it off its stand, and hung it on the cobalt tile wall overlooking the tub. Who needed candles by the Jacuzzi at night? The seashell phone cast its own radiance over the water, a magical moon of ethereal light.

So the bathroom was complete except for one thing. I had no idea what to do with the plain, unfinished wood cabinets and drawers below the yellow tile counter. One day, when was I voicing my dilemma, one of my guests offered a solution. "Cover it all with pale blue mirror," he said. "You know, the kind that was used a lot in Art Deco furniture and radios. The color will be soft and reflective and even reprise the Neil Winokur photograph."

"Great idea!" I concurred. Was it? I really didn't know. My eagerness to finish the cabinets short-circuited even the most elementary scrutiny.

When, after my guests had gone, Lloyd showed up, I told him of the plan. "It's a terrible idea!" he declared. "It's boring and uninteresting, and the glass will steam up from the Jacuzzi, and you'll constantly be cleaning it." I hated to admit it, but

In Your Space: Personalizing Your Home and Office

the blue mirrored glass **was** boring. I had been weak.

The next weekend, Lloyd was back at my house. "Okay, I have it," he announced, and opened his notebook to show me a sketch in which the doors and drawers were painted with different bathroom objects.

"When a guy's right, he's right," I cheerfully admitted.

Lloyd smiled. "Okay, let's get busy. What objects shall we use?"

So we came up with a first-aid kit and mouthwash and rollers and aspirin and a wig (a wig? I have no idea which of us ever thought of that or why). And we decided on used toothpaste tubes for one drawer, and a Keep Out sign for another, and Kilroy for a third. Lloyd painted the panels in his Brooklyn studio in those amazing colors of his and brought them up and installed them. Nothing, nothing, could have been better.

The bathroom was complete, and so, more or less, was Chill Hill. But as everyone knows, you're never ever really done, and thankfully things always change over time. How else would life stay interesting?

Lessons Learned Along the Way

1. Collecting for sheer pleasure is a wonderful occupation as long as you can afford what you buy and have the space to store it. With no place to showcase them, I've still bought innumerable objects I've loved. They've sat in darkness for years until, suddenly, the perfect spot presents itself. The 1930s and 1940s ceramic masks I'd found in England crowded a carton until I realized I could use them in designing the country fireplace. The silent butlers wordlessly occupied a storage bin until I imagined them marching up the stairs at Chill Hill. It's great to have collections at hand for the moment you might need them. But there will probably be some things you've purchased that will gather dust forever. Of course, it's possible to divest yourself of them. But doing so takes a certain kind of energy that, like me, you may never muster.

2. The world has become a global community. Why shouldn't décor be international, too? So when buying decorating magazines, don't confine yourself simply to American ones. England, France, Italy, Australia—they all have interesting publications that can be found domestically at any top-flight newsstand. Even if you don't understand the language, the pictures in decorating magazines are expressive. If you want to order from abroad but can't decode the words, find a friend who can. Too many fabulous things made in other countries are never shown here. Why miss out on them?

3. No matter what ideas you've come up with, no matter how in love with them you are, be prepared to alter them during the course of installing a project. It's impossible in conception to anticipate exactly how something is going to look. You have to execute. And when you do, there will usually be surprises. Sometimes you need to add something, sometimes subtract. And sometimes you have to discard your most cherished notion in favor of the larger effect.

4. There is a fine line between commissions and collaborations. When you choose an artist to make something you've conceived, it's because you respect his work. So there is a natural tendency, especially if the two of you are friends, to want to include his ideas. This, however, is slippery ground. In an effort to be collaborative, to have a genuine give-and-take, you might lose sight of the end results you really want. If the artist's suggestions improve upon yours, accept them with pleasure. But don't be afraid to say no. You can be gracious and respectful, but ultimately you are the client.

9.

My Harlem Renaissance:

Buying and Decorating a Landmark House

Outside my house on Strivers Row on
a beautiful summer's day.

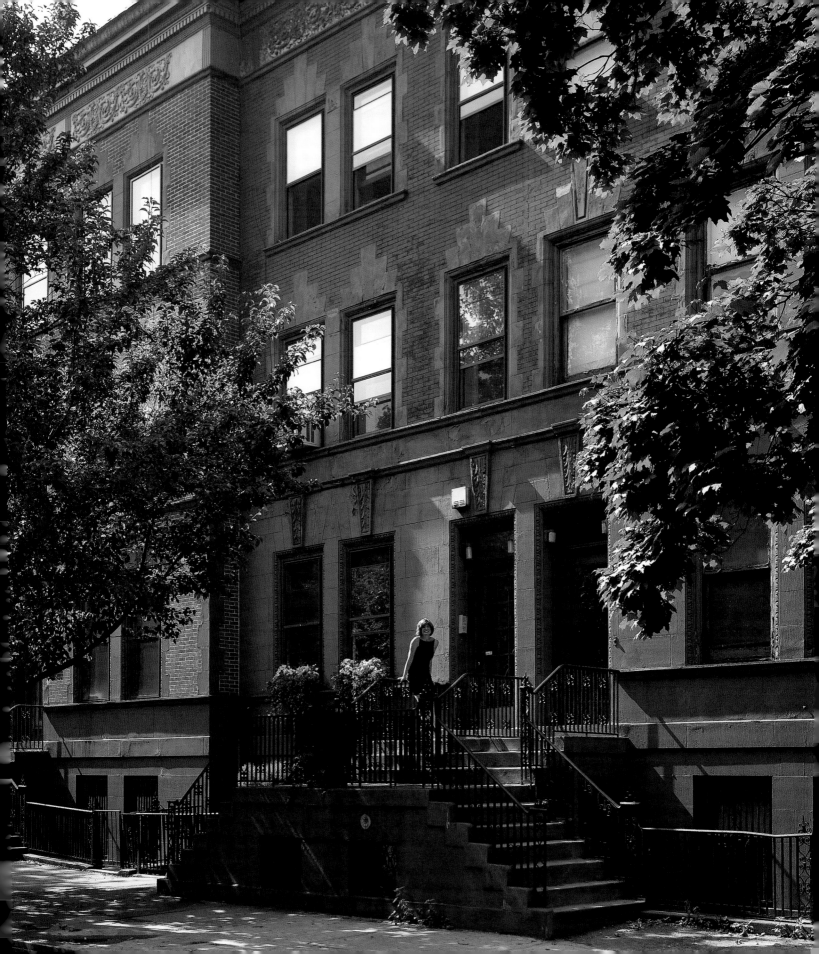

I was only twenty-five when I moved into the Century. Years had gone by, and I was still there. The apartment had endured my stumbling amateur efforts at decor and finally settled into my newer, more accomplished ones. I too had changed, and although my residency may have spanned only two decades, I felt as though I had lived several lifetimes at 25 Central Park West.

Still, I was not eager to leave. The Century was as comfortable and familiar as Archie Bunker's armchair. Everything was footsteps away, from the grocery store and drugstore in the building—both of which delivered—to the movie house around the corner, which showed the best of foreign films. Lincoln Center, home to opera, ballet, music, and theater, was two blocks behind the building. And it was only eight minutes to my office and twenty minutes to Madison Square Garden, home of the New York Knicks.

Time to Go

If I thought of moving at all, it was always to a larger apartment in the Century, preferably opening onto the front and the majestic views of Central Park. But I was in no hurry—2A was home, and there seemed no reason to leave the womb. Friends often wondered that I didn't seem to care about more space. After all, I was an inveterate collector, with more objects than most. And my apartment, the apartment of my youth, was small by adult standards. But when I finally made the decision to move, I realized I'd outgrown the comforts of the Century. I was ready for a new neighborhood, and if I didn't kick myself out of the nest, who would?

So I began looking the old-fashioned way, letting my fingers do the walking through the **New York Times** classifieds. I selected SoHo and TriBeCa because, despite the flight of galleries to Chelsea, they were still major centers for art. But long before my fingers caved, my spirits did. For the kind of space I wanted, anything downtown was financially prohibitive. I made an executive decision. If not downtown, then uptown, across 110th Street, Harlem.

The chorus from my friends, male and female, black and white, was unanimous.

"Jenette, this is the worst idea you've ever had."

"Yeah, tall white woman, short skirts, long legs. . . . I don't think so."

In 1996, the year of my search, Harlem in the minds of most people was still a taboo community. Even young black professionals who had money enough to choose where they lived tended to opt for more affluent neighborhoods with better schools and services. Perhaps I was naïve, but in those days I believed that Harlem was the best-kept real estate secret in New York, and anything was possible.

"No, Harlem it is," I declared. And to the naysayers I simply replied, "Don't worry, I'll be cool."

Since my twenties, I had known there were beautiful buildings in Harlem. Glancing through "Best Bets" in **New York** magazine, I had stopped to read about a Columbia student-turned-taxi-driver. A passionate lover of New York history, he knew not just the highways and byways but the nooks and crannies, the grottoes, the colorful but little-known enclaves, the neighborhood folk murals, the visionary efforts in community living. You could hire him and his van, fill it with friends, and cruise Manhattan, the Bronx, Queens, and Brooklyn with his informed and unabashedly biased commentary enlivening all you saw. For someone who had never been to Brooklyn or the Bronx, and had been to Queens only to go to an airport, this was an opportunity not to be missed. I dialed the number and booked a tour.

On the appointed morning, we all gathered at my apartment at the Century. Soon Jerry, if I remember his name correctly, pulled up in his van and we piled in. He crossed one of the park transverses to the East Side, and we began to head uptown to our first stop, Harlem, and two blocks known as Strivers Row. The streets were lined with attached houses, classically proportioned, the work of three different and important architectural firms. Even McKim, Mead and White, where the legendary Stanford White plied his trade, came on board, designing the north length of 139th Street. Just peering from the windows of the van was a revelation. I never forgot those blocks, and as the years went by, I learned there were others just as beautiful.

The Six-Month Search

So it was that with great confidence I began my search in Harlem for a place to live. I found Lana Turner, a preservationist and Harlem-based real

Looking through the middle parlor to a deconstructed Greek temple beneath Ingo Maurer's lamp of paper notes.

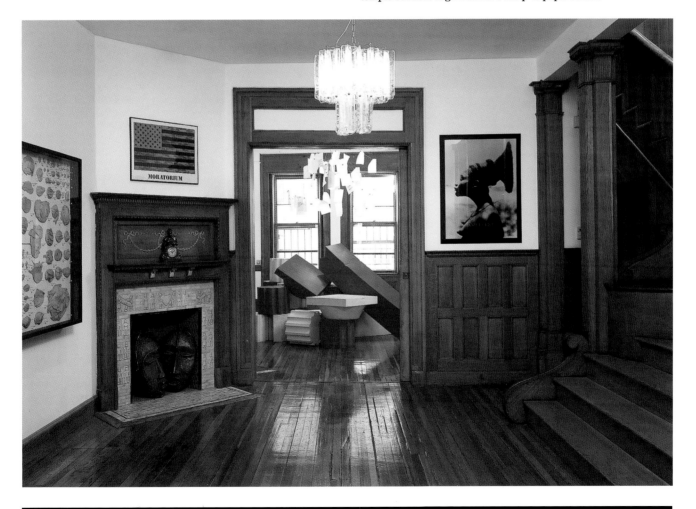

estate agent, and began looking at homes in one of the city's most remarkable landmark areas, Hamilton Terrace. My interest was first snagged by a magnificent corner building on Convent Avenue. It had been used for years as a City College fraternity house, and was in ruinous shape. But the architecture was stunning, and I felt sure that what had once been a one-family mansion could be rescued and restored.

Ah, the folly of neophytes and dreamers! The interior of the house had been utterly destroyed, the space carved up into as many rooms as possible, the original detail stripped and scrapped. My calculations estimated that buying the house and renovating it would exceed a million dollars—far more than I had. I was forced to abandon my first choice.

It was through Lana that I found my second possibility, a brownstone just three blocks down the street from the fraternity house. The building was owned by a lovely woman who was getting married and moving in with her fiancé. It had four floors and, although somewhat dark, was rich in beautiful detail, including the original separate dressing rooms for husband and wife. After several visits with artist friends and an architect, I felt I could make the house work. Not long after, I submitted an opening offer that was just 10 percent less than the asking price. The owner said she wanted to confer with her fiancé, and I expected a counteroffer in the next few days.

Nothing, however, could have prepared me for her response. My offer, she said to Lana, was far too low; she would not even enter into a discussion unless I raised my price. On principle, I refused to budge, and so did she. It was my second disappointment. But I had now toured many blocks in Harlem and seen truly beautiful homes; I was certain I would find the right one.

Only a day later another broker, Willie Suggs, phoned my office to say that she had several great exclusives in which I might be interested. Her timing was impeccable; the negotiations for the house on Convent Avenue had just fallen through. I told Willie I'd love to see the houses she was agenting (if Willie had exclusives, then Lana wasn't able to take me through them), but that I was leaving for Senegal in two days. The only time I could look at anything was that evening after work. Willie must have gone into hyperdrive, because by that afternoon she'd arranged to show me three homes.

I met Willie at the appointed time and we took, as everyone in Harlem does, a gypsy cab—yellow cabs were as scarce then in the community as all other customary services—to Jumel Terrace, a landmarked block on 162nd Street with buildings on one side and a park on the other. The house we saw was charming but small. I toured it quickly, and only out of courtesy, because I knew right away it was not for me. Harlem begins at 110th Street, but Jumel Terrace was fifty-two blocks beyond that, and 108 blocks from my midtown office. SoHo and Tribeca seemed like the other end of the world.

Another negative was the seeming lack of a neighborhood. While I'm sure the homeowners knew one another, the single side of one short block didn't really make a community. Although I had first come to Harlem simply to buy a wonderful house, my view had greatly expanded in the six months since. The best parts of Harlem, I quickly saw, were neighborhoods. People said good morning and good afternoon even to strangers, and if they actually recognized you, they would stop to chat. This was a phenomenon quite rare in a city where people tend to minimize contact even with residents of apartments down the hall.

"Don't worry," Willie replied when I expressed my concerns. "The next house is on Hamilton Terrace."

Hamilton Terrace? Good. I'd looked on Hamilton Terrace and loved it. And the residents on the terrace,

In Your Space: Personalizing Your Home and Office

along with those one block up on Convent, were a community. They had an enormously active neighborhood association, and for some time had been mounting an annual and lucrative house tour, with the proceeds going to improve the area even more.

But what a house! It may have had beautiful bones and original detail—I'll never know. The walls were covered with pebbly stucco that, although it could have been changed back to smooth plaster, made the interior look tacky and cheap. I'm amazed that I even noticed it, anyway; nearly every inch of space was crowded with knicknacks, pictures, mirrors, and photographs.

I had seen enough. I wanted to bolt, tour the next house, and go home.

And Then, the Perfect House

The third building—an attached house on 138th Street between Seventh and Eighth Avenues, or what are now known as Adam Clayton Powell Jr. and Frederick Douglass Boulevards—looked modest from the outside. The façade, brownstone and brick in a subdued Georgian style, dimmed next to the more ornate façades on Hamilton Terrace and Convent Avenue. But the moment I stepped into the house, my jaw dropped in wonder. Cascading through the middle parlor was a central staircase of quartersawn oak that started with the discipline and restraint of the Arts and Crafts movement but ended in a baroque flourish.

Central staircases are rare in brownstones. They take up more space than those stacked routinely on the side of a house and tend to make the room into which they flow less functional. But there is no denying their grandeur, especially when executed with the panache of this one. They also allow for beautifully proportioned rooms on the entrance floor; all the more so in this house, as it was a gen-

erous twenty feet wide. The width of the building, the harmonious proportions of the rooms, and the grand, flowing steps were the first things I saw. I was trying to be cautious, knowing there were three more floors to view. But at that moment I thought I had found the perfect house for me.

One man or woman's decor is another's nightmare. While the current owners had done a lot of work in their home, particularly in the kitchen and the master bath, for me it was aesthetically challenged. Fireplaces had been painted over and glass protectors fixed to the tile with concrete. Floor-to-ceiling closets had been added in the master bedroom, dwarfing the central fireplace and obliterating its function as the architectural focus of the room. A wall had been knocked down between two smaller rooms in the back to create an enormous nursery, but the new L-shaped room undermined the integrity of the original design, and the heavy support beam that remained when the wall was gone had the visual threat of a massive guillotine. And on it went. The kitchen was functional but totally brown—the floor, the wainscoting, the oak cabinets, the refrigerator, the tiles, the ovens, all oppressively brown. Perhaps to some it was wonderful, the perfect embodiment of masculine stolidity, but to me it was simply brown, brown and deadly.

On the other hand, minus the built-in closets, the master bedroom was a beautiful space. And although the fireplace needed a lot of work, there it was, a fireplace in the bedroom. Now how cool is that? Like the main bedroom, the room right above it was beautiful, too, with high ceilings and three large windows facing front. The kitchen may have been locked in a brown study, but it was also enormous; you could imagine anything from huge family dinners to an industrial cooking arena suitable for a medium-size restaurant. By actual count, the house had a total of six working fireplaces and a

My Harlem Renaissance: Buying and Decorating a Landmark House

possible seventh, if the kitchen hearth, which once had housed the original coal stove, was converted. Behind the kitchen, where first there had been a stable and then a garage, was a small open space surrounded by walls of painted cinder blocks. It looked like a prison exercise yard, but with time and imagination it could be turned into an intimate garden. And after looking in Harlem for six months, here I was again on Strivers Row, the first landmark section I'd toured uptown so many years before.

The decision was easy. So what if the house needed work? Transforming it would be part of the fun, even if doing so would suck up my cash flow for more years than I dared to consider. By noon the next day I had made an offer, and thirty-six hours after that I was on a plane to Africa.

If this house had been in almost any part of New York other than Harlem, it would have been worth between $2 and $3 million. But the public perception of Harlem was that it was drug-ridden, dangerous, and very, very black. In truth, Harlem is not only African-American but also Hispanic and West African. You can hear Spanish spoken in the streets and French as well. Yes, there are areas that are home to the drug trade, with its inevitable crime. But Harlem dwellers know where these are and, if they have a choice, live elsewhere. All in all, Harlem is not so much dangerous as it is poor. It is part of New York that until recently has been written off. White people seldom cross 110th Street, and neither does white money.

Before making my offer, I checked the sale prices of homes in the area. One building on Hamilton Terrace had sold for a good sum, although less than what the seller was asking for the Strivers Row house. And, in the instance of the home on Hamilton

Stately windows in the front parlor are suffused with the branches of a flowering tree.

180

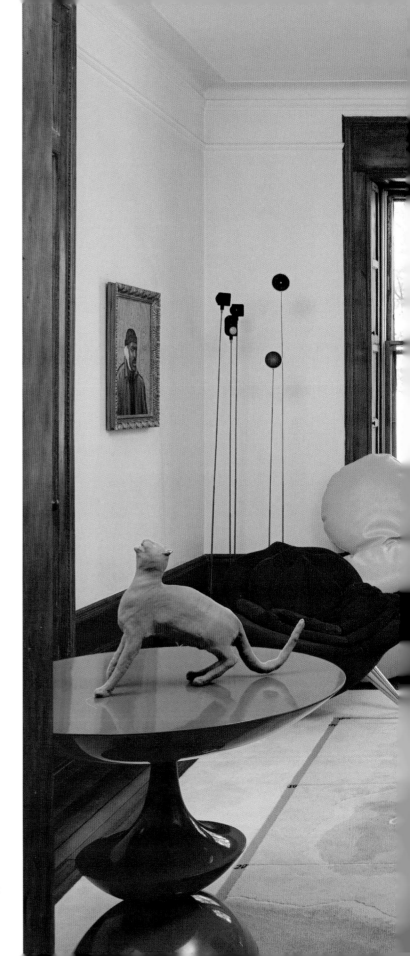

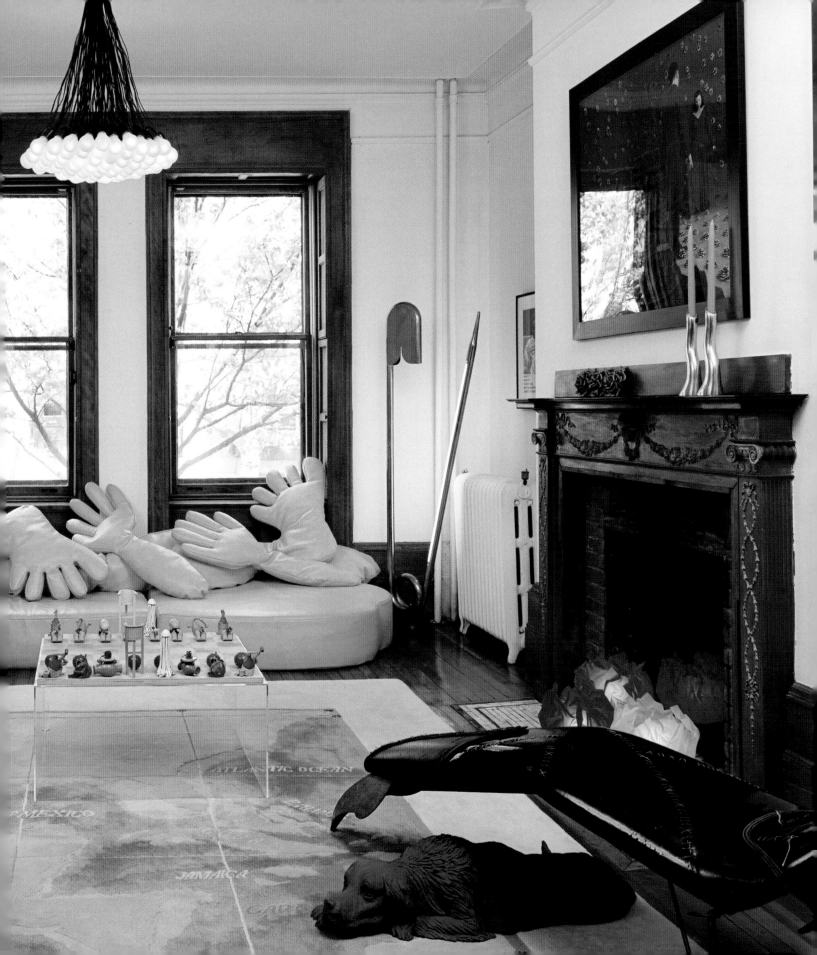

Terrace, I was told that the owner, as a point of pride, had wanted to set a record for Harlem. As such he was willing to wait a year to get his price, and it did indeed take that long for him to find a buyer. Only one residence on Strivers Row had sold for anything in a similar range, and it was hardly close. The owner and I were at odds, with Willie Suggs the go-between on our positions. She interpreted them and, I'm sure, defused them, so that neither of us became so outraged that we walked away from the table. Despite Willie's efforts at diplomacy, there were times when I was determined to toss in the towel, and others when the owner felt the same way. But Willie prevailed. I came to admire her statesmanship, and to this day believe that the sale would never have taken place were it not for her.

We finally agreed on a price sometime in July. But like the negotiation, the closing was difficult. It wasn't until December 23 that we sat down in the office of a mortgage bank and signed the numerous documents and checks that ultimately guaranteed the house was mine. My apartment was already packed, its contents loaded on trucks. I raced up to 138th Street to meet the owners only to find that they had not yet left. Countless men were marching up and down stairs, transporting their items, while my movers stood, nonplussed, in the road, wondering what in the world they were supposed to do. As night fell, the owners' movers finally quit, but just for the day. They would be back first thing the next morning to continue their labors, working until, mercifully, it was Christmas Eve.

Home at Last

Despite the frantic overlap of two sets of packing crates and two sets of movers working simultaneously, I somehow managed to settle into the bedroom on the night of the closing, putting fresh sheets on the mattress where my bed had been placed. It was the only oasis in a sea of brown cardboard. I opened a number of boxes looking for blankets, but the task was overwhelming and ultimately thankless. Luckily, although it was past midnight, there were a few minutes left before the phone line was disconnected. I called Craig Harris, one of my closest friends, who had been living in Harlem for years.

"Hey, J., how's the house?"

"I love it, Aq, I really do. I'm surrounded by boxes, the people I bought it from are still moving out, the place is a mess, but I love it."

"Well, nothing wrong with that."

"Yep. The only trouble is, I can't find my blankets. I've found sheets and pillows, but who knows where the blankets are."

"Well, let's see. I'm on 128th, ten blocks away. All right, J., I'll come on over there and bring you some stuff."

Not long after, Craig was at my house. His arms were overflowing, not just with a large down quilt but also with sheets and pillowcases just in case I had minimized my distress. The doorbell sounded with a ring so shrill I felt I should be sliding down a firehouse pole. One-thirty a.m., December 24th and I had my first visitor! I took the stairs as fast as I could, fumbled with the locks, and let Craig in.

"Thanks, Aq. I really appreciate it. And, hey, thanks for these," I added, turning toward the mound of bedcovers he'd brought me. "Just in the nick of time, too. The phone was turned off right after we spoke."

"I'm glad to do it, J. And I brought you something else. Now don't panic. I'm not going to light it in your room. I know how you don't like the smell. But you can't move into a new house without bringing some good spirits, too." And with that he took out a stick of incense, stuck it in a space between the wall and the recessed pocket door, and lit it, wishing me only happiness in my new home.

It is what I have felt ever since.

Which Would You Rather Have? A Great Contractor or a Husband?

The fact that my new home needed work was not a problem. I was eager to take it on and put my stamp on it. In attacking the renovations, I had two major factors in my favor. The first was a limited amount of money. This meant that I could not change the house all at once, even if I wanted to. Improvements could only be made a little at a time and, considering the size of the building, over a period of years. By living patiently in the house, I learned by heart the dimensions and the proportions of the rooms, the quality of light and where it fell, the rhythms of the space in relation to my own, the history secreted in details that had been added over time or stripped away. With the pace of the work slowed by my circumscribed assets, it was hard to make hasty decisions. I still made decisions I felt were wrong. But I seldom made rash ones.

My contractor was the other essential factor in realizing my vision of the house. I can't say that I found him—he came to me seemingly by accident—but I couldn't have hoped for anyone better. It started when I began to prepare my apartment for sale. To show it to best advantage, I wanted to repair the cracks and chips where water damage had taken its toll around the seventy-year-old window frames, to plaster and, where necessary, add a fresh coat of paint. Most importantly, I wanted to fix the mare's nest of wires that protruded from a twelve-by-twelve-inch square high on the kitchen wall, where a workman had tried to sort out the electrical nightmare that was my apartment. Some years back, when my former husband and I remodeled,

our contractor had convinced us to upgrade the wiring. But something was seriously wrong.

Several months after our designer Claudio's departure, I was using the hair dryer when the lights blew out in most of the house. I tried to think if anything was different from usual. Checking off the list, I realized that one of the window air conditioners was on. I switched it off, played with the circuit breakers, and once more everything was fine. A few weeks passed, and the same thing happened again—but this time the air conditioner was off. I searched the apartment for the variable. This time it was the toaster. It happened again when the TV was on, when the stereo was on, when more than a certain number of lights were on. As a defense mechanism I'd roam the apartment, turning off lamps and appliances, before daring to dry my hair.

Finally I asked my friend Lloyd Schwan if he knew someone who might fix the wiring. He suggested his friend David, who, I hoped, could analyze and solve the problem. And David did indeed find its source. Despite the elaborate circuit-breaker box with its many rows of switches, it turned out that everything in the bathroom, the bedroom, the kitchen, and the hall was on the same breaker. It was David who cut the hole in the kitchen wall so that he could begin to distribute the current evenly. The hole revealed a skein of tangled wires that seemed to lead everywhere and nowhere at once. As David tried to make sense of the fiasco, the building manager called me to task. I was to cease and desist all work until I indemnified the Century for every conceivable disaster.

The list was overwhelming. I dug a hole in the sand and put my head in as far as it would go. Only when someone visited, like my brother, would I be reminded of the potential danger.

"Jesus, Nets," Si would say, looking up at the raw hole, still gaping like an open wound. "You ought to get that fixed. That's a minefield in there."

And I would try to explain that I had tried to fix it, but . . .

Yet when it came time to sell the apartment, my conscience pricked me once more into action. It was one thing for me to live with a potential electrical storm, quite another to inflict it on somebody else. I had already asked Justen Ladda, an artist and friend, if he would help get the apartment into shape. He was ready to plaster and paint when I asked if he could fix the wiring as well. After spending hours trying to trace one colored strand, then another, Justen threw up his hands in despair. He tried to find a seasoned electrician, but was frustrated at every turn.

"Jenette, this is it. I can think of only one other person. He's my last resort. If he can't do it, well, I'm out of ideas."

Justen suggested Al Williams, a fellow artist. He convinced Al to meet him at my apartment one morning after I'd gone to work. It's all right, I thought, sitting in my office as the clock on my phone registered past twelve and Justen hadn't called. Al must have shown up. But just as I was sinking into this comfortable equanimity, the telephone rang. "Jenette, I am totally beside myself." It was Justen on the brink of despair, torn between killing himself or someone else. "So Al shows up at the apartment, and I show him the hole and the circuit-breaker box, and I say maybe we can fix it if we run some wires over the kitchen ceiling. And Al looks at it and says maybe we won't have to and leaves. He leaves! Just like that." But the next day, to Justen's surprise and mine, Al was back.

A week or so went by, and I was late for work. From somewhere in the apartment I heard a key turn in the lock, and a man I presumed to be Al walked in. He was carrying a battered leather briefcase (which hid his tools from the hawk eyes of the building manager) and wore a rumpled sport coat, a light blue denim shirt, and a tie. I would

have taken him more for a professor than an artist, and even less for a person with a talent for solving electrical bad dreams.

He seemed embarrassed that I was still at home, and I felt equally ill at ease, as though I had imposed upon his private space. Nonetheless, we began to talk, and soon we had established a comfort zone. I marveled at his work—smooth and clean, with no wires on the kitchen ceiling. In the course of conversation, I learned that Al was not only a sculptor but an internationally ranked chess master. Suddenly I understood what had happened the day that Justen had placed his frantic call, when Al had come to the apartment, said just a few words, and left. He had studied the components just as he would the pieces on a chessboard. Then he retreated to consider them, coming back only when he had an elegant solution.

I realized then that whatever house in Harlem I bought, Al would be the one to renovate it. He had the aesthetics of an artist, the refined problem-solving abilities of a chess master, and the mad skills of a contractor. In addition, he had fair prices and integrity. What more could I want? So immediately after Christmas, when I'd been in the house just two days, Al came over to inspect it. There was so much to do it was hard to know where to begin. But I wanted to have a housewarming party for everyone who helped me get the house, my new neighbors, and my old friends. After consulting Al, I set the date for February 18. We felt we could at least get the parlor floor in shape for the onslaught of guests. With this incentive in mind, we started work.

Fifty-four Days. What Can You Possibly Get Done?

Actually, it's possible to accomplish a lot more than you would think. It's amazing what a deadline will

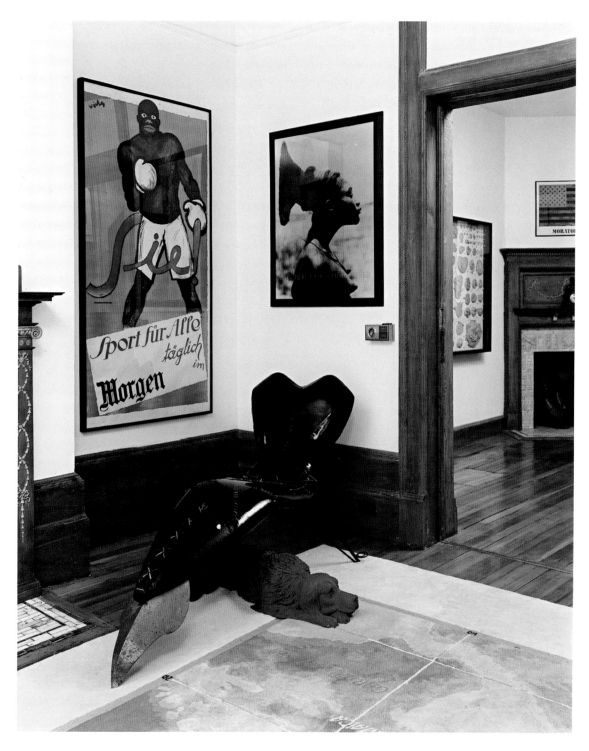

In one corner, a boxer promotes the morning paper,
while Sandy Skoglund's purple dog lazes under Alex Locadia's
Catwoman chaise.

My Harlem Renaissance: Buying and Decorating a Landmark House

do. The first things we attacked were the surfaces. Sometime in the 1920s decorative moldings had been added to the walls throughout the parlor rooms, in a bid to make the house more impressive. To me the moldings were an outdated idea of elegance, chopping up the space and undermining the classic bones of the interior architecture. In addition, they allowed only small pictures to be hung, imposing a daintiness as old-fashioned as your grandmother's antimacassars. Clearly the moldings would have to come off, and the walls, now yellowed with age, replastered and painted. The middle parlor was missing the baseboard on one wall, but Al found oak to match and laid it in. As I walked through the three connected parlors, I could hear the thin floors splintering underfoot, but replacing them would be a task for another day.

Other floors, however, required more immediate attention. Streaming down the majestic central stair was a ribbon of burgundy carpet. The previous owner had confided that it was very expensive and suggested that I keep it in place, but the stairs were too beautiful to hide. We pulled the carpet up and saw not only that the wood had never been refinished, but also that the carpeting had been held in place by nails, leaving a line of holes on every step that we could do nothing about. It seemed particularly unfortunate; there are so many ways to attach a runner without marring the wood below. For weeks I obsessed about these pockmarks, just as a teenager sees nothing but the pimples on his face. But Al brought in Henderson Greene, with whom he'd worked many times before, to sand and polish the stairs and cover them with a light coat of polyurethane. It was only then, when they shone with a dazzling beauty, that I could overlook their scars.

Needless to say, we didn't stop at the stairs. Wherever there was carpeting, we pulled it up, and Al restored the floors. With each newly renovated area my exhilaration mounted, almost as though I was on an archaeological dig retrieving treasures long buried by time and neglect. The original house, with its strong, clear lines, its wide plank floors, and its clean proportions, was beginning to emerge.

Old Contents and New Acquisitions

The next task was to arrange the furniture I'd brought from the Century. Amazingly, much of it worked. The front parlor easily accommodated Jody Harrow's map rug, Nicola's yellow vinyl sofa, the Takis signal-light lamps, and Yonel Lebovici's safety-pin lamp. The Nana Dietzel orange fiberglass table and Alex Locadia's Catwoman chaise looked equally at home in the room.

With the decorative moldings gone, there was room for art. Just as in the Century, I stacked Sandy Skoglund's **Revenge of the Goldfish** and **Germs Are Everywhere** on a wall beside the orange table. A goldfish still swam expectantly outside the top photograph, hung by an almost invisible plastic thread. The radioactive cat still paced the tabletop, its eyes only on the fish. And the heavy-lidded dog still gazed up at the cat from his position of safety beneath the Catwoman chaise. I had a Romare Bearden in the Century, a silkscreen of his collage **The Piano Lesson**, which supposedly inspired August Wilson's play of the same name. Now I placed it perpendicular to the fish and the germs, on a wall that at night, with the house alight, could be seen from the street.

A Rose Is a Rose Is a Rose

I made two related acquisitions that became part of the living room decor. One was a red velvet chair in the shape of a rose by the Japanese designer Masanori Umeda. The other was a new Sandy Skoglund photograph, **The Wedding**, which I hung above the

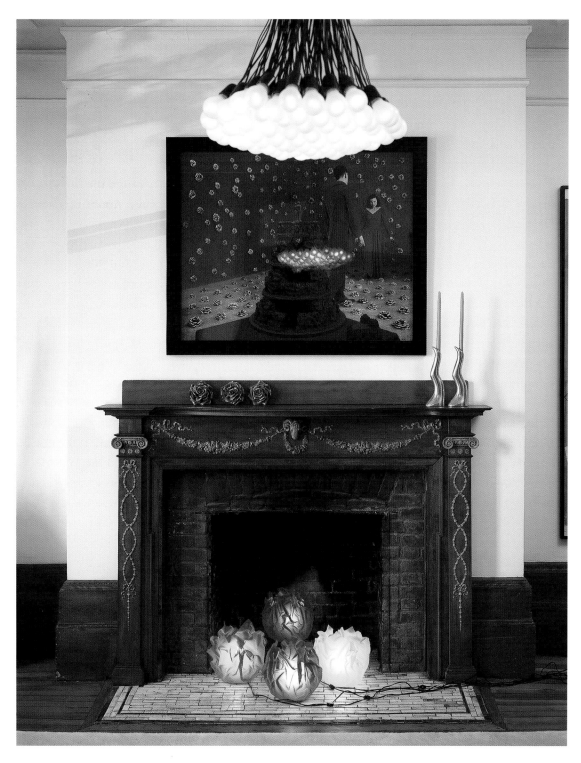

Sandy Skoglund's rose-covered photograph creates a glow above
the mantel as warm as the Godley-Schwan lights below.

My Harlem Renaissance: Buying and Decorating a Landmark House

fireplace. In the center of the picture is an elaborate wedding cake saturated in deep crimson. The bride-groom is dressed in the same color, as is the bride, who gingerly tries to step across the golden, viscous floor, which is smeared with orange marmalade. A coat of strawberry jam creates the glistening red walls. Sculpted roses dot the surfaces, forming a two-dimensional pattern that defies the depth of the interior.

Like so many of Sandy's photographs, this one is deceptively seductive. It is easy to dismiss the image as ingratiating, if a little skewed, with its roses, Technicolor hues, and towering wedding cake. But this is no marriage out of **Modern Bride**. We realize the bride, her step slowed by the thick, moist floor as tacky as tar on a hot summer's day, may never make it to the groom. The overripe, blood-red color of her costume, the groom's suit, and the cake suggest that the picture-book dreams of weddings may already have turned, their cloying expectations only an obstacle to marriage. I thought of the rose chair as an extension of the photograph, a red homage to the roses in the picture, drained of their color to a silvery brown and flattened by the camera.

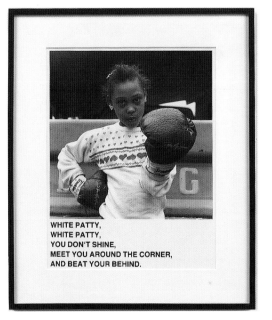

On the other side of the fireplace, Carrie Mae Weems's young boxer takes on a prejudiced white world.

Boxing Day

While I was looking at buildings in Harlem, I had bought a huge poster depicting a black boxer in white trunks against a soft green ground. His powerful fists are balled in gloves, and one of them is held directly at the viewer, delivering the punch of the message: "Sie!" in red letters outlined in black, scrolls like a challenge in front of him. On an angle across his calves is a white rectangle with the inscription "Sport für Alle täglich" and then, in black gothic letters "Morgen." "You! Sie!" The poster reads in German, grabbing your attention. "Sports for all, every morning." It is a bold and graphic ad for a newspaper.

My brother, who many years ago went south with the civil rights movement and has remained an activist ever since, eyed the poster with distaste. "That's pretty racist, don't you think?"

To be truthful, no, I didn't. The boxer's lips were fuller and redder than they ought to be, clearly a stereotypical rendering. But this nonetheless was a proud black man who held his body with dignity and looked you straight in the eye. Given the early date of the poster, most likely the 1920s, I was able to overlook the caricatured mouth and slightly overwide eyes to focus on the boxer's unabashed directness and power.

Yet if anyone scanning the poster wondered about my racial attitudes, another boxing picture in the living room had no ambiguity at all. The arresting black-and-white image, a photograph by my beloved friend Carrie Mae Weems, shows a young African-American girl, one hand on her hip, the other raising a boxing glove nearly as big as her head up toward the viewer. She faces the camera directly, and the pose and expression, even more than the boxer's in the poster, are steadfast and defiant. Printed on a field below the image are five lines, a child's rhyme. With sass and attitude she takes on a bigoted white world:

WHITE PATTY,
WHITE PATTY,
YOU DON'T SHINE,
MEET YOU AROUND THE CORNER,
AND BEAT YOUR BEHIND.

I never intended to have even a subtle boxing motif in my living room, but it seemed to occur spontaneously. In addition to Carrie's photograph and the poster, I eventually tried to add a third piece. Not long after one of boxing's most humiliating moments, in a sport as renowned for its roots in street brawls as it is for its sweet science, **Mad** magazine commemorated the episode in a classic back cover. Unable to outbox the defending heavyweight champ, Evander Holyfield, a desperate Mike Tyson lost it and sank his teeth into Holyfield's ear. Not once, but twice, and with bestial ferocity; part of Holyfield's ear went flying, along with Tyson's already dubious attempt at a comeback.

Probably the most famous of Vincent van Gogh's self-portraits is the one he made after he'd cut off his ear. The painting shows the artist from the shoulders up, his head wrapped all the way around

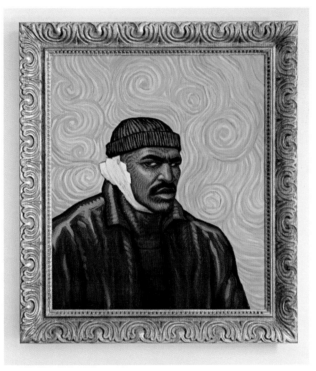

E. van Gogh Holyfield, painted by James Warhola for the back cover of **Mad** magazine, adds more colorful commentary to the front parlor.

with a bandage, both concealing and highlighting his self-mutilation. As recognizable as the portrait is, even more identifiable are van Gogh's thick swirls of impasto. To fuse the painting with the Tyson-Holyfield fiasco was an opportunity far too rich to be missed, and the editorial staff of **Mad**, better known as the Usual Gang of Idiots, jumped all over it. They commissioned James Warhola, a **Mad** artist and, coincidentally, Andy Warhol's nephew, to create a replica of the historic picture. This he did, except that van Gogh's visage was replaced by Holyfield's, his face, like the artist's, in three-quarter view, his head bandaged to cover up the offending ear. If ever a parody was literally picture-perfect, this, titled **E. van Gogh Holyfield**, was it.

Since DC Comics took over **Mad** following the death of its founder, Bill Gaines, we have returned all artwork to its creators. So as much as I coveted the portrait, I had to bid for it at Sotheby's like anyone else. I consulted Jerry Weist, one of Sotheby's pop culture advisers, to ask how much money he thought the painting would command. "I don't know what to tell you," he counseled, if that's what one can call statements so ambiguous that they are of no benefit at all. "The picture has aroused a tremendous amount of interest. It could easily go as high as $10,000, but on the other hand, it could go for considerably less."

Needless to say, I focused only on the outside end of Jerry's estimate. Ten thousand dollars? That was totally beyond my limit. I couldn't be at the auction to gauge the activity, or even on the phone, because I was going to be out of the country and nearly unreachable. Finally I threw myself on the mercy of **Mad**'s Nick Meglin, who was attending the auction with coeditor John Ficarra. Nick said he would bid on my behalf, and I authorized him to go up to $5,000, which, with buyer's premium and taxes, meant that the painting would cost a little over $6,000.

After the auction I asked Anna Ng, my dream assistant, if she knew what had happened. "No," said Anna, "Nick was rather vague. I think he wants to tell you himself."

I finally caught up with Nick. "Aw, Jenette. I'm so sorry. I really tried my best. I know how much you wanted the picture. But the amount you authorized for me was wrong. Yes," he continued, finally unable to contain his cat-that-ate-the-canary grin. "It was wrong. You got it! For a lot less!!" Should I kiss Nick or kill him? It didn't matter. **E. van Gogh Holyfield** was mine.

I couldn't wait to get the painting framed and hang it in my living room. All of my other work was mounted simply or not at all, in keeping with its contemporary content. But this was an exception. After all, Holyfield was painted in the style of van Gogh, and van Gogh had for decades been considered a modern master. Museums treated his pictures

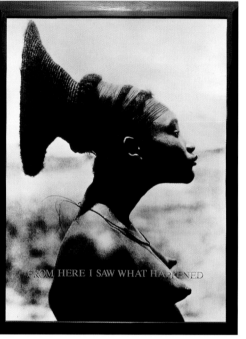

From the living room, you can see both this eloquent Carrie Mae Weems photograph and, farther away, its companion in the central parlor.

that way, encasing them in ornate gold frames. To make the joke complete, I felt I should follow their example and regard my painting with the same elaborate gravity. And so I selected a customized frame in gold leaf with a pattern of waves that echoed the swirls of the van Gogh–Warhola style. Although it cost nearly half what the picture had, it was worth it to add yet another layer to the double take.

I had actually considered spending three times as much for something truly excessive and baroque. But no matter how priceless a joke might be, it has no true equity. You can laugh, but not all the way to the bank.

From Parody to More Serious Social Commentary

After the Holyfield painting, there were three more additions to the living room. One was a chess set by the young and imaginative artist Roxy Paine. Exit Art, an extraordinary nonprofit cultural space in SoHo, had asked artists to design chess and checkers sets for a boutique then on its premises. The results were wonderful, from a set on checkerboard bedding where the checkers were condoms, to Roxy's cheerfully twisted board game, in which every piece was a fragment from a Hieronymus Bosch painting.

I loved the chess set. It was quirky, erotic, and inventive. I bought it and placed it in front of the couch in my living room. To protect the fragile pieces, all made of clay, I used a Plexiglas cover, a

plastic shield against clumsy hands and spontaneous bouts of cat hockey. As the one who bought
Roxy's creation, I always looked at it and saw chess
pieces in their starting formations, ready to do
battle, if someone would only lift the case that froze
them in place. But others, eyeing two rows of
buttocks with flowers in their cheeks, somehow didn't
see two rows of pawns. Instead they ignored the
specifics and read the whole,
knights and bishops, rooks
and royalty, plastic and board,
as a coffee table. An unusual
coffee table, but a coffee table
nonetheless. The fact was, I
didn't have a coffee table in the
living room, so Roxy's artwork
did double duty, although that
was never the plan.

The second addition was a
chandelier by the Netherlands
avant-garde collective Droog
Design. Called the 85 Lamps
chandelier, that's exactly what
it was: eighty-five naked but
muted light bulbs, bunched
like a bouquet on long wire
stems and hung upside-down
from the ceiling. It was such
a simple concept, but both radi-
cal and beautiful. And once it was installed, things
occurred that I hadn't expected, making it something else—magical.

I'm a girl who likes light, the kind of person
who rarely has curtains or blinds and seldom
closes shutters. When night falls, I walk into a room
and turn on all the lamps. They may be on dimmers,
but I always opt for the high beams. The dining
room is the only exception. My friend and fellow
party giver, restaurateur Alexander Smalls, has

made it painfully clear that I have no feel for atmospheric lighting, so when guests come for dinner,
I yield to Alexander's pressure and flick down
the rheostats.

But that's the dining room. If I'm in charge,
the front parlor is lit up like a Christmas tree. And,
with the shutters open, the 85 Lamps chandelier,
reflected in the night-blackened windows, gleams
like eighty-five Fabergé eggs.
Directly across from the light is
Sandy Skoglund's **Wedding**,
and the glass protecting the
photograph picks up the chandelier too, causing golden bulbs
to multiply and multiply until
all one feels is a festive warmth,
as welcoming as the Russian
Tea Room, where the holiday
decor is up all year.

The last addition to the
front parlor was another photograph by Carrie Mae Weems—
in this instance, one of a pair.
Carrie is a brilliant and provocative artist, never afraid to
cut to the bone. As friends do,
I try to go to every one of
her openings. But when an exhibition of her latest work was

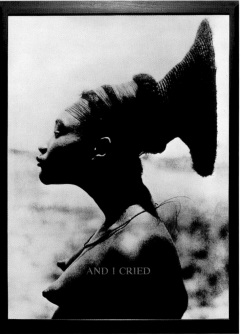

In the central parlor, the closing half
of Carrie Mae Weems's moving pair of
photographs.

mounted at the P. P. O.W. Gallery in New York, I
had the flu and was confined to bed. About a week
later, I felt well enough to walk, but still couldn't
talk. That, however, seemed no reason not to visit
Carrie's show.

So I journeyed downtown to P. P. O.W. and
entered the small front vestibule. The walls were
hung with photographs, first of majestic Africans
and then of the heartbreaking prisons on the island
of Gorée, where the internees were penned like

    My Harlem Renaissance: Buying and Decorating a Landmark House

animals, awaiting an even more horrible fate. The text accompanying each image resounded within me. I had been to Gorée and seen the inhuman conditions to which white slavers had subjected their black captives, even then stripping the men from the women and the children from their parents, forcing "recalcitrants" into a lightless hole. But nothing prepared me for the emotions I felt when I entered the main room. On the left side, beginning the exhibition, was a photo of a queenly African woman in profile, a picture taken in the 1920s that Carrie had found in a Paris archive and rephotographed in moving shades of blue. Printed over the bottom of the image were the words, "From here I saw what happened."

Following this picture was a series of nineteenth-century daguerreotypes of African-American slaves, enlarged and printed in bright crimson, each with text stabbing home the exploitation and degradation of a once-free people torn from its homes and sold into bondage. This cruel history was continued from the daguerreotypes through famous twentieth-century photographs, appropriated and reprinted in the same shade of outraged red. The exhibition ended with the blue photograph of the woman with whom the show began. But now the image was reversed so that she looked back on the angry history behind her. Where the text on the opening picture quietly declared, "From here I saw what happened," the text on the closing one mourned, "And I cried." Surrounded by this unflinching installation, which bore excruciating witness, that is what I did, too. In a gallery office hidden from view I dialed Carrie's number, needing her to answer the phone. My heart skipped when she did. "Carrie," was my hoarse whisper, in a voice strangled by laryngitis and dense with tears, "I'm at the show. It's so incredible. I don't even know what to say."

Through the thick of emotion I heard Carrie say, "Oh, baby . . ." And then she was crying, too. For the next ten minutes, with the phone a live wire between us, we wept together, not just for the searing beauty of the show but for the unbearable pain of being human and the irreplaceable bond of friendship.

Sometimes Less Is More

In the central parlor, where the sweeping staircase and quartersawn oak dominate the decor, I added very little. This was not necessarily by choice. I would have liked to have color and—what? seating? sculpture?—but the space seemed more like a platform for the central stair than a room with its own function. The previous owners had put a golden baby grand in the area, not a bad solution. But I don't play the piano, so introducing one seemed like movie-set pomp, as lacking in authenticity as the decorative moldings that someone had added long after the house was built, which Al had just removed. In addition, it was clear that the more sparsely furnished the central parlor, the more people you could entertain on one floor. If I decided to have a party, I couldn't just whisk the baby grand into a closet to get it out of sight.

So the central parlor remained empty. The few things I did add were on or near the walls. In a space that seemed made for a picture, between the pocket doors and a wooden pilaster, I hung a photograph of the Mexican magic-realist painter Frida Kahlo, who was known as much for her narcissism and melodramatic life as for her deeply personal and original art. The photo shows her sitting at her easel, painting a self-portrait, one that in later years would become particularly renowned. Standing behind her and watching her at work is her much more famous husband, the artist Diego Rivera. A big man, tall and corpulent, he appears at least for

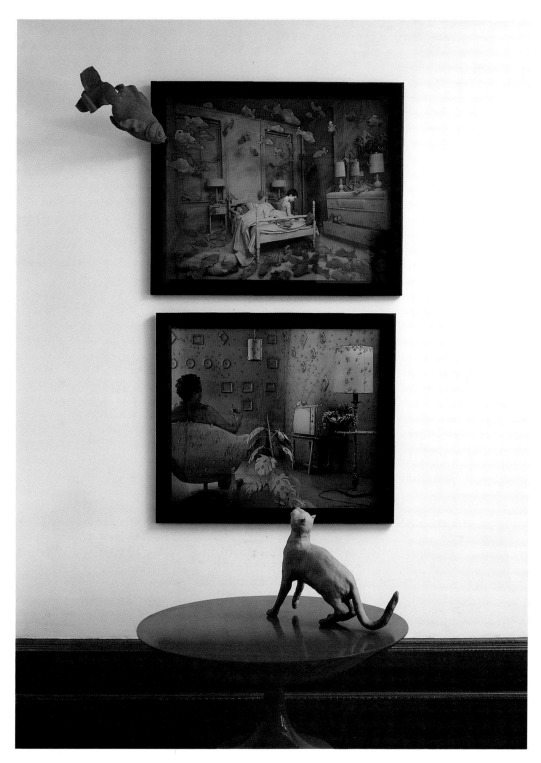

Sandy Skoglund's radioactive-green cat gazes hungrily up at a sculpted fish from her photograph **Revenge of the Goldfish**. Below it is another Skoglund photo, **Germs Are Everywhere**.

My Harlem Renaissance: Buying and Decorating a Landmark House

the moment to take a back seat to Kahlo, fascinated by watching her paint. At the same time, he also dwarfs her. Although the photograph makes no deliberate social comment, today's many champions of Frida Kahlo's work would find in it an implicit truth. One can debate whether Rivera was the better painter of the two, but the fact that he overshadowed his wife so completely has less to do with his size (and the size of his paintings) than with his being a man, when art criticism was controlled nearly exclusively by men.

On the other side of the pocket doors, in the corner, I stood three sculptures by Todd Siler. I'd purchased them several years before I bought the house on Strivers Row, only to discover that they were too tall for where I'd hoped to put them. And although it never even occurred to me that I might someday leave the Century, I nonetheless kept them in storage, thinking there might come a time and place when they could finally be installed.

It was at Ron Feldman's gallery on Mercer Street that I first discovered Todd's work. I love Ron and his wife, Frayda, and when I'm in SoHo I always try to visit them. I've bought art from the gallery over the years, but I'm always warmly welcomed as a friend, not a client. I'm usually a big fan of the artists Ron exhibits, but I had found his latest show so conceptual and dry that I was sure I'd drop from boredom each time I walked through the door. So now I was stunned to enter the front room and see not only that the exhibit was gone but that it had been replaced by a forest of metal totems against a lushly painted abstract field.

"Oh, thank God that other show is finally down!" I exclaimed to the empty room. I might as well have yelled, "Stel-la!!" Having announced my presence, I walked into the second room and a warm hug from Marc Nochella, who works in the gallery. Needless to say, he had heard me and came out to

say hello. This room, too, was full of sculptures and vivid, evocative paintings. Once again I was buoyantly outspoken, not just in relief that the other show had vanished but also because I was genuinely excited by what I saw.

In my voluble pleasure, I had failed to notice a ladder that, like Jack's beanstalk, seemed to disappear into infinite space. All of sudden I heard footsteps, but no one was moving across the gallery's hardwood floors. I looked up and saw feet, legs, a torso, and finally, a full human figure seemingly descend from the sky. All of these body parts finally landed on solid ground, turned around to face me, and, with a smile as wide as the ladder was tall, declared, "Now that's a voice I have to meet!"

"Oh, Jenette," Marc explained, "this is Todd Siler. He's the artist whose work you like so much."

And he had come down to find out who belonged to that voice!

Todd, however, expanded. "I've been up on this ladder for hours, and I hear everyone who comes and goes. But they sound, well, you know, regular. I know they're collectors, but I can't bother to stop what I'm doing to chat them up.

"But then I heard something different, this voice so spirited and full of energy that I had to come down off the ladder."

And so began my friendship with Todd. We walked through the show together, and I expressed my admiration for the sculptural totems in the front room. Todd, who may be the only visual artist to hold a doctorate from MIT, explained their significance: "To me they represent the spinal cord. Strip everything away, and it's the one area in which we're all equal. There are no issues of race or gender or sexual orientation or age."

Actually, there were issues of height; some of the totems were taller than others (a global hierarchy based solely on the length of one's spinal cord?),

In Your Space: Personalizing Your Home and Office

but I refrained from making this observation. I liked Todd's earnest idealism, and the sculptures, however interpreted, were powerful and unique.

In the end I bought three of the sculptures, all with somewhat different shapes, colors, and markings. My choices were determined not just by how each one looked individually but by how they complemented one other as a group. With myriad totems standing tall against a background of otherworldly colors, Todd had created his own exceptional environment. One could look at it and see a mysterious wood or a distant planet founded by a proud and regal race. I could not hope to approach Todd's creation, with its enveloping atmosphere and rich complexity, but I could at least hint at it. One totem by itself seemed singular and absolute, two, a couple unto themselves. But three gave a sense of varied interactions and activity that, in a small way, represented the larger world from which they came.

Reconceiving an Old Fireplace

The central stair and tightly grained wood wainscoting may be the first architectural elements one notices in the middle parlor, but there is another, quieter one that I loved the moment I entered the room. Across from the Frida Kahlo is a fireplace. Almost every fireplace adds to an environment, but this one's appeal lay not so much in its high oaken mantel but in its placement. It wasn't like most fireplaces, flush against a perpendicular wall; this one was on a short diagonal, exactly the length of the hearth. The staircase, pooling into the room with baroque flourishes, made the space exceptional. But so too did the fireplace, creating a second point of interest. If the staircase gave the parlor grandeur, the angled fireplace gave it charm.

Unfortunately, the opening of the fireplace was covered by heat-efficient glass doors that had

been cemented onto the original tile. When, at my request, Al removed the doors, the tiles inevitably came with them. Like the irreversible nail holes where the carpet had been tacked on the stairs, the broken tiles need never have occurred. The damage was compounded because, of all the fireplaces in the house, this was the only one that had the 1891 tile still intact. Using cement on it had destroyed what a hundred years of wear had left untouched.

The original tiles were butterscotch in color and glazed. Each individual piece was narrow and rectangular, about one inch high by four inches long. Al separated the whole ones from the broken and put them aside. As much as I regretted the broken tiles, their loss opened up a whole new realm of creativity. Had the tiles been intact, I would never have thought of replacing them. The house, after all, had won landmark status, and even though the statutes governing it protected only the façade, I felt an obligation to preserve the interior as well. Interestingly, this sense of obligation extended only to what was still there. A purist would have tried to restore every original detail. But, moving into the house a full century after it was built, I did not feel compelled to make it a perfect period piece. If I had a motto that guided me, it was: First, do no harm. The fractured tiles, a legacy of previous owners, lifted all constraints. Suddenly, it was open season on the fireplace.

At the same Exit Art store where I had bought Roxy Paine's chess set, I also purchased some wonderful tiles by the artist Tom Otterness. Whether in sculpture or two-dimensional art, Tom is known for his cartoonlike figures with perfectly round heads and features as minimal as dots and lines. But once lured into his work by the easy charm and surface playfulness, one notices that there is something else going on, something just a little subversive. Tom's work is about economics and class. A first

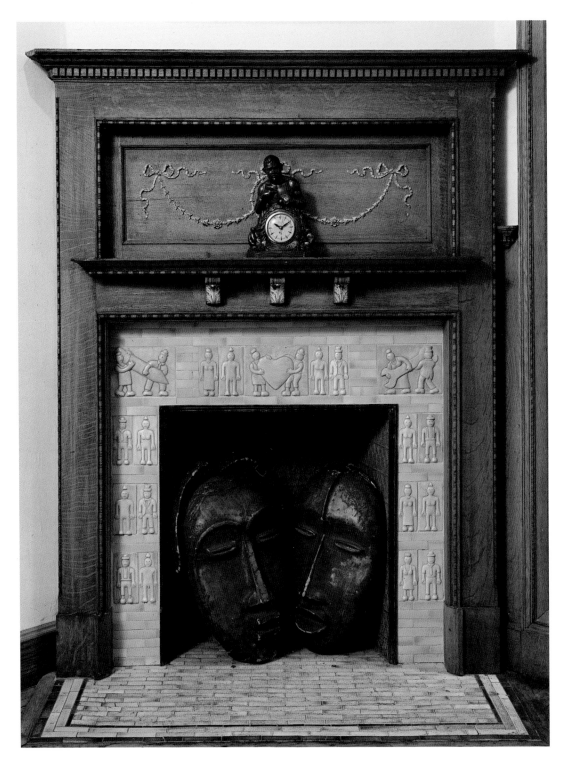

Contemporary tiles by Tom Otterness combine with original
pieces from 1891 to create a seamless fireplace surround.

In Your Space: Personalizing Your Home and Office

look might reveal a giant penny with a rotund Mr. Moneybags exulting on top of its rim. But closer inspection reveals a worker, so far below he might as well be invisible, slowly being crushed underneath. I like the fact that one sometimes encounters Tom's sculptures in the lobbies of large corporate offices. It's such a crazy incongruity. Do they get it? Or does the irony, like the worker, go unnoticed?

So there at Exit Art were Tom's tiles—political, witty, winsome, and totally affordable. I bought every one they had. Soon I was struggling to get two heavy shopping bags into a yellow cab. One was full of white tiles, and one of butterscotch. All this took place in December, just days after I'd moved onto Strivers Row. I had no plan for the tiles. But they were great. Something would come up. And it did.

It was nearly a month later that I realized that some of the Otterness tiles were the same color as the ones Al had salvaged from the original surround. We could combine them almost seamlessly. The Otterness tiles came in two sizes—large horizontal rectangles, about six inches high by eight inches wide, and small vertical rectangles, about three inches wide by six inches high. The fact that Tom's tiles were the same color as the originals was in itself an amazing occurrence. But just as amazing were their proportions. Like many fireplaces, the top bar of the surround was deeper than the sides were wide. There, the horizontal tiles fit perfectly. But they were clearly too large for the thin columns leading up to it. On the other hand, the small tiles, narrow and vertical, were perfect for the spaces edging each side.

The three groups of people Tom depicted in his tiles were emblematic of his class consciousness. Looking as if they'd stepped from a 1930s Helen Hokinson cartoon were the rich, posh, and well fed in their top hats and tails or small round hats and pearls. The Dilberts of the world, the woebegone middle class, were immediately recognizable by their standard-issue office uniforms of ties and short-sleeved shirts. And just as recognizable was your working-class Joe without even a shirt on his back.

Each horizontal tile had two characters carrying an oversize tool that was longer than they were tall. Some carried a pencil, some a screw, others a wrench. The tools were on the diagonal, and the people moving them were in profile. Luckily for my purposes, some of these handyman's helpers slanted from left to right and others from right to left. I chose ones in opposite directions for the top corners so that they pointed in toward the middle, helping to create a central area of interest. On the narrow, vertical panels I placed three rows of two small tiles side by side, mixing up gender and class.

In addition to the three classes Tom showcased in his tiles, there was a fourth that, like Todd Siler's totems, stripped people to their essence. These men and women, naked and fully frontal, devoid of any trappings of income or status, were critical to Tom's work, a Utopian plane against which to measure everything else. I mixed them with the other classes on the sides of the fireplace. But they deserved more importance, and mindful of that, I saved two for the fireplace's primary focus, the very center of the surround.

Of the horizontal tiles, one was different from the rest. It was a little saccharine for my taste, and I had thought twice before scooping it up with the rest of my loot from Exit Art. But sometimes, wholesale piggyness pays off. This tile, a man and a woman facing forward on either side of a gigantic heart, turned out to be the keystone of the fireplace. It was the only large tile in which the characters looked directly out at you, inviting your gaze. I flanked it with a naked man on one side, a naked woman on the other. Beside each I placed a repre-

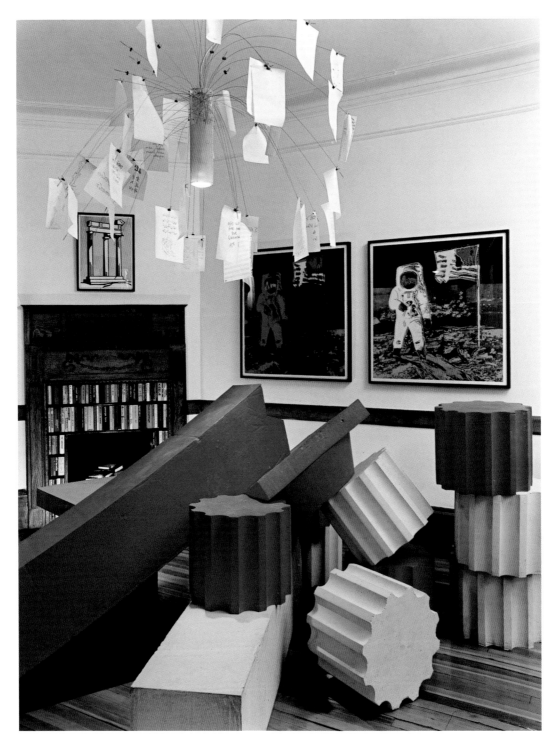

In the back parlor, a brief history of the world, with Andy Warhol's men on the moon overlooking pieces of a fallen Greek temple.

In Your Space: **Personalizing Your Home and Office**

sentative from the moneyed class in full upper-crust regalia. In arranging the tiles this way, I tried to convey what I saw as Tom's message: that beneath the baubles and the polyester, the frock coats and the overalls, are our true selves, where the heart and human connection lie.

In the spaces between the Otterness tiles, Al arranged the original ones in an interlocking grid that echoed the pattern on the hearth. When the old tiles were melded with the new, the combination seemed so much of a piece that most first-time visitors to the house assume that the 1891 fireplace is entirely intact. It is the rare person who notices that the surround is composed of two sets of tiles made a hundred years apart. But how could anyone appreciate the fireplace as much as Al and I? We both knew all that had gone into it, the coincidences, the complex planning, the thought and inspiration. And we also knew that this was a process shared by only the two of us, that the triumph of the fireplace was that the effort was hidden to all others behind the naturalness of the final effect.

Gazing with pride at the fireplace, the first of five that I was eventually to reconceive, Al announced, "Well, you'll never top this one."

As Al delivered his dictum, I could feel a slow burn start in the pit of my stomach. I, too, loved the fireplace, but those were fighting words. "We'll see," I threw back, "we'll see," and ground my shoe into the invisible gauntlet at my feet.

There was one last element to place in the room. As I mentioned, Carrie Mae Weems's regal portrait of an African woman was part of a pair. Printed on one were the words "From here I saw what happened," on the other, "And I cried." The first picture was in the front parlor beside the pocket doors leading into the next room. Diagonally across from it, in the central parlor, I hung its companion. Sitting on the yellow sofa, it was possible to see not just one photo

but both. Yet there was a distance between them, a distance measured in something far more human than inches and feet. For me the space was a constant and unstoppable ache. Another person, especially one less familiar with Carrie's work, might have read something quite different in the charged void between the photographs. But it was an active space, like the force field between two magnets, and impossible to dismiss.

The Back Parlor: A History of the World in Two and Three Dimensions

What was left? The back parlor, which, like the central parlor, posed a challenge. When the house was originally built, this space was actually the formal dining room. To the right was a butler's pantry, which you entered unseen from stairs that led directly up from the kitchen. A dumbwaiter, too, originated in the kitchen and ascended on pulleys to the pantry. The cooking staff would put food in the dumbwaiter and then hoist it to the parlor level, where all public entertaining took place. The butler would receive it, plate the food, and carry it with aplomb into the dining room through a private door at the pantry's end. At a time when the upper middle class could afford several full-time servants, this design enabled the family to enjoy nightly formal dining and to fete guests with a certain amount of ceremony. It wasn't grand dining on the scale that was de rigueur among New York's very rich, but it borrowed some of the trappings.

That era, however, was long past. The dumb-waiter, when I bought the house, was still intact, but the ropes were frayed with age, and it clearly hadn't been used for over sixty years. The former butler's pantry had been turned by the previous owners into a coat closet and a laundry room, more practical signs of a more practical age.

It was difficult to disagree with that thinking. Although I may not have put a laundry room on the parlor floor (it seemed gauche, just a closed door away from airing one's wash in public), it proved to be enormously convenient. I soon was used to dashing down the stairs to stuff my sheets and towels into the family-size washer. Left to my own devices, I'm sure I would have created a laundry room somewhere within the spacious ground-floor kitchen, but that would have meant running down two flights of stairs and, worse yet, lugging laundry up them. Soon the indecorous had become the unfailingly efficient, and as long as the laundry-room door remained fast shut, there was even a hint of elegance in that.

In this day and age, it no longer made sense to have the dining room on the parlor floor. I opted to put mine on the garden floor, where the kitchen was. But if the back parlor wasn't going to be the dining room, what purpose did it serve? Although my front parlor might not have been the essence of comfort, it was nonetheless the living room, the first line of defense in entertaining guests. Why would one need a second living room on the very same floor? While I struggled with this conundrum, help came in the form of a Christie's catalogue for an auction in London, a sleek, full-color siren song of modern design.

The cover, as I remember, showcased Gaetano Pesce's classic **Donna** chair, part of his Up series, which went on to set a staggering record price. It was a great chair, but mercifully I had one already and was therefore exempt from temptation—on that count, at least. Inside the catalogue was a photograph of something so foreign (and yet weirdly familiar), so odd and yet so amazing, that I could feel my pulse quickening without even having comprehended just exactly what it was. The small type clued me in. The object, or objects—this was a piece of many parts—was a foam construction made in 1971 by a radical design group called U.F.O. for an exposition in Italy. Half of the parts were yellow, half were red, but they all belonged to a humongous building set. When placed on top of one another, the parts could actually form two massive yet light-weight Doric columns, complete with capitals and connecting piers.

This was a wonderful notion, but what drew me was this foam Greek temple, not in its constructed state, but in its deconstructed one. When the drums that made up the columns were balanced so precariously that they looked like they might tumble to the ground, when they had fallen on their sides, when the piers crisscrossed on angles like rafters from a crumbling roof, then the temple had a complex beauty that could come only from the chaos of strong, colliding forms. It was a piece I felt I had to have. Within hours I had registered to be on the phone when it went up for sale, and a few weeks later I was enmeshed in a transatlantic bidding war for what I had begun to call the U.F.O.

It was one of those satisfying instances in which I won not only the battle but the booty as well. At a price that was high but still left me standing, I topped the competition and sealed possession of a piece that was equal parts architecture, sculpture, and design, both sendup and serious, and as capable of classical structure as it was of seemingly random disorder. It might not have been particularly functional (although one could use the drums as side tables, and thin people could even sit on them), but it filled a hole in my life. The once empty and unimagined back parlor was now enlivened by the endlessly dimensional U.F.O.

There were still things to do in that space, most of which would wait until after the housewarming. But to ready the room for the inaugural party, Al and I wanted at least to hang pictures on the walls. With a logic so understated I think it was known only to me, I chose works that, along with the shattered Greek temple in the middle of the room, summed up a brief history of the world. The first, in chronological order, was a wonderful Paul Colin poster showing an Easter Island head. The next was a Lichtenstein invitation to one of his shows that pictured a Greek temple, the perfect two-dimensional foil for the U.F.O. Leaping ahead a couple of millennia, I hung an Ib Andersen poster that showed a complex modern city, the buildings stacked on top of one another like planes at Kennedy International Airport. And, finally, I hung two Andy Warhol silkscreens of men on the moon whose celebratory neon colors promised a new era and new frontiers. Was that it? Well, naked light bulbs still hung overhead, the back fireplace still struggled under multiple coats of paint, but we were ready—or as ready as we were going to be. February 18 was upon us. It was time to open the doors and let the world pour in.

Lessons Learned Along the Way

1. When people say "everything happens for a reason," I discreetly raise my eyebrows. Does it? I don't know. The saying has a facile, pop-spiritual vibe that makes me somewhat uneasy. But I do know that when you lose something you hope to get—like a house or an apartment you're trying to buy—it's not the end of the world. There are other places to live that ultimately might make you happier.

2. When buying a house or an apartment, there should be things about it that make your heart beat a little faster. This doesn't mean that, under duress, you couldn't make the most of an uninspired space. But if you have a choice, don't commit to a home until you find one with certain aspects that genuinely excite you. It could be high ceilings, the view, the layout of the rooms, an architectural detail, or the trees in the backyard, but something has to thrill you. In my house, the fireplaces, the spaciously proportioned rooms, and the dramatic central stair were enough to ensure I would be happy there.

3. The first impression you have when walking into a space is of the overall effect. It might feel sophisticated or joyous or serene, but, if thoughtfully conceived, it will convey a unified tone. However, within that effect, there is so much more you can achieve. By choosing pieces carefully, you can establish a dialogue among them. The three boxing images in my front parlor commented on one another. So did the lush rose chair and the spare roses in Sandy Skoglund's photograph. The dog, the cat, and the fish started a chain reaction that began on the floor of one side of the parlor and crossed to the ceiling on the other. Smaller installations within the larger one create layers of interest and complexity.

4. While your interiors should convey a unified sensibility, they will be much more interesting if you strike different notes. Add the unexpected: anything from political commentary to historical references to tribal art in a modern home. While at first glance my front parlor feels exuberant, it gains its strength from the eroticism of Roxy Paine's chess set, the social commentary of James Warhola's **E. van Gogh Holyfield**, the sadomasochistic quality of Alex Locadia's Catwoman chaise, and the biting critique of Carrie Mae Weems's assertive young boxer.

10.

Strivers Row:

Settling In

The central parlor, with its quartersawn oak
and majestic stair.

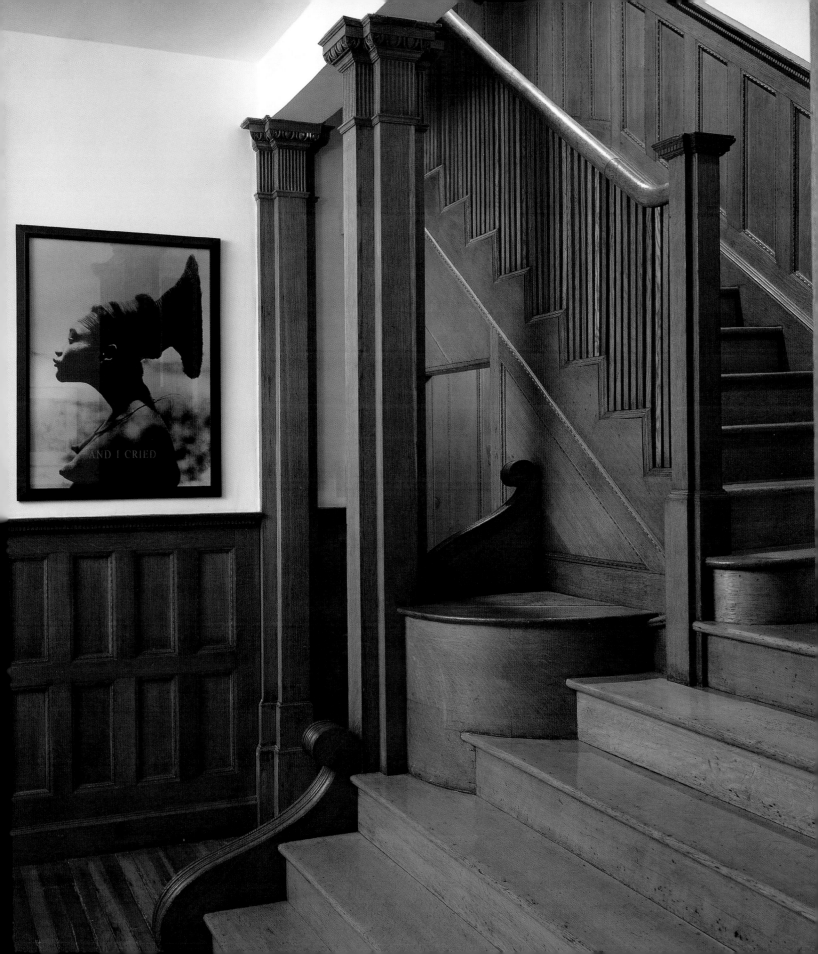

So how did the housewarming go? Well, the party, at least, was a huge success, owing in no small part to the fact that my great friend Alexander Smalls, opera singer, chef, and restaurateur, had made the food. Alexander, who grew up in South Carolina in the heart of low-country cooking, had brought to New York his personal version of an underrated category of American cuisine. To most people, low-country cooking means soul food— deep-fried chicken, barbecued ribs, and collard greens. But Alexander went well beyond these staples, calling his dishes Southern Revival cooking because he had taken all the classic recipes and reinvented them. Whether it was his vegetable and grits terrine or his bourbon praline ham, Alexander brought a new level of refinement and imagination to an old culinary tradition.

It was Alexander to whom I always went when I was entertaining. We had thrown many parties together when he lived in his vast downtown loft, including a strictly kosher southern dinner in honor of my father. Our entertaining days were temporarily put on hold when Alexander moved to a smallish apartment near his restaurant, Café Beulah, and I was still living in 1,000 square feet at the Century. But now that I had a house, things were different.

Alexander has never been one to stint on food. So when he arrived at my house with buffet dinner for eighty, there was enough food to feed about thirty people more.

The party, with its incredible edibles and a wonderful mix of people, was, as I said, a success. But the house? Well, that was a different matter. Most of my guests were still in shock that I'd bought in Harlem, and for many this was their first trip across 110th Street. They had come up in radio cabs and entered the house already fretting about how they'd safely get home. To the uninitiated, Harlem is a wasteland. They can't imagine that you can call a local car service, as I call Malcolm every day to go to work, and have a vehicle outside your door just three minutes later. Or that the drivers, most of whom are West African, are so genuinely warm and polite. Or that a Malcolm car costs no more than a yellow cab.

The Morning After

Wishing not to offend me, many friends tried to focus instead on how beautiful my street is, and how special it was to have found a house with so much detail and so many fireplaces. But others couldn't contain themselves.

"Do you really feel safe up here? Aren't you afraid to park your car on the street? You don't walk around up here, do you?"

Yes. No. Yes.

The truth is, I feel totally secure. Everyone on my street knows one another, and part of the culture is to keep a protective eye out for your neighbors. Jimmy Banks was born over seventy years ago in the same house in which he lived until his recent death. But his wife, Elois, as vigorous as they come, still rules, the official chairperson of our block association and the unofficial mayor of our street.

It's a closely knit community with small-town values, an oasis in the urban sprawl. But how do you convey that to people whose preconceptions have them seeing a mugger in every shadow, a drug dealer behind every lamppost?

Oh, well. So it goes. It's not that I was oblivious to the murmurings beneath the polite expressions of support. I just felt that they were wrong. Oh, not totally wrong. Harlem will never be like the white-gloved East Side, where doormen hover expectantly in the lobbies of their buildings and the streets are festooned with designer shops. And although it may happen someday, it will take years before Harlem resembles the bustling West Side, with its mix of families, yuppies, and senior citizens, its movie theaters, bookstores, and restaurants. But even in 1996, the year I bought my house, and five years before former president Bill Clinton decided to base his offices in Harlem, it was already on the move. Change was coming. You could feel it in the air.

The Fire Next Time: Conceiving Another Fireplace

Now that the party was over, I turned back to the interior of the house. Although the parlor floor was more or less complete, the fireplace in the back room still had to be rescued. Both the mantel and the surround were covered in heavy coats of white paint, which Al began to strip. There was no point in trying to salvage the small brick tiles around the firebox. They seemed to have lost whatever panache they might have had before someone years ago decided they'd look better with paint. The mantel, though, yielded up history. Behind it were three twenty-dollar bills that had been issued early in the century, and near them was an invitation from 1913 to a gallery exhibition on lower Fifth Avenue.

Only a week earlier, Al had looked appraisingly at the Otterness fireplace and declared that I would never top it. I nursed his pronouncement like a grudge; now I was even more determined to prove him wrong. So while Al was stripping the wood, I began a creative journey to come up with an idea for the second fireplace. It is difficult to say how the process works. For each person, I am sure, it is different. Mine begins with an active decision to define a problem and address it.

Once I've truly resolved to find a solution, my unconscious goes into high gear. When I put my head on the pillow at night, I involuntarily start to think. But the thinking is nonlinear. I let ideas flow freely, riffling through them as I would the pages of a book. It seems everything I've seen or heard or learned is part of this mental reference. I struggle—but not too hard—to connect the dots in new ways. If I don't get anywhere, I give it up, knowing that I've given my unconscious an assignment, and it will loyally keep at work.

And so it was that the idea for the second fireplace occurred, not long after I decided that I had to come up with one. I began to think about tiles—not their patterns or colors, but only their shapes. Tiles, as far as I knew, were either square or rectangular, but it seemed to me that we could cut the rectangular ones into narrow strips. An image flashed in my mind: the fireplace as a bookcase, with vertical tiles in different widths representing the spines of books. This illusion was enhanced by the warm, stained oak of the actual mantel, the kind of wood you might find in a gentleman's club. I made a crude sketch, just to see how it looked, and called Al.

"Alness" (I will languish in hell for the way I mangle people's names), "it's me. I had an idea for the second fireplace."

"Yeah?"

It is impossible to describe how much skepticism, doubt, and seeming lack of interest can be conveyed in one small word.

"Yeah!" I said as brightly as I could, to counter the flat, dull voice on the other end of the line. "You can cut tile, right? So why don't we get tiles in lots of different colors, cut them into slim rectangles, and stack them in rows like books?"

"It might work," he grudgingly conceded.

"Well, let's do it then!"

Despite his noncommittal tone, it turned out that Al was not unmoved by the idea. Two days later he showed up at my house with a polished freehand drawing of the design that we'd discussed.

Not long after, Al stopped off at a couple of stores and brought back some three-by-six-inch tiles in shades of white, moss green, dark blue, and gray. I, however, was unimpressed.

"Hey, that's all they had," Al said, defending himself. "It's not easy to find the colors you like."

"I did find these," said Al reaching for his brief-case. "But there's a problem with them." From his bag Al pulled out a small selection of tiles in orange, turquoise, and other offbeat but interesting hues.

"These are perfect. What could possibly be wrong with them?"

"They're scrap. Leftover tiles that are used for edging. I had to go down into basements and rum-mage through boxes just to come up with these."

"But there must be other tile stores."

"Sure there are. But how many pieces do you think I'll find in each? And you can't order these tiles. There are minimums, and you don't want more than two or three in each color."

Al observed my hangdog look and doled out a morsel of encouragement.

"I'll try, though."

And he did. But he was right—he'd find five tiles in one store, eight, if he was lucky, in another. Nevertheless, he almost always uncovered a couple of interesting ones whose shapes we hadn't seen before. When I conceived the fireplace, my imagination, as often happens, had been limited by what I knew. To my mind, all standard-issue tiles were flat. But Al was bringing back the occasional dimensional tiles, curved from one edge to the other, often with stria-tions on the side. These tiles were as fabulous as they were unexpected. If we ever were able to amass a sufficient number of tiles to make the fireplace, these dimensional ones would add volume, forging a varied surface, a more credible sense of real books.

But rounded or flat, we had to find some more. It was a lengthy process. Al hit all the tile stores, let a little time go by, and hit them again. Twenty-five tiles, thirty-seven, fifty-four. Bit by bit they were slowly adding up. Only sixty-some tiles to go.

It's rare to have an idea so fully thought out from the get-go that it isn't modified along the way. Rather, it evolves and is refined and redesigned as one assembles the parts and interacts with them. And so it was that as Al continued the hunt for tiles, another notion occurred to me. Maybe we should put titles on the "books." Al rejected my suggestions for how we might accomplish this, so I pushed him for his. Finally he volunteered that Letraset, or press type, might work. But computers had made press type obsolete. No one did pasteups of layouts any more.

When press type was essential to the printing process, magazine companies and large design firms bought it in bulk, while art supply stores sold single sheets to individuals. But did they still? The next day I detoured past Lee's Art Shop on Fifty-seventh Street to see if they had a stash of Letraset. It took several mystified young clerks before I finally found a seasoned veteran who was able to process the word. He led me to some shelves tucked behind a pier toward the back of the store. While the quantity was limited, I felt as though I had struck oil. There was Letraset in sizes and typefaces from discreet to bold, in elegant fonts, playful fonts, and powerful fonts. I filled my arms with everything I thought might have a chance to work, even some sheets in gold.

But at the cash register, my enthusiasm crashed. Press type had never been expensive, and I had picked up sheets willy-nilly without bothering to look at the prices. However, as the clerk started to ring them up, my mouth dropped in disbelief.

"Six dollars for a sheet of press type?! Nine dol-lars? This is crazy. I thought no one used it any more."

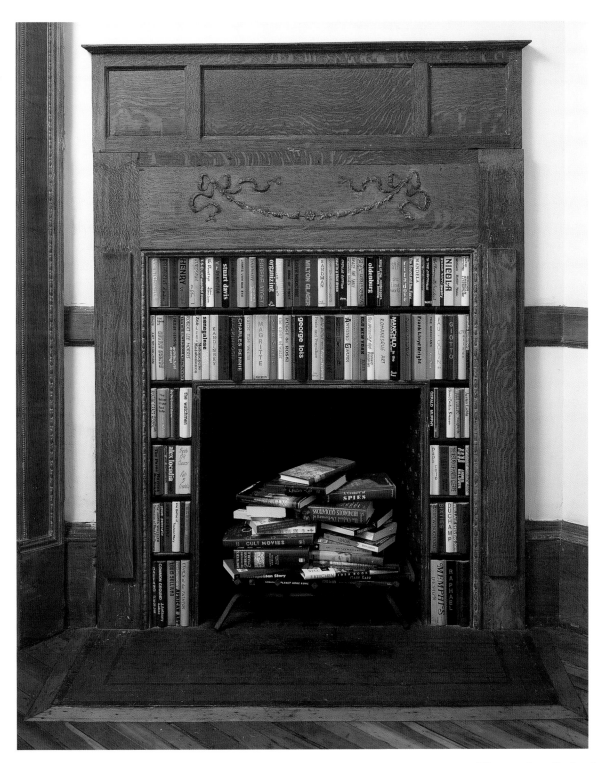

In the back parlor, a very personal library, where the fireplace's vertical tiles hold the names of beloved authors, artists, and books.

Strivers Row: Settling In

"Yes, but there won't be any more. So the prices are higher."

I knew I should have said thanks but no thanks. But I was like a bride at the altar who, having suddenly heard unsettling news, feels she's in too deep to call the wedding off. No doubt about it, this was highway robbery. But I was dying to see how the press type looked on the tiles. I held up my hands, handed over the cash, and let myself be mugged.

The good news was that the press type did in fact look terrific on the tiles. Al, of course, was the one who executed the experiment. Positioning and applying press type is a tedious and painstaking occupation. To do it well, one not only has to be detail-oriented but also must possess extraordinary reserves of patience. In addition, the spacing between letters requires a keen eye for balance and proportion. Luckily, Al has all of these qualities, and the initial results convinced us we were on the right track.

With that behind us, Al and I divvied up assignments. We followed the Marxist maxim of each according to his abilities, so Al had three tasks, and I had one. Mine was to come up with a list of book titles I wanted to see in the fireplace. Al's missions were to find more vertical tiles and more press type, preferably as cheap as possible to help amortize the damage I'd done at Lee's Art Shop. His third assignment was the hardest. From my list of books Al had to choose a title, then a tile for it, and finally a typeface he thought would be most appropriate. Following that, he had to print each title, letter by letter by letter.

As difficult as Al's last assignment was, mine, creating a list of titles, promised to be a breeze. Nonetheless, what at first had seemed so easy actually proved to involve unexpected complexities. This fireplace, after all, was public. It was on the parlor floor, and therefore accessible to casual comers and

goers in a way that the fireplaces in the dining room and on the bedroom floor were not. The choices I made would say a great deal about me. Was I comfortable with that?

Not only did I determine that the answer to this question was yes, I decided to let it shape my selection. The books I chose were those that I'd loved as a child and those that moved me as an adult, books by artists and designers whose work I admired, and books by my friends. For my friends who didn't yet have books but deserved to, I made them up. My choices showed a pilgrim's progress, from **Pride and Prejudice** to **Zen and the Art of Motorcycle Maintenance**, from W. B. Yeats to W. E. B. Du Bois, and from Jonathan Kozol's **Amazing Grace** to Alexander's own **Grace the Table**, a memoir of a life shaped by music and food. My friend Ornette Coleman, the extraordinary musician and composer, had been working for years on a book that explained his theory of music. It's anybody's guess when Ornette will finish **Harmolodics**, but meanwhile it took its place beside **Organizing**, by my brother Si, on one side, and **The Rose of Tibet** on the other. Craig Harris, also a composer and musician, may never write a book, but I love his work, and he's one of my closest friends. So I placed a title for him in the fireplace, calling it **F-Stops** after one of his CDs. The same was true for my friend the poet Sekou Sundiata, who prefers to perform and record his work rather than commit it to print. But he got a volume, too.

It was during the course of working on the fireplace that I began to realize that it was something deeper than a witty trompe-l'oeil conceit. It had become an actual piece of autobiography. The books I'd been selecting all had had an impact on my life, and if you chose to pay attention, they spoke volumes about me. Neither of my parents had published a book, but they had influenced me in ways more

In Your Space: Personalizing Your Home and Office

critical than I could ever count. In this diary of images, ideas, and intimate connections, it was enormously important to acknowledge them. I created a volume for each, the first titled **To Nettie** (my childhood name), by Rosalind Kahn. It stood for my mother's desire to leave me with her ardent appreciation of the world even after she died too young. **The Wit and Wisdom of Ben Kahn** was in honor of my father, who throughout his life lovingly shared his commitment to Judaism and his impish, irrepressible humor.

At the close of a day's work, Al would take several tiles from the pile and meticulously place a title on each one. Week by week, the "library" grew until finally, all but two of the tiles were complete. It was at this point that Al considered the project far enough along to arrange the entire group on the floor in front of the fireplace.

"You take them," Al said, gesturing toward his layout of would-be books. "I know you. You'll want to decide what order to put them in. You have your own ideas about color."

He was right, of course. The tiles fell naturally in place according to their dimension: two large rows of books on top of the surround, three short rows of books on either side. The only exception was a set of thick black one-inch tiles with a gentle curve. Rather than use these tiles for titles, we saved them to make horizontal borders under each row of books, to create the illusion of shelves. The tiles were still on the floor when I suggested to Al that he should have a book. It would be a way he could sign his work; he had been so vital to the fireplace, contributing aesthetic decisions as well as his craftsmanship.

"I'll think about it," Al only grudgingly allowed.

The days turned into weeks, but eventually Al did pick a title for himself. Among his many talents, Al is a formidable Scrabble player; although he doesn't participate in tournaments, he commands the respect of some of the country's highest-ranked players. Al's interest in the game has led him to amass more arcane words than most literate people encounter in several lifetimes, and he knows every anagram that can be made from them. It was no surprise, then, that Al chose an obscure word for his title: **Tumulu**. He signed it A. Williams in gold press type on a soft blue tile. This decision—it had to be conscious—caused the letters to shimmer against the muted field so that they seemed to merge with the background, elusive and illegible. It was an abstract, cryptic signature for someone just as enigmatic himself.

Al hired Michael Wu, a masterful Chinese craftsman with whom he'd worked before, to come with his crew and set the tiles in the fireplace surround. Only Michael spoke English, but the delight of all the men was palpable. As Michael explained, they had done so many bathrooms and kitchens in multimillion-dollar homes that he'd lost count. But they'd never worked on something so original. After a few hours, everyone was laughing and drinking tea, and I brought out my Polaroid camera to document the event.

Later, when they had picked up their work again, Al reminded me that there was still one tile for which I needed a title. Despite Al's advisory, I let Michael Wu place all the tiles in the surround, including that one slim volume without a title. In a way, it was my signature. It represented all the books I had yet to read and love, all the artists and designers I had yet to meet, all the poets and musicians whose words and music I had yet to hear. This book stood for the future. Its pages were still to be filled. I wanted the book to be as open-ended, as full of adventures and joys and possibilities, as the rest of my years on Strivers Row.

One Story Up

While working on the bookcase fireplace, we began to tackle my bedroom, where certain things that I'd brought from the Century were already in place: the two tall Sottsass prototype King lamps with their elegant yellow columns, the rhythmic Atlantique bureau, also by Sottsass, with its curved yellow door-pulls and its black-and-white sawtooth laminate, the prototype bed by Michele de Lucchi, which seemed to float off the floor. All these had come from Karl Lagerfeld's 1980s Paris apartment, the contents of which had been sold at Sotheby's in Monaco.

But although these pieces had started to make the bedroom feel like home, there was still a tremendous amount of work to be done. Perhaps the most important task was reestablishing the original proportions of the room. The previous owners had built floor-to-ceiling closets on either side of the fireplace. While these certainly made dressing more convenient, they also blurred the geometric focus of the space. The fireplace was the bedroom's central organizing principle. It jutted into the room with a sense of primacy; the architect, James Brown Lord, had built a substantial pier to house it. Nine feet long and protruding twelve inches beyond the rest of the wall, it framed the fireplace and gave it a magisterial presence—or had, until the closets were built. Deeper than the pier, these extended into the room even farther, robbing the fireplace of its role as the key element, the anchor to everything else in a bedroom of grand proportions. The closets had to come out.

Where the closets had been, I asked Al to build bookshelves. Although I wanted to make room for as many books as possible, I also was careful that the shelves were neither too high nor too deep. Anything else would have repeated the equation of the closets, convenience muffling architectural form.

Al built the shelves with a kick space at the bottom that echoed the height of the baseboard, cementing them within the room's geometry. Whereas the pier and the vertically oriented fireplace underscored the height of the bedroom, the horizontal shelves emphasized the serene grace of its width.

"You Can Always Repaint"

Three beautiful windows in my bedroom face out to Strivers Row and the pale yellow Italianate town houses across the way. It is a northerly view, but the sun hits the houses opposite full force, bouncing off their façades and back to the shaded side of the road. My bedroom is suffused with reflected light, my windows clotted with branches from the tree beyond my door. Through my windows and up, I can see blue sky and clouds filtering through the classical columns of the distant balustrades that cap these buildings with a restrained but ornamental flourish. On my quiet block especially, this view takes on a hushed magnificence, framed like a painting by the clean, handsome lines of the windows.

It is a magnificence augmented by interior detail. Each window is surrounded by a four-inch frame edged with a generous egg-and-dart molding that gives it a more articulated presence. The frame begins at the floor on one side and ends at the floor on the other. Underneath the windowsills are low, recessed wainscoted panels that also start at the floor. Combined with the frames, they turn each window into a distinct architectural element, a majestic vertical column nearly nine feet tall. The windows' importance in the room cannot be overestimated.

Nonetheless, it is possible to understand this importance and still make egregious mistakes—something I did in such a major way that even now it is painful to recall. Downstairs on the parlor floor the two windows in the living room had massive

In Your Space: Personalizing Your Home and Office

frames of quartersawn oak. These frames and the wainscoting below them were not painted but stained. The unpainted wood, which was echoed in the fireplace, the baseboards, and the pocket doors, called attention to these elements and gave the room distinction. Upstairs, by contrast, all the wood in the bedroom was painted white. I kept looking at it and thinking of the proud oak downstairs. The white, I concluded, was a mistake. I decided to strip the bedroom wood.

As always, I enlisted Al for this grueling task. Day after day he chipped away at layers of paint until finally the wainscoting below the windows and the frames around them were exposed. Al sanded them down and then brought over a full spectrum of stains. We tried one sample, then another, never quite satisfied. Although it wasn't my ideal—and by this time I had lost any sense of what exactly my ideal was—we finally opted for a medium oak hue with a hint of red. The choice made, Al moved from one daunting labor to another. Because the wood was old and had been painted many times, it was difficult to achieve an even stain. Progress was tedious and often frustrating, compounded all the more by noxious fumes. And then one evening I came home from work, and the wood was done.

Did I love it? Actually, no. The exposed wood was critical to the character of the parlor floor, and where it occurred in other parts of the house I found it beautiful. But while I didn't have the same response to it in the bedroom, I couldn't manage to acknowledge this fact even to myself. I was a coward. It had been my idea to strip the wood, and Al had labored in the desert for so long. How could I tell him it was all for naught?

While Al was working on the wood, my friend Lloyd Schwan, the designer, dropped by.

"You know," he counseled, "the wood on the upper floors of houses like these was meant to be painted. The parlor floor is different. That wood's of the highest grade. But up here? See for yourself. It's pine. It was never meant to be exposed."

I loved Lloyd, and his point of view always weighed heavily with me. On the other hand, I had heard many conflicting opinions about these Harlem houses, even from people who knew them inside and out. What Lloyd was postulating might be right, but how, then, did one account for how good the unpainted wood looked around the windows on the top floor of the house, particularly in the front room, where it warmed the space without overwhelming it? I noted what Lloyd said but at the same time disregarded it. Al's work was far from complete. Why should we turn back just because of a theory that wasn't proved and might not even be relevant?

So the stripping and staining continued, and finally, as I said, it was done. Although I was far from ecstatic, I made a few positive comments to Al (he had, after all, slaved away on a thankless task) and resigned myself to living with the results. This, of course, was another mistake. One can only suppress one's unhappiness so long. I was in this state, despondent but equally reluctant to ask Al to scrap his work, when Lloyd, channeling the Oracle of Intelligent Design, showed up again. He looked at the stained wood with disdain.

"You really should paint it all white," he proclaimed.

It was just the statement I needed to hear, the outside judgment that enabled me to shake off my lassitude and finally declare myself. "You're right. And, boy, was I wrong! I hate the stain!"

That felt so good. Now to tell Al. "Lloyd knew what he was talking about," I confessed. "I guess I just had to see for myself."

Which, in decorating, as in all other things in life, is often the case. But it was also Lloyd who had told me many years before that, at least in design, nothing is truly dire. You can always repaint, he said. And that is exactly what we did.

Meanwhile Al made a wonderful discovery. The previous owners had had shades on their bedroom windows. However, it was clear from the structure of the window frames that they were built to have pocket shutters. By some incredible fortune, the pocket shutters in the dining room and front parlor had weathered over a hundred years of use, multiple owners, and decades of transient boarders to survive intact. But the shutters for the master bedroom were missing. I took this in stride. To have two of the three original sets of shutters was just short of a miracle.

But the miracle was complete when Al emerged from the cellar with his arms filled with wood. "I found these shutters," he announced. "I don't know if they're the right height, but maybe they'll fit in the bedroom windows."

And to my immense delight, they did. In fact, upon inspection, these clearly were the original shutters from 1891. They were coated with a dense, white film of lime, a mineral testament to their history of neglect, but Al reclaimed them from their distress and painted them white. There was a beautiful organization to the shutters that parsed them into sections and confirmed that they had been designed as part of the rest of the room.

The drawback was their louvers, which were sealed shut and no longer let in light and air. Several years later I considered trading the shutters for a contemporary version, in which the louvers actually functioned. As an experiment, Al took down an original shutter and put up a new one. The louvers, clean and pristine, rotated like a spanking new machine—mechanically, they were a success—

My light-struck bedroom, filled with pattern, color, rhythm, and music.

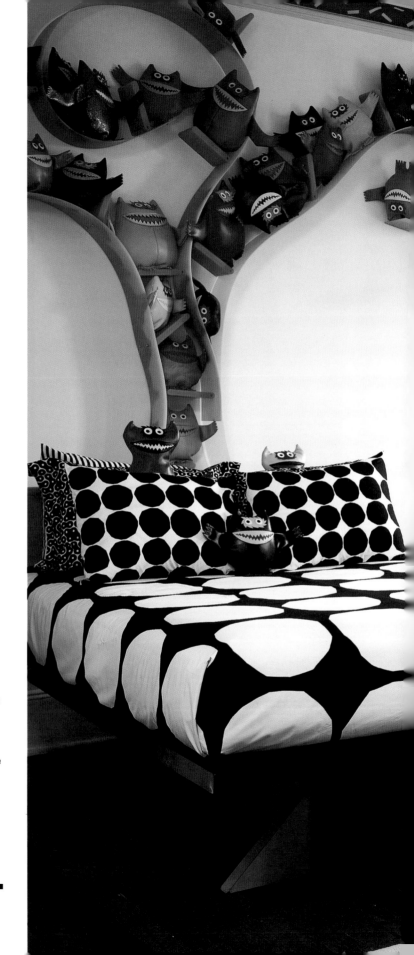

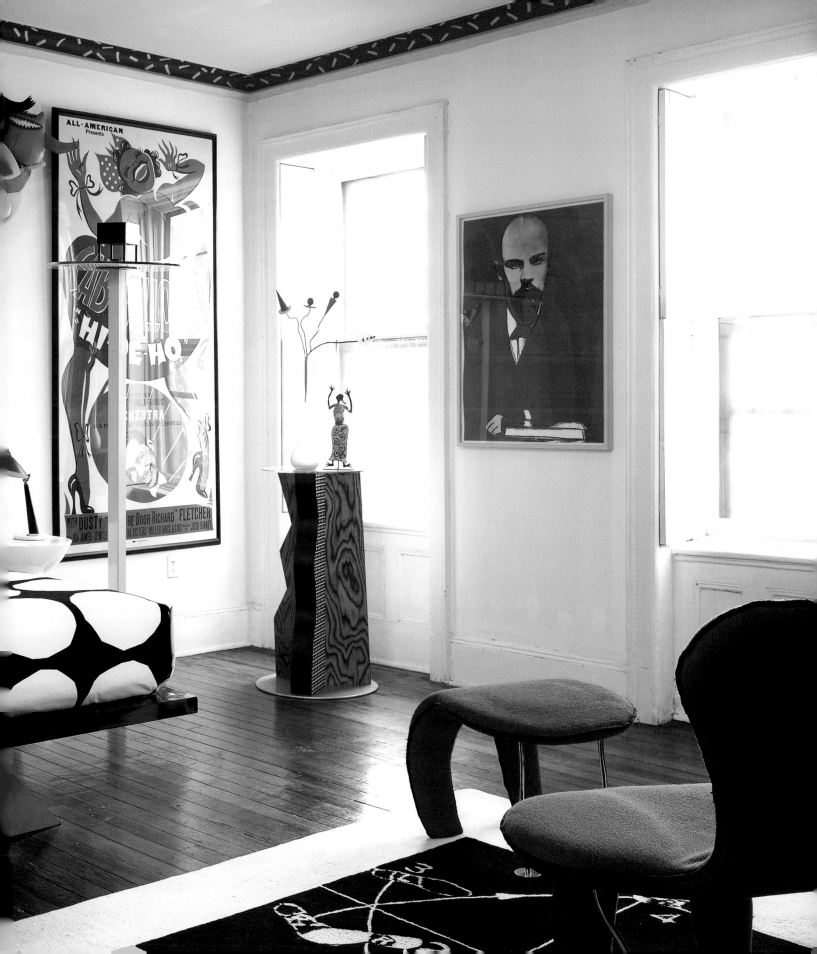

but visually the shutter was a dud. On the other hand, the white paint looked great. It was so close to perfect, I wondered how I'd ever taken such a perilous turn through the dark stained woods. We coated the fireplace in white, too, including the crossed-feather design at the center of the mantel, which had previously been emblazoned in gold.

Beauty and the Bold

The white on the bedroom woodwork and walls was only a staging ground for the bright palette to come. The ceiling soon was yellow, and in this instance there was no need to second-guess myself. The yellow ceiling lifted the bedroom into a coherent environment, where bright hues occurred not just in the furniture or the bedding but circulated throughout the space. To pop the bedroom ceiling even more and to continue the Memphis patterns that had already been established by key pieces of furniture, I wanted to paint the cove molding in a bold graphic of one-inch-wide yellow rectangles against a ground of red. Al achieved this by first painting the molding yellow. He waited for it to dry, and then cut masking tape into the same size as the rectangles I'd chosen. He placed them rhythmically around the

Above Ettore Sottsass's Memphis bureau, Ida Applebroog's deceptively simple painting sounds notes of missed opportunities and love lost.

perimeter, pausing always to ask if I thought the spacing was correct. Okay, I'd reply. No, move that one in the center a little more to the left. A little more. Just a tiny bit more, maybe an eighth of an inch. Okay, okay, that's it. And in that way, not by measurement but by visual impression, we established the design.

With the pattern locked in place, Al then covered the yellow with a coat of red. When it too had dried, he pulled off the masking tape, and the yellow rectangles it revealed danced like free spirits in an open field.

There was one last area to address with color. The pier that housed the fireplace was, as I said, a commanding presence in the room. To underscore its architectural importance, I chose to paint it entirely in blue, with the exceptions, of course, of the white baseboard and the fireplace mantel. The blue was of medium intensity, and neither too bright nor too sweet. If anything, it was closer to gray in spirit, and I could just as well have selected a gray if I hadn't wanted the extra play of more color. The blue was beautiful. While it was easy to look at (a bright color on a bedroom wall might have been too taxing), it nonetheless emphasized the height of the ceiling

---

and framed the fireplace, pushing it gently forward into the room. I was happy with all these choices—the yellow ceiling, the blue of the pier, the red-and-yellow pattern in the cove molding—when Lloyd, with his impeccable timing, showed up for a third time.

"Hey, that looks good," he said, surveying the new paint in the bedroom. "Just one suggestion. See that narrow molding just below the cove molding and right above the wall? You should paint it yellow. Red against white is static. Nothing really happens between them. But the yellow will be a positive transition. Try it. You'll see. It will make everything work better."

"How about yellow against the blue pier?" I wondered, not anxious to put those colors together.

"Don't worry. With the red right above, it will look okay."

This time I took Lloyd's counsel to heart. He had been so overwhelmingly right about the stained wood that it seemed foolish to do otherwise. Al painted the lower molding around the room with the same bright yellow as the ceiling. It made,

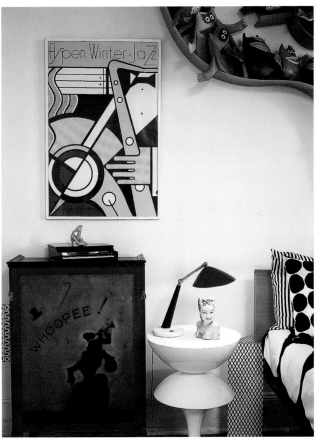

Music and rhythm to the left of the bed: a 1920s bar celebrating hot jazz, Roy Lichtenstein's 1967 poster for a jazz festival in Aspen.

as Lloyd predicted, a world of difference. With the additional line of yellow, all the colors resonated in a new way. It is good to have friends. And it doesn't hurt if they're talented.

The Determining Shape of Squares

Like the fireplace surrounds in the central and back parlors, the one in the bedroom also had to be replaced. This time Al didn't question whether I could top the other two, although it must have taken some effort for him not to. I took his silence as a muted vote of confidence and began to focus on the design.

When I studied art history at school, there was a tremendous emphasis on the role of a picture's shape in determining its inner logic. This was not a new thought; since the early Renaissance, artists had instinctively understood the relationship between the size and proportions of a painting's edge and the placement of the components within it. But in the 1960s, a group of artists began to challenge conventional notions of a picture's shape. Eschewing traditional rectangles, squares, and the occasional oval, they conceived new forms to paint on. Frank Stella in particular started to build huge canvases that ranged from X's to trapezoids. These paintings were executed in a single color. The second color, the "subject" of the painting, came from the canvas fabric, which had been left exposed in parallel lines that followed the picture's

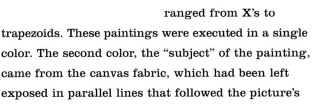

contours. What had been done quietly for 500 years was now thrust into the spotlight. The internal components of these paintings, in this case the unpainted lines of the canvas, dramatically showed their allegiance and subordination to the picture's edge.

As spontaneously as minimalism, as this new movement was called, seemed to burst upon the scene, just as rapidly did a whole corresponding body of art-critical discourse. It permeated the fine arts departments at colleges and art schools and became, until it was supplanted by the next discipline du jour, the presiding method for thinking and writing about paintings. Needless to say, it was also a particularly limited way of experiencing art, and it was inevitably pushed to the sidelines. Nonetheless, the lessons of this new art criticism stayed with me long after they ceased to hold sway. So when I contemplated the fireplace in my bedroom, I involuntarily returned once more to questions of shape, particularly the shapes that tiles come in.

Almost all tiles, as I've said before, are produced in rectangles and squares. Working not from the outside in, which is the philosophic approach of shaped canvases, but from the inside out, I began with the unit of the square. What could I come up with where the square was the essential building block, where the final image would emerge from massing the squares together, but where each unit would still stand alone as a unique and indispensable part? The solution seemed to come quickly, perhaps because I'd so clearly narrowed the outline of the problem. A crossword puzzle. In a crossword puzzle, every square has meaning. Each white square is a holding place for a letter to come, each black one a form of punctuation that stops the words from running together.

Although seemingly skeptical, Al was nonetheless taken with the idea. It appealed to the Scrabble player in him, the lover of word games who daily exercised his mental muscles on the **New York Times** crossword puzzle. Now it was a matter of figuring out how to create a puzzle on the fireplace, a process that proved more complicated than I'd originally thought.

The first thing I did was buy crossword-puzzle books to find a pattern we could work from. There were two immediate problems. This was a working fireplace, so a huge part of the puzzle would necessarily be missing to make room for the firebox, that blackened open area where one actually stacks logs and lights them. The only place for tiles was on the three narrow sides surrounding it. In this confined space, the layout of blacks and whites would have to be so graphic and strong that, even with a gaping hole in the center, one would still immediately grasp that the tiles formed the outer edges of a crossword puzzle. For the image to read, it was necessary to find a puzzle with a heavy proliferation of blacks near the perimeter. Surprisingly, patterns like this are quite rare. Only after much searching did I find one that we could use as our springboard.

The second problem involved proportion. Crossword puzzles, as enthusiasts must know, but I had never realized, aren't just composed of squares, they are squares. The puzzles break down into quadrants, the upper left mirroring the lower right, the upper right mirroring the lower left. But the surround of my fireplace wasn't square. It was taller than it was wide, in irritating defiance of the Crossword Puzzle Rule Book. We would have to subtly alter the design we were coopting.

The third issue was the size of the tiles. I chose two-by-two-inch squares—large enough to have presence, but small enough to create compelling patterns within the surround. The white tiles I opted for were matte, but I picked a high gloss for the black ones to stir more surface interest. After that, all the hard work fell to Al. It was Al, the master problem solver, who compensated for the vertical

In Your Space: **Personalizing Your Home and Office**

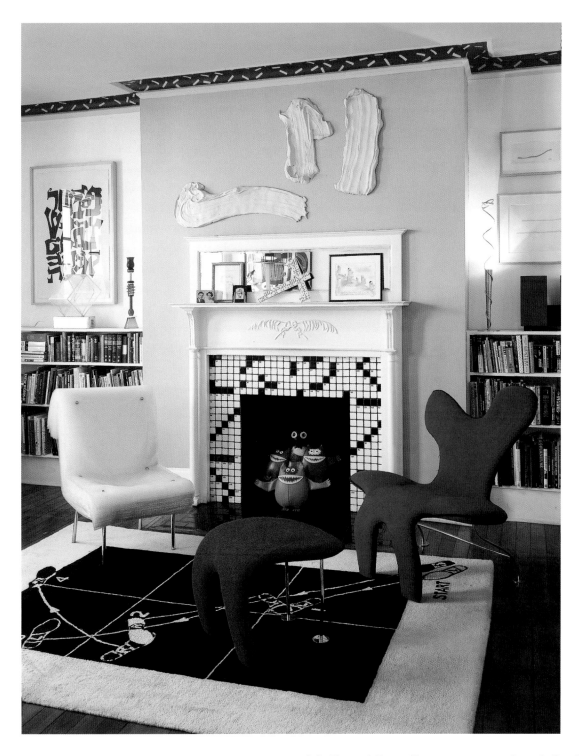

Jody Harrow's Dance-Step rug, a crossword-puzzle fireplace, and a Memphis pattern in the molding, move rhythmic graphics from the ceiling to the floor.

Strivers Row: Settling In

shape of the surround. And it was Al who laid out the tiles so that they not only formed an aesthetically strong design but also held true to the logic and conventions of working crossword puzzles.

When the squares were in place, even without the numbers, which we had yet to add, the effect was startling. The dramatic black-and-white patterns, striking but not overly complex, set up a series of rhythms that circulated with those laid down by the Memphis pieces in the room and with the lively yellow strips in the cove molding. Just as the yellow ceiling helped establish the bedroom as a total environment, so, too, did the crossword-puzzle fireplace. It continued the sense of visual music, ensuring that the wall on which the fireplace stood shared the same syncopated energy as the rest of the room.

The fireplace is opposite my bed, where I spend more time than any other place in the house. As I sit against the pillows on my headboard, writing or reading or talking on the phone, I am struck over and over again by how good the puzzle looks, how graphic it is at first glance, and how witty at the second. No matter how much time goes by, it always holds my interest. The true triumph of the fireplace is how much pleasure it gives me.

Over time I added a few more items to the bedroom: Godley-Schwan's whimsical blue Cartoon chair with its red ottoman, Jody Harrow's Dance-Step rug (which, seemingly sullied beyond repair, had toured over seven carpet cleaners to finally find one who restored it), and, much later, Fernando and Humberto Campana's elegantly subversive Bubble Wrap chair, with its shimmering translucence. Andy Warhol's powerful and radiant **Red Lenin**, a work he finished just before he died, went on the wall between two of my three windows. It was the first thing you saw through the door and, like the Ida Applebroog I placed above my bureau, created ballast for the lighter motifs in the room.

There was one last great addition, and it came to me as the crossword-puzzle fireplace had, although more slowly, perhaps because it took me longer to define the problem. Although art was everywhere in the bedroom, there was nothing over the bed itself. The bed was flanked on one side by my small 1920s jazz bar, over which hung Roy Lichtenstein's poster for the 1967 Aspen Jazz Festival. On the other side was my joyously spirited movie poster featuring Cab Calloway in **Hi-De-Ho**. But as I looked around the room, almost every piece of art, no matter how personal or intense or deeply felt, was described by a square or rectangular border. It made one think twice about the welcome contributions of shaped canvases. I hesitated to add yet another framed piece to this stiff geometry. With the exception of three thick impasto brushstrokes over the fireplace by Roxy Paine, the shape of the art on my walls had a formulaic rigidity. One more picture, however wonderful, seemed just one rectangle too many.

A Tree Grows in Harlem

This is a maxim I have often employed. Why rush something toward completion if the idea is not exactly right? Needless to say, it takes special circumstances to be able to bide one's time, holding out for the eureka that will lift something out of the ordinary into the realm of the perfect. Many projects, especially those involving other people, have real-world deadlines. In those cases, you have to go with not your best idea, but your best idea at the time, one of the compromises we make so as not to halt the calendar of progress, that singular schedule of expectations and forward movement whose very raison d'être demands delivery on time.

In a personal project, however, there is much more latitude. If you can sufficiently subdue your alpha instincts, then you can allow yourself to wait for just the right idea. This, of course, applies most when form, not function, is involved. It is a great deal harder to hold out for the perfect toilet or the perfect sink than it is for the perfect painting. And so, although the space above my bed was conspicuously empty, giving the bedroom a quality of anxious incompleteness, I did nothing. As much as possible, I ignored the bare spot on my wall, knowing, without yet having any ideas, that the solution was not one large, impressive picture or even an assemblage of smaller ones, but something quite different, something free-form and organic and definitely not square.

Some maxims, however, can be taken too far. I had become so accomplished in ignoring the space above my bed that two years went by without my giving it a thought. When finally, after twenty-four months, I decided to make it a priority, I was struggling with another problem. In the Century, herds of Naugas, those grinning, pointy-toothed vinyl beasties, had cavorted on my dining room shelves. I loved my Naugas, and they were everywhere I called home: not just in the Century but at my office and in my house in the country. But here on Strivers Row, they were still in the same cartons in which they'd made the move uptown in Padded Wagon trucks. Worse, they had been relegated to the cellar; in 4,000 square feet of house, I could think of no place to put them.

For one brief moment I thought of selling them. I had single-handedly driven up the Nauga market, and I could certainly get my money out or more. But selling just wasn't a possibility. Naugas are the most animated of inanimate objects, and I felt a strong emotional attachment to them. In fact, the more I thought about them stuffed in boxes in my basement, the more I felt like some evil stepmother who would surely get her comeuppance were there any justice in the world. So my problem was: what to do with the Naugas?

And here it was that two struggles converged in a single creative solution. There was just one room in the house where the Naugas truly belonged. Their bright colors, their playfulness, their double-edged smiles, full of warmth and multiple incisors, were at home in the bedroom as nowhere else. And the only place to put them, of course, was over the bed. But not on shelves—at least, not on straight, conventional shelves like those I'd had in the Century. That would only be perpetuating my rectilinear crisis. No, they would have to go on something different, something free-form and organic and full of curves, and I knew just what it was.

Ron Arad is an Israeli designer who lives and works in England. I had started seeing his furniture some twelve years earlier, as photos of it appeared in design magazines, particularly European ones. I was immediately struck by Ron's work, by its sculptural audacity, by the way he'd transformed steel into something strong and sensuous and unexpected. And I was never more impressed than when I saw Ron's bookcases, bookcases so radical they took your breath away. Forged from metal in unprecedented monumental shapes, they suddenly pushed all previous bookcases to the background. These bookcases looped, they curved, they spiraled into circles, but with such power and scale that one could believe that Ron might be Richard Serra's identical twin, separated at birth. As modern as they were, they also had a primitive magnificence. One of them was aptly called the War Wheel, its circular form and staggering size bringing to mind an ancient, brutal military machine. I fervently wanted one of these bookcases. But I didn't even investigate. In my heart, I already knew it was out of my range.

And then something wonderful occurred. Ron created an affordable version of his bookcases—the Bookworm, he called it—for Kartell, a European company that issues great design in a variety of plastics. Ron's Bookworm for Kartell was the ordinary mortal's model, a do-it-yourself edition that lacked the brute power of the original but retained its possibilities for unconventional forms. It came in six colors—amber, green, red, cobalt, charcoal, and clear, which was really a pale gray—and in three different lengths. The plastic itself was hard, but with just enough flexibility that one could bend it into any number of curved shapes, depending upon one's whims and physical strength. Of course, there were limits to how much the plastic would give, but the opportunity for self-expression was there.

I loved everything about Ron's Bookworms. They were witty and unique. They were interactive. And they were egalitarian. Not long after they came out, I bought a green one for the master bath in my country house. Later, I bought two cobalt blue Bookworms for the media room in my home on Strivers Row. And now I realized that the Bookworm would help me fill in the space above my bed with the perfect idea.

Usually people buy one Kartell Bookworm and, depending upon how daring they are and how much wall space they have, create forms from modest pinwheels to roller coasters of dips and swirls and loop-the-loops. A roller-coaster design would require a tremendous strip of plastic, but Ron had allowed even for that eventuality by making the Bookworm available in a giant twenty-seven-foot length. Like the rest of the world, I had only two thoughts in buying my first Bookworm: what color should it be, and how long? But when I decided to use the Bookworm in Harlem, I broke with the norm. Rather than buy one Bookworm, I bought two of equal lengths, installing one on top of the other in a pair of gentle horizontal waves. One Bookworm in this unassuming position would probably have looked incredibly bland, reflecting a total lack of imagina-

tion. But when one was placed over the other, they seemed like two parallel lines of music. When Ron Arad was brought by a friend to a party at my house, he admired how I'd used his invention. "I always enjoy seeing something done with my work that I haven't thought of myself," is how he put it, causing me to beam through the rest of the night.

But now I was thinking not of one Bookworm or two but of three, even possibly four. Accompanying the purchase of each Bookworm was a booklet that contained examples of possible shapes one might create. Although it showed a number of schematics, all the forms were abstract. In fact, only Ron's steel War Wheel had any figurative allusions. But figurative was just what I had in mind. If I took several Bookworms, grouped them together at a base (in this case, right behind the headboard of the bed), and then curved each one separately up the wall, they would give the impression of a tree. I ran to my notebook and, with pen in hand, drew this image. Between the dividers that came with each Bookworm to stabilize the books, I drew something else. Not books, although I had used my other three Bookworms for them—no, Naugas. Laughing, playing, mischievous, multiple Naugas, grinning from the branches of the tree.

When Al came over the next day, I showed him my primitive sketch.

"I guess it's possible," he said graciously.

With Al on board, I called Moss, a top-notch design store in SoHo, to see if they had the Bookworm in stock in the so-called clear or light gray. I'd already decided that with the many colors in my bedroom, and the even larger number of colors in the Naugas, gray was the only conceivable choice. Luckily, of all the colors in which the Bookworm comes, Moss had only gray in supply.

When the Bookworms arrived at my house the next day, Al immediately got to work. Having installed the cobalt blue ones in the media room

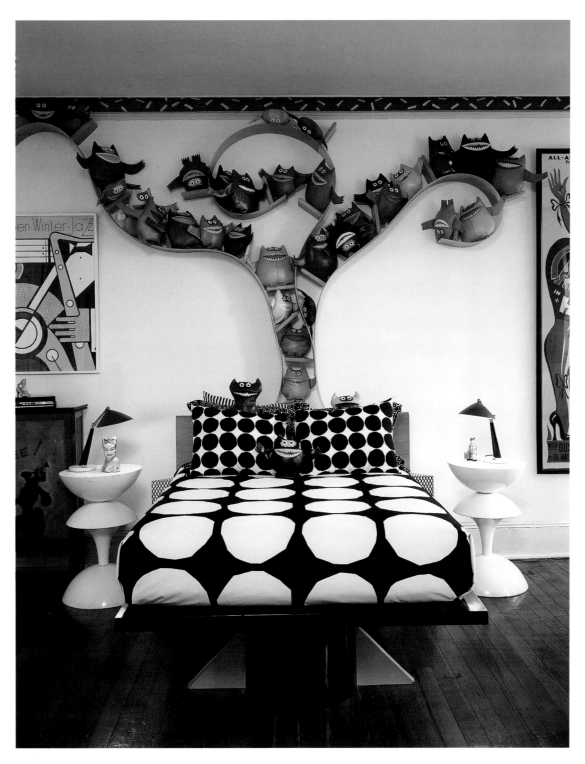

Naugas! George Lois's joyous creations celebrating Naugahyde.
Here they are, in a family tree.

upstairs, he knew the plastic well—where it had stresses and strains, where it would bend and where it wouldn't. It was no small task to shape the Bookworms into some semblance of a tree, but Al surpassed himself. He gathered the three lengths of plastic tightly together at the top of the headboard. When he had built the base high enough so that it could be seen only as a tree trunk, he separated the plastic lengths and curved each piece out in a different direction, like a large and flowing branch. One rose up to the left and climbed over the Lichtenstein poster for the Aspen Jazz Festival. The second shot up the center and then veered somewhat toward the right. The third moved even farther right, curving in on itself as it neared the Cab Calloway poster. The effect was thrilling. These three lengths of hard gray plastic had actually come together, bending and arcing against the tenacity of the material, until they grew up the wall as proud and strong as any tree found in nature.

Now it was time to liberate the Naugas. As Al brought them up from the cellar, the putrid scent of mildew filled the air, and I felt even more like Cruella de Ville. These poor guys! How they'd suffered! And how they smelled! I washed each one, sprayed and cleaned him* with Febreze, sprayed him with Lysol, and rinsed again. It didn't work. They still stank. It was clear that the Naugas needed an airing. We stuffed them between the screens and the storm windows and hoped for the best. Days passed. The dank scent, though fainter, still clung like stale perfume. And then one evening, I sniffed a Nauga,

*Although the Nauga's creator, George Lois, referred to it as his son, I do believe there are female Naugas as well. But that is a scientific thesis better left for another book.

and he smelled, well, just like a Nauga. I sniffed another, and another. One by one, although sometimes in twos and threes, they began to pass the sniff test. Another spray with Lysol, just to make sure, and I gathered up my brood to place them on the tree that was waiting for them with outstretched arms.

When I finished, I stepped back to enjoy the view. There were Naugas everywhere, big ones and little ones, yellow and turquoise ones, glitter-rock Naugas, and plain brown wrapper Naugas. But every one was exuberant. Some did cartwheels, others stood upside-down, and yet others lay on their stomachs to peer over the edge. A tree was growing in Harlem, and it bore strange fruit. But it was the fruit of unbounded joy.

Blooming Naugas

I had waited a long time to come up with this idea—obviously, a lot longer than I had to. The Naugas had been in the house all along, and I'd used the Bookworms before. The tools for the solution had been available to me from the beginning. Would I have come up with this idea two years earlier? It's impossible to know. I may have thought of something else that I felt was just as wonderful, there being, I am sure, more than one perfect solution for any given problem. The delay came from my lack of focus, from the fact that I never made the blank wall behind my bed a priority. Now, of course, it doesn't matter. The Nauga tree is in full bloom, and I love it with all my heart. But I've learned something for the future. If I want other solutions, other ideas, other Nauga trees, I can't expect them to grow on their own. It will happen only when I decide to break ground and plant the seed.

Lessons Learned Along the Way

1. It can't be helped. Your imagination is limited by what you know. Believing that all standard-issue tiles were flat, I never thought about how dimensional my bookcase fireplace could look if I used rounded tiles to indicate the volumes' spines. When Al unexpectedly found some in tile stores (they were made for edging), they helped make the surround seem all the more realistic. In order to expand your imagination, it's essential to expand your knowledge base. View everything you can, read everything you can. And familiarize yourself with new materials. When you see grass made out of recycled tennis shoes, or delicate gold chain mail encased in sheets of glass, you'll have ideas you never dreamed of. Although membership is required to use the resources of Material ConneXion in New York, it is well worth the visit. You'll find cutting-edge materials there that will open up a whole new world of possibilities.

2. Even the most banal of rooms usually has an architectural orientation. It may be where the windows are placed, or something as simple as the way the door opens into the space, but it's important to respect the architectural integrity of your interiors when deciding where to put your furniture. There are times when you'll want to make built-in additions to a room, like bookshelves or closets. But in doing so, make sure that they don't overwhelm the basic lines of your environment.

3. We all make mistakes. And when we do, sometimes it seems easier just to shrug our shoulders and live with them. This, however, is not a good idea. Although it always takes time and money to set things right, the alternative is living with something that most likely will make you increasingly unhappy over time. Clearly, if you're depressed about something major, like a bathroom you've installed, it would probably be foolhardy to tear it out. But if it's the color of the paint you've chosen, or some wallpaper or fabric, don't feel guilty about changing it. This is your home, and it's most important that you be happy in it.

4. Sometimes it's best to leave well enough alone. But at others, you might look at the architectural elements in a room and decide they could be enhanced. If there's a strong pier you want to bring forward, you can paint it a color or find an unusual material in which to cover it. If you have interesting moldings, you might consider painting them for emphasis.

5. Boring, boxlike rooms need help so that they don't look cold and spare. But even rooms full of detail— those with a fireplace, strong windows, high ceilings, cove moldings—can also look rigid. It's possible to have too many straight lines even in well-conceived interiors. To break the monotony, add an unexpected shape. The Nauga tree in my bedroom gave it an energy it never would have had if everything had been rectilinear.

11.

An Exhilarating Adventure:

The Dining Room from Scratch

Plaster heads on the fireplace, a George II mirror,
and nineteenth-century swirled candlesticks create
drama at one end of the room.

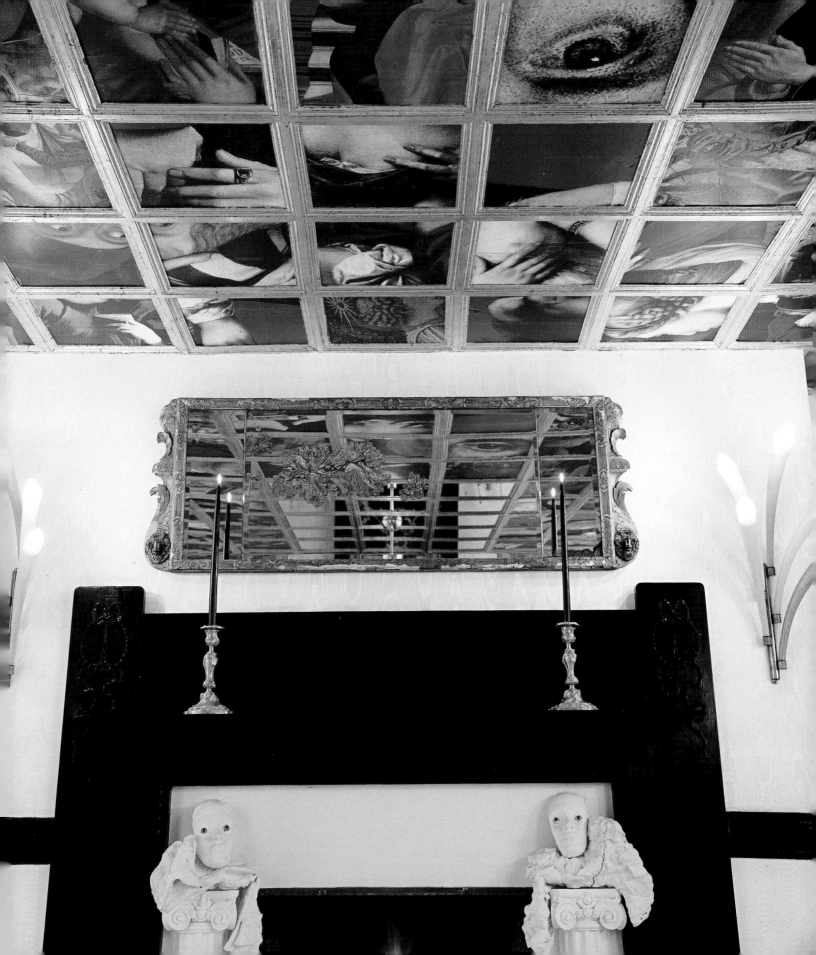

Creativity is one of life's most exhilarating pleasures, right up there with great sex and great food. And just as with sex and food, it can become addictive; the more you do it, the better you get at it. The better you get at it, the more fun it is. The more fun it is—well, you get the point. There are many wonderful reasons for personalizing the spaces where you live. But one of the best is the incredible rush that comes from opening the creative valve.

The Germ of a Guiding Idea

After the crossword-puzzle fireplace and the bookcase fireplace, and long before the Nauga tree, I was already feeling the wind at my back when I thought of the dining room. Unlike the front parlor or my bedroom, where I was working with pieces I'd brought from the Century, the dining room owed nothing to my past. It was virtually a blank, three-dimensional canvas, but I had a strong notion for it from the time I bought the house. This notion was no more than a phrase, but it guided me, despite countless alterations, through two and a half years of work to the final result: "I want to do a skewed version of Versailles."

Now, I had never been to Versailles. And although I could have researched it through books of lavish photographs, I wasn't interested in mining the images for inspiration. No, it was not actually Versailles but rather the idea of it—a glittering world of excess—that shaped my thinking of the room. I wanted to create this feeling in my dining room by constructing a formal, self-contained environment of rich surfaces and glistening materials. But that was not all. My version of Versailles would have twists and turns and references that formed an ironic commentary, challenging not just the effect but also the roots of such fabulous ornamentation.

Although the original dining room was on the parlor floor when the house was built, I chose to put mine on the garden floor, which also housed the kitchen in the back. From a point of convenience, this made total sense, and equally persuasive were the generous proportions of the front room where the dining room would go.

Mirrors, Gold-Leaf Ceilings, and Faux-Marble Floors

The only drawback was the ceiling. It was just eight feet high on the garden floor, the lowest in the house. To create the illusion of more height and in keeping with my notion of a skewed version of Versailles, I asked Al to create a modest coffered ceiling. Coffered ceilings are traditionally composed of thick beams that form a pattern of squares overhead. If well done, they add a powerful dimension to a room, connecting the ceiling execution with the rest of the space. The squares between the beams can be plain, or filled with complex, painted designs. But they almost always occur in high-ceilinged rooms, which have the scale to support them. My dining room was certainly not meant for a coffered ceiling. But if I could do a skewed version of Versailles, then why couldn't I also do a skewed version of a coffered ceiling? Rather than use thick beams to divide the ceiling into squares, I suggested to Al that we use thin moldings covered in gold leaf. Within each square we would place a mirror, over 180 in all. The gold leaf would be part of the Versailles motif, a luxurious material with a centuries-old history in the decorative arts. Between the gold, the mirrors would cause the room to dance with light, reflecting it in myriad ways while seeming to double the ceiling height.

Using both math and his artist's instincts, Al

composed a layout of fourteen-by-fourteen-inch squares and then brought back possible moldings so that I could pick the one I thought best. When I'd made my selection, he put up a few squares, covered the moldings in gold leaf, and added mirrors. This was a test run to see if the effects I imagined would be borne out in reality. And they were. Even though we'd barely begun the dining room, the moldings and mirrors were incontrovertible emblems of sparkling luxe, lifting the space from the banal to the opulent and creating the illusion of greater ceiling height.

But before Al could proceed with the ceiling, he had to address the floor. When I bought the house, the floor was composed of thin brown hardwood strips. I immediately knew that I wanted to paint it over in a classic marble pattern—large white squares on the diagonal, with black diamonds at the points of intersection. Why not use real marble? "Skewed," here as throughout the dining room, was the operative word. A real marble floor would have been a literal re-creation of the ornamental extravagance to which I wanted to bring a fresh and knowing perspective. It was essential not to ape this style but to refer to it and, in doing so, bring it into question. Painting the floor would suggest the effect of marble, but it would also allow the wood strips to come through, emphasizing the floor's more humble and utilitarian origins.

So Al brought back Henderson Greene, who had restored the stairs as closely as possible to their original condition. Henderson sanded the floor down to its bare wood, dispatching decades of accumulated wax and grime. When it was primed, Al drew a grid, opting, with my input, for sixteen-inch squares, whose gracious amplitude echoed the proportions of the room. Smaller squares would have created an overly busy pattern, while larger ones would have made it look too spare. Al then laid down the paint, a creamy white for the large squares,

a deep black for the small ones at the intersecting points. When the paint dried, the underlying wood added its own soft variations to the color. Some strips were lighter, some warmer, some had a faintly yellow cast. These unexpected slight changes in hue, as though the house had decided to contribute subtle rhythms of its own, made the floor more beautiful than I had ever dreamed.

With the floor complete, Al returned to the tedious task of putting up the moldings and gold-leafing them in place. Before one adds gold leaf, it is necessary first to apply an undercoat of paint. Although there is no rule as to the color—it could be green or blue or black—red is the foundation most often used. Al adhered to this tradition, painting the moldings with a coat of red paint and then, when it had dried, layering gold leaf on top of it. Needless to say, I regularly visited Al in his Sistine Chapel mode, stopping to chat and to check on his progress.

It was on one of these trips that I was struck so hard by something that it changed the course of the ceiling and of many other components in the room. Although Al is nothing if not meticulous, his application of the gold leaf was not seamless. Instead, on every molding, red flecks of the undercoat were showing through. Whether this was by design or not I never asked, because the red beneath the gold had caught my imagination, bringing up memories and powerful associations.

"Al, you see how the red comes through the gold leaf? It reminds me of the frames on old master paintings when they start to chip with age."

"So?"

"So, wouldn't it be wonderful to fill the squares not with mirrors but with details from Renaissance paintings?"

It was such a radical change in direction that Al, who seems to have a response for everything, was silent.

"You know," I expanded, "not whole paintings but fragments—the close-up of a hand or a piece of jewelry, the embroidery on a garment, a nose, an eye, a lace collar, the border of a robe."

"And how would you do this?" Al had recovered sufficiently to retreat to his twin harbors of safety, pragmatism and logic.

"We'd pick the details and then enlarge them to fit the squares. I know there's a photoreproduction process that can get high resolution on paper."

"So you're not thinking of painting these?"

"Oh, no." It was my turn to be surprised. "That would be impossible. And besides, it would never look as good as the original."

Original, naturally, was a pointedly absurd term, although I brandished it with conviction. After all, I was talking about a third- or fourth-generation image, an enlargement of a detail from a printed page, reproduced from a transparency of a painting.

"I guess we could do it," Al conceded. He didn't say so, but, as an artist himself, he was intrigued by the idea. So while the gold-leafing continued, Al also scoured the used-book market to find reference works we could cut up with a minimum of guilt. I opted only for Italian Renaissance paintings, wanting the warm, lush styles of the south.

When he finally had enough variety to get started, Al made a template, a two-by-two-inch square, and put it like a frame over the pictures in the books, moving it this way and that until he'd isolated a detail that met the parameters I'd set. These parameters required that the detail not only had to be compelling when it stood alone but also had to look like a detail. Many Renaissance paintings are so complex that you could pull a fragment from one and, not knowing the source, think you were look-

The dining room, with Renaissance paintings on the ceiling, opulent details, and surreal themes.

228

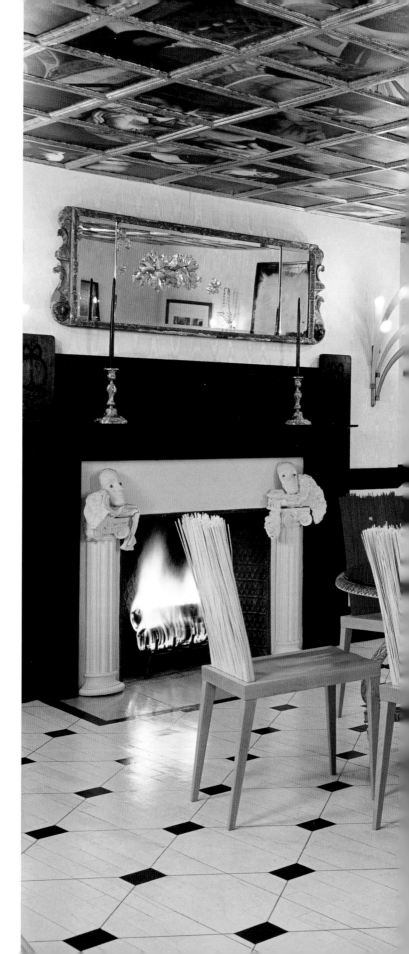

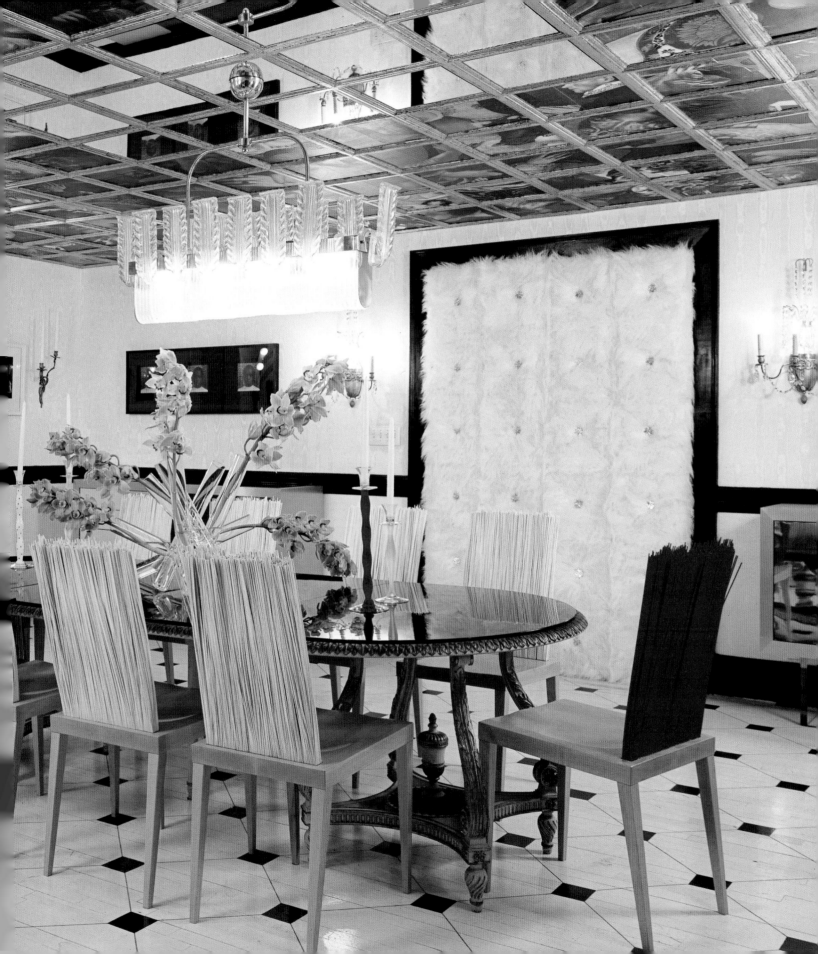

ing at a fully realized picture. But if the devil is in the details, I believed the beauty of the ceiling would be in the details, too. We ran out of images, forcing Al to buy more books. Meanwhile, we made a decision to keep some of the mirrors overhead, just enough to shoot light about the room while seeming to vault the ceiling. In planning how many mirrors to use, I had to consider the approximate size and placement of the dining room table. It would have to be large enough to seat ten and be positioned lengthwise, creating a strong horizontal that would be seen as soon as you passed through the dining room doors. Using estimated proportions for the table, we saved fifteen squares to be mirrored: five for the length, and five sets of three for the width.

To help me visualize the ceiling in miniature, Al took a large sheet of posterboard and drew a layout of the ceiling: blank squares for each detail, and fifteen shaded ones in the center to indicate where the mirrors would go. He then laid in the two-by-two-inch fragments he'd cut from our mounting pile of books. Although Al put these details in an order he liked, he knew I'd want to play with them, changing their final positions. In doing so I tried to distribute color, intensity, and content in ways that were neither repetitive nor formulaic. When this small-scale template of the ceiling looked as good as it was going to get on paper, it was time to work on the real thing.

While Al was diligently completing the gold leaf, searching out art books, and cutting them apart, I'd been investigating how to blow up his small squares into the full-size fourteen-by-fourteen-inch ones. The process I had first mentioned to Al turned out to be terrifically expensive, approximately $80 an image. Fourteen thousand dollars just for paper copies! There had to be another way, and it was Al the chess player, the consummate problem solver, who came up with it.

Al had already investigated Kinko's, which, as every student knows, is the place to go for inexpensive color copies. It seemed like the logical place for us to go as well, except that the largest size paper Kinko's handled was eleven inches by seventeen. But we needed to enlarge each detail to a fourteen-inch square, and that size was immutable because the gold-leaf moldings that determined this dimension were already in place. Stumped at first, Al revisited the problem until the solution emerged. If he cut each of his two-inch-square details in half, he could blow them up, then blow them up again.

The resulting fourteen-inch square would have to be arrived at by piecing two halves of the image together. This meant each detail would have a central seam. Yet it was amazing how readily it vanished in the interest and complexity of each image. If I point out the seams to friends, they have no trouble seeing them. But guests left to their own observation are so taken by the beauty of the details and the overall effect of the ceiling that their eyes and minds are selective, focusing on the whole and not upon what it took to get there.

Elegant Sconces and Moiré Walls

Even before Al started work on the ceiling, when my thoughts were of mirrors, gold leaf, and faux-marble floors, I had a number of other ideas for the dining room. A brown wood chair rail ran around the perimeter, neatly bisecting the walls. I wanted to cover the two sections in fabric, pink moiré for the bottom, white moiré for the top. This leaned more heavily toward the feminine than is my wont, but what was Versailles if not that? I also imagined sconces on every wall, and busied myself on a quest for them. The very first sconce I bought was relatively contemporary. Made in the early 1950s by the Italian design company Fontana Arte, it was based on a sixteen-inch rod of solid glass in an emerald green so deep that it felt like an ancient treasure, the staff of a king or a mage. But the shape of the rod was modern, the lines pure and clean. Four brass candelabra jutted from the glass, but what caught my attention was the hardware that gripped it on one end and was meant to be affixed to the wall on the other. The hardware was bronze, and it was fashioned in the shape of a hand.

The Expansion of an Idea

Even if I had no reference points, I would have been captivated by the jewel-like gleam of the glass, the power of its shape, cast as a single, uninterrupted piece, and most especially, the hand that held it. But seeing the sconce, I immediately thought of Jean Cocteau's **Beauty and the Beast**, one of the most beautiful films ever made. Shot in France during World War II, **Beauty and the Beast** was a triumph of vision over budget. Wartime had made all supplies scarce, but Cocteau was an artist as well as a poet, and he had hired the wonderfully imaginative Christian Bérard as his production designer. Moving from location to location to escape the Fascists on the one hand and their creditors on the other, scrambling for the next two francs to shoot another scene, Cocteau and Bérard fashioned a surreal and visually lyrical film with a minimum of means.

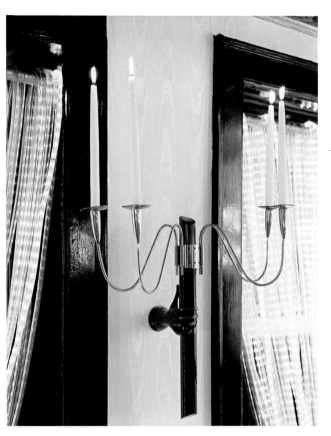

Between the windows, a hand holds aloft a candelabra, recalling similar lamps in Jean Cocteau's **Beauty and the Beast**.

When Beauty arrives alone and frightened at the Beast's castle, she is propelled by invisible air currents down a vast corridor, her feet never touching the ground. Sheer curtains billow into the passage as she floats by, and candelabra, held aloft by arms and hands, swivel to follow her journey through the hall. As befits a true fairy tale, it is a world of sparkling enchantment troubled by dark ripples just beneath. So while Beauty's progress through the Beast's grand hall is stirring, it is disturbing too. It is this unsettling combination, the stunning lushness of the scene, the surreal signs punctuated by sinister entrapments, that make Beauty's passage some of the most visually memorable footage in the history of film.

The emerald green sconce clutched by a bronze hand had resonated in me and inspired me to expand my vision of the dining room. The old definition was: a skewed version of Versailles. The new one read: a skewed version of Versailles, joined to the disconcerting ambience of **Beauty and the Beast**.

A Search for the Surreal

The sconce was my first acquisition to conform to this altered definition. But there were more to come.

While I searched out other sconces and a chandelier that could possibly be hung from an eight-foot ceiling, I also stopped to see some work by my friend Justen Ladda. Justen is an immensely creative and dedicated artist, so deeply curious, so fascinated by different materials and new ideas, that it is impossible to categorize him.

Justen had told me that he was in a group show at the National Academy of Arts and Letters. So one Saturday afternoon, just as the exhibit was about to come down, I took a taxi over to 155th Street and Broadway and walked through a mall of stately buildings to the one that housed the academy. Once I'd discovered the room with Justen's work, it was hard to concentrate on anything else.

Most people, when they mentioned Justen's art, talked about an installation he'd made of Marvel Comics' brutish Hulk climbing over the seats in the basement auditorium of an abandoned school in the Bronx. It had caused quite a stir, but that was many years before, and Justen had pursued any number of different ideas since then. Not surprisingly, there was nothing at the academy even faintly reminiscent of the work that had created so much buzz. Instead, there was a selection of pictures from Justen's series of mirrors. The forward surfaces were printed with photographs of elaborate ornamental frames, and recessed behind them were shiny, almost reflective skins containing a striking image. An ape hovered in the corner of one frame. A mask floated at eye level in another. I had never seen anything quite like them. They were stunningly beautiful, but equally provocative, bringing into question how we present ourselves and who we truly are. That night, I called Justen.

"Justen, hi, it's me. I absolutely loved your work. Is any of it available? I especially love the one with the mask."

"Well, the mask you saw with the sepia surface is sold. But I have another with a black surface that's still available."

I couldn't contain my excitement. What luck that Justen had made two versions! The gold frame in this picture was opulent enough to have been hung in the Grand Palais, while the bodiless mask brought to mind masquerade balls where disguise blurs not only identity but also boundaries of restraint. It called up the countless masks we wear in public, and even those we wear in private, when we look in the mirror and believe we truly see ourselves. It was a brilliant, potent work—and for my purposes a perfect one, referencing the glistening world I was building in my dining room and the uneasy, surreal currents of **Beauty and the Beast**.

Naturally, I was down at Justen's studio in a flash. Once there, I looked not just at the mask but at several more works in the mirror series. But, ultimately, for me, the mask was the most powerful. And philosophically, with its issues of surface and substance, it fit best within the context of the dining room. I bought the mask but left it with Justen, who graciously agreed to keep it until the dining room was finished enough for it to be installed.* I already knew where it would go—on the center of the wall opposite the fireplace.

*I have done this many times with items I have bought, but it is a truly terrible idea. One should always take one's purchase, no matter how inconvenient it might be. There are many horror stories about what happens if you don't, and I have more than my share of them. However, in this case, all went well, for which I have only Justen and good fortune to thank, not one whit of common sense.

The Light Fantastic

In this period I had picked up a number of other objects for the dining room. From Fred Silberman, a store now in Chelsea that specializes in Italian design, I bought a pair of beautiful 1950s lights. By Barovier, they were composed of handblown glass horns in subtle pastel colors, flecked almost imperceptibly with gold. Light bulbs peeked out of each, like tight blooms about to unfurl. I loved them and thought they would look great with the pink moiré fabric I was planning to put in the room. There was a chandelier there, too, but it was the first one I'd seen with any possibilities, and I wasn't sure enough to commit.

At an antiques show I also bought a pair of early-twentieth-century French sconces, each with three candles that had been electrified. Their bases were silvered, and they were draped with ropes of crystal beads. Over-the-top, clearly—but so was Versailles. And they were fabulous. I never thought I'd be looking at something made so long ago, let alone buying it. But I was about to discover that even the nineteenth-century world held interest for me, and treasures that I wanted.

I hit the indoor antiques market on West Twenty-fifth Street and, on the basement floor, found two brass sconces in the shape of women, their breasts bare, their arms extending forever to hold the candles up. They had the same unsettling quirkiness as **Beauty and the Beast**, and I bought them. As always in my quests, I wondered if the dealer had any other sconces that I hadn't seen. Yes, he did. Nothing that satisfied my criteria, but it was imperative to ask.

Finally he mentioned that he had a pair with an Egyptian motif at an antiques show at the Eastside Armory. I couldn't afford not to look, so I got the address of the armory and the booth number where the sconces were and scurried across town. The Egyptian women were not for me—too small, without enough impact—but since I was there, I cruised the corridors to see what else I might find. At another booth, pay dirt—not sconces, but candlesticks. They were heavy, and brass, with the metal swirled in a sensuous way that presaged Art Nouveau. Late

nineteenth century, said the good-looking man whose booth it was. I thanked him—candlesticks were not on my list—and told him I would think about them. This is such a common response in antiques shows that no one takes it seriously. So when I returned some twenty minutes later to find the owner engaged in conversation, his peripheral vision didn't even pick me up. I hovered expectantly as long as I could, then gave up, returning only when I saw he was alone.

"Hi, I'm back," I said, in case he hadn't noticed. And he must not have, because his gaze was polite but blank.

"The nineteenth-century brass candlesticks. I'd like to buy them. I tried to catch your attention before, but you were busy."

He fell over himself with apologies. "I'm so sorry. I didn't think you wanted them. Here, let me get them for you."

I asked if he had any sconces. The design detective, leaving no stone unturned.

"No, but the man that I was talking to, Michael Hall, is one of the most important connoisseurs of art, particularly Renaissance sculptures, which he sells to museums around the world. There's nothing he doesn't have. Let me get his number for you."

But he didn't have to. Michael Hall returned while I was there. He gave me his card, and I made an appointment to visit him in his town house near the Metropolitan Museum. It was jammed, top to bottom, with incredible things. And he had sconces, of course. I bought two nineteenth-century pairs from him, and later a truly extraordinary George II mirror whose early, flawed silvering created a gorgeous, rippling shape in the glass.

I now had more than enough sconces. In my enthusiasm, I had even snatched up another stunning set, their glass profiles sleek, sculptural, and futuristic. I didn't know where they would go, but I was getting carried away. Now it was time to concentrate on the chandelier. I made the rounds of dealers, hoping for something glittering and imaginative that could be hung over a dining table from my painfully low ceiling. Justen suggested I visit his friend Louis Bofferding, who was renowned for impeccable taste and one-of-a-kind pieces.

"Go see Louis," he urged. "I've seen chandeliers at his place that look like helium balloons and sailing ships."

Well, that was recommendation enough. But when I visited Louis, those chandeliers were gone. They were rare, and he couldn't say when he'd come across another. What he did have, however, was a table. A long, oval table with a glistening black lacquer top, gilding on the carved edge around it, and gilding on the two carved, cagelike bases that held it up. It bore no resemblance to anything I'd owned, or wanted to own, or had ever appreciated even from afar. It was opulent and decidedly not modern, and just as decidedly not to my taste. But now that I was paying attention, it was also, I had to admit, pretty wonderful.

"How about the table?" I finally asked after we'd discussed everything in his flat, from chairs and photographs to mirrored valances. Louis was full of fascinating information, a dealer who had scrupulously done his homework.

"Oh, that was made in the thirties by the House of Jansen in Paris. There were only three of them as far as I know, each with slight variations. The duke and duchess of Windsor had one that sold recently at auction for a staggering amount." And, so saying, he brought out books that showed the Windsors' table as it had sat in their dining room. Despite the dearth of chandeliers, it had been, after all, a very rewarding visit. We talked a little longer; then I thanked Louis and left.

Having struck out in my quest for chandeliers,

I began to think again about the first one I'd considered at Fred Silberman's, an Italian light made by Venini in the 1930s. Two attributes made it quite unusual: the lamp was fashioned not from crystal but from heavy cast pieces of cut glass, and, rather than cascading loosely like most chandeliers, its form was rigid and horizontal. This last fact, especially, made the light exceptional and, for my needs, close to perfect. But I had barely noticed it.

Although I like to think I'm quite adventurous, in this instance I was probably more conservative than I realized, too stuck in the world of crystal beads to consider that one could have just as much drama without them. A horizontal chandelier was clearly the solution. And to have found one so beautiful was nothing short of a miracle. But was it really beautiful? It was so different, so conspicuously opulent compared to anything I owned, that I could feel the clay oozing from my feet. It's not that I hadn't bought large pieces that made even larger statements, like Nicola's twelve-foot sofa in the shape of a woman, but they'd always had a witty turn that took the edge off any self-importance. But this chandelier was neither lighthearted nor knowingly ironic. It was grand, and it was serious. It was one of those few times—at least with questions of design—that I felt unsure of myself. There was nothing to do but pick up the phone and ask for a second opinion from Jim Walrod, a good friend who I was sure would have seen the chandelier.

When he confirmed it was an amazing piece, I added the Venini chandelier to my shopping cart. And Jim was right. I truly love the lamp, my appreciation growing each time I see it hanging from the mirrored section of the ceiling. It is serious and grand, but it is also subtle, with a geometry that makes it more modern than most other chandeliers. And while it lacks the glittering verve of crystal, the cut glass gives it a subdued opulence, closer to candlelight, a rich complement to the Renaissance details surrounding it. It creates an effect that is not unlike that of the interior scenes in Stanley Kubrick's visual masterpiece **Barry Lyndon**, which were shot without electric lighting, not just for historical accuracy but also to achieve the mellow glow that comes when you let a thousand candles burn.

A Table Fit for a Duke

The dining room was shaping up. I now had a number of major anchors in place—the floor, the ceiling, a commanding piece of art, the Fontana Arte sconce, which established the surreal secondary theme of the room, and the most important piece of lighting, the chandelier. On the other hand, I was still missing many things. And there was one glaring central gap, the table. Now I did have an idea for one. Once the Fontana Arte sconce had triggered memories of **Beauty and the Beast**, I decided to dot the room with similar motifs. In the Cocteau film, a statue of an archer guards the treasure house of the Beast. I wanted to build a table with a similar statue underneath, a table that also evoked the look of the light-struck curtains that billow as Beauty is propelled down the hall. It seemed possible to achieve this effect by surrounding the tabletop with sheer fabric, but in sections, so that when it parted, one would catch glimpses of the statue lit by pinpoint beams. Somewhere—in the corners?—my thought was to place small fans that would cause the fabric to move, blown by an unseen source. I decided to start with the statue.

When I had free time on weekends, I raced to all the places that sold the salvaged remains of razed New York buildings, where extraordinary attention had been paid to every element, from gargoyles to elevator doors. To my surprise, I found nothing. Meanwhile, Al and Alexander voiced a chorus of objections. Ordinarily, I would not have paid much attention to their grumbling, but this was an exception. How could I ignore Alexander, Alexander, the black belt in entertaining, when he postulated the discomfort that this design was sure to cause my guests? And even more, how could I dismiss Al's skepticism, since he was the one who would have to build the table, and he believed that my ideas—hidden fans, buried pinpoint lights—were totally impractical? Unable to find a statue, I buckled under their pressure, and decided to call Louis Bofferding to see if his dining table was still available. I also wanted to ask again about the price, which I remembered as being very high—not high for the table's value, but very high for me. Louis hadn't yet sold it, but the price confirmed my fears.

At Louis's I waffled. If I thought the Venini chandelier was different from everything I owned, the table belonged to a yet unnamed species. And then there was the price. Starting with my first set of doubts, I tried to assemble the pros and cons. Okay, so the duke and duchess of Windsor had had the nearly identical piece. Aside from the fact that they led spoiled, feckless lives, and he was most likely a Nazi sympathizer, did that necessarily make it bad? Well, no, not exactly. Maybe it was even a plus, because the duke and duchess were surely the direct spiritual descendents of Louis XVI and Marie Antoinette.

At any other time I wouldn't have given the table a second glance. But if I switched gears and took it on its own terms, it was actually a drop-dead piece with classic proportions, given an unexpected sense of fantasy by the cagelike bases. The lacquer top picked up the black in the painted floor and in Justen's mirror picture. Without diminishing the ceiling, the table would give much-needed weight to the most important function of the room, dining. The gilding worked too, echoing the gold-leaf moldings and the bronze sconces I had bought. Even the table's oval shape was welcome, an antidote to a room full of rectangles and squares. Okay, I was convinced. But what about that price?

Louis was willing to work with me, and assured me that I could pay for the table over time. Trying to bolster my confidence, he reminded me that the table would always do well at auction. And, when he saw I was still not sure, he offered to send the table up to my house to see how it looked in the dining room.

When the table was delivered and set up under the Renaissance ceiling, there was a collective sigh of relief from the critics. Al and Alexander were thrilled. They felt I'd finally come to my senses. The only obstacle continued to be the price, and I knew I was hooked when I called Louis to see how much better he could do.

Well, you know the rest. Louis and I worked out something I could live with in a quick and simple discussion. With the table entrenched in the center of my dining room, I was a fairly pathetic negotiator. Yet I had no regrets—the table was truly spectacular. All it needed was something to take just a little edge off its fabulousness. And that would come later, with the chairs.

A horizontal 1930s Venini chandelier is the perfect fixture for the dining room's low ceiling.

The Importance of Being Flexible

In a project like the dining room, certain cherished ideas inevitably fall by the wayside. My Cocteau-inspired table was the first to bite the dust, but so did the pink moiré fabric that had been one of my earliest notions for the room. Al had picked up a few sample pieces of the fabric and tacked them to the wall to see the effect. When they first went up, they looked wonderful, a graceful, luxurious transition between the black-and-white floor and the mirrors and gold-leaf moldings overhead. But, as I changed course and traded an overall mirrored ceiling for an assemblage of Renaissance details, it became clear that the pink moiré would have to go. It had to do with color. The number of pigments available during the Renaissance was limited, but artists made the most of what they had, and looking at their pictures, you don't feel that whole spectrums of hues are missing. Nonetheless, when you view close to two hundred details at once, it becomes apparent that red predominates. The red is warm and strong, but the pink moiré was pretty and, though light, still assertive. Each color had its own distinct sensibility, and they were at odds with one another. There was nothing wrong with the white moiré, which provided both a welcome break from the ceiling's intensity and a clear background against which to hang art. But I needed something other than pink below the chair rail, a neutral with some warmth.

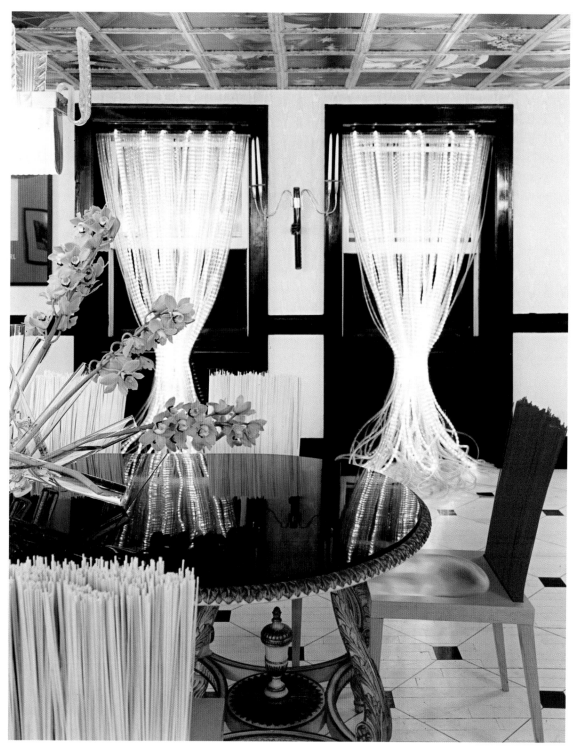

Reflections from curtains of beaded lights bounce off the lacquered sheen of an ornate French 1930s table.

An Exhilarating Adventure: The Dining Room from Scratch

Once again Al hit the fabric stores, returning with every color that fit this description from mushroom moiré to beige. Ultimately, a cream moiré won the Great Fabric Swatch Switch-off. It was close to the white above the chair rail, but had more yellow in it. The wall was now more of a piece, but subtle differences still made it interesting. At this point Lloyd, his timing as always unassailable, showed up with another incisive pronouncement.

"Paint all the wood black," he declared.

"Black? Lloyd, I don't know. There's a lot of wood in this room. If it's all black, I'm afraid it will look heavy."

"Well, marbleize it with gold if you want to lighten it. Someone in my building does faux painting. I can ask him for you."

I mentioned this to Al, who was not about to concede his primacy as master artist to someone else. He had never attempted faux painting, but that was only a detail. With a book on the subject in one hand and a paintbrush in the other, Al came up with numerous variations on black marble veined with gold. But there wasn't one of them I liked. It wasn't Al's fault. The gold and black just didn't seem to work. At this juncture, Lloyd, summoned by some unseen force, appeared again. He assessed the chair rail covered with failed experiments and proclaimed:

"Oh, just paint it solid black."

What was there to lose? Wherever there was wood, Al painted it with a glossy black enamel. The change was dramatic, and the black did seem heavy. But after such a strenuous effort, I was not about to suggest trying something else, at least not right away. And that proved to be a blessing. Because bit by bit, the black grew on me. In fact, it soon became impossible to consider any other option for the wood. Yes, the black was a dramatic change, but it also was a change with drama. And it gave a framework to everything else—to the black-and-white

floor, to the dining room table with its black lacquer top, to Justen's black mirror picture, and to the warm reds in the Renaissance ceiling. Even the white and cream moirés looked richer, their subtle byplay heightened by the strong blacks flanking them.

Yes, There Is a Lesson in All This

I'm basically a believer in snap judgments. They represent a synthesis of all one's experiences, all one's observations, all one's trials, one's errors, and one's triumphs. They are honest and direct, unfettered by the countless modifications that come from too consciously thinking something through. Yet they can be wrong. In the case of the dining room wood, I would have scrapped the black. But black, without question, was the ideal solution for the space.

Why, when most immediate responses are the best ones, did my instincts fail in this instance? I think it comes down to our human comfort with familiarity and our innate resistance to change. No matter how enlightened we feel, at times, when faced with something different, we falter involuntarily. We may not even realize how attached we've been to something until it suddenly no longer exists and we're uncomfortable with its replacement. So what is a person to do?

Whenever possible, trust your instincts. The more you hone them, the better they'll be. But know, too, that there is room for error, that every once in a while your instincts might lag behind your intellect, particularly when change is involved. Try to give the change a chance. Again, this is an emotional process, not a conscious one. If two weeks later you're still unhappy, the change was wrong, just as my decision to stain the wood in my bedroom was wrong. But if positive feelings are starting to replace more negative ones, if what looked bad is beginning to look good, then you know you made the right decision in the end.

The Dining Room Chairs

In late summer of 1998, I was having lunch with my friend Paola Antonelli, a curator of design at the Museum of Modern Art. Paola is a visionary and courageous curator, and I'm always eager to know what she's looking at and thinking about.

"So what's your next show?" I asked, interested as ever.

"I'm doing something in the Projects Room this fall," Paola replied. "I'm combining Ingo Maurer's lighting with the furniture of two young Brazilian designers, Fernando and Humberto Campana. You know Ingo's work, of course, but you probably don't know the Campana brothers'. It's great, and it's just the kind of thing you love."

"Honestly? Oh, I'd love to see it. Do you have any photographs?"

"Of course, tesoro." Paola is Italian and employs the nicest endearments. "I'll send some over to your office."

Paola was right. When the photos arrived, I was thrilled. Fernando and Humberto had combined unexpected materials—bubble wrap, garden hose, heavy rope—with more traditional, even elegant shapes. Their furniture looked fresh and modern, and I felt the same kind of rush I had ten years earlier when I first saw the work of Lyn Godley and Lloyd Schwan. The opening, Paola had told me, was in November. And suddenly, because I love Paola, because I've revered Ingo's lighting for more years than I can count, because Fernando and Humberto were already inspiring me with their humble materials and sophisticated imaginations, I volunteered to have a party for them all on the night of the opening. Make up your guest list, I told Paola, and ask Ingo and Fernando and

Humberto to do the same. I'll mix in some of my friends, and we'll have dinner afterward at my house.

And that is what happened. Ingo and Fernando and Humberto were all as special as their work, and the first lines of friendship were charted that night. I went to Brazil for the holidays. Fernando and Humberto came back to New York and stayed with me. When their show at the Modern came down, I bought from it two of their chairs, including the Bubble Wrap chair for my bedroom. And I asked Fernando and Humberto to design the chairs for my dining room.

They said yes with enthusiasm, made sketches, built prototypes in their studio in São Paulo, and sent me photographs. When I returned to Brazil a year later, I saw what was now named the Jenette chair. It was fashioned from a pale, hard wood, with four straight legs and a slightly curved seat to support long stretches at the dining table. A normal chair so far—but the back pushed it into wholly new territory. It was composed of over a thousand long plastic bristles, the kind of bristles used in brooms, jammed and glued together at the bottom to create a dense cushion that fanned out at the top. It was both beautiful and comfortable.

Fernando and Humberto had built the prototype so that it could be taken apart and packed in a small package to send to the States. This way, Al could analyze the construction and make all the chairs in New York, a far more economic solution than shipping a dozen chairs from one continent to another with freight and duty to pay. Humberto and Fernando promised to visit soon after the chair arrived so that they could help refine the details.

We decided that eight of the chairs would have backs with cream bristles, four with red. After a frustrating search for bristles in New York, Al found an out-of-town supplier who would manufacture them to a specified length and color, with a minimum order of 30,000 feet. Amazingly, we met that requirement, and I chose a bright red from my Pantone book. Meanwhile, Lloyd took the seat and legs from the prototype to a Mennonite woodworker in Pennsylvania who, as well as crafting pieces for Lloyd, made furniture for Knoll, the renowned manufacturer of classic American design. There was also an iron frame hidden among the bristles of the chair to help hold them in place, and Lloyd took charge of having twelve of these fabricated, too.

Ultimately, Al assembled all the parts and built the dining room chairs, using only early photographs to guide him, since parts of the prototype, like the seat and legs, had been lost in the process of farming it out. Just as they said, Fernando and Humberto returned, adding their comments, which Al incorporated into his work. The final chairs were beautiful, and the perfect counterpoint to the table.

At the dining room's far end, Tina Barney's photograph, **The Bridesmaid**, describes an insular world of privilege.

While things still remained to be done, I decided it was time to inaugurate the space by having a party in it, the guest list comprising everyone who in one way or another had contributed to the dining room's success. Yes, there was more to do. But it was time to celebrate.

Pictures with a Point

When I decided to turn the dining room into a skewed version of Versailles, I was determined to provide a modern commentary that would challenge the assumptions of wealth and privilege on which it had been built. This, I knew, would come from the art on the walls, the centerpiece of which was Justen's mirror with the floating mask. Other than Justen's picture, which employed photographic means to achieve its effects, every other piece I chose to hang was a photograph.

I selected two large color photographs by Tina Barney, who has made a career of documenting the insulated social world of her extended family and friends in New York on Park Avenue and in the Hamptons. One of these, **The Bridesmaid**, shows a young woman getting ready for her wedding portrait. Her hair is long and blond and pulled back from her face. Her dress, a sophisticated dark blue taffeta, falls to the floor. To her left are three young men in black tie, laid-back and loose-limbed as they watch the proceedings. These are all children of wealth. They show their youth but no awkwardness at being either in formal wear or at a formal occasion.

The second photograph I chose is my favorite of the two, and also one of my favorites in Tina's entire body of work. Titled **The Curator and the Trustee**, it shows two people and two interior rooms at the Metropolitan Museum of Art. The first room at the

In Your Space: Personalizing Your Home and Office

left contains a famous painting by the French artist Jean-Auguste-Dominique Ingres of a fashionable nineteenth-century woman in, coincidentally, a blue taffeta dress. Closer to the camera is the second room, full of medieval religious paintings, all reds and blues and gold leaf. The walls on which they're hung are covered with a red velvet so faded and worn that it's easy to think that it is medieval, too. In the room is the curator of the title, looking prissy and uptight as he paces off the length of the room. Hovering at the periphery is the trustee—Tina's brother, in fact—well put together but far more at ease in his pastel summer suit. It is truly a great photograph that also complements the dining room themes. The Ingres painting depicts a wealthy exemplar of one era, the trustee a modern-day version. Meanwhile, the medieval paintings in the photograph segue into the Renaissance details on the ceiling.

The Curator and the Trustee, also by Tina Barney, speaks to relationships of money, art, and class.

From Louis Bofferding, I also purchased two small black-and-white photographs that I had seen in his flat. They were shot in 1930s France by François Kollar, and I was totally taken with them. One showed the corner of a luxurious tufted bed, the other a complex, expensive interior. I was not familiar with the photographer, but it didn't matter; his work spoke for itself. Although Louis gave me a book that showed Kollar's wider range, the pictures that Louis had were like great fashion photographs, only of interiors, calling to mind the images of Horst, Irving Penn, and Richard Avedon. In addition, something about these photos, as with Cocteau's **Beauty and the Beast**, which they predate, is simultaneously opulent and surreal. I placed one on either side of the fireplace, between two nineteenth-century sconces.

My friend and photography dealer Janet Borden bid for me at auction on a picture I wanted by the German photographer Candida Hofer. It showed an empty restaurant, the tables all draped in white, waiting expectantly for the time when they'd be set with fine china and silver and the hustle and bustle would begin. There was a surreal quality to the image that I liked. But in addition, the restaurant had tall columns with grand gold ornaments, a wall of mirrors reflecting back the room, and a black-and-white marble floor that looked surprisingly close to my faux painted one. In many ways, the photograph was an echo of themes and motifs in the dining room, and I liked the counterpoint of an interior where they were taken a great deal more seriously than I took mine.

The last two photographs, in some ways the most important photographs in the room, were by my friend Carrie Mae Weems. Taken in 1989, they

An Exhilarating Adventure: The Dining Room from Scratch

were part of a series she called Colored People. Highly political, challenging notions of color both outside and in the black community, they played with the knee-jerk phrases people use to describe degrees of pigmentation. **Blue Black Boy**, a magisterial triptych I'd owned since 1993, showed the same proud young African-American face printed three successive times in shades of blue and black. The word blue was beneath the first image, black beneath the second, and boy beneath the third.

I wanted the single image called **Burnt Orange Girl**. It was not so much the words as the image that moved me. A young girl sits sideways on a chair, her left arm draped over its back. Her posture is erect, her profile poised, her hands clasped together with natural grace. Like the subject of **Blue Black Boy**, she has an incomparable nobility. Together they throw into question all the other photographs in the room. Dignity, they say, has nothing to do with background or status or money. It is a self-realized human quality and cannot be bought. Ultimately, when Carrie hand-delivered the photograph to me, it was printed not in orange but in yellow, and the words beneath it read **Golden Yella Girl**. "I knew that yellow would look much better in your dining room," she said. And, incredible friend that she is, she had made it just that way for me.

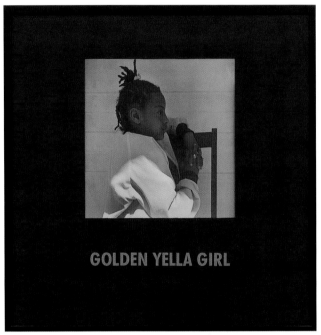

Carrie Mae Weems's **Golden Yella Girl** depicts an intrinsic nobility that has nothing to do with class or wealth.

Crowning Touches

I have no curtains to speak of, not in my office, not at Chill Hill, not in Harlem. There are shades I designed but never use in my office, and café curtains in the guest house in the country, but that's it. For whatever reason, I don't respond to curtains, although there must be some sort of innovative window treatments I would like, if I only paid more attention. Luckily, I was spared the need for them in my Harlem bedroom because it was built with pocket shutters that fit my aesthetic perfectly. The dining room had pocket shutters, too, but I was reluctant to consider them the right solution for the room. The shutters had a spartan quality that was at odds with the opulence I was trying to achieve. One way or another, I needed drapes, but I had no idea what they could be other than some magnificent carved faux fabric valances I had seen in a photograph of a grand nineteenth-century home. Lacking immediate inspiration, I put off the issue, knowing, however, that the time would come when I would have to deal with it.

One day Lyn Godley called to say she would like to talk to me about some ideas she had that were about neither expressly art or exclusively design but something in between. I was delighted, of course, to see anything she was working on. Lyn, by this time, had gotten divorced from Lloyd, and rather than compete with him in making furniture, she had carved out lighting as her bailiwick. I had always loved Lyn's lights, and the last piece on which she and Lloyd collaborated, the Crinkle lamp, had been acquisitioned into the Museum of Modern Art's permanent design collection. We made a date for her to come up to the house and go over her ideas.

Lyn arrived with a notebook full of sketches. She wanted to make full-size dresses out of plastic and then light them. Her drawings covered the gamut of fashion from prom dresses to—what was this? an ancient Greek gown? There was something about the Greek dress that so surprised me that I momentarily stepped out of my role of counselor and friend.

"Lyn, I'm amazed. Can plastic really drape like this? I didn't think it could be so flexible."

"That's plastic rope. I learned about it from one of my students at Parsons, who used it for a project."

Lloyd Schwan's sideboard with its gently curved façade simultaneously reflects and distorts the dining room floor.

"Wow, if it can really do that, then I know just what I want to do for the dining room curtains." I whipped out my notebook and made a sketch of what I had in mind. It showed a large number of pieces of plastic rope hanging from a rod at the top of a dining room window. The ropes were gathered tightly together about two-thirds of the way down, and then freed to puddle onto the floor. It's clear plastic rope, I explained, and I want to thread lights through it.

"If it's possible, I'd want you to make them," I proposed. And happily, Lyn agreed to take the project on.

So Lyn left my house not only with my total support for her lighted dresses, one of which was later showcased in the window of the American Craft Museum, but with a commission for plastic drapes threaded with lights. It took close to a year for the curtains to be done, but one day I received a call from Lyn asking if Al would be at my house. The curtains were finally finished, and she was going to need help installing them.

I came home from work to find Al and Lyn still there. They had just gotten the curtains up, complete with rheostats, and I was able to try them out at every degree of intensity, from the brightest to the most subdued. It is impossible to describe just how magical they were. Their forms softened the hard lines of the window frames, and the lights within them were festive, welcoming, and radiant. Radical, luxurious, and slightly unreal, the curtains satisfied the different themes of the dining room. Lyn had done an incredible job.

When I commissioned Lyn to make the curtains, I had also asked Lloyd to design the sideboards for the room. Although we brainstormed about different ideas that expanded on the work Lloyd was then doing using photographs on laminate, in the end we abandoned them as too competitive with the Renaissance details on the ceiling. Instead, Lloyd came up with a design that was wholly his own. It was sleek and sophisticated—silver-faced cabinets framed in gold with black insets on the top. The cabinets themselves were built on bases of thick Plexiglas, so that they seemed to float. There was a slight, almost imperceptible curve to the silver fronts, so that the reflection in them subtly distorted the room and created complex, ambiguous surfaces.

"You can't imagine how difficult it is to be the last person to make something for the dining room," Lloyd would say as he worked on his design. And it was true, he had the unenviable task of accommodating everything that was already there. But Lloyd needn't have worried. His sideboards were perfect.

Two things still remained to be done: the fireplace surround and the doors. From the moment that the Fontana Arte sconce brought to mind **Beauty and the Beast,** I had the idea for the fireplace. In the Beast's castle is a great room where Beauty is summoned to have dinner every night. Aside from the resplendent table, the most arresting item in the room is the massive stone fireplace.

At first glance it is what one would expect in a baronial space—an immense fireplace with carved stone heads on either side. It is only when you realize that the eyes in the heads are bright with motion, following Beauty's every move, that the fireplace takes on a slightly sinister, otherworldly presence.

The fireplace in my dining room is minute by

A focal point of the dining room, Justen Ladda's dramatic artwork raises questions about the masks we wear.

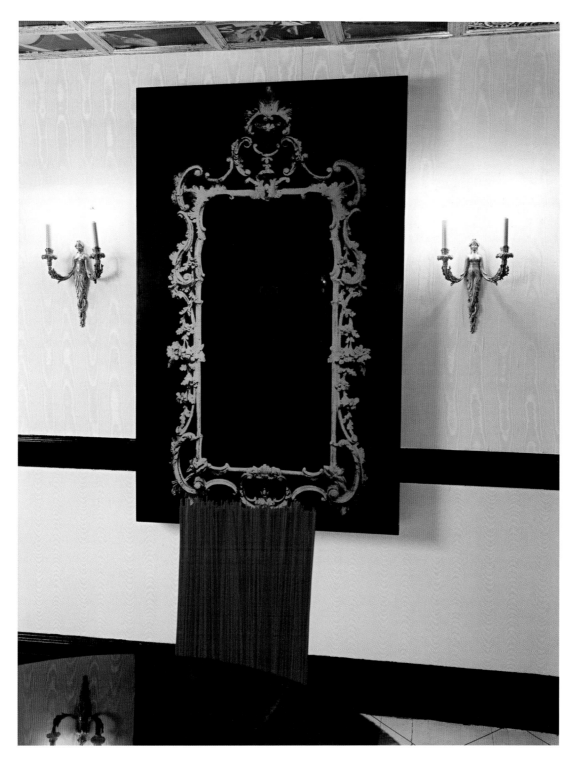

The Campana brothers' bristle-backed chairs provide a provocative foil to the luxurious materials used throughout the room.

An Exhilarating Adventure: The Dining Room from Scratch

comparison, but there was just enough room to put a head on each side of the surround. Rather than try to emulate the stone from **Beauty and the Beast**, I chose instead white plaster, which has an eerie quality of its own. From a friend who works at Madame Alexander's doll company I got dolls' eyes that proved to be just the right size, as well as rather alarming. Al cast the heads for my fireplace from a hollow plastic face I had bought because it reminded me of the cutoff ones in Jasper Johns's target paintings. With the eyes set into the plaster heads, the fireplace was a clear homage to Cocteau and Bérard, while still a reinvention with its own distinct sensibility.

The doors? Well, that was another matter. When I bought the house there was just a framed, wide-open space between the kitchen and what I'd decided would be my dining room. Al had early on put up temporary wood doors, primarily to keep my cats from wreaking the exquisite destruction of which only felines are capable. But once the doors were up, Al began to press me for what I really wanted to do with them. Eventually, the answer just popped out. "I'm going to cover them in white fake fur," I said.

Now, there is no fake fur in **Beauty and the Beast**, except perhaps for the hairy coat of the Beast himself. So, unlike the fireplace, my desire to use fake fur was less a reference to the film than a spiritual tribute to its visual invention. Nonetheless, I expected Al to protest. The fake fur was a pretty outrageous idea, even for my dining room. But the artist in Al paused for a few moments to absorb what I'd said, and then declared: "Well, that's okay. There's a surrealist tradition for it in art." He may well have been thinking of Meret Oppenheim's famous fur-lined teacup and saucer in the Museum of Modern Art.

I had no question about what kind of fake fur I would use. Several years earlier Jeanette Kastenberg,

a fashion designer and one of my closest friends, had made me a short jacket out of fake monkey fur. The monkey fur had not been expensive, and for that reason it was neither silky nor smooth but rough and thick, with high definition to individual strands. These were all qualities that I loved. The fur had volume, and it looked frankly, unequivocally fake. I called Jeanette and asked what I thought was the easiest of favors, if she could order several yards of the monkey fur for me. Jeanette looked for the fur at fabric fairs. No luck.

Despite the fact that I had no fur in hand, I still knew that I wouldn't cover each door with a single large piece. Even my great, inexpensive monkey fur with the giant articulated strands went in only one direction. But I wanted the doors to have something of the feel of the upholstered leather ones found in serious men's clubs. To achieve this kind of definition, I would have to cover the doors in a series of tufted rectangles. And the rectangles themselves would have to be assembled from four opposing triangles so that the fur would seem especially abundant, emanating from a central point. The finishing touch, adding to the dimensionality, would be some fabulous medallion in the middle of each block.

Jeanette knew this is what I wanted. I had drawn a sketch to explain it almost every time we got together. So occasionally she would pick up some monkey fur, cut it into triangles, and sew it together to create the multidirectional look that I kept talking about. These were wonderful gifts, the efforts of a friend to help me realize the fake fur doors to which I was so committed. I'd take the samples home and tack them on the doors, thinking how great the fur would look if only I could find some with the density and volume of the fabric of my jacket.

Two years went by. To anyone paying attention, my quest was simply pathetic, but I was not about

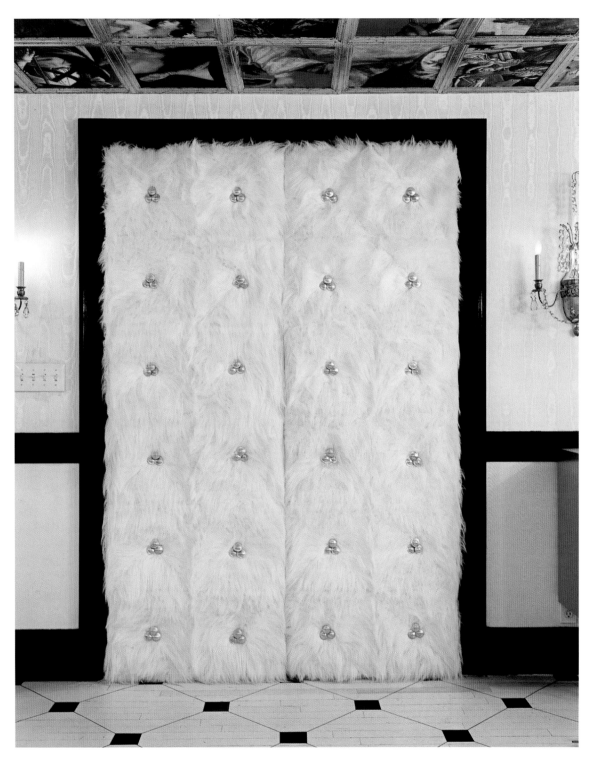

Robert Lee Morris's sculptural gold pins give structure to the dining room's tufted fake-fur doors.

An Exhilarating Adventure: The Dining Room from Scratch

to yield. Not even when Lloyd said, especially now that the doors were painted black, "You know, Al and I don't think the fake fur is going to work. On the other hand, I've thought most of your ideas for this dining room wouldn't work, and I've been wrong every time. Somehow or other you've pulled it off. It couldn't be more spectacular."

It was such an enormously generous statement, especially from someone with so many unbudging opinions of his own. It was also the last time that Lloyd and I talked in person. The Christmas holidays came and went, and not long after, in the winter of 2001, Lloyd committed suicide. It was a loss that I will never get over. He challenged me and argued with me, collaborated with me and supported me and made me better than I was. And he was my friend. I love him for those last words, which, like his maxim—you can always repaint—will stay with me always. They summed up our relationship at its best, the no-holds-barred debates, the shared passion for design, the ultimate human kindness. I believe he would have liked the fur doors. And he would have told me so.

The fur doors actually went up about three months after Lloyd died. **House and Garden** was about to photograph my house, and I was despairing to my friend Greg Garry, the photo editor of **HomeStyle**, a newly reenvisioned shelter magazine, that the shoot would take place without them. But Greg had the answer. There are two guys, he told me, Kevin Fitzpatrick and Jim Jackson, who can fabricate anything. They do work for Ralph Lauren and Donna Karan and for magazines like **Wallpaper** when they need a special set for a shoot. They're expensive, but their work is flawless and they're fast. And this is weird, Greg added, but I was just speaking to them the other day, and they said they had some French monkey fur left over from a job.

Greg gave me the number of their company, Design Support, and I phoned them right away. This was Wednesday. The **House and Garden** shoot was just five days away. Why was I even calling? But Kevin came up with one of his associates that very night, and they laid out a grid on the doors, suggesting a different and better division of the space than the one I'd originally planned. We'll have it for you Monday, Kevin said. I was dreaming, right? But, true to their word, they showed up right after the weekend to install the doors. And even though the monkey fur was smoother than I'd wanted, the doors were fabulous. The fur was the ultimate surprise, something you saw only after you'd entered the room and thought you'd seen everything. It made the doors the epitome of decadence, although the fakeness of the fur gave them a modern spin. They were wild and totally surreal.

Several months later, my friend Robert Lee Morris, whose modern jewelry has set the standard for everyone else, came up with the missing piece, the ultimate capper, the medallions. I needed twenty-four of them, no small number, and thought that Robert would have to create a new design, sculpt it, make a mold, and cast the entire set. But Robert had a better idea. He had a stash of signature rounded stickpins in gold plate. One alone was too small for the size of the fur rectangles, but Robert suggested putting three together to create a larger, pyramidal form. He sent me up a sample, even offering to come and install the pins if I liked it. When I put the sample up, there was no doubt—the pins were exactly right, the crowning touch.

In a dining room where there was something amazing to see no matter where you looked, the fake fur doors with their gleaming medallions caused mouths to drop. As I said, Lloyd would have liked them.

Lessons Learned Along the Way

1. What can you do about a low, oppressive ceiling? Adding mirrors is a great way to give the illusion of extra height. But be careful: it's easy to end up looking like a Las Vegas hotel where circular beds hover under flashy, reflective glass. Other solutions include lighting a ceiling so that it seems to float, bordering it with an airy pattern, or covering it with a rich and buoyant design.

2. The geometry of a room rules its internal logic. But within that geometry it's important to vary the spatial relationships. When Al painted my dining room floor, we agreed that sixteen-inch squares were the right proportion for the room. But when we turned our attention to the ceiling, we instinctively knew not to repeat those dimensions. Instead we chose fourteen-by-fourteen-inch squares to create interest and variety.

3. There are so many ways to treat a floor. A great rug can make a room. A stone floor, whether it's rusticated slate or highly polished marble, can determine the entire tenor of a room. But when assessing your options, consider painting a pattern on the wood. There are so many designs to choose from, or you can create your own. A painted floor can be a wonderful hybrid, allowing the wood to show through while adding a level of engagement and sophistication.

4. Repainting, as my friend Lloyd Schwan averred, is really quite simple. It's not a hardship to change a color once it's in place. But there are times when, in the middle of a project, you'll have a radical idea that will dramatically change the course of what you're working on. Should you scrap your original concept, throw out all the work, and go with the new notion? Unlike repainting, this is a weighty decision. If, after much thought, you believe the second idea will make all the difference in the world, go with it. Just try not to do it too often.

5. In America, we tend to put a premium on luxury. Marble and granite are better than laminates, mahogany is better than maple. We've been socialized to believe that if something costs more, it must be worth more. But this is not always the case. Often, cheaper materials and processes are the ones that yield the maximum results. Don't be afraid what the neighbors will think. If inexpensive solutions create the best effects, the Joneses should be keeping up with you.

12.

Strivers Row :

Other Visions, Other Rooms

In the office, smashing pumpkins, gleaming skeletons, and DC Comics heroes fight an intergalactic battle above a Prouvé desk.

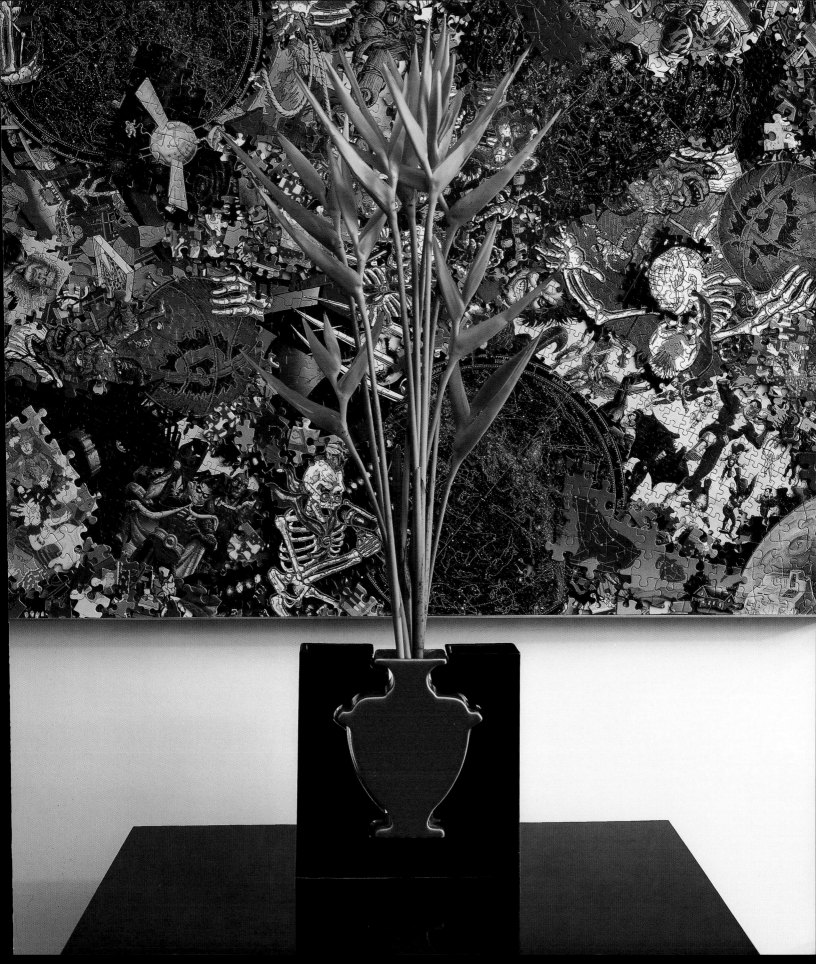

Was it possible to have an antidote to the dining room, where every period and every style was merged somehow together, where materials ranged from the luxury of hand-applied gold leaf to the banality of extruded plastic bristles? The media room, which I was already working on, promised a similar level of intensity. But two other rooms in the house show remarkable restraint. Compared to the dining room with its riot of ideas, these rooms are subdued, as close as I am ever going to get to a Zen interior. One of these is my office, the other a small guest room on the topmost floor. Even now, when I walk into the office, I am amazed at how spare it is. Which is not to say that either of these rooms lacks invention or that one might think for a moment that they were designed by someone else.

Finding One's Train of Thought

My office is on the same floor as my bedroom. It is more narrow than it is square, but that is compensated for by two large windows at the far end facing south. For most of the day, the room is filled with radiant natural light, and I regularly find my cats stretched out on the floor in pools of sun. It is a graceful room, limned by light wood around the window frames and doors. But the most extraordinary thing about it is the fireplace. As you enter the office from the door at the top of the stairs, the fireplace is the first thing you notice. It is directly in your line of vision on its own dedicated diagonal stretch of wall, and it is the diagonal that is the arresting detail. Although the fireplaces in the middle and back parlors are on the diagonal, too, this diagonal has a more powerful presence.

When I bought my house, this fireplace was in

every other way undistinguished. But when I looked at it, I saw only one thing—René Magritte's famed surrealist painting **Time Transfigured**. It depicts a fireplace, on the diagonal, with a smoke-spewing train jutting out from its back wall. This picture has always been one of my favorites. It is painted with the same disinterested precision and meticulousness that characterizes all of Magritte's work. The collision of images is what one remembers most: the total incongruity of a small but lifelike train plowing through the opening of a marble fireplace. There are other details—a black clock and two brass candlesticks on the mantel, a mirror in a gold frame that reflects them, floorboards that go straight to the fireplace without a hearth between. But it is the train steaming out of the firebox that stays long after the other aspects of the painting have been blurred by time.

So strong was my connection between the fireplace in the Magritte and the one in my office that it impelled me to re-create the painting in the room. This could be a daunting task, more difficult even than the bookcase fireplace, because it involved so many kinds of invention, both two- and three-dimensional. But I already had some ideas of what I wanted to do, and I knew this was a challenge Al could not refuse.

Furniture: Combining Vintage Pieces with Present-day Reissues

Before tackling the fireplace, I started choosing the furniture. Happily, as with the dining room, I was able to start from scratch. As I've mentioned, I had collected 1950s furniture when I was married, only to divest myself of it when my husband and I separated. With a few exceptions we had specialized in European design, and some pieces from that period still held my interest. One of them especially was Osvaldo Borsani's Tecno chair. We had had two of them as well as the couch, covered, thanks to our designer, Claudio, in deep turquoise leather. Interestingly, I liked our set a great deal less upholstered this way. But several years later, when our Tecno chairs had been sold and I had totally redecorated the apartment, I happened to walk into a back room of Leo Castelli's famed eponymous gallery. Facing each other were two Tecno chairs and a Tecno couch, all covered in black. They looked so dramatically modern that they took my breath away, and I felt once again the same excitement I'd experienced upon seeing my first Tecno chair in Alan Moss's crowded loft. Suddenly I missed mine tremendously, and it was a Tecno chair that was first on my list when I started shopping for furniture.

I called Jim Walrod, friend and design resource, for possible dealers who might have not only the chair but also some objects by two wonderful French designers, Jean Prouvé and Serge Mouille. He directed me to Michael Benevento, who dealt out of his downtown SoHo loft. Nothing by Mouille, but Michael did have some furniture by Prouvé. And he had the Tecno chair. I chose a graceful Prouvé desk, small enough not to overwhelm the room, and a Prouvé chair with the back and seat in a golden stained wood but the frame in black. Michael had half a dozen of the Prouvé chairs, each with the back and seat in better or worse condition, and with the color of the stain vivid in some, duller in others. Needless to say, I wanted the optimum: the best condition, the warmest stain. Although no single chair met both requirements, I voiced my wish—the only way there is any chance of having it granted. And Michael was a prince. The seats and backs unscrewed, so he let me choose a back from one chair, a seat from another, until I got as close as I could to what I wanted.

Michael also had daybeds for sale. One was by

Eileen Gray, a Scottish woman who, early in the twentieth century, became a pioneer of modern architecture and design. The other was by Jean Prouvé. They were remarkably similar, although the Prouvé had a small tabletop that could rotate out if you needed it, or be tucked under the bed if you didn't. There were other subtle differences between the two, but the tabletop clinched it for me. Naturally, I wanted to re-cover the chair and the daybed in fabrics of my choosing, and Michael volunteered to go with me to Knoll. Normally Knoll sells only to designers, but Michael had contacts who allowed me to pick the fabrics out myself. I selected a slightly textured red for the Tecno chair, a tightly woven yellow for the daybed, and a rich purple to make into a bolster.

There was only one other piece of furniture I wanted, a combination cabinet, bookcase, and display case. What I would have loved most of all, had I been able to afford it, was one of the extraordinary shelving units designed by Charlotte Perriand and Sonia Delaunay. Charlotte Perriand collaborated with Le Corbusier and was equally responsible for many famous designs attributed until only recently exclusively to him. No matter how talented and vibrant you were—and Charlotte Perriand was both, as well as beautiful—it was almost impossible for a woman to get recognition in art or design if she partnered with a man. Sonia Delaunay was married to a famous painter, Robert Delaunay, but she had visibility early on because her own career as an artist and designer was separate from his. Yet had they collaborated, she almost certainly would have suffered the fate of Charlotte Perriand. The Perriand/Delaunay shelving units were attributed to them because no man was involved to overwhelm their remarkable achievements. Charlotte Perriand designed the units, Sonia Delaunay selected the colors. They were made of wood, and although in many ways they followed classical forms, they were often asymmetrical. Each unit was unique, with Perriand establishing different rhythmical grids in which Delaunay laid the color. The colors varied from unit to unit, but the combinations were always rich, often involving black, ocher, red, and white, as well as the warm stain of the wood. I considered the units masterworks because of Perriand's strong architectural designs and Delaunay's painterly deployment of color. But the prices for them were, as I said, out of my reach.

Some years later, Americans Charles and Ray Eames came up with their own similar but affordable shelving systems. With Herman Miller as manufacturer, they created a mix-and-match design made of plywood and metal. Although not nearly as sturdy or substantial as the earlier Perriand/Delaunay units, the Eameses' concept had far more flexibility, allowing the buyer to customize her purchase. She had the option of selecting different colored panels for the back and fronts of her system—they came in white, red, yellow, blue, and black—or perforated metal, or a minimal metal support in the shape of an **X**. Sliding, dimpled plywood doors were another option, as were narrow wooden drawers. One could also get large, single-colored drawers for storage or for files.

In recent years, prices for vintage Eames cabinets have skyrocketed, approaching, if not matching, those for the Perriand/Delaunay units. But simultaneous with this wild escalation in going market rates, a store in New York called Modernica reissued the Eames system, following their original specifications exactly. This I'm sure would have pleased its creators, who wanted to make good design egalitarian, not the precious commodity that their original units have become.

Vintage has always been an important monetary factor in the collector markets for art and design. And sometimes the aesthetic difference is so clear-cut that this factor is worth paying for. With the Eames systems, most vintage units have a warmth and patina that results from age and wear, but these qualities were not inherent in the units when they were first produced. Why, then, spend the money on an original system? For me there are just three good reasons for buying vintage design: (1) it is the only version available; (2) there is a real aesthetic difference between the vintage version and its reissue; and (3) one is collecting only museum-quality pieces. Because none of these factors was at play with the Eames cabinet, I went down to Modernica and ordered a new one. Not only was the price right, I was also able to customize my system according to both my functional needs and my visual preferences. I like to think that that is how the Eameses would have wanted it.

A desk and desk chair, an easy chair, a daybed, a cabinet for books, storage, and display—that was the only furniture I needed, and the only furniture that I put in the room I'd decided to make my office. For lighting, I chose a beautiful Ingo Maurer hanging lamp composed of three descending circular tiers of paper, each one slightly larger than the next. A small vermilion ring perched on an angle above them. It altered, when one wanted, the height of the light, and added both a zing of color and an asymmetrical counterpoint to the classical shades below. All that I still needed to do was place objects on the Eames cabinet, hang artwork on the walls, and consult on the fireplace with Al.

Shelf Life: An Animated Eames Cabinet

I love my work at DC Comics, and my office there is full of references to our characters in every incarnation. But there is hardly a trace of what I do at home, and it has always been that way. Unconsciously, I must have felt the separation was necessary, even though I'm on the phone every night to California talking about our projects for movies and TV or propped against my pillows reading comic books and scripts. Yet when it came to my office on Strivers Row, I suddenly wanted to display some pieces that spoke eloquently about DC and the pleasure it has given me for so many years.

For the Eames cabinet, I chose a life-size green lantern for our larger-than-life character Green Lantern, whom we have been publishing in one form or another for sixty years. Every comic-book fan knows it—it's the power battery against which every twenty-four hours Green Lantern charges his ring while uttering the famous oath: "In brightest day, in blackest night, no evil shall escape my sight. Let those who worship evil's might beware my power, Green Lantern's light." Our retail products group at DC produced the lantern, complete with ring, in a limited edition. The design, by staffer Georg Brewer, is inspired. When you hold the ring

An Eames cabinet, filled with cherished objects, art, and books.

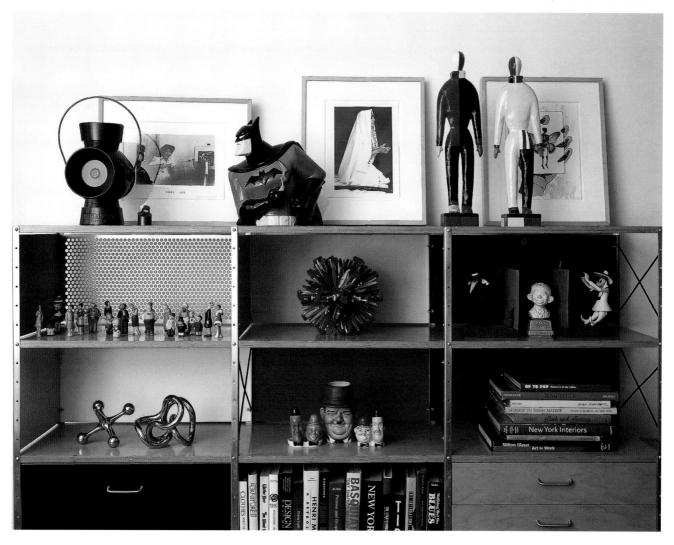

up against the lantern, it lights—just long enough for you to say the oath. It is a piece of sculpture and a wonderful, witty homage to one of our best-loved characters.

I also selected a Batman cookie jar that had been made for the Warner Bros. stores. Based on the majestic animation designs by Bruce Timm, the jar depicts an iron-willed Dark Knight, his jutting jaw in profile, his upper body twisted in a torque, ready to spring into action. I placed it on the top shelf along with Green Lantern's lamp. On a lower shelf I placed a four-inch ceramic bust of **Mad** magazine's grinning icon, Alfred E. Neuman. Made in the 1960s, it was now a coveted collectible. But for me, as the head of **Mad** as well as of DC, it had special meaning. I flanked it with bookends we'd recently produced of **Mad**'s infamous spies— the black one on one side, the white on the other.

I love these objects, but I didn't devote the Eames cabinet solely to pieces from DC and **Mad**. For me, the pleasure in designing comes from the odd juxtapositions, from mixing things up and enjoying how good they look together. So on the top shelf, along with the Batman cookie jar and Green Lantern's power battery, I placed two tall multi-colored figures inspired by the work of Russian suprematist artist Kasimir Malevich, issued by the Guggenheim Museum in conjunction with a show. Roxy Paine had given me a small multiple based on one of his mushroom installations, and that went on the top shelf too. For a birthday, Justen Ladda had made me a miniature of his latest work, a dress fashioned from chandelier beads, and that also went on the shelf. So did a grouping of early bisque comic-strip characters, pint-size but full of attitude.

Architectural Lines, Painterly Swirls

Behind all these objects, leaning against the wall, I placed three framed prints by young emerging artists. The first piece of art I actually hung on the walls was a poster by Ib Andersen, who had also designed the modern cityscape in my back parlor. This poster, inscribed **Bygge Bolig** in bold black letters, was one I bought with the room in mind. I had loved it for many years, but lacking a place to put it, I'd exercised a surprising semblance of self-restraint and passed when I had the chance to purchase it. Now, however, it felt like a necessity, and I embarked on a do-or-die mission to uncover it (the Internet proved amazingly helpful in this). The poster, on a white field with red, yellow, blue, and black, showed a cutaway of the interior of a building, with a few pieces of contemporary furniture inside.

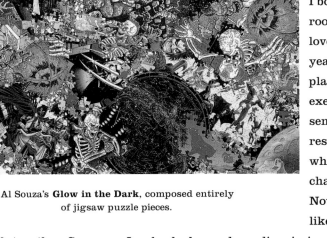

Al Souza's **Glow in the Dark**, composed entirely of jigsaw puzzle pieces.

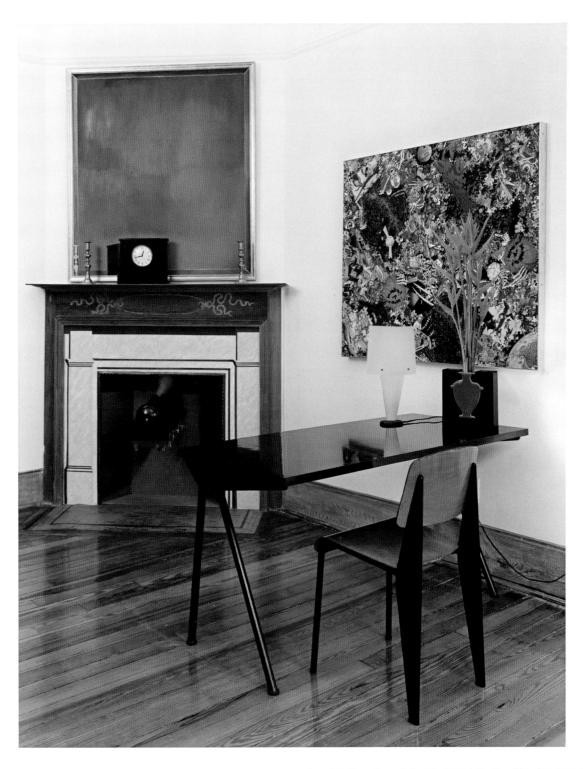

A re-creation of a painting by Magritte, the office fireplace explores
the tension between real and faux, two dimensions and three.

Strivers Row: Other Visions, Other Rooms

The building's clean straight lines, the primary colors, the modern chair sitting in a room, were a tribute to the Bauhaus design movement, which created an environment in which the Prouvé desk, the Tecno chair, and the Eames cabinet could flourish. Together with the furniture, the **Bygge Bolig** poster triggered an implicit and active dialogue about the roots of contemporary design, giving the furniture in the office both context and meaning. I placed it on one side of the Eames cabinet, a two-dimensional echo of the three-dimensional form it was next to.

On the other side of the Eames cabinet I hung the same Roy Lichtenstein gallery invitation that I'd had in my bedroom in the Century. Created for a show of his at Leo Castelli's, it was printed with Roy's famous swirled brushstroke, yellow and black against a field of tight blue benday dots. If the **Bygge Bolig** poster was architectural and disciplined, the brushstroke was totally painterly, full of joyous abandon. The primary palettes of these works on paper drew from the same well, but the impulses driving them were worlds apart. Using the pictures as parentheses, with the Eames cabinet between, triggered a second provocative dialogue about art and design, painting and architecture.

But not every one of my choices for the office was so painstakingly thought out. On the narrow wall to the left as you entered the room, I hung a Milton Glaser poster for the Juilliard School of Music. I did so only because I loved it, and knew I'd enjoy looking at it wherever I was in the room. Yes, the colors worked well in the space, and the overlapping cubist forms related in some ways to the Eames shelving unit. But the truth was, I simply liked the poster's spirit, and that, in most cases, should be reason enough.

The last three pieces of art went on the far wall of the office as you entered the room. Two, which at first glance looked like superrealist paintings, were actually photographs by an Israeli artist living in Chicago, Iris Bonor. I had found them at Exit Art in a portion of its space called the Warehouse. The Warehouse is a place where you can purchase work by a wide range of artists, some of them established but many relatively unknown and not yet represented by galleries. It's hard to beat the prices in the Warehouse, and while it's potluck in terms of finding pieces that you like, each has a level of quality to recommend it.

I was immediately struck by these photos, which were from a series of eleven thematically linked images. There was a vividness to the orange and aqua backgrounds, and a somewhat surreal quality to the figures, whose bodies are turned, their faces hidden and cut off. This surreality is heightened by the furniture in the pictures, which veers between flatness and three-dimensionality. Constructed this way by the artist, it emphasizes the tension between surface and depth. The more I looked at the photographs, the more I was drawn to them. And there was a bonus, too. The few pieces of furniture in the pictures, signposts really, are files and shelves, the stuff of which offices are made. I bought both, because the images in tandem enhanced each other, and hung them in my office as a pair.

Finally, over my desk, I hung a picture by Al Souza. I'd met Al through Janet Borden, who urged me to join her at Al's studio one day after work. There was a picture, she said, that I had to see. When I got there, I understood why Janet had dragged me all the way downtown. Tucked away in the picture she was sure I had to have were several DC Comics characters.

Despite Janet's enthusiasm, this was not the picture of my dreams. Even so, Al's art was unique and well worth the trip. What made it fascinating was that Al worked solely with jigsaw puzzle pieces, which he deployed as masterfully as if he were working with paint. I did buy another picture, less flashy than the others but also more poetic. When Al and I went out to celebrate the sale, he mentioned his continuous quest to find puzzles so that he could cannibalize the parts. I wondered what we might have at work, and found we had licensed a jigsaw puzzle based on a DC Comics poster by artist Jerry Ordway. It featured countless numbers of our heroes, from the classic characters to virtual unknowns. Needless to say, I dispatched it to Al.

Nearly a year later, I received an invitation in the mail to Al's first opening in New York. He had been picked up by the Charles Cowles Gallery, and its announcement of his exhibit included a small note from Al saying that he hoped I could come. For the invitation, the gallery had selected two pictures of Al's to represent the show. One of them was filled with skeletons and pumpkin heads. But suddenly I saw Plastic Man in the upper left-hand corner, then

The clean lines of a Tecno chair and Prouvé daybed are lit by the sun and Gaetano Pesce's resin lamp.

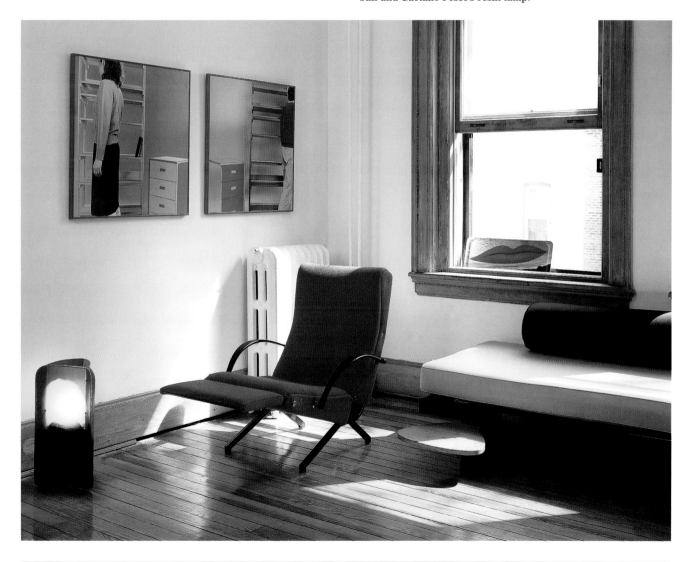

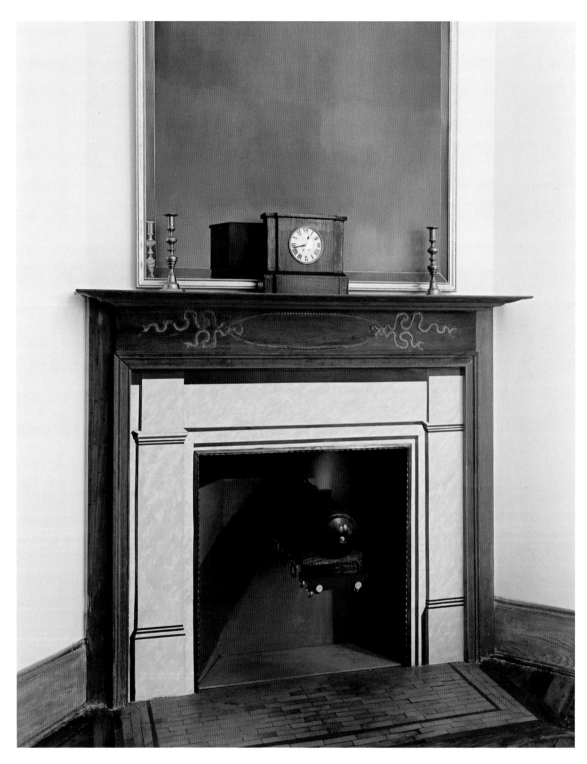

A close-up of the fireplace with its painted shadows and real
steam pulsing from the chimney of the train.

In Your Space: Personalizing Your Home and Office

Supergirl, Captain Marvel, Nightwing, Aquaman, Lobo, Impulse. . . . It dawned on me that Al had used huge portions of the puzzle that I'd given him. And he'd done it so artfully that I'd responded to the overall drama of the picture without even realizing at first that it was full of DC heroes.

I couldn't go to the opening, but as soon as I returned from out of town I headed down to Chelsea. Although the show was rich and varied, I found myself spending most of my time in front of the piece with our characters. Aside from the vivid distribution of color and the dynamic play of darks and lights, there was something magical in the use of imagery. Al had mixed black-and-white puzzles of celestial spheres with ghoulish skeletons and the DC heroes in their bold, bright uniforms. The picture worked first and foremost as art, but for me there was another appeal, the mythic presentation of our characters. Hovering above starry, ebon realms, besieged by otherworldly enemies, their heroism is on an intergalactic scale. By the time I left the gallery, I had bought the picture. It was just the right piece to complete the art on my office walls.

The Magritte Fireplace

I loved the things I purchased for the office, but nothing in it compared to my feeling for the Magritte fireplace. It was a true tour de force, and for this, as with so many other exceptional things in the house, I had to thank the other Al, Al Williams.

Every inch of the fireplace was slathered in white paint, from the wooden mantel to the tiny bricks in the surround. Al stripped the mantel down to its brown wood and removed the bricks, which weren't worth even trying to salvage. Now we could begin to adapt the Magritte. The questions at hand were, What would be real, what would be faux, what would be two-dimensional, what would be three? In

the Magritte, the surround is marble. Rather than install real marble in mine, I asked Al to replicate the Magritte in paint, complete with its architectural details and corollary shadows. Although there was no wood mantel in the Magritte, I elected to keep mine intact. This was, after all, an adaptation, not a literal re-creation (which would have been no more than a painted copy), and my mantel was part of the original house. It would provide not only a frame, but also a framework, for the differences as well as the similarities between the actual Magritte and the installation we were creating.

As much as I wanted the marble to be faux, I wanted the train to be real. Well, as real as a locomotive charging through a fireplace can be. Al and I first thought of buying a model train. My friend Justen gave me train catalogues to pore through, but I couldn't find anything that resembled the engine in the Magritte. Al tried some model train stores, but also without luck. "I'm going to have to build it, I guess," said Al. And that is what he did, with assorted spare parts and imagination to spare. Al created the body from a galvanized steel pipe once used as a flue. He coopted a dome from a lighting fixture to form the engine's nose. A cylinder from a lock became the chimney, while the lamps on the engine's front were made from tiny metal door-pulls. Al took a piece of wood, painted it, and made the wheel bed. And finally, using industrial-strength foil, he fashioned the wheels themselves.

In addition to the train and the marble surround, there were other issues to consider in adapting the Magritte. The painting shows a mirror above the fireplace, encased in a narrow gold frame. Should I get a real mirror, find a similar gold frame? In this instance, my instincts were immediate, and I didn't question them. No, I did not want a real mirror, a piece of shiny glass that would sparkle and gleam with reflections. It seemed totally contrary to the spirit of the painting, where Magritte had exercised spartan control. Yes, his mirror had reflections, but it was highly discriminating, recording nothing in the room except one of the two brass candlesticks on the mantel and the back of the black clock. This particularity, and Magritte's subdued rendering of the mirror, were essential to the painting's surreal effect. I wanted to capture it, and therefore, for our installation, asked Al to make a painting of a mirror. This, of course, is exactly what Magritte had done. But when it came to the frame, I had a different feeling. I believed that for the installation to work, some things in it had to be tangible. So while Al painted a mirror with all the subtle lavenders and grays of the Magritte, he built a real gold frame to surround it.

The candlesticks on top of the mantel were also real. With a color photocopy tucked in my purse, I traveled about the city, hoping to find a pair with the same sensibility and relative scale as those in the painting. Luckily, one of New York's triple-pier antiques shows was coming up, and it was there that I found a set that did the trick.

The clock was a slightly different matter. It, too, had to be three-dimensional, but it would be impossible to find one with the same structure, proportions, and deadpan look as the one in the Magritte. Once again, Al would have to fabricate part of the installation. Yet for it to be credible, the clock had to incorporate at least some elements of hard reality. Luckily, Al found these in my basement, a repository, vast and unorganized, of my collecting forays over the years. One afternoon he emerged from the cellar with an Art Deco clock in a brown wood case. "Are you ever going to use this?" Al asked. No, I didn't think so. When anything has been in a cardboard box for over four years, it's probably destined for oblivion. So Al appropriated the hands from the clock, as well as its glass cover. A friend of his made a rendering to scale on her computer so that the

dial looked exactly like the one in the Magritte. All of these were installed in a housing Al built that replicated the one in the painting. The final effect was so artful, it was easy to believe that the clock was in production, on sale by the dozen on every other street corner.

"Do you want it to work?" Al asked, because the Art Deco clock still functioned, and it was easy to transfer the mechanism.

"Oh, no," was my immediate response. "I just want the hands to be in the same position that they are in the Magritte. And no matter what the real time is, that's where they should always be."

There were just two details left. The firebox in my fireplace was lined on its three sides with metal blackened by age and use. It was forged with a discreetly raised and subtle pattern. Both Al and I assumed that we would leave the lining in. But when Al temporarily installed the train, it was clear that the lining would have to go. As restrained as it was, it still had none of the flat, uninflected quality of the firebox in the Magritte. In addition, its dark background undercut the impact of the train, which was black itself. And finally, the train in the painting cast a shadow on the firebox walls. Al and I had failed to realize how critical that one detail was to the overall effect. So the metal lining went out, plain walls went up, and Al painted them in mushroom colors with the telling shadow intact.

The last detail to resolve was the steam. Somehow we had to manufacture smoke that would not only run through the train and out the engine's stack but stream backward, as it did in the Magritte. I tried the Internet for smoke machines, dry-ice machines, and theatrical props. But the solution was starting to feel familiar. Some way or another, Al was going to have to build this, too. Not long after, he came over, carrying a cappuccino machine from his loft. He answered my quizzical look rhetorically:

"It makes steam, right?" It was hard to argue.

Soon Al was drilling holes in a bathroom closet wall and funneling plastic tubes through it to the fireplace on the other side. He ran the tubes into the train and up the main chimney of the locomotive. A bottle of water, a plug in a bathroom socket, and the experiment began. K-chung, k-chung, k-chung. The cappuccino machine was rattling in the first throes of getting started. And then we saw it—smoke pouring out of the engine's stack. It still needed some refinements, but Al had done it. The Magritte fireplace, with its dialectics of genuine and faux, of two-dimensional and three, and of real and surreal, was complete.

A Room of His Own

There are two small guest rooms on the top floor of my house. Because I had two rooms, my plan was to make one somewhat more masculine, the other a little more feminine, although hopefully people of both genders would be happy in either one. The room slated to be the more feminine of the two was constantly occupied, so I turned my attention to the other, the masculine one, at the top of the stairs.

I was pursuing my usual occupation of cruising design magazines, when I started to see full-page ads for an Andrew Martin fabric. Tobacco colored, covered with black Chinese calligraphy and red Chinese seals, it was graphic and warm. Despite my love of bright, clear colors, I decided to cover the guest room walls with it. In doing so, I wanted to create an intimate, denlike quality. The guest room is only ten feet square, and there was the chance that the fabric might overwhelm such a tiny space. But I hoped that pale woodwork and a light ceiling would keep it from becoming too intense. The fabric was sold only to the trade, a category for which I didn't qualify, but Jody Harrow had the right credentials, so I asked her to purchase it for me. Of course she said yes, but she was surprised that I liked the pattern. It reminded her, she said, of overdecorated Long Island homes. Perhaps this should have been a warning sign, but I was determined that the fabric would work.

When it arrived, Al couldn't wait to apply it to the walls. But he was unable to do this until he had painted the ceiling, and I had yet to choose what color it would be, if in fact it made sense to paint it at all. As with the dining room doors, Al stepped up a campaign to urge me to make a decision.

"So what's it going to be?" he kept asking. "You know I can't do anything until you make up your mind."

He was right, of course, but I stubbornly held my ground. And when I finally committed to a ceiling treatment, I'd decided not to paint. Surprising even myself, I announced, "I'm not going to paint the ceiling. I want to make it a cubist collage."

Where did this concept come from? I truly have no idea. As much as I would like to demystify the creative process, sometimes it is totally inexplicable. There is only one trigger I can think of. I was envisioning the guest room in shades of brown and black, and cubists like Picasso and Braque had limited themselves to this palette. But that is hardly a total explanation.

The next task was to pick a collage that would work on the ceiling. I rummaged through a book in my library that was replete with pictures of cubist collages as well as paintings. I tagged the ones that I thought had possibilities, and Al made photocopies of them so that we could compare them side by side. It was a Braque collage that made the final cut. In true cubist tradition, it combined a number of items from daily life—a menu, the top half of a newspaper, an advertisement for Gillette. It also used faux materials, in this case, two tightly grained panels of wood. But the artist's touch was also there in Braque's

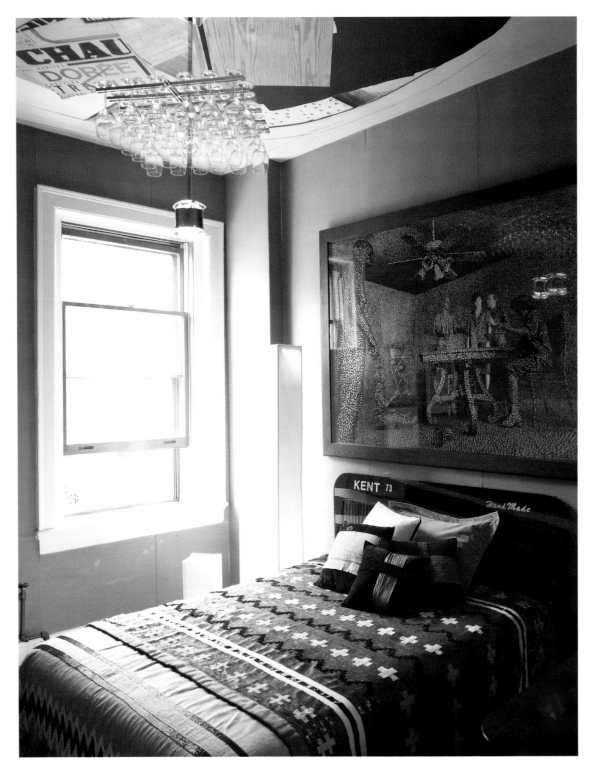

The masculine guest room, a study in browns and black.

In Your Space: Personalizing Your Home and Office

charcoal freehand drawings—a wineglass, a horse's head, some abstract patterns, a blush of soft shading.

Al began the process of transferring the collage by taking an enlarged photocopy of it and parsing it with a coded grid. In this way the upper left corner became a square that read 1A, a middle section read C4, a lower one E5. Al drew the same grid on the ceiling, therefore ensuring that every element in the collage would fall in its proper place. When the collage was complete and the grid erased, the effect was truly astonishing. I would lie on the bed in the room, the lone piece of furniture I'd installed, looking up at the ceiling in awe. How great it would be, I thought, to stay in this guest room and wake up to a sky full of art.

"I guess I can put the fabric up now," Al only half-queried, sure of my answer.

"Well, not exactly. I'm afraid I can't use it anymore. The ceiling is French, and the fabric's Chinese. They'll clash. And things have changed. The ceiling is now the most important element in the room. Any printed fabric would detract from it."

"So what are you going to do?"

And from somewhere I heard myself saying: "I'm going to cover the walls in corrugated cardboard."

As with the cubist collage, I'm hard-pressed to say how I came up with this idea. Despite the fact that I had paid for the fabric, I was able to put it aside without regret. Had Jody been right all along? It wasn't that I'd ceased to like the pattern. But it obviously was no longer going to work. I had long since learned that a certain number of missteps are part of the process, even though there is almost always some sort of price to pay—in this case, fiscal.

It seems that the same thought process that triggered my idea for the ceiling also triggered my concept for the walls. I considered painting them, but quickly rejected that notion as not interesting enough. Yet I'd also rejected any sort of patterned fabric—or patterned paper, for that matter—as too distracting once the collage was up. The definition of the problem was narrowed on both sides. I needed something monochromatic, but with surface texture. Any number of materials could have answered these concerns. But here, without examining all of them, I made a creative leap and decided intuitively upon corrugated cardboard. The brown of the cardboard was soft and warm, the ridges in it forming a gentle relief of low peaks and small valleys. And it was a utilitarian material, as common as the restaurant menu in the collage or the folded newspaper. The choice of corrugated cardboard in one way differentiated the walls from the ceiling, but in another made them all of a piece.

Pipe Dreams

Next on the list was the headboard for the bed. I'd explored a number of ideas, all inspired by my desire to have a masculine feel to the room. And strangely, as with my office, it was a Magritte painting that influenced my initial thinking of what the headboard might be. The Magritte in this instance depicts a man's pipe floating on a greige-colored field. What makes it pointed and funny and gives it its conceptual spin is the title written below the image: **"Ceci n'est pas une pipe"** ("This is not a pipe"). From the Renaissance to the twentieth century, artists struggled to achieve a mastery of reality so credible that one could look at, say, a painted courtesan and believe it was possible to enter her world, feel the firmness of her flesh, touch the velvet ribbon around her neck, and finger the satin texture of her sheets. And Magritte had painted a pipe in this vernacular, with a three-dimensional authenticity that made you think you could pick it up, hold it, even put it in your mouth and smoke it. But just as you were wrapping your mind and hand around the pipe, he slammed you with the true reality. This is not a pipe, he wrote. In other words, this was only the painting of a pipe, a mere two-dimensional simulation, and anything else you might have believed was simply an illusion.

When I was in college, I bought a reproduction of a painting. It was a pink Man Ray of three apples, and the color was so yummy I couldn't pass it up, even though generally, reproductions have always felt like a cheat to me. It's not that I'm a snob; I love works on paper and have a large collection of posters. Yet I loved this particular Magritte. It was so dead-pan, but spoke volumes about the seductive falsity of painting. I couldn't resist it, even when it wasn't the actual painting but only a paper copy. So one day, several years before I moved uptown, I bought a reproduction, framed it, and put it aside for when the time was right to bring it out again.

Now that we were working on the guest room, it seemed that time had come. The background of the Magritte was an undefinable shade of brown, and the pipe, well, the pipe was a quintessential male object. I thought I would hang it somewhere in the room and add other objects with masculine motifs. All this was before the Braque collage on the ceiling, even before I'd bought the tobacco-colored cloth covered in Chinese calligraphy. Already I had some pieces of art I thought would work—a striking war poster we'd produced for a DC Comics miniseries, **The Unknown Soldier**, and a sexy, grainy Jane Dickson print of a woman seen voyeuristically through a window.

From Cigar Boxes to Combs: The Headboard

I then began to think about the bed. I loved cigar boxes, with their faux wood exteriors and elaborate images on the inside lids. Larry Rivers, with his paintings of Dutch Masters cigar boxes, had made

us aware of their odd allegiances, referring in these works both to Rembrandt and a good old-fashioned smoke. Having started with the Magritte pipe, it was easy to envision a cigar-box bed, fake wood grain on the sides and a fabulous painting on an opened lid as the headboard.

For reference, I began buying up old cigar boxes, which, although long empty, still released the pungent smell of strong tobacco. It is not an odor that I like, and each time I lifted a lid to inspect the art inside, I would quickly slam it down as though it were the cover to Pandora's box. The scent that seeped from the boxes seemed to contaminate any-thing nearby, so I bagged them in plastic while I worked on a possible design. As I did, I began to realize that for the inside lid to double as a head-board, it would have to open on the short side of the box. I tried drawing the bed this way, with the lid opening at the short end, but it was patently false. A cigar-box bed would succeed only if it looked exactly like a cigar box. Changing the position of the opened lid was too drastic a switch for the bed to have any integrity, and therefore any wit. Open-ing lengthwise, it still could have made a daybed, but this was a guest room, and I needed a real bed with a headboard at the proper end.

Rather than force the cigar-box bed into some-thing it was not, I abandoned the concept altogether. But the Magritte pipe was guiding me still, taking me further into the field of masculine accoutrements. If a cigar box wasn't going to work, what else could I mine from that terrain? Mentally I'd pick up dif-ferent objects, explore their possibilities, and put them down, sometimes as a discard, others as the seed of an idea to visit later from a fresh perspective. But when my thoughts fastened on a comb, I knew that that was it.

The comb I saw in my mind was a tortoiseshell one, handmade, not too long, rounded at the edges and stamped with gold lettering. A classic comb, it was relatively expensive compared to the standard-issue pocket-size ones in black plastic. I knew of two companies that made different versions, Kent and Speert. They were both European and had probably been fashioning tortoiseshell combs since the beginning of time. Their old-world displays and the gold letters on their combs gave them a luxurious mystique decades before the marketing world seized the concept of branding as the Holy Grail of contemporary marketing.

I stopped by my drugstore to pick up several examples. A comb, I thought, would make a perfect headboard. It was just the right shape, and the glowing, mottled browns of the tortoiseshell would be a rich counterpoint to the corrugated cardboard, its interest lying not in color but in texture. In addition, a comb would be subtle, reading as a headboard first and only on second glance as a pop object.

Happily, Al embraced the idea. The question now was how to fabricate it. We both agreed that the material to use would

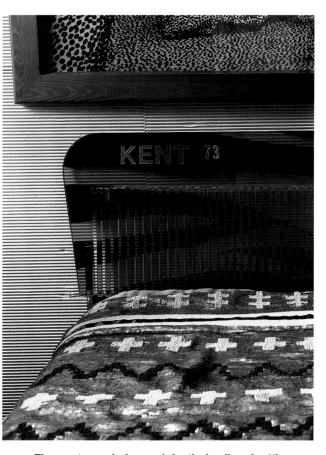

The guest room bed: a comb for the headboard, with Jeanette Kastenberg's sequined Indian blanket as a bedcover.

be Plexiglas. But in this assumption I was totally naïve. While I couldn't say with certainty that Plexiglas came in tortoiseshell patterns, I was totally convinced that we'd find it in amber. Plexiglas, after all, is made in a variety of colors, and amber is

a fairly conventional one. But no matter where Al looked or what supplier I called, no one had Plexiglas in a color that came close. I hoped that Al's name was really short for alchemist, because somehow he was going to have to turn clear plastic into a precious substance.

Because Al needed to simulate the dappled pattern of tortoiseshell, he made two life-size watercolors of combs showing how the variegated color might be distributed. They also showed how the teeth would look. I felt it would be more interesting if, as in some combs, half of them were thicker and farther apart, the others thinner and closer together. Working from the paintings, we agreed on the essentials: the size, the shape, and the pattern of the comb. Although there might have been a plastics company that would agree to custom-make the comb, Al elected to build it himself. He had a thick piece of plastic cut for the top and sides, and miraculously found Plexiglas dowels, in amber no less, to use for the teeth. The question was, how would he transform the rest of the comb into amber too?

After thinking through different options, Al came over one day with a roll of amber-colored acetate. He had an experiment to perform. The acetate was adhesive on one side, and Al was curious what would happen if he covered the front of the comb with it. Would the color seem ingrained in the plastic, even though it was only a facing? And the answer was yes. Even close up, with the acetate on it, the Plexiglas had the appearance of amber throughout. But there was a serious obstacle to achieving this effect over a large area. The acetate had to be applied as a solid sheet. Any seams would ruin the illusion. Yet because it was sticky, so ready to adhere to another material the moment contact was made, it was extraordinarily difficult to cover anything more than several square inches without getting bubbles and ripples. It took Al numerous tries—putting the acetate down, peeling it back when it riffled and dimpled—until he finally got it to lie smoothly across the entire comb. Then, using paint on the reverse side of the comb, Al limned in the tortoiseshell pattern. And everything worked! The paint, the acetate, and the clear plastic had all merged to create a perfect illusion. The headboard was almost complete. I

Above a Paul Frankl desk, Eduard Samso's mirror splinters the room like a modern cubist painting.

was committed to only two other additions, the gold lettering, "Kent" in block letters (I was biased, having used Kent combs over Speert all my life), and "handmade" in script. And here, as with the bookcase fireplace and the crossword-puzzle fireplace, we fell back on Letraset, the near-obsolete press type that had made so many of our projects possible.

Furniture for a Small Space

While Al was working on the headboard, I turned to other aspects of the room. There was very little space for furniture, and left to my own devices, I don't believe I would have assigned a desk priority. But my brother Si, a frequent and welcome visitor, made a pitch for one. Although I feel that no workspace is ever quite so ideal as a bed, Si unaccountably believes there is something to be said for sitting in a chair pulled up to a clean, flat surface. When he visits me, he works from the moment he gets up, and the lack of a desk would send him three flights down to the kitchen where he could have both privacy and space. There is so little he asks for, I took his request to heart. And when I was in Los Angeles, it seemed I'd found the exact right piece.

I had stopped by Off the Wall, one of my favorite haunts for unusual objects, when I spied an Art Deco desk. Brown with black detailing, it had curved, wraparound bookshelves on one side, and lines that suggested it had been designed by Paul Frankl,

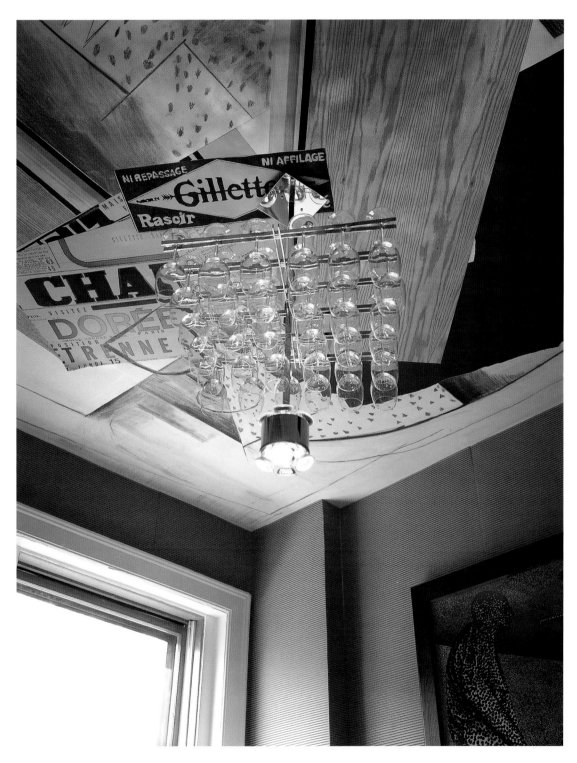

Lit by Vico Magistretti's wine-rack lamp, a Braque collage
dominates the ceiling.

Strivers Row: Other Visions, Other Rooms

which it had. The desk had a masculine feel, but it was also small, a necessity for the size of my guest room. I bought it and arranged to have it shipped to New York.

Although I planned to hang art on the guest room walls and had been stockpiling it in anticipation, I also wanted a mirror to lighten the brown palette and expand the space. And I knew just which one. Issued in 1991, the creation of Spanish artist Eduard Samso, this mirror was like no other I'd ever seen. It broke with all conventions and was so beautiful that I considered it a work of art in itself. Called the Mirallmar, it consisted of seven connected reflective squares, most of which you could twist and turn according to your taste. Each mirrored pane was a different size, from 4.85 inches square to 27.5 inches square. I'd wanted the mirror from the moment I'd first seen it, but I had no place to put it. Even when I moved to Harlem, I couldn't think where it would go. But suddenly, it seemed made for the guest room on the wall right over the desk.

A store in New York called See carried the mirror, but as with most items from Europe, it took several months for it to arrive. By the time it did, the ceiling was finished and Al was on to the next challenge. But I was back in the guest room, lying on top of the bed. If I'd gone there before just to admire the ceiling, now I went to see how the mirror splintered the room into a kaleidoscope of images, each square holding a facet of it on its silvery surface.

My last major quest was for a lighting fixture to hang from the ceiling. I combed my mental images and asked friends of mine in design, but none of the lamps I liked seemed like possibilities. They were either too significant or not significant enough. And there was another problem. It was essential that whatever light I got not obscure the Braque collage. During this period of searches and dead ends, Fontana Arte issued a new lamp by Vico Magistretti.

It was based on the overhead wineglass racks one finds in the bars of European bistros, composed of metal rods from which the glasses hang upside-down, held in place by their bases. What Magistretti had done was push a rod through the center of the rack to a cylinder of lights below. Half of the bulbs faced upward toward the glasses and the ceiling, while the other half faced down.

As was usual with international design, I had found the light only in foreign magazines. Curious, I asked my friend and curator Paola Antonelli if she'd seen it in Italy and liked it. One of the difficulties of buying European design is that it is hard to view it in person. Only a small amount of it comes here, usually to New York and sometimes to L.A., where the larger manufacturers have showrooms. Paola had seen the light and, yes, she did like it, although she had doubts about how it would look against the Braque collage. "But Fontana Arte must have a showroom here," she advised. "You should go see for yourself."

It turned out that there was no showroom in New York, but there was one in Los Angeles, so I made a note to drop by on my next business trip. I arrived at the showroom on my way back from work, a photograph of the light clutched in my hand, even though I was sure it would be on prominent display. Failing to find it, I offered my crumpled picture to a salesman.

"Oh, no, we don't have it," he said, stating what should have been obvious by now. "The fixture is wired strictly for Europe. We're not selling it in the States."

"But supposing I'm willing to rewire it? Would you sell it to me then?"

He fixed me with a dubious glance, but said he would check, and told me to call in several days. Here I was, eager to buy a lamp not simply sight unseen, but also one that would work only if it was taken apart and put back together again. But by now

I was fixated on the Magistretti light, certain, despite these drawbacks, that it was perfect for the room.

Needless to say, I was on the phone to Fontana Arte as soon as I'd observed just enough waiting time not to be considered grossly impolite. And the answer? Yes, they would sell me the lamp, but only at my own risk. If I was going to disregard the company's wisdom, then it would take no responsibility for what happened to the light once it crossed into foreign territory, as lacking in rights and warranties as any illegal immigrant. But none of this mattered to me. I ordered the Magistretti and mentally marked the calendar for when it would arrive.

When it did arrive, I immediately called an electrician, the Museum of Modern Art's expert-in-residence, renowned for assembling and rewiring European lamps without so much as a sheet of instructions. We made a date for him to come over and inspect my contraband light. But now it was Al who was impatient. While I was at DC, he unpacked the Magistretti, and he had it up and working by the time I came home. So much for the master electrician. I called to let him know that I wouldn't be needing his services after all. There was just one more issue—the wineglasses. Before the lamp arrived, all of us who had seen it either in person, as Paola had, or in a magazine, as had I and Al and Alexander, too, debated whether the fixture came with wineglasses or not. Paola and I said yes. Al said no. Alexander maintained a politic neutrality. In the end, the light showed up without glasses.

"Aha!" beamed the triumphant Al.

Ordinarily his victory would have meant more work for me, a trip to Midtown to find thirty-six wineglasses to hang from the rack. But in this case I was lucky. Months before, I had invaded Crate and Barrel to buy four or five dozen inexpensive wineglasses for large parties, where a certain breakage rate was inevitable. The ones I'd chosen had simple,

modern lines, and now I had more than enough to fill out the Magistretti lamp. A four-mile journey was reduced to six flights of stairs as I flew down to the kitchen and back. Soon they were installed upside-down in the rack, the four upward-facing bulbs illuminating not only the Braque collage but the glasses as well, which gleamed with light as only glass can. I was in decorating heaven. The Magistretti met all my criteria: it had scale and panache but, because of the glasses' transparency, in no way obscured the artwork on the ceiling. In addition, I felt it was the exact thematic fit.

"You know," I explained in my exuberance to Al, although he was as well versed in the subject as I, "so much about cubism and the cubists revolved around café life. That's why you always see wine bottles and pipes and words like **Le Journal** in the paintings. And that's why this light is so perfect."

"Well, of course, the Braque has a wineglass in it. Did you forget?"

And that's exactly what I had done. There was so much going on in the collage that over time my memory had become selective. So I followed Al upstairs, and there it was, a wineglass, part of the freehand charcoal drawing. I'd like to think I had subliminally retained its image when I chose the Magistretti light, but in truth, I doubt it. The parallel of the wineglass in the collage and the glasses hanging from the fixture was an artistic accident, something that wasn't intended but miraculously happened anyway.

Interestingly, when the art went up on the walls, the Jane Dickson was not among it, nor was the **Unknown Soldier** poster, or the Magritte pipe. I loved them all, but other works for other reasons took precedence. Yet these first choices, and the Magritte most especially, were still there in the room. They were its creative underpinnings and, like the struts behind the plaster, had determined its shape.

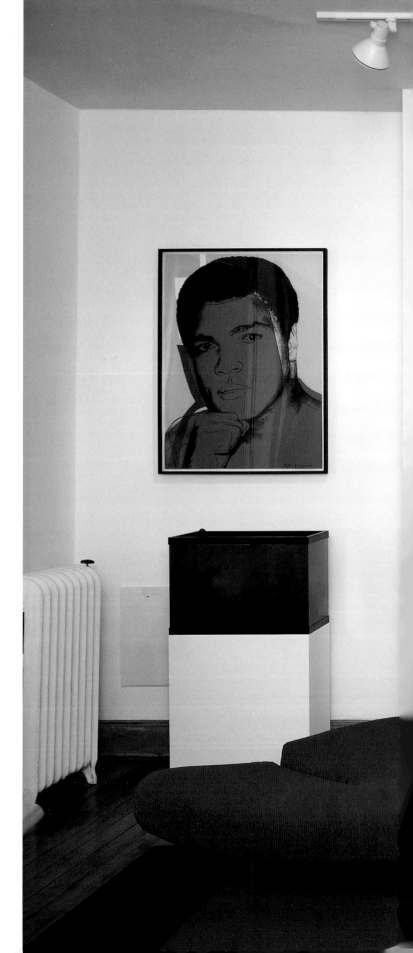

In Media Res: Baseball, Boxing, and Art in a Large Room for Friends

Aside from a small kitchen on the top floor, the kitchen on the bottom floor, the "feminine" guest room, and the second guest bathroom, which some-day would need a gut and purge, only one room was left to design. It was a beautiful room, facing front with three windows overlooking Strivers Row. From the beginning I referred to it as the media room. Like my bedroom below it, it was large, a little longer than it was wide, with high ceilings and warm, natural light. In my fantasies it would be the ultimate hangout space where my closest friends and I could laugh and drape ourselves over the fur-niture and watch the Knicks on a large-screen TV.

The first thing Al and I did was remove the two closets in the room. One jutted into the space and detracted from its beautiful proportions. The second was no more than a door leading to a storage area hidden from view, but it interrupted what would otherwise have been a wonderful expanse of wall, suitable especially for hanging art. Once the closets were gone and the plaster had dried, I asked Al to paint the ceiling yellow. I knew already that the media room was going to be the cheery room.

At the same time that I was looking for a home in Harlem, I had started to design a rug. It's not that I had a place for it, of course, but I knew that when I had a house, I would find one. The odd thing about this rug was that it took its inspiration from baseball. I am a crazed, obsessed basketball fan, but at that time in my life I thought baseball was the slowest, most painfully boring sport on the face of the planet. I was clearly benighted in this perception and had yet to understand the classic beauty of the

On either side of Bruce Pearson's monumental painting, two very different testaments to boxing.

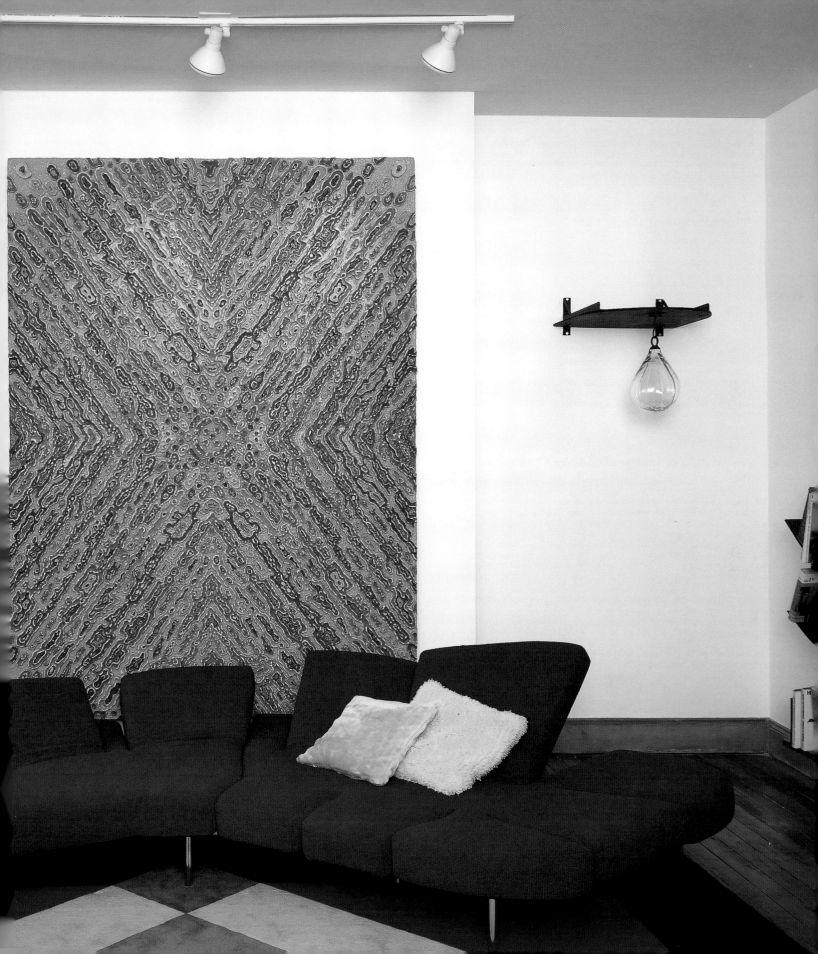

game. But nonetheless, I respected it as a uniquely American invention, replete with lore and traditions, statistics and superstitions, and the joy of kick-back summer afternoons where time seems stuck in its tracks. Somewhere deep inside me a soft spot for baseball had taken root. And, without realizing it, I'd acted on it already.

Several years earlier at the annual folk art show on the Hudson piers, I was stopped by a display of vintage baseball gloves and several catchers' masks in the booth of my friends Jolie Kelter and Michael Malcé. Michael had them all together on one small wall, and they looked just great to me. Was any of them particularly special, steeped in history, or a rare design? I didn't know and didn't think to ask. Probably not—Michael would have stepped up his pitch and told me, if so. All they had to recommend them was their age and their appearance, but that was more than enough. To me they were artifacts with stories to tell. And they were beautiful. I bought every one and stored them in a box—for what? for when? I didn't know. I was still living in the Century and hadn't yet thought of moving. But I couldn't pass them up.

This latent soft spot for baseball had manifested itself in a second way. There was a chair I loved by three Italian designers: Jonathan De Pas, Donato D'Urbino, and Paolo Lomazzi. Issued in 1968, it was called the Joe chair, in tribute to Yankee great Joe DiMaggio. A piece of pure pop art, the Joe chair was a giant baseball glove. It was large enough for two people to fall into, a soft leather womb for one. As with other classics of modern design, I'd always wanted the Joe chair, but I simply didn't have the space. Now, with the Harlem house in sight, I placed my order. Several months later the chair arrived, and soon there was a huge baseball glove in my media room, the first piece of truly comfortable furniture in my house. The chair installed, I dusted

off my vintage gloves and brought them up to the media room to hang on a wall between two of the three windows. They were the first thing you saw as you entered the room, these aged, worn, and cherished hallmarks of our national pastime. Once, they had been held on someone's hand. Now, in front of them, was the Joe chair, their modern counterpoint, a glove so large it could hold a person rather than a person holding it.

It was not surprising, then, that the rug I'd conceived was baseball themed. On the one hand, it was a diamond in a square, a pattern found among traditional Amish quilts. It was also, of course, a baseball diamond, albeit abstracted. As every fan knows, playing fields today are no longer true diamonds composed of straight edges on all four sides; instead, they have a giant curve that extends from first base to third. But cut away the curve, and the diamond is still there, a sacrosanct ninety feet between every base, including home plate. So I drew an actual diamond—this pure underlying shape—and at the corners sketched in four small squares to signify the bases. Then, starting at home plate, I drew a series of balls arcing up and to the left, each one growing larger than the next until there was one outside the diamond, outside the square itself, a separate ball, the largest of all for the exalted liberation of a home run hit clear out of the park.

Sketch in hand, I got together with Jody Harrow, who had made four of the rugs that I owned. I arrived with many of the colors thought out—yellow for the diamond, brown for the corner squares, green within the diamond to indicate grass, red on the outer side, and a strong black frame to surround it all. I had yet to choose the colors for the baseballs, but I knew that each would not only be different from the next but would have different color laces as well. Jody was delighted to execute the rug, and made a polished computer rendering from my clear

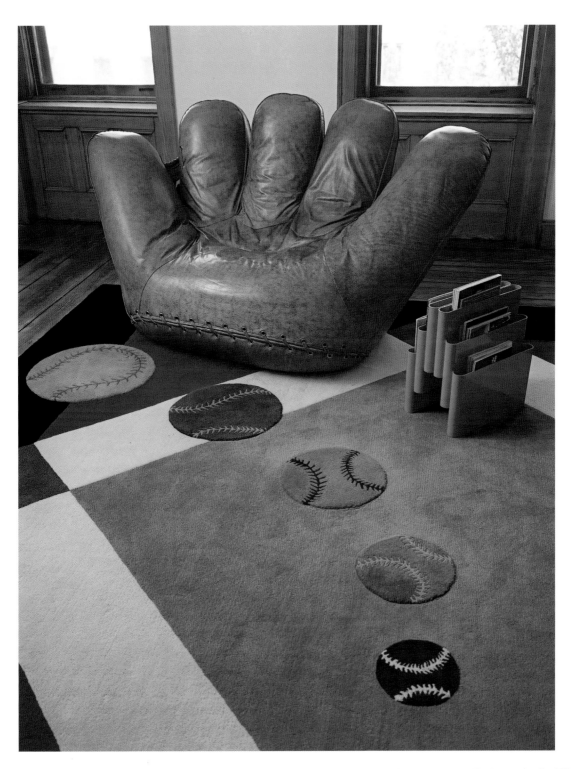

The Joe Chair, an Italian homage to Yankee great Joe DiMaggio, on top of a graphic baseball rug.

Strivers Row: Other Visions, Other Rooms

but amateurish sketch. It seemed that in no time the floor of the media room would be turned into a vivid playing field.

But nothing could have been further from the truth. Jody tried factories as far away as Europe and Asia and as close to home as Georgia. Strike-offs, small samples of the larger rug, would arrive, but there was always something wrong. The colors would be off, the lines not crisp, the pile incorrectly looped. One disappointment followed another, and three years amazingly flew by. Jody had now found a factory in New Jersey. Its strike-off also raised doubts, and Jody found the people hard to deal with. But the closeness of the New Jersey factory was an advantage because you could be on-site, pointing out the errors, raising the level of execution, and pumping up workers when they felt you'd asked the impossible. Although it's become easy to believe that all things can be effected through e-mail and fax, there really is no substitute for giving input in person. So we gave them the go-ahead, with Jody constantly checking

Between two windows of the media room, a collection of vintage baseball gloves plus two catcher's masks.

their progress, and six weeks later the rug was complete. And end result was truly beautiful, beautiful enough to make any unbeliever reconsider baseball.

Clearly the media room was taking on a strong sports theme. Baseball dominated, with three other additions. Mark Chiarello, a gifted comic-book artist and truly exceptional colorist, had created a set of trading cards based on players in the Negro League.

The Negro League had held my interest since my early twenties, when I first learned about the great African-American pitcher Satchel Paige, one of the most phenomenal figures ever to play the game. It wasn't until 1947 that Jackie Robinson became the first black player allowed into the majors. By then Satchel Paige was forty-seven, and his best years, like those of so many other talented players, had been confined to the segregated Negro League. Yet the Negro League, while an outgrowth of America's shameful treatment of blacks, was still a vivid piece of history, as steeped in its traditions, tales, and personalities as the major leagues were in theirs.

When Mark Chiarello's cards were issued, I asked if I could buy some of the beautiful watercolors on which they were based. Two were already promised, but Mark graciously gave me my choice of the rest. I purchased five, including the one I wanted most, Satchel Paige in profile winding up for a pitch. To give the paintings more presence, I framed them all together. They hung for several years in Alexander's restaurant, along with early photographs of several black families, including Percy Sutton's and Gordon Parks's. But I retrieved them when I bought the house on Strivers Row. If they truly belonged anywhere, they belonged in Harlem.

The two other pieces came from the Curt Marcus Gallery, which was having a summer show devoted to baseball. It was an invitational exhibit, with artists from Jeff Koons to Andy Warhol contributing a baseball-themed work. Since baseball was part of the media room, I hastened downtown to check it out. Summer art shows are often lighter than those during the rest of the year, and this one was not only fun but affordable. I walked away with a life-size painting by Jane Dixon of a suburban door on green AstroTurf. It hung flat against the wall and continued onto the floor. Sitting on the fabric on the floor, as though it had just been hit out of the sandlot, narrowly missing someone's window, was a well-worn ball. The second piece was a small sculpture, a low box no more than five inches square. It contained some fake grass, what looked suspiciously like moldering excrement, and beside it, a spanking-new white ball. This baseball, too, had been hit out of the park, but with slightly less savory results. The title of this tiny installation piece was, appropriately, **Now You Owe Me a New Ball**.

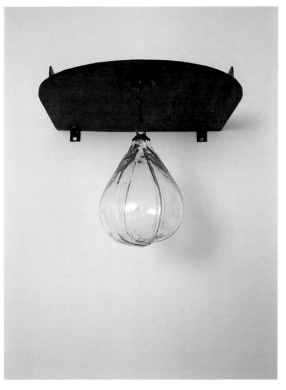

The ultimate visual oxymoron, Tony Stanzione's glass punching bag.

Walking into the baseball-filled media room, I hoped visitors would be arrested by the many different ways one could view this American sport. The vintage gloves and the paintings of players in the Negro League provided prisms of history and social commentary. The Jane Dickson ball and door, and the second ball cradled by grass and dung, spoke to baseball's pervasiveness, to endless pickup games, and a sport belonging as much to amateurs and neighborhoods as it does to the pros and stadiums. The Joe chair? An homage, but overblown and cartoonish, a foreign perspective on an American obsession. And the rug? Well, perhaps the rug was simply my field of dreams.

Other Themes, Other Dreams

So that was it for baseball. I had collected other related memorabilia I thought would work in the space, but it turned out there were limits. It was important to sound other notes, and I did this with furniture and objects that had no connection to baseball, and many that had no connection to sports at all.

The most exciting piece of art I bought for the media room was a painting by Bruce Pearson. My friends Jeanette Ingberman and Papo Colo, who have often been my guides through the international labyrinth of emerging artists, had suggested I look at his paintings. Concerned always with provocative works of immense integrity, they have spent more than two decades searching out and showcasing the best the art world has yet to discover. Always generous with their advice and passions, they are available to anyone—a seasoned collector, a museum curator, or an absolute novice who simply stumbles on their space. The more interested you are, the more time they'll spend with you.

I had seen and looked at a few works by Bruce at Exit Art, although there was no single picture I'd warmed to enough to want to own. But both Colo and Jeanette were high on Bruce, and urged me to see more. One weekend afternoon, on my way to Brooklyn to visit Roxy Paine, whose work Jeanette and Colo had shown before anyone else, I called Jeanette from the car.

"You're going to see Roxy?" she exclaimed. "You should go to see Bruce at the same time. Their studios are near each other, and they're the best of friends."

When I was at Roxy's, he also urged me to go see Bruce, since I was already in Brooklyn. As I was readying to leave, Roxy called Bruce for me and managed to reach him on the phone. Yes, said Bruce, of course I was welcome to come over.

If I had liked Bruce's work at Exit Art, I was wowed by what I saw in his studio. The paintings were enormous, most of them six feet by eight, and the colors jumped off the surfaces. The surfaces themselves were

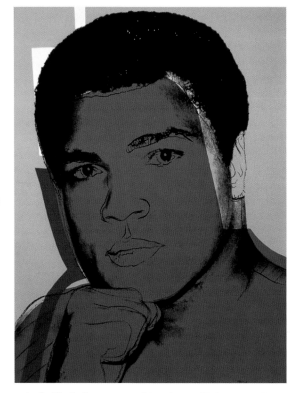

Andy Warhol's young and handsome Muhammad Ali.

crenellated; Bruce, using a hot wire and a sewing machine, had carved the foundations out of Styrofoam and fitted them together like pieces in a puzzle. Almost all the pictures were works in progress, but still, there was one I couldn't take my eyes off. It had a vibrant, bright blue background and a pattern of vividly colored ellipses that swirled diagonally outward from the center into each of

the four quadrants. The painting was aflame with oranges, yellows, magentas, and reds, each with the lacquered sheen of enamel.

"Oh, is that one available?" I gasped, dreading that it was already spoken for. But no, it wasn't. Bruce and I discussed price, and I walked out his door in promissory possession of a thrilling work of art.

Before the painting came to me, it detoured to the Museum of Modern Art, where it hung with other works of Bruce's in the Project Rooms for a month and a half. After Al had received it and hoisted it two flights up to the media room, I hung the painting on a large pier at one end of the space, where it served as the vertical connection between the vibrant rug on the floor and the yellow ceiling above. The picture had a pulsating presence; without question, it was the visual centerpiece of the room.

Directly opposite Bruce's work, I hung a sculpture by David Henderson, as calm and serenely textural as Bruce's work was electric. This piece, like so many others, was an Exit Art find. On one side of it I placed Jane Dickson's AstroTurf door, on the other, Al Souza's collaged maps, with a plane flying overhead. The maps were intricate plans of different states, from north to south and from east to west. Together, they gave a sense of the breadth and diversity that is America.

On the perpendicular wall, above the waving library shelves made from Ron Arad's Bookworms,

I hung a wonderful work by the artist Allan Wexler. Called **24 Unfolded Houses**, it was just that—twenty-four Plasticine houses, each one deconstructed into a different schematic of six squares. In a row at the bottom of the picture were twenty-four fully realized houses, each corresponding to one of the numbered patterns above. Intellectually it was brilliant, and emotionally it could not have been more satisfying. Beneath its seeming surface simplicity, Allan's work was like a Zen rock garden, deeply complex and rewarding.

I believed that these varied works of art made the media room a much richer experience; a room that is precisely themed tends to deaden over time. I always have mixed feelings when I see houses in Aspen or Telluride with explicit western motifs. Yes, the vintage furniture is great, the Indian blankets beautiful examples of native artistry. The wood is warm; the antler lamps and buffalo heads, while sordid trophies in my mind, nevertheless evoke life on the open range. But after a while all of these homes start to seem the same. There are no surprises, no humor, no commentary, and ultimately no challenges. A room holds up over time when there are unexpected choices, choices that have no obvious connection but are often intuitive, keenly felt and serious.

I felt this way about the couch that I bought, called the Flap sofa and manufactured by Edra in Italy. I first saw it in a black-and-white photo in

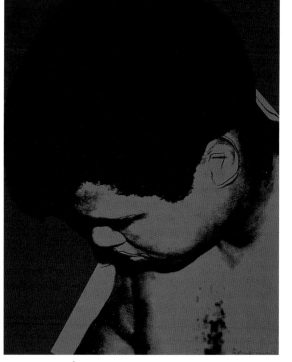

The private, introspective Ali, also by Warhol.

the **New York Times**. It was April 2000, and the annual furniture fair in Milan was under way. Despite the low resolution inevitable with newspaper reproduction, I was fascinated by the photograph of this new seating unit. It was curvilinear in shape and sectionalized, so that you could individually adjust different parts of the back. One portion could be placed all the way down, another at a thirty-degree angle, yet another practically straight up.

In addition to the personal comfort afforded by this design, the sofa was varied and exciting and full of visual possibilities.

My friends Humberto and Fernando Campana had attended the fair, and because Edra manufactures several collections of their furniture, I was sure they must have seen the sofa.

"What did you think of it?" I queried as they passed through New York on their way back to Brazil.

"Oh, it looked good, Jenette, it looked good."

They gave me the name of a contact person at Edra from whom I could get measurements and fabric samples, too. It turned out that there were two versions of the sofa; one had the greatest width on the left side, one on the right. I thought the first design would work best in the media room, but before I ordered it, Al insisted on making a paper pattern cut to the sofa's full shape and size. The Flap sofa was a very big piece of furniture; placing the pattern on the floor would give us some sense of how much area it would take up. Clearly, with the Joe chair and the Flap sofa, there would be no room for other furniture. You also had to imagine the sofa in three dimensions. If the seat were high or the sofa a solid block of upholstery, it would overwhelm the room. I had to believe that the varied back positions would offset its dimensions and make something quite large still look graceful and light.

Although Edra had more than fifty colors and fabrics to choose from, I selected an electric blue; made deeper and more interesting by having been woven with black, it had punch, and it had weight. I knew it would take the usual three months for the Flap sofa, like all things from Europe, to arrive. This was a huge commitment to something sight unseen. I tried to let the time go by peacefully and hoped there would be no unwelcome surprises. Luckily, when the sofa was delivered, the surprises were all positive. It didn't look good, it looked great. And it was not only wonderfully flexible, it was wildly comfortable, too. It was interactive, it was personal, it was sculptural, and it was fun.

In the last five decades a dozen or so designers have altered the sofa's traditional form. In the 1950s Vladimir Kagan and Isamu Noguchi gave it sensuous curved shapes, and George Nelson introduced his Marshmallow sofa, with its circular cushions. In the 1960s, Nicola's pop creations wittily re-created male and female forms. In 1971, Cini Boeri designed the Serpentone, which, true to its name, was snaking and sinuous. In the 1980s, Masanori Umeda contributed a Memphis icon, a padded boxing ring, a playpen for a convivial, informal group of friends. And a few years later, Antonio Citterio created Sity, a sectionalized sofa that straddled Bauhaus straight-line sensibilities with contemporary interchangeability. Now, looking at the Flap sofa, I felt that it too had taken its place on the short list of ground-breaking classics. It was beautiful, and I loved it.

The media room was almost complete. A sculpture I'd owned for many years, a punching bag fashioned from transparent glass by the artist Tony Stanzione, launched a second sports theme. At first glance it was transparent and airy—almost pretty, like a handblown vase. It was only when you realized its oxymoronic quality—a glass punching bag!—that the piece hit back. We hung the bag to the right of Bruce Pearson's painting. On its other side and on the small left wall as you entered the room, I placed two Andy Warhols of Muhammad Ali. I had had the enormous pleasure of working with Ali. But even if I hadn't, he would still always be one of my heroes.

Of the suite of four silkscreens Andy did of Ali, I chose the one that showed his face full frontal, handsome and clear-eyed on a yellow field with a large magenta accent. It was the colorful, public Ali, the man who had an uncanny sense of self-promotion, ushering in the modern boxing era with his rhymes, bravado, and showstopping personality. The second, on a dark and bluesy ground, showed the introspective Ali, the one who was willing to sacrifice his peak years for his principles, who refused to be patronized, who changed his name from Cassius Clay, whose convictions would not permit him to serve in Vietnam. For these acts of courage he risked everything, and consequently was reviled and stripped of his titles. Both faces of Ali were equally true, and these portraits spoke not just about the man but also about our country and our times.

There were just three other additions to the media room—a yellow surfboard coffee table by Andrea Ruggiero (on which I placed a vintage **Life** magazine with Ali on the cover), a translucent resin door by Gaetano Pesce originally made for the advertising offices he designed for Chiat-Day, and a sculpture by Austrian artist Iris Andrashek, a fish tank with a light and a pump in which a T-shirt endlessly folded and unfolded like an exotic plant.

When Manny Gerard, one of my oldest friends, whose delight in razzing me has never abated, first saw the room, he erupted, with all the glee of someone who's just achieved a major scientific breakthrough: "Where's the media? This is the first media room I've ever seen that doesn't have any media!" I have to admit, I was speechless. But after he left, as I watched the T-shirt twist and turn, as engrossing as the Knicks' Latrell Sprewell in midair or any Hitchcock thriller, I realized that media comes in many different forms. It was the media room after all.

Lessons Learned Along the Way

1. When buying something, whether from a manufacturer, a retailer, an artist, or a dealer, don't be afraid to express your wishes, no matter how extreme they might seem. Do you want a chair in a color not in the line? To change the proportions of a rug? To have the sofa legs in chrome instead of wood? Say so, as politely as possible, but say so. Often the answer is no. And if the answer is yes, you may have to pay a premium. But you'll never know if you can have exactly what you want unless you ask.

2. A lot of great design is still in production. Other pieces appear on the market as reissues, faithfully following their original specifications. Purists will scoff at these, valuing only the earliest editions of an object. But if there is no real aesthetic difference between an item issued at the time of its design and the same one manufactured now, consider the more recent one. It won't have the resale value of a vintage piece, but it will cost a lot less and be in considerably better shape.

3. Harmony makes a space livable, tension makes it interesting. I have a soft spot for dichotomies and odd juxtapositions, like mixing pop-culture icons with serious art, or painting a tape measure around an organically shaped swimming pool. If you establish an overall sensibility, you can play numerous games within it.

4. Faux-finish painting, like many decorating trends, has become too popular; it tends to be used indiscriminately. But applied judiciously in just the right spot, it can add layers of interest and wit. By detailing the surround with faux marble, my Magritte fireplace referenced the artist's painting far more successfully than if I'd employed real marble. The painted-marble floor in my dining room was warmer than stone, and nodded to other wood details in the space, like the chair rail and the fireplace mantel. Before you opt for faux, check out books on the subject to see how it's used for maximum effect. Then apply what works best to your own interiors.

5. Conventional wisdom says that small, intimate pictures should go in a small, intimate room. And conventional wisdom is right. Small pictures in a small space can have a lovely effect, creating the sense of a private, almost sequestered interior. But what about unconventional wisdom? What happens when you have a large artwork on a small wall? You might lose the feeling of quiet introspection, but by converting expected notions of scale, you can create drama in a pocket-size room.

Acknowledgments

So many people helped to make **In Your Space** possible. But there is one person I must mention above all others, the one person to whom I owe the deepest, most heartfelt thanks: Bob Abrams, the president and publisher of Abbeville Press. It was Bob's idea that I write a book in the first place, something that had never occurred to me to do. He promised to be my publisher, even before I had written a single sentence. And when I waffled, it was Bob who kept telling me he was serious. His perseverance made me serious, too.

Through the protracted process of completing my first book, Bob had the patience of a latter-day saint. And even after the World Trade Center disaster, when Abbeville was forced out of its offices across the street, Bob remained dedicated to publishing **In Your Space** this year. When has an untried author ever been so lucky?

There are other people at Abbeville to whom I am also indebted, most especially my incredible editor, Susan Costello. With wisdom, humor, and immense sensitivity, Susan has made **In Your Space** an infinitely better book. While we jointly groaned about the rotten play of our beloved Knicks, Susan cheerfully took in stride the pitfalls of working with a first-time author. Thanks, too, to Louise Kurtz, Abbeville's production manager. Her imprint can be found in the quality details for which Abbeville is famous, and in the fact that there is a book at all.

Julietta Cheung is the inspired art director of **In Your Space**. I love her aesthetic choices, from the bold primaries and colored heads to the open layouts and expansive spreads. I also cannot say enough about Jason Schmidt's luminous photographs with their sophisticated naturalism, their clarity of vision, and their rich and balanced palette. Thanks to Tom Booth, who represents Jason, for facilitating his work on the book. And thanks to Michael Reynolds, who brought his imaginative styling to Jason's Harlem shoot.

On the home front, no one has been more critical to **In Your Space** than Anna Ng, my assistant on the book. Anna has been my adviser, champion, and confidante every step of the way. Through all the hard work, all the deadlines, the innumerable additions, deletions, and last-minute changes, Anna has been a shining jewel—forever positive, good-natured, supportive, and unflappable. I could not ask for a better helpmate or a better friend.

Special thanks to my brother, Si Kahn, who in this last year has been my supportive reader and valued counselor. During the many months of writing before work, after work, on weekends, and during vacations, he constantly encouraged me, coining what became my daily mantra, The Book Rules. Thanks, too, to my sister-in-law, Elizabeth Minnich, for her kindness and insight.

Among my friends, none deserves more thanks than Greg Garry, who not only read the majority of the manuscript but contributed some of the best chapter headings. Jeanette Ingberman has been my most steadfast booster, reading the book in installments over the space of two years, and somehow managing to remain engaged. Thanks also to my friends who read only small portions of **In Your Space** but believed in the whole, and to those who read nothing at all but had faith.

I am indebted to **House & Garden**, and to Dominique Browning, Lucy Gilmore, and Betsy Pochoda in particular. They commissioned Jason Schmidt to photograph my Harlem house for a feature in the magazine (**House & Garden**, April 2002) and generously gave me full access to those images. Thanks, too, to the galleries who so graciously made available photographs of artwork for the book: Janet Borden, Inc., Charles Cowles Gallery, Exit Art/The First World, P.P.O.W., and Ronald Feldman Fine Arts.

Finally, thank you to my treasured caretakers, Tony and Joanne Bilotta, who have been looking after my house in the country since it was built; to the best of neighbors there, Brean Yates and Drew Dyer, who make my garden grow; and to Carolyn Campbell, who sees that my house in Harlem shines.

Source Guide

Allan Wexler
See Galleries—Ronald Feldman Fine Arts.

Al Williams
521 West 26th Street
New York, NY 10011
Phone: 212-563-2563 or 917-716-6191

Auction Houses

Auction houses publish catalogues on up-coming sales. If you want to see the range of what they offer, contact them to send you a calendar of the auctions for the year. You can subscribe to catalogues by category or purchase them individually.

The Blue Chip Houses

Christie's
20 Rockefeller Plaza
New York, NY 10020
Phone: 212-636-2000
Fax: 212-636-2399
www.christies.com

Phillips, de Pury & Luxembourg
3 West 57th Street
New York, NY 10019
Phone: 212-570-4830
Fax: 212-570-2207
lschiff@phillipsny.com

Sotheby's Incorporated
1334 York Avenue
New York, NY 10021
Phone: 212-606-7000
Fax;: 212-606-7107
www.sothebys.com

The More Affordable Houses

Christie's East
20 Rockefeller Plaza
New York, NY 10020
Phone: 212-636-2000
Fax: 212-636-2399
www.christieseast.com

David Rago Auctions, Inc.
333 North Main Street
Lambertville, NJ 08530
Phone: 609-397-9374
Fax: 609-397-9377
email: info@ragoarts.com
www.ragoarts.com

Los Angeles Modern Auctions
7601 Sunset Blvd.
Los Angeles, CA 90046
Phone: 323-904-1950/323-436-5415
Fax: 323-904-1954
sloughrey@butterfields.com

Treadway Gallery/John Toomey Gallery
2029 Madison Road
Cincinnati, OH 45208
Phone: 513-321-6742
Fax: 513-871-7722
email: info@treadwaygallery.com

William Doyle Galleries
175 East 87th Street
New York, NY 10028
Phone: 212-427-4141

No Catalogues, No Frills, But Bi-Weekly Bargains

Tepper Galleries
110 East 25th Street
New York, NY 10010
Phone: 212-677-5300
Fax: 212-673-3686
www.teppergalleries.com

Catalogues

Design within Reach
A catalogue of well-designed modern furniture, lighting, and accessories. There is also a retail store in San Francisco.
455 Jackson Street
San Francisco, CA 94111
1-800-944-2233
www.dwr.com
info@dwr.com

Oriac Design

Another excellent catalogue for contemporary design.
275 Grove Street
Suite 2-400
Netwon, MA 02466
Phone: 866-GO-ORIAC
www.oriacdesign.com

Lillian Vernon Corporation

User-friendly catalogues specializing in highly affordable home décor and personalized gifts.
For a free catalogue or to order, call 1-800-LILLIAN
www.lillianvernon.com

Contractors and Architects

Al Williams

General contractor with a specialty in custom artistic solutions.
Williams Construction
521 West 26th Street
New York, NY 10011
Phone: 212-563-2563 or 917-716-6191

Arthur Zweck-Bronner

Interior Architect, residential and commercial.
194 West 10th Street
New York, NY 10014
Phone and Fax: 212-989-4013

Philip Hayes Builder, Inc.

841 Middlesex Turnpike
Old Saybrook, CT 06475
Phone: 860-388-4428

Dealers

Bruce Hershenson

Movie posters.
P.O. Box 874
West Plains, MO 65775
Phone: 417-256-9616
Fax: 417-257-6948
mail@brucehershenson.com
www.brucehershenson.com

Harris Diamant

American folk art.
27 West 20th Street
New York, NY 10011
Phone: 212-627-3964

John Sakas

Bakelite and Catalin radios.
Radio Craze
P.O. Box 362
Walden, NY 12586
Phone: 845-778-4064

Kelter Malcé Antiques

Jolie Kelter and Michael Malcé
American folk art including rugs, quilts, weather vanes, and Native American textiles.
74 Jane Street
New York, NY 10014
Phone: 212-675-7380
Fax: 212-675-9529
keltermalcé@mac.com

Norman Brosterman

Architectural and techno-futuristic drawings.
Phone: 917-648-5120
nbrosterman@nyc.rr.com

Orange Group

Michael Benevento
Modernist and Post-War furniture by French Architects.
515 Broadway
New York, NY 10012
Phone: 212-965-8617
Fax: 212-334-4703
orangegroup@angelfire.com

R. Louis Bofferding

18th-Century French and Italian furniture, 20th-Century interior design pieces.
Phone: 212-744-6725

Super Rare Immediately Now

Michael Ralphs
Post-War Italian and radical design.
Telephone: + 45-33-16-33-26
Fax: + 33-04-93-26-47-78
Mobile: + 45-40-86-67-89
Majic@worldnet.fr

Designers

Harriette Bauknight

Beautiful plastic frames, mirrors, and pocketbooks
by commission.
Phone: 864-855-4252
email: Harriettebauk@aol.com

Alex Locadia

Fabrication of futuristic lighting, furniture,
and interiors.
371 Canal Street
New York, NY 10013
Phone: 212-226-5349
Fax: 212-219-9295
www.afuture.com
afuture@spacelab.net

Casual Thought Corporation

Steve Kursh
Interior design, decoration, and fabrication.
Phone: 917-806-8636

Gaetano Pesce

Architect and designer who has pioneered
the use of resins.
543 Broadway
New York, NY 10012
212-941-0280

Groundplans, Ltd.

Jody Harrow
Custom rugs, carpets, and textiles.
136 East 56th Street
New York, NY 10022
212-888-9366
j.harrowdesign@worldnett.att.net

Lloyd Schwan (1955–2001)

Although Lloyd died in 2001, Lyn Godley, his former
wife and partner, still has some of his seminal pieces for
sale. In addition, Lyn and Lloyd shared a sensibility, and
Lyn, along with her own style, still creates pieces and
interiors that reflect it. For information, see her contact
information below.

Lyn Godley

Custom designed innovations in lighting, furniture,
and interiors.
504 Walnut Tree Drive
Blandon, PA 19510
610-944-9838
nlgodley@aol.com

Mardi-jo Cohen

Custom fabrication of innovative silver tableware from
forks, knives and spoons to salad servers, cake cutters,
candleholders, and menorahs.
147 Poplar Street
Philadelphia, PA 19123
215-592-8667
MARDIONEANDONLY@aol.com

Nicola

Imaginative, functional art.
222 West 23rd Street Suite 929
212-627-1240
nicolal@earthlink.net

Pucci De Rossi

Highly personal furniture and lighting.
Phone: 011.33.1.4024.1048
Fax: 011.33.1.4024.1158
email: pucciderossi@gonline.fr
www.made75.com

Rhodes West Inc.

Brenda White and Jesse Rhodes
Limited edition art pieces and ceramics.
P.O. Box 215
Eastport, Maine 04631
Rwest@midmaine.com

Robert Lee Morris

Award-winning contemporary jewelry,
including plates, bowls, and candlesticks.
Robert Lee Morris Gallery
400 West Broadway
New York, NY 10012
Phone: 212-431-9405
www.robertleemorris.com
Morris's work is also available at Bergdorf Goodman,
Bloomingdale's, Neiman Marcus, Saks Fifth Avenue,
and fine jewelry stores.

Studio Campana

Fernando and Humberto Campana
Unique, modern furniture, often using unexpected materials.
Rua Barão de Tatuí 219
São Paulo SP 01226-030
Phone/Fax: 55-11-3825-3408
Campanad@aol.com.br

Wendy Gell Designs

Jewelry, and jeweled mirrors, picture frames,
canvases, and dolls.
608 Lake Drive
Guilford, CT 06437
203-457-1397
http://wendygell.com
wendella@wendygell.com

Galleries

ACA Galleries

Specialists in Romare Beardon's work.
529 West 20th Street
New York, NY 10011
Phone: 212-206-8080
Fax: 212-206-8498
info@acagalleries.com

Charles Cowles Gallery, Inc.

Contemporary art including the work of Al Souza.
537 West 24th Street
New York, NY 10011
Phone: 212-925-3500
Fax: 212-925-3501
www.cowlesgallery.com
info@cowlesgallery.com

Exit Art/The First World

Highly affordable work of quality, emerging artists.
548 Broadway
New York, NY 10012
Phone: 212-966-7745
Fax: 212-925-2928

James Cohan Gallery

International contemporary art including
the work of Roxy Paine.
Phone: 212-755-7171
Fax: 212-755-7177
www.jamescohan.com
jane@jamescohan.com

Janet Borden, Inc.

Contemporary fine art photography (including
works by Sandy Skoglund, Tina Barney, Jan Groover,
and Neil Winokur).
560 Broadway
New York, NY 10012
www.janetbordeninc.com

Louis K. Meisel Gallery

Photorealism, pop art, and the American pin-up
including the work of Mel Ramos.
141 Prince Street
New York, NY 10012
Phone: 212-677-1340
www.meiselgallery.com

Newbury Fine Arts

Contemporary art including the work of Randy Stevens.
29 Newbury Street
Boston, MA 02116
Tel: 617-536-0210
www.newburyfinearts.com

Paul Morris Gallery

Contemporary art, including the photographs of
David Levinthal.
530 West 22d Street
New York, NY 10011
Phone: 212-243-3753
Fax: 212-243-3668

P.P.O.W.

Contemporary painting, sculpture, and photography, including the work of Carrie Mae Weems.
Pilkington-Olsoff Fine Arts, Inc.
476 Broome Street, Third Floor
Phone: 212-941-8642
Fax: 212-274-8339
info@ppowgallery.com

Ricco/Maresca Gallery

Self-taught, outsider, and American folk art.
529 West 20th Street – 3rd Floor
New York, NY 10011
Phone: 212-627-4819
Fax: 212-627-5117
www.riccomaresca.com
info@riccomaresca.com

Ronald Feldman Fine Arts

Contemporary art, including the work of Ida Applebroog, Komar and Melamid, Bruce Pearson, Todd Siler, Andy Warhol, and Allan Wexler.
31 Mercer Street
New York, NY 10013
Phone: 212-226-3232
Fax: 212-941-1536
www.feldmangallery.com

Manufacturers

Herman Miller

Manufacturers of modern American furniture classics including the Eames lounge chair and ottoman and George Nelson's Marshmallow sofa.
800-646-4400
www.hermanmiller.com

Knoll

Contemporary furnishings and fabrics.
Showroom—open to the public
105 Wooster Street
New York, NY 10012
Phone: 212-343-4000
Fax: 212-343-4180
www.knoll.com

Vitra

Home and office contemporary furniture including designs by Ron Arad.
888-278-2855 (for retail locations)
800-33-VITRA (for office furniture)
www.vitra.com
info@vitra.com

Museum Stores

American Craft Museum Store

40 West 53rd Street
New York, NY 10019
Phone: 212-956-3535
www.americancraftmuseum.org

Metropolitan Museum Store

1000 Fifth Avenue
New York, NY 10028
Phone: 212-535-7710
To order a catalogue call 1-800-468-7386
email: visitorservices@metmuseum.org
www.metmuseum.org

MoMA Design Store

44 West 53rd Street
New York, NY 10019
Phone: 212-767-1050
To order a catalogue call 1-800-447-6662
ProductService @moma.org
www.momastore.org

Museum of African Arts Store

593 Broadway
New York, NY 10012
Phone: 212-966-1313
www.africanart.org

Solomon R. Guggenheim Museum Store

1071 5th Avenue at 89th Street
Phone: 212-423-3615

Studio Museum of Harlem Store

144 West 125th Street
New York, NY 10027
Phone: 212-864-4500
Fax: 212-864-4800
For complete listing of publications call 212-864-0014
www.studiomuseuminharlem.org

Whitney Museum Store

945 Madison Avenue at 75th Street
New York, NY 10021
Phone: 212-570-3614

Retailers

Affordable Lighting

No high design, but a wide variety of inexpensive lights.
727 Boston Post Road #2
Guilford, CT 06437
Phone: 203-458-7116

Alan Moss

High-end 20th-Century American and European art,
furniture, lighting, and objects.
436 Lafayette Street
New York, NY 10003
Phone: 212-473-1310

Beverley

Clarice Cliff, Keith Murray, Shelley pottery, and
other Art Deco objects.
30 Church Street
MaryLebone, England
London NW8 8EP
Phone/Fax: 0207.262 1576
Mobile: 077.7613.6003

Carole A. Berk, Ltd.

British ceramics including Clarice Cliff, Keith Murray,
and Shelley pottery.
By Appointment
Bethesda, Maryland
Phone: 301-365-3400
Fax: 301-365-8837

Crate & Barrel

Nationwide stores selling good, clean design
at affordable prices.
For Store Locations: 800-996-9960
Catalog: 800-323-5461
www.crateandbarrel.com

DeLorenzo 1950

Top French 1950s design, including the work
of Charlotte Perriand and Jean Ròyere.
440 Lafayette Street
New York, NY 10003
Phone: 212-995-1950

Design 70

Post-War design with a specialty in esoteric objects.
Items found upon request.
3, rue Saint Francois de Paule
06300 NICF
France
Telephone: + 33-04-93-80-42-62
Fax: + 33-04-93-80-42-28
Mobile: + 33-06-09-53-89-09
www.design70.com
info@design70.com

Fontana Arte

Lighting and glass including designs by Gae Aulenti
and Vico Magistretti.
8807 Beverly Blvd.
Los Angeles, CA 90048
Phone: 310-247-9933
Fax: 310-247-1668
www.fontanaarte.it
Fontanaarte@hotmail.com

Fred Silberman

Italian furniture and lighting from 1920-1960.
36 West 25th Street
New York, NY 10010
Phone: 212-924-6330
Fax: 212-924-6360

IKEA

A great source for inexpensive contemporary furniture, lighting, rugs, and objects.
1100 Broadway Mall
Hicksville, NY 11801
Phone: 516-681-4532
www.ikea-usa.com
Check Web site for other store locations or to receive a catalogue.

Making Light

The innovative lighting designs of Ingo Maurer.
89 Grand Street
New York, NY 10013
Phone: 212-965-8817
Fax: 212-965-8819
email: making-light2ingomaurer-usa.com
www.ingo-maurer.com

Irreplaceable Artifacts

Salvaged architectural elements, from vintage bathtubs to decorative gates.
14 Second Avenue
New York, NY 10003
Phone: 212-777-2900
Fax: 212-780-0642
www.irreplaceableartifacts.com
info@irreplaceableartifacts.com

International Poster Gallery

Vintage posters from around the world.
205 Newbury Street
Boston, MA 02116
Phone: 617-375-0076/800-624-7441
Fax: 617-375-0079
info@internationalposter.com

Lost City Arts

Vintage furniture and reproduced classics.
18 Cooper Square
New York, NY 10003
Phone: 212-375-0500
Fax: 212-375-9342
info@lostcityarts.com

Modernica

Precise reissues of Charles and Ray Eames designs.
57 Greene Street
New York, NY 10012
Phone: 212-219-1303
Fax: 212-219-1699

Mood Indigo

Vintage objects from the 1920s to the 1960s including Bakelite, Fiesta Ware, Russell Wright and Eva Zeisel dinnerware, and New York World's Fair memorabilia.
181 Prince Street
New York, NY
Phone: 212-254-1176

Moss

Cutting-edge modern design, including tableware, home accessories, lighting, and furniture.
146 Greene Street
New York, NY 10012
Phone: 212-226-2190
www.mossonline.com

Off the Wall Antiques and Weird Stuff

An array of 20th Century antiques and weird stuff.
7325 Melrose Avenue
Los Angeles, CA 90046
Phone: 323-930-1185
Fax: 323-930-1595
email: weirdstuff@earthlink.net
www.offthewallantiques.com

Palazzetti

Modern European furniture classics, including a Noguchi sofa and Poltronova's Joe chair.
515 Madison Avenue at 53rd Street
New York, NY 10022
Phone: 212-832-1199
Fax: 212-832-1385
email: info@palazzetti.com

The Pop Shop

T-shirts, posters, and other collectibles featuring
artwork from Keith Haring.
292 Lafayette Street
New York, NY 10012
Phone: 212-219-2784
Fax: 212-274-8743
www.haring.com
popshop@haring.com

Poster America

Vintage American and international posters.
138 West 18th Street
New York, NY 1011
Phone: 212-206-0499

Pottery Barn

Good, simple, affordable design.
1965 Broadway
New York, NY 10023
Phone: 212-579-8477
www.potterybarn.com
Go to Web site for other store locations and a free catalog.

Primavera Gallery

High-end 20th-Century furniture, decorative objects,
and jewelry.
808 Madison Avenue
New York, NY 10012
Phone: 212-288-1569
Fax: 212-288-2102
www.primaveragallery.com
info@primaveragallery.com

Restoration Hardware

High-quality items for the home including cabinet
hardware, interior and exterior fittings, gardenware,
fixtures, tools, furniture, and lighting.
935 Broadway
New York, NY 10010
212-260-9479
www.restorationhardware.com
Go to Web site for other store locations and
a free catalog.

Second Hand Rose

19th-Century exotic furnishings.
138 Duane Street
New York, NY 10013
Phone: 212-393-9002
Fax: 212-393-9084
www.secondhandrose.com
shroseltd@aol.com

SEE Ltd.

Contemporary European furniture including
Eduard Samso's Mirallmar mirror and Mansanori
Umeda's rose chair.
920 Broadway
New York, NY 10010
212-228-3600
800-258-8292

Totem Design Group

Contemporary American and international design.
71 Franklin Street
New York, NY 10013
212-925-5506
www.totemdesign.com

Urban Archeology

Salvaged architectural elements as well as some
manufactured ones.
143 Franklin Street
New York, NY 10013
Phone: 212-431-4646
Fax: 212-343-9312
www.urbanarcheology.com

Special Resources

Andrew R. Dyer

Weekend gardening in the Connecticut area.
Phone: 203-457-4239
email: ardyer@earthlink.net

Branford Paint & Wallcovering

Every possible kind of paint; proprietor Joyce Peterson
can mix any color you imagine.
288 East Main Street
Branford, CT 06405
Phone: 203-488-2774

Brean T. Yates, Bldr.

Authentic restoration, fine carpentry, and natural landscaping in Connecticut.
144 Quonnipaug Lane
Guilford, CT 06437
Phone: 203-457-2087

Design Support, Inc.

Kevin Fitzpatrick
Unique custom designs and installations executed with precision and speed.
270 West 38th Street, Suite 703
New York, NY 10018
Phone: 212-869-9008
Fax: 212-869-8991

George Lois

One of the true geniuses in advertising, marketing, promotions, and design.
37 West 12th Street
New York, NY 10011
212-645-0386
Llphoto1@aol.com

Henderson Greene

Expert wood flooring services in greater New York area.
Contact: Al Williams, Williams Construction
Phone: 212-563-2563 or 917-716-6191

Material ConneXion

A unique resource and library for innovative materials and processes.
127 West 25th Street – 2nd Floor
New York, NY 10001
Phone: 212-842-2050
Fax: 212-842-1090
www.materialconnexion.com

Marc Wilson Design Flowers & Special Events

Marc Wilson
Exterior and interior planting and floral design.
460 West 128th Street
New York, NY 10027
Phone: 212-749-2266
Fax: 212-749-2246
www.marcwilsondesign.com

Michael Wu

Accomplished tile work in greater New York area.
Contact: Al Williams, Williams Construction
Phone: 212-563-2563 or 917-716-6191

Milton Glaser Inc.

A living legend in design, art, and visual problem-solving.
207 East 32nd Street
New York, NY 10016
Phone: 212-889-3161
Fax: 212-213-4072
www.miltonglaser.com

Neal's Wood Flooring, Inc.

Suppliers and installers of high-quality wood flooring, specializing in staining.
7 Business Park Dr.
Branford, CT 06405
Phone: 203-488-4915
Phone: 203-488-2950
Fax: 203-488-3427

Thomas V. Ruta

Behan, Ling & Ruta, CPA's, P.C.
Expert accounting and financial advice.
358 5th Avenue 9th Floor
New York, NY 10001-2209
Phone: 212-695-7003
Fax: 212-695-3031

Alexander Smalls

Catering, hospitality event company, and restaurant consultant.
Smalls & Company
Phone: 212-491-4060
Fax: 212-491-4099
email: smallsandcompany@aol.com

Willie Kathryn Suggs Licensed Real Estate Brokers

Harlem-based real estate firm unrivaled in the area.
412 West 145th Street
New York City, NY 10031
(212) 690-7636

Index

Page numbers in italic refer to illustrations.

Photography Credits

Unless otherwise indicated, all photographs are by Jason Schmidt. Other photographers and sources of photographic material are as follows:

Collection of Carole A. Berk: 29.

Madeleine Blaustein: 15.

Courtesy Charles Cowles Gallery, New York: 256.

D. James Dee, Courtesy of P.P.O.W. Gallery, New York: 188, 242.

D. James Dee, Courtesy Ronald Feldman Fine Arts, New York, www.feldmangallery.com: 146.

D. James Dee, Courtesy Ronald Feldman Fine Arts, New York, www.feldmangallery.com; Copyright © 2002 Andy Warhol Foundation for the Visual Arts, Artists Rights Society (ARS), New York: 278, 279.

Copyright © E. C. Publications, Inc. All rights reserved. Used with permission: 189.

Copyright © 2002 Succession H. Matisse, Paris/Artists Rights Society (ARS), New York; Copyright © 2002 Giraudon/Art Resource, New York: 9.

Courtesy Herman Miller, Inc.: 25, 27.

Courtesy Janet Borden, Inc.: 129, 133, 147, 172, 240, 241.

Courtesy Justen Ladda: 244.

Alex McLean: 37, 45, 54-55.

Christof Piepenstock, Courtesy Ingo Mauer, GmbH: 22.

Copyright © 2002 John Sakas, Radio Craze, Walden, New York: 30, 31.

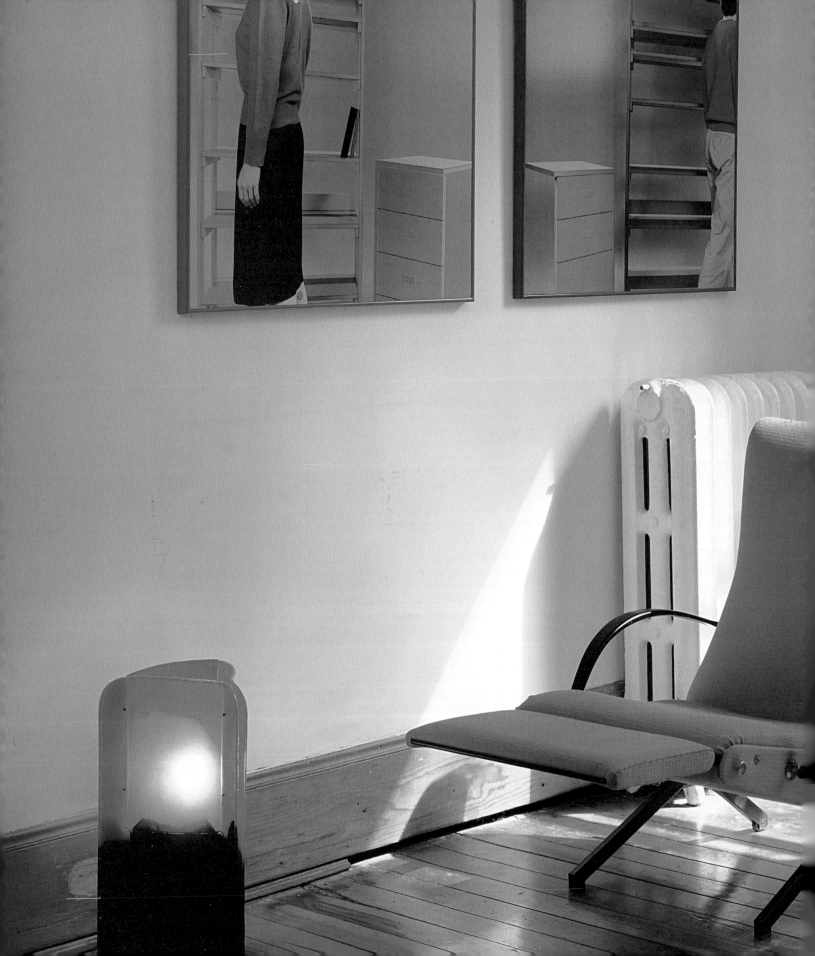